Nazi Propaganda and the Second World War

D0901601

2008

Also by Aristotle A. Kallis

THE FASCISM READER (*ed.*)

FASCIST IDEOLOGY: Territory and Expansionism in Italy and Germany 1922–1945

Nazi Propaganda and the Second World War

Aristotle A. Kallis

palgrave
macmillan

First published in 2005 in hardback, and 2008 in paperback by
PALGRAVE MACMILLAN
Houndmills, Basingstoke, Hampshire RG21 6XS and
175 Fifth Avenue, New York, N.Y. 10010
Companies and representatives throughout the world.

PALGRAVE MACMILLAN is the global academic imprint of the Palgrave
Macmillan division of St. Martin's Press, LLC and of Palgrave Macmillan Ltd.
Macmillan® is a registered trademark in the United States, United Kingdom
and other countries. Palgrave is a registered trademark in the European
Union and other countries.

ISBN-13: 978–1–4039–9251–2 hardback
ISBN-10: 1–4039–9251–7   hardback
ISBN-13: 978–0–230–54681–3 paperback
ISBN-10: 0–230–54681–1   paperback

Printed in the U.S.A.

A Book Club Edition

Contents

List of Abbreviations   ix

Acknowledgements   xiii

**Introduction: 'Totalitarianism', Propaganda, War
and the Third Reich**   1
  Propaganda, propagandist and the audience   1
  Effective propaganda and the limits of NS
    'totalitarianism'   6
  Main premises   12
  Structure and foci of the book   13

**1 Propaganda, 'Co-ordination' and 'Centralisation':
The Goebbels Network in Search of a
Total Empire**   16
  Cinema   19
  Press   26
  Broadcasting   31

**2 'Polyocracy' versus 'Centralisation': The Multiple
'Networks' of NS Propaganda**   40
  Polyocracy and 'charismatic' power in the NS regime   40
  The role of Goebbels in NS propaganda:
   power-base and limits   43
  The 'Dietrich network'   47
  The 'Ribbentrop' network   49
  The case of Alfred Rosenberg   51
  The rise of Martin Bormann   53
  The 'OKW network'   56
  Himmler and Speer   58
  The 'Goebbels network' strikes back: 1943–45   59

**3 The Discourses of NS Propaganda: Long-Term
Emplotment and Short-Term Justification**   63
  NS propaganda and long-term positive integration   65
  Negative integration: the (powerful) common denominator   70
  The early common denominator: 'plutocrats' and 'the Jew'   71
  Anti-Bolshevism   76
  The construction of a negative mega-narrative:
   the 'Jewish–Bolshevik–plutocratic alliance'   83

4   From 'Short Campaign' to 'Gigantic Confrontation': NS
    Propaganda and the Justification of War, 1939–41   93
    Justifying 'war', 1939   93
    From plan to invasion: the campaign against
      Poland and the first 'triumph'   98
    The campaign against the west: the second 'triumph'   100
    NS policy (and propaganda) at crossroads: Britain
      or Russia?   104
    Towards the attack on the Soviet Union ('Barbarossa')   106

5   From Triumph to Disaster: NS Propaganda from the
    Launch of 'Barbarossa' until Stalingrad   111
    The first stage of 'Barbarossa' (1941)   111
    The first adversities: Pearl Harbour, 'General Winter'
      and the extension of the war   117
    The 'year of decision': 1942   121
    The turning point: Stalingrad
      (September 1942–January 1943)   125

6   NS Propaganda and the Loss of the
    Monopoly of Truth (1943–44)   130
    The Stalingrad aftermath: NS propaganda and
      'public opinion'   130
    Bouncing back after Stalingrad: 'Total war' and 'fear'   133
    The subversion of the regime's monopoly of truth   137
    The 'Hitler-cult': staying power and disintegration   145
    The withdrawal of Hitler – a new role for Goebbels?   148

7   The Winding Road to Defeat: The Propaganda of
    Diversion and Negative Integration   153
    NS propaganda from consensus to negative
      integration   153
    In search for 'victory'   154
    Allied 'terror attacks' and 'retaliation' (*Vergeltung*)   160
    The eastern front: defeat, 'shortening' and
      'planned evacuation'   168
    Diverting attention from the east and the west   173
    Preparing for the final showdown   178

8   Cinema and Totalitarian Propaganda: 'Information'
    and 'Leisure' in NS Germany, 1939–45   185
    The Wochenschau (newsreel)   188
    Documentary as reality   194
    The historical film as contemporary narrative   198

Commercial and politically valuable?
The 'entertainment film' and NS propaganda   207
Managing German cinema, 1939–45   213

Conclusions: Legitimising the Impossible?   218

Notes   224

Bibliography   266

Index   284

Abbreviations

AA	*Auswärtiges Amt* [German Foreign Ministry]
APA	*Außenpolitisches Amt*
BA	*Bundesarchiv* [Federal Republic of Germany (Berlin)]
BDO	*Bund Deutscher Offiziere* [League of German Officers]
DACHO	*Dach organisation der Film schaffender Deutschlands* [Umbrella Organisation of German Film-Makers]
DAF	*Deutsche Arbeitsfront* [German Labour Front]
DD	*Drahtlose Dienst* [Wireless News Service]
DFT	*Deutsche Filmtheater-Gesellschaft*
DGFP	Documents on German Foreign Policy
DNB	*Deutsche Nachrichtenbüro* [German News Agency]
DRZW	*Das deutsche Reich und der zweite Weltkrieg* [The German Reich and the Second World War]
DW	*Deutsche Wochenschauzentrale GmbH* [German Newsreel]
FO	Foreign Office
IMT	International Military Tribunal
KA-R	*Kulturpolitische Abteilung-Rundfunkreferat*
KPD	*Kommunistische Partei Deutschlands* [German Communist Party]
MGFA	*Militärgeschichtliches Forschungsamt*
NA	US National Archives
NKFD	*Nationalkomitee Freies Deutschland* [National Committee of Free Germany]
NS	National Socialist
NSDAP	*Nationalsozialistische Deutsche Arbeiterpartei* [National Socialist German Workers Party]
OKW	*Oberkommando Wehrmacht* [Wehrmacht High Command]
OKW/WPr	*Oberkommando Wehrmacht/Wehrmacht-Propaganda* [Wehrmacht High Command/Propaganda Division]
PK	*Propaganda-Kompanien* [Wehrmacht Propaganda Troops]
PO	*Politische Organisation der* NSDAP [Political Organisation of the NSDAP]
PRO	Public Records Office (London)
RFD	*Reichsfilmdramatung* [Reich Film Dramatist]
RFK	*Reichsfilmkammer* [Reich Film Chamber]
RGB	*Reichsgesetzblatt*
RKK	*Reichskulturkammer* [Reich Culture Chamber]
RMVP	*Reichsministerium für Volksaufklärung und Propaganda* [Reich Ministry of Popular Enlightenment and Propaganda]
RPA	*Reichspropagandaämter* [Reich Propaganda Offices]

RPK	*Reichspressekammer* [Reich Press Chamber]
RPL	*Reichspropagandaleitung* [Reich Propaganda Head Office]
RRG	*Reichsrundfunkgesellschaft* [Reich Radio Company]
RRK	*Reichsrundfunkkammer* [Reich Radio Chamber]
RVDP	*Reichsverband der Deutschen Presse* [Reich Association of German Press]
SA	*Sturmabteilung* [Storm Division]
SD	*Sicherheitsdienst* [Security Service]
SPD	*Sozialdemokratische Partei Deutschlands* [Social-Democratic German Party]
SPIO	*Spitzenorganisation der deutschen Filmwirtschaft* [Parent Organisation of the German Film Industry]
SS	*Schutzstaffeln* [Protection Troops]
UFA	*Universum-Film AG* (later renamed as UFI)
VB	Völkischer Beobachter
VDZV	*Verein Deutscher Zeitungsverleger* [Association of German Newspaper Publishers] (later prefixed with 'Reich' – RVDZV)
VfZ	*Vierteljahrshefte für Zeitgeschichte*
WB	*Wehrmachtberichte* [Wehrmacht Reports]
WFst	*Wehrmacht Führungsstab*
ZSg	*Zeitgeschichtliche Sammlungen* (Bundesarchiv)

Acknowledgements

The idea for this book on National Socialist (NS) propaganda during the Second World War began during a research colloquium held by the *Militärgeschichtliches Forschungsamt* (MGFA) in Potsdam, Germany in 2002. Whilst working for a long chapter on the same topic, I conducted more extensive research that eventually resulted in this more detailed study. I am therefore indebted to colleagues took part in the colloquium for their observations during the proceedings, as well as to the organisers of the event for inviting me to contribute a chapter to their publication. During the editing of the initial chapter for the publication, *Das deutsche Reich und der zweite Weltkrieg*, Vol. 9/2, I received invaluable assistance from Joerg Echternkamp and Michael Thomae (MGFA Potsdam), whose meticulous reading of the draft and detailed comments helped me to improve my clarity and acquainted me with aspects of the German literature on the subject.

I would like to thank all those who have contributed to this project in different ways. Phil Payne and Allyson Fiddler, my colleagues at the Department of European Languages and Cultures in Lancaster University, kindly agreed to read chapters of the manuscript and offered both constructive criticism and much-needed encouragement. Roger Eatwell helped me with his expertise on fascism/totalitarianism. Roger Griffin invited me to participate in an exciting exchange of views on fascism, hosted by *Erwägen, Wissen, Ethik* in 2004, that brought me into direct contact with the ideas of many scholars on fascism and enhanced my own analytical perspective on the subject matter of fascist propaganda. Both of them have followed my overall work with touching interest and immense support – for which I will always be indebted to them. Antonio Costa Pinto always eager to share his work and expertise offered informal commentary on aspects of this book in the context of a workshop organised in Lisbon in May 2004. At Palgrave, Daniel Bunyard, Luciana O'Flaherty, Ruth Ireland and, particularly, Michael Strang supported the project (even when they heard of the final word count!) and did everything possible to ensure its smooth publication. I am also grateful to the two anonymous reviewers for their feedback and suggestions for improvement.

All my present colleagues at the Department of European Languages and Cultures, Lancaster University, provided me with an inspirational context for my research and teaching activities; Ann Thomas, Annik Taylor, Brigitte Theunissen–Hughes and Linda Gilmour tried (with partial success, due to my own shortcomings) to add an element of order in my everyday academic life. They all were instrumental in making my work in Lancaster rewarding, exciting and humane. My past colleagues at the School of History, University of Edinburgh and at the Department of Historical Studies, University of

Bristol were equally supportive and willing to share their expertise. I would like to thank especially Jim McMillan, Tim Cole and Ian Wei. Finally, I owe a very special thanks to Jill Stephenson who has always been my academic *guardian angel*, willing to impart her humbling knowledge on National Socialism and offering her unqualified support at all stages of my academic trajectory.

Archival and bibliographical research in Germany was greatly assisted from two generous grants: one from the Faculty of Arts Research Travel Fund, University of Bristol in 2003; and the other from the Faculty of Arts Small Projects Fund, Lancaster University during 2003–04. During my work in the Bundesarchiv (BA), Berlin, I received a lot of support and guidance from Jana Blumberg, especially in terms of locating relevant material and gaining swift access to them. I should also acknowledge my gratitude to the staff of the British Library, the National Library of Scotland, and the libraries of the universities of Lancaster, Edinburgh, Manchester and Sheffield for granting me access to their resources at very short notice and meeting requests beyond their call of duty. In an age of increased availability of excellent web resources, I feel that the study of NS propaganda has been greatly enhanced and crucially democratised through a series of online material. Apart from the convenience of consulting electronic publications whenever (and wherever) needed, I should also acknowledge a very big debt to Randall Bytwerk of Calvin College, Grand Rapids, Michigan, for creating a real gem of a website on NS propaganda. The material featured there provided me with a compass for the arduous task of charting the territory of primary sources, acting as both a point of reference and an incentive for further archival enquiry that enhanced the empirical aspect of this book.

A number of people very close to me were forced to endure my long working hours, volatile mood, rambling fascination and occasional anguish with this project – a project that became part of their lives far more than they would have wished for or I would have intended. My apologies to them come with my gratitude for helping me maintain a more balanced perspective on life and work alike. My parents and close friends have a share in this book to which I could not possibly do justice with words.

During the time I spent on this project, Iain 'Robbie' Robertson died very unexpectedly and prematurely. I had always admired his intellectual *élan vitale*, his eagerness to engage any subject and his ability to turn any conversation into a process of unconditionally sharing his extraordinary life and thought. He, his wife, Hilary and his family have made Scotland feel far more like my second *home* than I would have ever imagined. When he hastened to buy my first monograph, I promised to give him a copy of this book once it was published. It seems that, regrettably, I ran out of time. To dedicate this work to him is only a partial and belated redress.

Whilst this book owes so much to the kind help and advice of others, I alone am responsible for any error of fact or judgement in it.

Aristotle A. Kallis

Nazi Propaganda and the Second World War

Introduction: 'Totalitarianism', Propaganda, War and the Third Reich

Propaganda, propagandist and the audience

What exactly is *propaganda*? Nowadays, the word is usually associated with deception, lies and manipulation. And yet, propaganda did not always have such a clearly negative meaning. In the first decades of the twentieth century, it was deployed generically to indicate a systematic process of information management geared to promoting a particular goal and to guaranteeing a popular response as desired by the propagandist. As such, propaganda remains a sub-genus of mass communication and persuasion, developed in the context of modernity to deal with two parallel developments: on the one hand, the increasing expansion and sophistication of the 'public sphere' with its ever-growing thirst for information and opinion-forming; on the other hand, the exponential proliferation of available information, making it very difficult for the individual to identify, absorb and analyse the material. As one of the leading theorists of propaganda and communication, Jacques Ellul, noted,

> [i]t is the emergence of mass media which makes possible the use of propaganda techniques on a societal scale. The orchestration of press, radio and television to create a continuous, lasting and total environment renders the influence of propaganda virtually unnoticed precisely because it creates a constant environment. Mass media provides the essential link between the individual and the demands of the technological society.[1]

Propaganda arose out of a need to prioritise, organise, correlate and then transmit information to the interested public, thus making full use of the opportunities offered by technology (mass media) and modernity (aggregation of population, access to media) to that effect. State propaganda possessed sufficient legitimacy to make such choices on behalf of its citizens and then perform its function of supplying information as an expression of its *raison d'etat*; in other words, apart from simply informing the public, state propaganda also became the vehicle for the promotion of communal desired objectives and of the state's own continuity. Indeed, it is no coincidence that the debate about the formulation of a systematic approach to 'propaganda' emerged in the context of the First World War, in Germany and elsewhere. At a time of full mobilisation for the attainment of a national goal (such as victory in the military confrontation), the need for methodical and efficient information strategies that would bolster the morale of the home front and mobilise society was particularly highlighted.[2]

Thus, propaganda did not simply provide information; it performed a wide variety of further functions – many of which were on behalf of its recipients. It was intended to respond to fundamental societal needs, such as *integration, correlation, guidance, motivation/mobilisation, adaptation, continuity* and even *diversion/relaxation*. 'Integration', in particular, is one of the most fundamental functions of propaganda, even more so because the modern mass society has an inherent tendency for fragmentation that runs counter to the functioning of society as a 'system'.[3] By promoting a common cognitive environment for information acquisition and interpretation, as well as a constant 'cultivation' of perceptions of the world, propaganda aims to integrate the person both as an individual and a member of a social group into a shared context of symbols, meanings and desired objectives. The existence of such a common and widely accepted anchor helps the other functions of 'correlation' or 'emplotment' (i.e., linking information in intelligible ways and thus bridging past, present and future) and 'guidance' (namely, indirect orientation of the audience towards particular patterns of predisposition, expression and often action). But the rest of the functions are also vital: 'motivation' refers to the provision of justifications and incentives for internalising the propaganda message, whilst 'mobilisation' is more directly geared towards propelling people into modes of individual or collective action as desired by the propagandist; 'adaptation' pertains to the bolstering of the audience's psychological ability to adjust to changing circumstances; 'continuity' of cognition and perception helps the public correlate the present with both the past and a desirable future; whilst diversion or relaxation constitute the essential punctuation of propaganda, providing a controlled respite for the audience and thus avoiding the danger of weariness.

Systematic application of the above elements of propaganda thus entails both providing and withholding information. Sometimes, the continuity of the wider context of reference is best preserved through omission (e.g. by withholding adverse information), distracting attention (through displacement of responsibility or focus) or by providing necessary relaxation (e.g. by avoiding an overflow of information). Entertainment and leisure are essential punctuations of modern life, providing stress-releasing valves for the individual and society. But even in this case, the audience remains the recipient of cultural symbols which it then processes with reference to its overall perception of reality. Therefore, it is impossible to separate mass information from mass entertainment. Again, the demands of deploying the full media technological apparatus at the service of state propaganda functions led the leaders of wartime Germany in 1917 to enlist cinema, to the effort of providing a combination of news and entertainment to the home front. By that time radio broadcast had already started to find its place inside the households and thus to attract the attention of state authorities as a medium of communication between authorities and citizens. In the 1920s and particularly during the 1930s, technological advances and systematic state policies led to a rapid expansion of the number of appliances used inside German houses, as well as in cinema infrastructure across the country.

The Nazis were not the instigators of the process that saw broadcasting and cinema – in addition to the already established press – as potential purveyors of dominant symbols and images geared towards societal integration; nor were they innovators in perceiving media, in their dual function of providing information and entertainment, as crucial for shaping and/or bolstering attitudes in the longer term. Attitudes, unlike perceptions (that relate to short-term events), concern value-systems and fundamental beliefs. In this respect, effective propaganda anchors incidental arguments in the wider environment of attitudes and values; and altering the latter necessitates systematic but subtle cultivation of the desired alternative. In 1940, the National Socialist (NS) regime commissioned a film about euthanasia at a time when its own secret operation against the mentally ill (code-named T–4) had already been secretly underway. The film, a social drama (and not a documentary) titled, *Ich klage an*, premiered in 1941 and was received with mixed audience reactions – as for many, it dealt with a taboo issue that ran counter to the notion of the sanctity of human life.[4] In commissioning a film that broached the subject of an operation that it had already started in utter secrecy, the NS regime recognised the immense difficulty of effecting a swift attitudinal change on this issue and chose an indirect way to initiate a change ('subpropaganda'),[5] by correlating the taboo issue with other, widely shared values (e.g. merciful termination of a tortured life as an act of utter humanism). The conclusion it drew from audience reactions (as well as by vocal criticisms from the Catholic constituency) was that it still had a long way to go before effecting a real change in societal perceptions on the matter. By contrast, the negative depiction of 'the Jew', in the press and films such as *Jud Süß* or *Der ewige Jude* (both released in 1941) was far more acceptable to a public long-steeped in dominant anti-Semitic images.[6] Understanding and acceptance in this case was easily and convincingly performed without necessitating changes in broad attitudinal norms.[7]

This observation leads us to another significant point, relating to reception of the propaganda message by the targeted audience. The suggestion that any form of effective propaganda results in 'brainwashing' fails to take account of the recipient's ability to resist a particular message, however successfully this may be presented to them. As in the example used above, although the treatment of the 'euthanasia' issue was highly sensitive and careful, the majority of the population resisted the allusion, as they were reluctant to challenge their long-embedded beliefs and values. The active complicity or even passive consensus of the audience cannot be taken for granted, even in putatively 'totalitarian' systems where individual issues become related to a one-dimensional world-view. This is because, even in a 'revolutionary' situation[8] of break with the past, the replacement of traditional values with attitudes derived from a 'revolutionary' ideology requires a long-term process of careful, step-by-step cultivation. In the interim period, propaganda cannot afford to assume that such values have lost their emotional and psychological significance for its target audience; otherwise, it risks losing the latter's attention and encounters a far stronger resistance. In this context, the most effective propaganda is one that maintains a dialogue between traditional social principles and its own alternative prescriptions by using some of the vocabulary, terminology and fundamentals of the existing value system. This would indeed suggest to the audience that the propaganda anchor is firmly fixed in the sea-bed of social fundamentals. In this way, the audience can be brought to believe that the way the propagandist adresses a particular pressing issue of the day either accords with convictions and attitudes that have long been held within society, or at least does not violate them. Such congruence is, of course, often illusory. By undermining the validity of entrenched attitudes very slowly and in interconnection with other values that the society also shares, successful propaganda opts for long-term, gradual attitudinal change through sustained exposure to an alternative.[9]

Once an attitude has been seriously subverted or overshadowed by an alternative set of values, the behaviour that was originally associated with it would also change accordingly – and at this point, propaganda may become more aggressive in providing the necessary guidance for translating attitudinal change into behavioural adjustment. Interestingly, Goebbels had always operated on the basis of a distinction between *Stimmung* (sentiment, morale) and *Haltung* (observable behaviour),[10] underlining their correspondence and also a crucial difference: the latter was more difficult to change, whilst the former remained far more volatile and vulnerable to short-term news. Goebbels realised that behaviours emanate from fundamental beliefs and may change only after a long-term attitudinal shift.[11] Therefore, effective propaganda requires constantly addressing both, but with different strategies and tools, in order to maintain their correspondence or to channel their conflict in the desired direction.[12]

Tensions between profound attitudes, *Stimmung* and *Haltung* may arise in a host of contexts and forms. For example, in the light of the impressive military victories of 1940 and of the first half of 1941, NS propaganda capitalised heavily on the improvement of the population's *Stimmung*, in order to effect changes in their deeper attitudes towards the war (which from the beginning had been at best circumspect). By contrast, in the aftermath of the Stalingrad defeat, in the winter of 1943, propaganda efforts were concentrated mainly on shielding attitudes and behaviour from the adverse effect of short-term morale disintegration. Then, in 1944–45, when belief in victory or even in the alleged infallibility of Hitler began to crumble, Goebbels used different strategies aimed at bolstering the *Haltung*, even if morale continued to collapse. Whilst he found that the breakdown of the *Stimmung* was virtually irreversible in the absence of positive developments in the military field, he strove to maintain a broad correspondence between population attitudes and behaviour, noting that a positive psychological identification with the regime's war goals was no longer an option. So, instead of the confident, triumphalist and self-congratulatory discourses that had characterised NS propaganda output in the first three years of the war, he resorted to what may be described as 'fear appeals' and 'negative integration'.[13] This rested on the premise that, whilst the majority of the German population would no longer identify positively with their previous attitudes (many of them forged under the influence of earlier NS propaganda activities), they should remain attached to them through fear of the consequences of defeat. This tactical, pragmatic shift in propaganda strategy expressed itself in negative discourses – such as 'betrayal of the fatherland', anti-Bolshevism, anti-Semitism and 'anti-plutocratic' themes against the western Allies – that had been consistently articulated in the past (hence their plausibility) but now had to be strengthened in order to make society remain psychologically ready to resist as a lesser evil than defeat. Propagation of a positive commitment to National Socialism and to the active defence of its alleged achievements largely faded in the background; safeguarding the Vaterland against the prospect of 'collapse' (*Untergang*), and 'chaos' increasingly became the common denominator of resistance, fighting power and integration.

Overall, the propagandists have an array of *techniques* at their disposal that they may use for formulating a message. They specify the content of day-to-day communication with their audience, run campaigns lasting for weeks or months, provide guiding principles for understanding the events presented, use ideological referents to supply meaning to the fragments of information that they have chosen to impart and thus maintain the consistency and continuity of their specific message. The latter's resonance with the public depends on a number of variables that, whilst nearly impossible to diagnose accurately in their full complexity, require the propagandists to take calculated risks about the most appropriate form(s) of communication, based on both good identification and deep knowledge of the target audience. Broadly speaking, any propaganda campaign addresses four interconnected needs: to bolster the moral validity of the state's actions and at the same time minimise knowledge or embellish perception of the less pleasant aspects of its own side's behaviour; and to exaggerate the alleged immorality or errors of the opponent(s) whilst consciously underestimating their more positive attributes.[14] At any given moment the goal of audience integration is performed by a combination of 'positive' and 'negative' themes, depending on the circumstances and the desired psychological effect. Shifts in the techniques of propaganda are often dictated by variables beyond the control of the propagandists; but the latter may still achieve a desirable reaction from their audience by making effective choices from their panoply of available techniques. Thus, whilst the propagandists' control over what actually happens is seriously limited and their response often reactive, the power of their position lies in their ability to organise the information and present it through a plethora of versatile techniques and devices to their carefully chosen recipients.

Effective propaganda and the limits of NS 'totalitarianism'

In one of the classic accounts of wartime NS propaganda, Edward Herzstein described the overall record of Germany's efforts in this field as 'the war that Hitler won'.[15] This description encapsulates the essence of wartime propaganda as psychological warfare and makes an unmistakeable judgement about its overall effectiveness. How does a regime win a propaganda war, especially in the context of a situation whose outcome is largely and crucially determined in distant battlefields? Propaganda cannot and does not win wars, at least not in the literal sense of the word. Besides, it is ironic that Herzstein uses this categorical judgement for NS Germany – that is, for a regime and system that suffered a crushing defeat in the Second World War. Could it be that propaganda may be effective *regardless of the military situation* – that in fact its degree of success is irrelevant to military realities?

The benchmarks for success or failure of propaganda activities remain extremely hard to define in unequivocal terms.[16] What might appear effective in swinging short-term attitudes does not necessarily influence dispositions in the long-term; equally, failure of a particular theme, slogan or campaign does not necessarily entail a wider shift of population attitudes. Wartime propaganda is primarily concerned with sustaining and enforcing long-term integration, as well as facilitating mobilisation along desired lines of behaviour. But a rigid separation of short- and long-term propaganda dimensions is impossible: whilst a single message is not in itself enough to effect fundamental psychological changes (desired or undesirable), short-term techniques blend with long-term strategies and vice versa. In ideal-typical terms, successful propaganda anchors specific perceptions on desired psychological attitudes, emplots convincingly the particular in the desirable broader narrative, maintains its psychological authority by corresponding to its audience's perception of reality – which it has helped to shape in the first place – and manages a favourable set of developments. In the specific circumstances of war, the effective functioning of a propaganda network also depends on the centralisation of the whole operation, which ensures overall control of the sources and the flow of information, in order to maintain unity and coherence.

War effects fundamental changes in the organisation and functioning of any propaganda network, regardless of overall political orientation. As Michael Balfour has shown in his comparative study of German and British wartime propaganda, the two countries' strategies to information control converged substantially from September 1939; and this happened more because of the adoption of aggressive information management techniques by the latter, rather than due to the radicalisation of practices employed by the former.[17] Whilst before 1939 propaganda in Britain operated in a more pluralistic context in interaction with a developed 'public sphere' (in a way that the NS regime had rejected ever since 1933), the needs of the war caused a profound inhibition of plural public discussion and a parallel tightening of the official handling of information. Although the convergence should not be exaggerated (for example, the British shift towards control and centralisation was incidental and tied to the exigencies of war, while for NS Germany it was the default and desired mode of operation), clear distinctions between allegedly free and controlled information flow became increasingly blurred and problematic.

The NS propaganda network had long before developed a trend towards ideological *co-ordination* and administrative/political *centralisation*, in tandem with a demobilisation of the developed 'public sphere' that it had inherited from the Weimar Republic. The outbreak of the war supplied opportunities for stepping up a gear or two and bringing the system closer to an ideal-typical mode of mono-dimensional operation. Unlike the case of Britain or the USA, this was no deviation or temporary concession; it made possible a permanent, ever-evolving alignment of propaganda with a totalitarian management of information, subjecting to its rigid logic every other aspect of societal activity, from mobilisation and education to entertainment. In this crucial respect, NS authorities had a head start in 1939 – capitalising on previous achievements and operating in a largely familiar territory. No wonder then that they were better placed to play the game and indeed 'win the war'.

Or did they? Against the conventional wisdom of a tight, Machiavellian monopoly exercised by the Minister of National Enlightenment and Propaganda, Dr Joseph Goebbels, some historians have detected ambiguities, divisions and contradictions. Their Goebbels remains a supremely able manager of propaganda, a central agent with clear views and strategies, who was however operating in a plural, non-normative decision-making process and was not always capable of translating his ideas into practice. Such an analysis serves as a cautionary tale that is relevant to all accounts of NS rule from the viewpoint of 'totalitarianism' – that reality was often substantially different from intention or rhetoric.[18] Thus, when Friedrich and Brzezinski talked of '[a] technologically conditioned, near-complete monopoly of control, in the hands of the party and of the government, of all means of effective mass communication, such as the press, radio, and motion pictures'[19] as evidence of 'totalitarian' rule, he was referring to an organisational process of 'co-ordination', bringing all information and leisure networks under the full control of the authorities, eliminating pluralism and the possibility of alternative versions of 'truth' reaching the public.[20] Concentration of authority, however, in the state does not necessarily mean effective exercise of power. Even in Brzezinski's statement above, the dualism between 'government' and 'party' was extremely problematic in NS Germany, since Hitler had resisted a definitive normative regulation of relations between state and party after the seizure of power.[21] But even within each of these two domains, power was neither crystallised nor exercised in mono-dimensional terms, as will be demonstrated in this book. Therefore, to talk of a fully-fledged 'totalitarian system' of propaganda in the Third Reich would involve a troubling confusion between intentions or rhetoric, on the one hand, and a fluid reality, on the other.

In fact, even the word 'system' is misleading in the context of NS propaganda. It conveys an impression of organisational clarity and division of labour, integration and coherence that eluded the NS system of rule almost immediately after the *Machtergreifung* and simply became even more convoluted in subsequent years. In this respect, war accentuated pre-existing centrifugal tendencies in the whole organisation of the NS regime that affected adversely the conduct of propaganda. This book places the whole debate on NS wartime propaganda into the analytical framework of *polyocracy* that undermined from within the project of producing a genuinely 'totalitarian' propaganda 'system'. Whilst ideological co-ordination and accumulation of jurisdictions proved easier to achieve, drawing firm lines of authority amongst the competing state and party agencies was another matter. Hitler's charismatic leadership proved impervious to bureaucratic rationalisation, creating a network of semi-autonomous 'networks' that often cancelled each other out in terms of achieving centralised control over propaganda. It is argued that the output of NS propaganda cannot be adequately understood in terms of a Goebbels monopoly over strategy and output; the result was more akin to a tangle of threads, guidelines, discourses and initiatives that were bound together only by vague objectives: to ensure NS domination and 'cultural hegemony' (qua Antonio Gramsci); to support the psychological structures of Hitler's charismatic authority (qua Kershaw's scheme of 'working towards the Führer'); to sustain or even bolster the staying power of the domestic front; and to win the war. Beyond these broad elements of convergence, there were indeed multiple *propagandas*, managed by different agencies ('networks') to different short-term goals, that cumulatively (through their joint effect but often through their profound contradictions) made up what we may schematically call NS propaganda.

The highly porous nature of NS 'totalitarianism' in the field of propaganda extended beyond the mere sphere of administrative control. The absence of a truly internally centralised and normative decision-making process established parallel networks of information-gathering and dissemination. In every classic propaganda schema, the role of 'the propagandist' is crucial in terms of making short-term decisions about *what*, *when* and *how* to say (and, by implication, to omit); of maintaining the correlation between the specific and the generic; and of working out long-term strategies of communication and persuasion. The propagandist stands on the crucial junction between gathering of raw material and transmitting the propaganda message. Their central position ('gatekeeper'[22]) theoretically ensures a wide appraisal of the available data, a careful choice of themes and strategies, as well as a co-ordinated diffusion of the propaganda message through a combination of available resources (in this case, mass media and events, such as speeches, public gatherings etc.). They make choices on the basis of his profound knowledge of their audience (knowledge supported by frequent assessment of the effectiveness of propaganda through opinion reports) and then are responsible for revisiting their overall strategy in the light of the message's reception. The division of labour should emanate from a clear delegation and exercise of partial power within the parameters of a single overall strategy, as defined and articulated by the head of the system and carried out through a clearly defined hierarchical structure. At the same time, the propagandist himself is integrated in a wider hierarchical schema (the state), in which he becomes the recipient of delegation of power by his superiors in a structure that extends from the highest echelon of political power downwards. In other words, the propagandist functions as the crucial mediator between the overall orientation of the regime as communicated to him from above and the ancillary work of agencies under his administrative control.[23]

According to the administrative hierarchy of the Third Reich, this person should have been Joseph Goebbels, with his institutional power-base in the Ministry of Popular Enlightenment and Propaganda [*Reichsministerium für Volksaufklärung und Propaganda* (RMVP)] acting as a sorting-house working towards the fulfilment of its figurehead's strategy with the rest of the relevant agencies following its lead. Yet in NS Germany, this pattern of division of labour never worked. On the one hand, the non-normative character of Hitler's 'charismatic' power and, on the other, the polycratic nature of decision-making, even within allegedly separate and specific spheres of jurisdiction, rendered centralisation and continuity practically impossible. The roots of this administrative confusion and ambiguity reach deep into the time before the outbreak of the war; the military conflict simply aggravated the trend through proliferation of information sources and data, as well as through an even less normative exercise of power from above. That it became more visible from 1941–42 onwards and damaged the effectiveness of the whole propaganda operation had more to do with the rapidly deteriorating fortunes of the Third Reich on the battlefield. In early 1943, Goebbels had predicted that,

> [t]o praise a Blitz campaign needs no toughness … [W]e must prepare our
> minds and hearts for bitter experiences.[24]

At that point, the whole NS leadership was only starting to realise the
practical significance of a diachronic truth: that propaganda alone does not
make victories or defeats.[25] The striking contrast in the Third Reich's military
performance between the initial period of triumph (1939–41) and the subsequent wave of defeats on all fronts (1942–45) constituted the raw material of
reality that no propaganda apparatus could ignore, silence or twist beyond
recognition without losing credibility or effectiveness. During the 1942–44
period, the dramatic reversal of fortunes on the military front and the cumulative effect of the war on the civilian population within the Reich (restrictions
imposed by 'total war', destruction by Allied air warfare, drop in standards of
living) served to illustrate the inability of the regime's propaganda network
to juggle a plethora of conflicting expectations and ambitions: to convince
public opinion of the gravity of the situation whilst upholding morale;
to warn of the dangers whilst rallying public enthusiasm for the war, the
regime and the Führer; to display sensitivity to the privations of German
soldiers and civilians whilst continuing to spread the gospel of eventual
'victory'; and, even more crucially, to forewarn the Reich's citizens of the
trials that lay ahead at the same time that it still strove to keep the longed-
for triumphal conclusion of the military effort in (visible) perspective.
Setbacks forced the regime to change its propaganda effort, in terms of both
discourse and method, by trading triumphal optimism for a mixture of stark
realism and a fair amount of escapism. However, propaganda remained
essentially bound to the reality that it was meant to embellish, celebrate or
mitigate, depending on the situation. In this respect, its degree of success
depended on many complex factors, only some of were directly under the
control of the regime.

The result was that, little by little after 1941, the official regime propaganda discourse became discordant with the perceptions of the vast majority
of the German civilian population. National Socialism had established
a hegemonic control over communication – what I refer to as 'monopoly of
truth' – and upheld it through an equally hegemonic handling of communication devices. This monopoly operated on two levels. First, it described a
system of information exclusively directed by the regime authorities after a
period of ideological and institutional 'co-ordination'. Second, by virtue of
its 'total' signification of reality through references to its one-dimensional
ideological core, NS propaganda was able to mediate in a wholesale manner
between 'reality' and population, thereby establishing a filter through which
the former would be viewed and assessed by the latter. This resulted in the
cultivation of a 'substitute (*ersatz*) reality'[26] that often (and increasingly after

1941) lay in dissonance to the actual developments, but could be sustained in the absence of alternative sources of information. The case of the sinking of the passenger liner, *Athenia* in early September 1939 provides a case study of how this 'monopoly of truth' operated and how it could nurture an 'ersatz reality'. After an initial period of confusion about the circumstances of the incident, the NS propaganda authorities found unequivocal evidence that responsibility lay with one of their own U-boats. Nevertheless, the authorities continued to accuse Britain of sinking the boat. In the November bulletin of the *Reichspropagandaleitung* (RPL) – Reich Propaganda Head Office, to low-level party propagandists, it was claimed that,

> [n]o means is too evil for these puppeteers and warmongers. They even sink their own ships, as in the case of the 'Athenia', letting innocent people perish.[27]

In the case of the *Athenia* incident, an 'ersatz reality' completely divorced from the facts was actually created at the upper echelons of the NS hierarchy and then distributed as 'truth' throughout the propaganda network (even Hans Fritzsche, the then head of the Home Press Division of the RMVP, maintained at Nuremberg that he had no idea about the truth until he discussed the issue with Admiral Raeder in prison[28]) and to the public. The German population, shielded from enemy counter-propaganda and alternative sources of information, were expected to believe the official version of the story – and in this case they duly did.

However, the 'monopoly of truth' that the NS regime claimed was challenged and eroded in subsequent years. Although counter-propaganda from within the Reich had been effectively eliminated in the pre-war years, alternative channels of information-gathering and opinion-forming could never be fully eradicated. Radio broadcasts from the Reich's enemies could reach Germany and, in spite of the introduction of severe sanctions for tuning in to foreign stations, a substantial part of the German wartime society did listen – sporadically at the beginning, but more consistently later. Then, when the western Allies achieved superiority in the air warfare and flew over the German skies almost uninhibited in 1943–45, they repeatedly showered the civilian population with leaflets offering a very different perspective on the military developments. In parallel, the exposure of German society to a first-hand experience of the Reich's deteriorating military fortunes (spiralling number of soldier-deaths; reports by soldiers on leave; effects of air raids; deterioration of standards of living) underlined a discrepancy between the official propaganda line and the everyday perceptions of reality (see Ch. 6). As a result, full control over information and perceptions of reality was never really achieved by the authorities, who saw the authority of their propaganda output suffer considerably under the weight of a very different 'reality' that, contrary to their desires, came crushing in on German society. This meant that during the period of 'defeat' NS propaganda was gradually deprived of its 'monopoly of truth' – if not on a purely organisational level, then certainly in mass psychological terms.[29]

Main premises

This book is about the conduct of propaganda under an aspiring 'totalitarian' state and in the context of 'total war' – a war that started amidst strong reservations and scepticism and entered a period of what appeared as unassailable triumph (1940–41) before sliding into disaster and defeat (1942–45). It aims to revisit two conventional assumptions about NS propaganda: that it operated in a purely totalitarian fashion, whereby ideological/political co-ordination, institutional centralisation and 'monopoly of truth' were taken for granted after six years (1933–39) of radical changes in state and society; and that it remained effective throughout the war period, making a crucial contribution to the mobilisation and staying power of the German population until the very end, even to the point of claiming that this was a war within the war that the regime 'won'. While there are elements of truth in both these statements, the book intends to show that our perceptions of NS wartime propaganda have been shrouded in exaggeration – about the generic role of propaganda in modern societies; about the 'totalitarian' nature of the NS regime in practice; about the degree of central control exercised over propaganda activities by Goebbels and the RMVP; about the attitudes and behaviours of German society; as well as the role of propaganda output in directly shaping them.

For the purpose of the subsequent analysis, 'propaganda' is understood as a standard function of political legitimation[30] and societal integration in all modern environments. It is borne out of the need for communication between state and its citizens, the provision of information for the 'public sphere', the cultivation of shared dominant symbolic patterns that serve as points of reference for processing reality and the channelling of societal energies into modes of action/behaviour deemed by the authorities as desirable. Because of such broad functions, propaganda should be understood not simply in the narrow sense of information-provision through established networks of opinion-shaping, but also in an expanded manner, encompassing and saturating the cultivation of dominant norms of cultural perception through language discourses, art, entertainment and 'media events'.[31]

The impact of a war situation – especially a 'total' modern conflict requiring full mobilisation over an extended period of time – has a 'totalising' effect on the functioning of state and society, hence on propaganda as well, thus placing it at the heart of information flow and shaping perceptions of a reality that the population is ill-equipped to grasp in its entirety. However, even in this context of monopoly and direct opportunities for mass opinion-shaping, propaganda mediates between events and interpretation, without controlling the former or assuming the effectiveness of the latter. Herein lies the value of Herzstein's provocative statement about NS propaganda: it can be effective and successful in spite of the outcome of the military effort it supports. Military defeat in this domain, when resulting from strategic or logistical factors, does not reflect a failed propaganda effort; and, equally, a war may be won on the battlefield in spite of propaganda per se. Thus, the effectiveness of propaganda should be judged on different terrains: ability to integrate, ideally in positive and voluntary but, if need be, also in negative and even coercive terms; capacity for sustaining its 'monopoly' of truth, in institutional and psychological terms alike; aptitude for intelligible correlation of events that maintains continuity and anchors popular perception in a familiar and resonant common ground of values; ability to manage behavioural and attitudinal patterns amongst the audience in order to generate the desired action; but also unity of purpose and continuity in the propaganda output itself, based on institutional and political coherence.

In other words, *effective* propaganda involves success in a chain of interrelated processes and functions – from data collection to the formulation of the message, the choice of devices for its dissemination, the timing and, finally, the reception of the output as well as its effect on attitude-behaviour.[32] It is not a matter of one-directional communication between the person who transmits the message and passive receivers but a complex process of negotiation, shared knowledge and trust, reassessment and reformulation. It is also crucial to stress that effective propaganda operates on two linked time-frames: one *short-term* and incidental (conducted within a specific timeframe), the other *long-term* (appealing to deeper cultivated attitudes, beliefs and perceptions). In this respect, the successful (as outlined above) conduct of propaganda at any given moment derives from a combination of effective communication per se and equally effective cultivation of generic shared attitudes. And the converse is also true: ineffective propaganda may be the result of inappropriate message-formulation in the short term or of the failure to correlate even the most sophisticated message with established attitudinal patterns or specific audience needs. To put it differently, an appeal to fundamental values and perceptions is more likely to be effective in spite of weaknesses in the handling of short-term issues than a communication – however well planned and well executed – that fails to appeal to deep, shared beliefs or is untimely.

Structure and foci of the book

Analysing the structure, conduct and effectiveness of propaganda involves passing through various stages: the ideological context in which it takes place; the question of institutional agency; the specifics of administering a propaganda network; the reasons behind the choice of particular communication techniques and media devices for its dissemination; the nature of the target audience and its reactions; and, finally, the evaluation of this feedback by the propaganda authorities. This study has an analytical bias towards agency and the conduct of propaganda rather than towards its reception and effect on public opinion. The latter aspect has been meticulously explored in authoritative studies, both classic and recent.[33] Rather than charting population reactions in an exhaustive manner, the book offers insights into the organisation, management and conduct of NS wartime propaganda, whilst at the same time probing the relation between the desired and actual effect on population. Chapters 1 and 2 cover the whole NS period, because one of the methodological assumptions of this project is that wartime propaganda inherited powerful (and often irreversible) tendencies from the first six years of NS rule. In order to understand how the system worked in 1939–45, it is essential to examine its basic organisational principles and processes, as well as to chronicle the ways in which co-ordination and centralisation was (or was not) attained. The notion that Goebbels and the RMVP (or, for that matter, any other single party or state institution) reigned over a clearly delimited and centrally commanded system of propaganda will be revisited and challenged. In fact, it will be shown that war accentuated previous tendencies, intensified inheritances of the past and whetted the appetite of those already involved in the propaganda effort to claim a further stake in the formulation of the regime's propaganda policy. Another powerful assumption that will be questioned is the intentionalist account of political 'co-ordination' (*Gleichschaltung*) as an ideological and linear project; instead, co-ordination will be examined as an open-ended process that often contradicted the parallel goal of centralisation and whose timing and initiatives were largely defined by structural factors (e.g. economic considerations, power-struggle within the regime or the party, etc.).

This discussion sets the scene for the main analysis of NS propaganda during wartime. Chapter 3 provides an overview of the main themes ('discourses') that the regime used throughout the war. Here the focus is on long-term narratives that formed the backbone of NS propaganda until its defeat in 1945, providing its overall message with a gloss of cognitive and psychological 'consistency'.[34] The basic methodological premise is a distinction between *positive* and *negative integration*. By examining broad discourse subjects (such as 'national community', 'mission', 'anti-plutocratic' struggle; 'anti-Bolshevism' etc.), the chapter shows how NS propaganda gradually shifted its emphasis from positive to negative schemes of integration and how it reverted to a 'common denominator' [defending Germany against a concerted campaign by its time-long international enemies] that ensured its coherence and a modicum of integrative success. Chapters 4–7 provide a roughly chronological account of NS propaganda during wartime. Emphasis is placed on how short-term events were communicated to the public and emploted into a broader context of objectives and beliefs. Whilst Chapter 4 deals with the period from the outbreak of the war until the launch of

Operation Barbarossa (1939–41), Chapters 5–7 deal with the management of an increasingly inauspicious 'reality' and with the strategies employed in order to accentuate positive developments, divert attention, justify setbacks and maintain the integrative power of its propaganda message for the domestic front (1942–45).

Chapter 8 deals with cinema. The decision to separate more traditional types of propaganda from a theoretically leisure activity such as cinema is a conscious one. Whilst printed matter, speeches and radio broadcasts had a specific regularity and 'frequency', films were far more complex undertakings, planned over a far longer period, destined for the whole Volk (as opposed to broadcasts or press that tended to include a high degree of regional diversification) and were not weighed down by the need for direct information. Furthermore, celluloid necessitated different communication strategies, as well as a far more complex balance between indoctrination and entertainment, politics and art, and factual accuracy and diversion. Even newsreel – by definition more akin to standard 'news propaganda' – served a bridging function between information and leisure, depicting war as a sort of epic battle in a way that printed propaganda was ill-suited to do. The methodology of this chapter is rather different as it deals with complex questions of art-versus-ideology, entertainment-versus-propaganda etc. Such distinctions, it is argued, existed only on the level of *perception*, not of function; in other words, whilst technically different films were perceived by the public as belonging to different genres (and were labelled as such by the regime), this does not justify a differentiation between 'propaganda' and 'light' cinema. Three interesting trends in the RMVP's cinema policy are discussed in detail: first, the monitoring of every film – regardless of its propagandistic or not content and theme – for cultural symbols and political references; second, the attempt to unify the spheres of indoctrination and leisure; and, third, the effort to align film production to contemporary or projected political prerequisites (e.g. anti-Soviet films after Stalingrad, anti-American films after Pearl Harbour; films about the Jews at the time that a planned radicalisation of anti-Jewish policy was underway etc.).

1
Propaganda, 'Co-ordination' and 'Centralisation': The Goebbels Network in Search of a Total Empire

One of the most unrelenting orthodoxies in the analysis of interwar fascist regimes concerns the alleged commitment of the fascist leaderships to promote an integral 'co-ordination' of the structures of power that they had inherited. Adolf Hitler forced the political establishment of the stillborn Weimar Republic to surrender authority to him and began the process of improvising his NS state. Within three years, the NS leadership had succeeded in appropriating, centralising and establishing an uncontested hegemony over Germany's political, economic, social and cultural life.[1] The existence of a plan behind the legal and political measures, introduced with conspicuous speed by the NS regime immediately after the handing-over of power, was claimed to reflect its 'revolutionary' nature[2] and its wholesale intention to colonise, transform or appropriate the structures of power on the basis of an integral vision of 'total' authority and direction.[3] It was precisely the totality of this vision and the disdain for alternatives not sanctioned by NS world view (*Weltanschauung*) that points to a degree of correlation between intention and political action.

The main objective of the NS regime, immediately after 30 January 1933 was its political and social consolidation. This priority was determined by the very practical deficits of the 'seizure of power' – neither a seizure in revolutionary terms, nor an unchallenged monopoly of power. The pressure of international and domestic respectability, of wider economic necessities, of inter-systemic political bargaining, and of co-habitation with strong pillars of the *ancien régime* vigilantly tolerant towards the new radical NS project and often strikingly lukewarm vis-à-vis Hitler's initiatives, generated a realistic attitude to the goal of 'co-ordination' that (at least in 1933 or in 1934) appeared anything but assured in its scope and direction.

Even in propaganda – a field so vital for an aspiring 'totalitarian' system – the NS regime was confronted with an elaborate network of competing interests and elites, whose support or co-operation was crucial in three different ways: first, as a structural prerequisite for the consolidation of NS rule in the first difficult years of power-sharing and potential challenge; second, in order to maintain the impression of *voluntary* co-ordination (as opposed to aggressive requisition) as the fastest and least disruptive strategy for 'total' control over information, indoctrination and leisure; and, third, in those cases where the NS movement lacked in expertise, clarity of vision and competitive advantage when faced with the power of entrenched interests in the same field that had been permitted to survive the *Machtergreifung*. A snapshot of NS Germany in 1933 or even in 1934 would have offered the impression of striking continuity in crucial areas such as press ownership and activities, cinema production and cultural patronage in general. With the exception of the swift elimination of socialist-communist activities and the beginning of the process of removing 'Jewish influence' (*Entjudung*) that would gather significant momentum in subsequent years, 'co-ordination' seemed remarkably orderly and consensual. However, even this gradualist and long-term approach to 'co-ordination' was not accompanied by a consistent policy of totalitarian centralisation. The more the 'charismatic' Hitler hesitated to authorise a radicalisation of attitude vis-à-vis traditional elites and interests, and the more he refrained from empowering specific agencies and figures to proceed with the accumulation of the spoils of 'co-ordination', the more centrifugal the system became and the more the internal jurisdictional battle for control over slices of the NS empire was complicated.

Any account of NS propaganda centres on the person of Dr Joseph Goebbels. Appointed minister of Propaganda and Public Enlightenment in March 1933, he retained his party identity as Gauleiter of the crucial Berlin area and belonged to the select circle of Reich leaders (*Reichsleiter*), courtesy of his long *Nationalsozialistische Deutsche Arbeiterpartei* (NSDAP – National Socialist German Workers Party) membership and his political talent. An 'old fighter' with strong organizational skills, he came from the radical wing of the party and had opposed Hitler's centralising and 'normalising' strategy in the mid-1920s; but, unlike the Strasser brothers, he was flexible enough to adjust to the new realities of Hitler's 'charismatic' authority and played an instrumental role in the crucial months between the Führer's appointment in January 1933 and the decisive NSDAP electoral victory two months later. Goebbels shared with his leader a deep appreciation of the potential of modern propaganda and of the importance of establishing patterns of long-term political hegemony, not simply on the basis of coercion but also through positive popular identification with the new regime. He was also quick to grasp the organisational ramifications of Hitler's appointments as Chancellor, hastening to combine his party rank with a clearly defined institutional role in the new NS state. His dual role as RPL since 1930 and official minister with the same remit since 1933 reflected the fundamental process of a party-led takeover of the German state; his subsequent efforts to conduct and co-ordinate

NS propaganda from his ministerial office epitomised the prevalent culture of legalism that inspired early NS policy, concerned with curtailing the more radical forces of 'constant revolution' within the NSDAP and with granting a degree of normativity to the dual nature of party–state relations after 1933.

Goebbels was forced to wage a dual battle throughout the lifespan of the NS regime: first, along with other NS party and state agencies, to bring the broad remit of propaganda activities under the control of the regime in a totalitarian direction that involved the complete elimination of non-NS influences and jurisdictions; second, against these very same NS party and regime institutions that interfered in the domain of propaganda, thus contesting and subverting Goebbels's grip. Technically, the Propaganda minister was right in asserting that a fully co-ordinated and centralised network of propaganda – extending over all involved media and agencies of information, indoctrination and leisure – was the necessary and sufficient condition for the exercise of a fully-fledged 'totalitarian' control over society. For his regime and party opponents, however, co-ordination and centralisation were far from intertwined; in fact, so long as the latter was synonymous with control by the RMVP alone, it was deemed as undesirable. Instead, decentralising the initial 'propaganda' remit of the RMVP by dividing it into distinct spheres of activity (e.g. radio, press, cinema, etc.) and then centralising authority over each of them was the alternative strategy of all Goebbels's competitors. In parallel, this involved a conscious challenging and subverting of the RMVP's authority over all fields of activity as a means for averting full centralisation. The result of this ongoing internecine struggle was not simply administrative and jurisdictional disarray, but also obstruction of the primary process of 'co-ordination' per se.[4]

It is perhaps fashionable to talk of 'waves' of co-ordination ('fascistisation') in the study of NS propaganda.[5] There is, however, an unmistakeable pattern of stock-taking and resumption in the take-over and reconfiguration of hegemonic structures. The first wave coincided with the institutional entrenchment of NS rule immediately after Hitler's appointment – establishment of the RMVP; Reich Culture Chamber; Editors' Law; Cinema Law; re-organisation of broadcasting and so on. The second wave followed in the 1935–37 period – 'Amann ordinances' for the German press; beginning of the financial restructuring of the film industry under the command of Max Winkler; centralisation of broadcasting and so on. In preparation for, and with the start of the Second World War the prerequisites of the military effort effected new far-reaching changes on the network of information and leisure, as well as a closer relation between the two from the regime's point of view. Finally, from 1942 onwards the ultimate phase of co-ordination witnessed a radicalisation of state control over propaganda media – full nationalisation of film industry; control and streamlining of broadcasting, and so on. However, while *co-ordination* (in the sense of administrative subjugation, ideological alignment and political monopolisation) proceeded with rather spectacular – if gradual – results, *centralisation* (from an internal point of view; i.e., control exercised by the de jure legitimate institution of the Propaganda Ministry) remained a far more muddled affair (see Ch. 2). The two processes, however intertwined, followed divergent rhythms and involved different strategies. Simply put, co-ordination of propaganda structures and output proved relatively easier than centralisation under the auspices of any single authority. By focusing on these three case-studies – the co-ordination of the film industry, the press and broadcasting – I will be seeking to elucidate the pragmatic, often haphazard nature of the NS 'co-ordination' project – the process of seeking an improved environment for the attainment of open-ended, long-term goals without an essential agreement on how, when and by whom, as well as without a clear direction from the highest echelons of the NS leadership. Then, the following chapter (Ch. 2) will examine the parallel efforts of the RMVP leadership to 'centralise' control of propaganda devices in the context of the polycratic complexity and non-normative pluralism of the Third Reich, paying particular attention to the way in which external structures and tendencies impacted on Goebbels's intentions thereby thwarting the desired 'centralisation'.

Cinema

Film occupied a special position in the history of NS propaganda. Although the NSDAP did not engage in relevant activities in a systematic, extensive and centralised manner prior to the *Machtergreifung* (in spite of Goebbels's efforts, as head of the RPL, to create a central party authority[6]), the new medium exerted a mesmerising influence on many crucial NS leaders, including Hitler and Goebbels. In his first address to the representatives of the German film industry on 28 March 1933, the recently appointed minister spoke with enthusiasm about the wider significance of film and promised a new era of greatness for the country's cinema production:

> [t]he ability to make a film is not the only important thing. The inner greatness of the ideas must coincide with the external means. When this happens, German films can become a force in the world, with limitless opportunities for development. Vague, formless films are not capable of making this kind of impact on the world. The more closely a film reflects national contours, the greater are its chances of conquering the world. If the film industry starts to exercise a dangerous influence, then it is the duty of the state to step in and exercise control.

The speech was well-received by the expert audience, particularly as it combined promises of financial independence with a commitment to a degree of cultural autonomy. Even if Goebbels's charm offensive was punctuated by veiled allusions to the approaching ideological 'co-ordination' of German cinema, the message was clear: there would be no revolutionary take-over of the industry by the party, no artistic straightjack and no heavy-handed nationalisation. Instead, the Propaganda minister spoke of continuity, cautious reform and anticipated co-operation:

> [i]t is not the intention of the government to meddle in the affairs of the professional organisations. These organisations will, in fact, be granted greater rights. The government wants to proceed in full co-operation with the artistic film world and to follow a common path with it. For this it is not necessary for the artist to be associated with the Party, but they must clearly acknowledge the new basis of society [and] raise themselves to the general spiritual level of the nation.[7]

It is indicative of the cautiousness of NS policy-makers that the co-ordination of cinema was often justified by appeals to un-ideological considerations. Many of the legal and institutional measures that the regime implemented from the spring of 1933 onwards carried the official label of 'rationalisation' – a term that *stricto senso* referred more to economic viability and administrative enhancement than to ideological subjugation. In June 1933, Goebbels announced the establishment of the *Filmkreditbank* – a credit mechanism for supporting the battered German film industry after years of economic crisis and competition from abroad,[8] thus sending out the right kind of signals to the representatives of the cinema industry. The almost concurrent reduction of entertainment tax (from 11 to 8.5 per cent) was a further significant measure in the same direction,[9] received with a mixture of relief and gratitude by big studios and small producers, alike.

Throughout 1933, Goebbels had expended considerable resources in order to establish a framework of mutual trust between the regime authorities and the traditional representatives of the film industry. On 28 March 1933, when he addressed the joint meeting of *Spitzenorganisation der deutschen Filmwirtschaft* (SPIO – Parent Organisation of the German Film Industry) and *Dachorganisation der Filmschaffenden Deutschlands*[10] (DACHO – Umbrella Organisation of German Film-Makers), he combined a clear statement of the regime's determination to rescue German cinema from its cultural and financial 'crisis' with a reassuring reference to a continuity of operative patterns. This was a typical statement of the sort of 'stick and carrot' policy that would become a trademark of the regime's approach to 'co-ordination' in general.[11] The subtext of this – and other initiatives that the RMVP undertook in the first two years of NS rule – was that viability, protection and improvement would be guaranteed, but at a price. Even before March 1933, the NSDAP had already felt free to intervene in the functioning of SPIO, demanding the election of the party favourite, Engel, as the organisation's head. Throughout the spring and summer of 1933 the dissolution of all trade unions resulted in the institutional absorption of employee organisations into the structures of the NS labour movement – first, the NS *Betriebszellen Organisation*, and eventually the German Labour Front [*Deutsche Arbeitsfront* (DAF)].[12] Then came the institutional re-organisation of cultural life in Germany under the auspices of the new RMVP. The establishment of the *Reichskulturkammer* (RKK – Reich Culture Chamber) in the autumn of 1933 brought the various branches of cultural activity (radio, press, art, literature, theatre and music) under the direct unitary control of the NS regime. All branches of cultural and leisure activity in the Reich were placed under the exclusive aegis of the newly established RMVP, controlled by Goebbels himself. In spite of the introduction of hierarchical patterns and principles of division of labour (each type of activity was amalgamated into the Ministry as a separate Directorate with its own 'experts'), the overriding role of the minister was initially assumed and, later, legally entrenched.

By 1935, the first 'wave' of co-ordination of German culture had already taken institutional shape. In February 1934, Goebbels introduced a new concept in the management of film activity that betrayed his intention to re-define the field of artistic activity through more rigid interventionist structures of controlling film content. Apart from the traditional (not only to Germany, as it had been in operation throughout the Weimar years, but also across Europe) function of *negative* censorship, the Propaganda Minister spoke of the special value of *positive* censorship. The introduction of the *Reichlichtspielgesetz* (Reich Cinema Law) placed the whole issue of censorship on a fundamentally new basis.[13] Rather than targeting end-products and assessing their individual merits on a post-production level, the regime made clear its intention to engage with both the themes and methods of film production, from the inception of the project through to its official release.[14] To this purpose, the position of *Reichsfilmdramatung* (RFD – Reich Film Dramatist) was created as the first stage of active state censorship. According to the new, far more rigid process of film approval, a summary statement about the film had to be submitted to the office of the RFD in order to elicit the RMVP's approval for production. Provided that this approval was granted, it remained conditional upon the final sanction of the Ministry, through various stages of monitoring of the script and production.[15] Negative censorship at the post-production stage was maintained as the final diaphragm, but the 1934 law introduced a further measure designed to reward stylistic and thematic conformity through the award of special 'certificates' (*Prädikate*). An elaborate table of categories of distinctions, both qualitative (politically, artistically, culturally, nationally, suitable for the youth etc.) and quantitative (especially valuable etc.), created a hierarchy of official regime approval and indirect promotion that was significant in at least two ways: as a guarantee of sorts for the film's financial success in the short-term (also accompanied by progressive reduction of entertainment tax levels for artefacts carrying 'certificate' status), and as a vote of confidence to those involved in the film's production, enhancing their career prospects in the Third Reich's film industry.[16]

Positive censorship performed the crucial function of shaping the cultural artefacts in ways that conformed to the regime's political planning and actively promoted its long-term ambitions. The advantage of this system over the traditional functions of 'negative' censorship lay in its ability to guarantee, at least in theory, an increased supply of 'valuable' films for the purpose of societal indoctrination and propaganda. This function very soon rendered 'negative' censorship of the end-product all, but redundant. After an initial retrospective censorship of a series of films that had been produced under the Weimar Republic (including *Das Testament des Dr Mabuse*), the number of banned films at this stage fell to two in 1936 and one in 1938, and remained at roughly these levels until 1943, with an increase taking place in the last two years of war because of Goebbels's determination to prohibit the showing of films with 'defeatist' content.[17]

The special role of Goebbels in the process of prioritising themes, personalities, producers and distribution networks cannot be underestimated at any stage of the regime's involvement in cinema production between 1933 and 1945. The 1935 revision of the 1934 Cinema Law, however, provided the Propaganda Minister with extraordinary powers that reflected the non-normative approach of National Socialism to state administration. The minister could, 'independently of the outcome of the film inspection procedure ... decree the prohibition of a film, if he deems it necessary for urgent reasons of the public well-being'.[18] Such a power had more symbolic, than actual ramifications. Although, it essentially meant that the minister could sidestep the 'orthodox' procedural networks established through his own political patronage of the 'co-ordination' process, in reality, it constituted an emphatic restatement of his exceptional role in the decision-making process and an eloquent statement of his intention to dominate cultural production as his own personal 'feudal' domain.[19] This involved both undercutting the normative authority of his subordinates (e.g., the RFD[20]) and intervening in a series of production, stylistic and artistic matters at the expense of the creative freedom of directors, script-writers and actors. The more 'politically valuable' a film was judged by the Propaganda Minister, the more it was tied to wider propaganda purposes and objectives, and so the freedom of those involved became more vulnerable. This trend accelerated dramatically during the last stages of the war, when the absence of an auspicious 'reality' (news from the military front, developments inside the Reich etc.) accentuated the significance of propaganda allusions through film and forced Goebbels himself to demand far more rigid products from his artistic associates (see Ch. 7 and 8).

By 1935–36, Goebbels's measures had borne fruits in the direction of bringing cinema production in Germany under the regime's yoke within administrative, legal and political terms. The RKK had overseen the process of the *Entjudung* of German culture, by openly marginalising Jewish artists or by indirectly forcing them to emigrate.[21] NS film production had risen substantially, although comparing figures to the pre-1933 situation were essentially distorted, given the impact of the 1929 economic crisis on Germany, and on its film production in particular.[22] However, the recovery of film production and the success of ideological or administrative 'co-ordination' of NS cinema did not translate into financial recovery. In fact, the opposite was true: spiralling production costs (up to three times higher, compared to 1933), coupled with a devastating loss of revenue from exports (reaching 7 per cent in 1937)[23] and a growing hostility of international distributors vis-à-vis German films (not least because of the regime's anti-Jewish legislation, but also because of their blatantly political/propagandistic content) brought NS cinema to the threshold of a shattering financial crisis. At exactly this point – that is, in 1936 – Goebbels decided to implement a series of measures that amounted to a de facto nationalisation of the German film industry.[24] It is reasonable to assume that the Propaganda Minister would have wished to see this step taken from the beginning, as it was in line with his thinking on the nature and mechanics of film production under National Socialism. Balancing, however, the priority of ideological co-ordination against the need to reassure those involved in cultural production about their artistic 'freedom', avoiding negative international repercussions or even adverse financial consequences, as well as preventing a further haemorrhage of talent from Germany, was a formidable task for the embryonic – and far from secure – regime in the first two years of domestic consolidation.[25] So, did this decision – and the way that it was implemented – reflect ideological conviction, a logical and pre-meditated step, or a reflexive, reactive and desperate attempt to deal with deadlocks that the NS policy itself had produced?

The new wave of 'co-ordination' might appear at first as the logical outcome of the regime's approach to cultural production and of its totalitarian intentions; but it seems that both ideological convictions and forced structural challenges were at play in 1935–36. Both Hitler and Goebbels had repeatedly spoken of their conviction that film was the most potent means of psychological and emotional hegemony over the masses – and, for this reason, an indispensable tool of ideological propaganda.[26] At the same time, the Propaganda Minister had set himself the task of both 'co-ordinating' German cinema *and* making it commercially successful. The struggle for international prestige, fought between US cultural dominance (Hollywood, in particular), and Soviet cinematic innovation and fascist aesthetics, implied that the battle could not be fought simply within the confines of the Reich. The regime's credibility and its prospects of influencing the ideological debate on a European or even global scale presupposed the extension of the National Socialism's hegemonic status. In the context of mass culture, and given the popularity of cinema as a means of projecting national symbols of values, beliefs and more subliminal messages, consumption of cinematic artefacts was a crucial qualifier of cultural 'hegemony'. It was exactly on this level that the decline in German cinema's appeal abroad, during the mid-1930s, had both financial and political connotations, which the regime could not afford to ignore. The financial problems of the largest and most significant German studio, *Universum-Film AG* (Ufa), was in itself a sound enough commercial reason or justification for regime intervention; similar problems faced by the other heavyweights of German film production, such as Tobis and Bavaria, opened up the prospect of a co-ordinated action and facilitated the handling of the crisis in the context of a uniform administrative and financial scheme.

Thus, the establishment of a monopolistic framework of film production in the Third Reich appeared a highly desirable solution, both from the regime's ideological point of view and from the film magnates' interest in capitalising on their compliance with NS desiderata.[27] No policy choice or direction, however, should be seen as fortuitous, even if it appears to constitute a measure of structural readjustment. The de facto nationalisation of the German film industry in 1937–38 was pursued by the RMVP in a manner that betrayed both comprehensive intentions and caution. Goebbels used Max Winkler, a prominent media magnet with parallel activities in the press (see below), as the co-ordinator of the gradual re-nationalisation process. Winkler, since 1935, in his capacity as Reich Plenipotentiary for the German Film Industry, set up the *Cautio Treuhand Gmbh* as the institutional medium for the purchase of majority share-packages, first, from Ufa and Tobis (in November 1937, renamed *Tobis Filmkunst* Gmbh and absorbing a series of smaller companies), then from smaller companies such as Bavaria Film AG (in February 1938, renamed Bavaria Filmkunst GmbH) and, after the incorporation of Austria, *Wien Film Gmbh*.[28] The purchase of shares took place without any publicity by the regime authorities and without any attempt by the RMVP to exploit the propaganda dimension of this crucial step of 'co-ordination'. However, once the accumulation of control over the beleaguered big studios had been accomplished, Winkler embarked upon a comprehensive restructuring of German cinema's financing regime. In 1938, he founded the *Film Finanz GmbH*, an organisation that was meant to work in tandem with the RMVP and the *Filmkredit Bank* in order to promote the commercial and financial recovery of cinema production in Germany. The substantial increase in capital and state aid to the acquired companies throughout 1937 and 1938 did improve their financial position, with the *Cautio* and other companies controlled by Winkler (such as the *Allgemeine Film-Treuhand*) continuing to acquire share-packages in all big studios and overseeing the latter's capital increase.

The onset of the Second World War contributed to the radicalization of NS policy-making, extending and deepening patterns of 'co-ordination' in all spheres of political, economic, social and cultural life.[29] In January 1942, the complete nationalisation and centralisation of German cinema was achieved through the absorption of all studios under the new organization of *Ufa-Film GmbH* (now referred to as Ufi to distinguish it from the old Ufa studio).[30] On hindsight, this step can be interpreted as either the culmination of a step-by-step approach to the intended administrative centralisation and ideological monopolisation of cinema production, or as an upshot of the extraordinary circumstances produced by the transition from peacetime to 'total' war. Whether the war released the regime from the burden of accountability and thus facilitated the pursuit of crystallised long-term intentions, or it simply forced its authorities to deal with extraordinary factors that could not have been initially envisaged but at any rate demanded radical action, remains a moot point. The impressive expansion of the Reich's territory in the period between the *Anschluß* (March 1938) and the attack on the Soviet Union (autumn 1941) created not just new markets for German cultural artefacts, but also the preconditions for the exercise of an almost uncontested cultural hegemony over the continent. The potential economic benefits of this new situation were evident, not just to Winkler (who stated his conviction that the NS film industry should seek to maximise its quantitative output) but also to Goebbels and the RMVP. Winkler's ideas, in terms of both production levels and commercial success, had proved to be wishful thinking by 1941 – again not necessarily because of the failure of NS policy-making but, at least partly, as a result of the circumstances of war: rising production costs, scarcity of film personnel and material, competition from the equally ambitious fascist Italy in this field.[31] In this respect, it is tempting to see at least the *timing* (if not the essence too) of the full nationalisation–centralisation of the German film industry as evidence of the relative insufficiency of the 1936–38 measures and of the aggravating effect of the war.

On the other hand, January 1942 was a real turning point for the NS regime. A latent process of ideological and political radicalisation had been set in motion since the summer of 1941, with ideological priorities gradually taking precedence over rational-economic planning. The concurrence between the regime's new policy vis-à-vis cinema and the radicalisation of the regime's policy towards the 'Jewish Question' may be little more than a coincidence; but what remains indisputable is the intensification of NS ideological fanaticism, regardless of the practical implications of policy-making in this direction. The safeguarding of film production per se, and the guarantee of its ideological-propaganda value, were of paramount importance for the regime for a combination of economic and political reasons. However, as the German war machine started to crumble after 1942, Winkler's intention to exercise a virtual hegemony over the continent was superseded by external circumstances; what mattered in the last stage of the war was the sustenance of public morale within the Reich in the face of privation and potential defeat.

Overall, NS film policy never untangled the multiple dilemmas raised by National Socialism's idiosyncratic relation to modernity.[32] Faced with pressure from below – the local party rank-and-file, for example – for a complete, immediate 'nazification' (that is, both centralisation and complete 'co-ordination') of the film industry, and from financial and professional interests upon which it had to rely in the absence of full party expertise and capacity in the field, the regime chose to reconcile the irreconcilable. Commercial success, prestige on the international level, political influence, propaganda consistency, ideological indoctrination, cultural hegemony, the personal vanity of Goebbels himself – all these diverse motives and objectives intertwined, making NS policy-making in this area appear at times unswerving but, more often than not, pragmatic or even opportunistic. In fact, it is difficult to detect a rigid programmatic coherence in Nazi measures in the light of antagonisms between party and traditional interests, and shifting structural/economic caveats. Nevertheless, through an auspicious combination of the smooth voluntary co-ordination of the various agencies involved in film production, the absence of party encroachments and the relatively successful execution of the 1934–41 measures, Goebbels and the RMVP were in a position to wield substantial power and influence in this domain. This did not happen in the case of press.

Press

Max Winkler, the man who Goebbels turned to in the mid-1930s in order to rescue German cinema from commercial disaster and support it in its ability to perform its anticipated propaganda functions, had made his reputation as the 'trustee for everything' and financial saviour of many troubled commercial interests long before the Nazis came to power in 1933. Upon moving from West Prussia to the Reich, after the signing of the Versailles Treaty and the transfer of his native region to Poland, Winkler amassed responsibilities as trustee and supervisor of many activities relating to press. His interest in maintaining German influence on his homeland in the 1920s and 1930s put him in charge of a press network of newspapers targeting minority areas outside the Reich.[33] In order to both finance his activities and extend his commercial influence, Winkler proved particularly prolific in setting up purchasing and auditing GmbHs, for which he remained the principal or even sole shareholder. By the time he was introduced to Hitler and Goebbels, he had acquired the reputation of a man with commercial acumen, ideological elasticity and a vast knowledge of the German press.

Winkler's role in the 'co-ordination' of the German press under the Third Reich was perhaps less direct and overt than in matters relating to cinema. In this case, he was integrated in a hierarchical structure that had crystallised at least a decade prior to his introduction to the NS 'inner circle'. The undisputed driving force of the financial side of the NS press was Max Amann – unlike Winkler, an 'old fighter' (he had joined the party in 1920) – a party financial director and director of the *Eher Verlag* (the party's publishing house) since 1923.[34] Upon Hitler's appointment, Amann was the unquestionable, de facto press supremo of the regime. The establishment of the RMVP and the subsequent re-organisation of cultural life under the aegis of the RKK (with press being incorporated as a separate directorate in this administrative structure[35]) brought Amann to the position of the nominal head of a press branch [*Reichspressekammer* (RPK – Reich Press Chamber)] of the organisation. But even before the NS regime proceeded with the institutional re-organisation of the newspaper industry in Germany, the official association of press publishers, *Verein Deutscher Zeitungsverleger* (VDZV – Association of German Newspaper Publishers) had already taken the first steps towards a highly pragmatic 'voluntary co-ordination': in June 1933, following a meeting of its representatives with Goebbels, the executive board of the Association (in February 1934, re-organised and prefixed with the epithet 'Reich' – hence RVDZV) resigned and Amann became its new president. Given Hitler's lip-service to the alleged autonomy of the press and the degree of control that independent publishers still wielded over German press, this measure was undertaken with relative tact; tact that was certainly not repeated in the case of the union of the journalists [Reichsverband du Deutschen Presse (RVDP), Reich Association of German Press], whose 'co-ordination' was announced by the regime after a meeting that had elected Otto Dietrich, the party's Chief of Press (*Reichspressechef* and, from 1937, *Pressechef der Reichsregierung*), as its new chairman.[36] Therefore, in the following November, when the institutional structure of the RKK/RPK was finally in place, Amann could easily combine roles and powers, as well as facilitate the absorption of the previously independent associations (not just the VDZV but also the RVDP).

By then, the field of newspaper publications and publishing houses in Germany had already been seriously qualified by a generic measure. The order for the 'Protection of the State and the Nation' that was put in effect in the aftermath of the Reichstag Fire (28 February 1933) resulted in the immediate closure of more than 230 left-wing [*Sozialdemokratische Partei Deutschlands* (SPD) and *Kommunistische Partei Deutschlands* (KPD) affiliated] publications.[37] The de facto take-over of the socialist–communist press was effectively legalized five months later, with the law for the expropriation of 'hostile and subversive people's property' (*Einziehung volks- und staats-feindlichen Vermögens*), without any significant protest from the RVDZV, in spite of the blatant violation of ownership rights by the NS authorities and local organizations.[38] However, the normative dimension of the principle of unassailable independent ownership of press assets had been infringed. In the following October, in one of the last official meetings of the cabinet, Goebbels presented the draft of a law for the institutional 'co-ordination' of the German press – the so-called Editors' Law (*Schriftleitergesetz*).[39] Given the Propaganda Minister's perception of propaganda as an 'orchestra',[40] he stressed that the press should be 'in the hand of the government like a piano ..., on which the government can play' and 'a tremendously important instrument of mass influence ..., that can serve the government in its significant work'.[41] Thus, the law bestowed upon the editors the sole responsibility for 'the total content and attitude of the textual part of the newspaper'.[42] In spite of the earlier pleas from the RVDZV – wholly supported by Amann himself – for the protection of the publishers' status and influence on their publications, the RMVP chose to reduce them to nominal proprietors, leaving instead all decisions about press coverage to appointed editors.[43]

At the same time that Amann and the traditional publishing interests were subjected to a humiliating political defeat with the Editors' Law, the *Eher Verlag* scored a crucial victory against the autonomy of the *Gau* party press, in spite of the Gauleiters' efforts to ensure their control over press activities in their regions. Through the organisation of the RPK, Amann oversaw the creation of the *Standarte GmbH* as the major shareholder of the previously independent *Gau* press interests. In reality, the latter company acted as an extension of the *Eher Verlag* itself (which was its sole shareholder), thus supplying Amann with enhanced powers over the overall structure and administration of the NS party press.[44] Yet, even this seeming triumph was more symbolic and qualified rather than normative: even under the new system of direct central supervision, Gauleiters continued to press for (and often force) a radicalisation of policy vis-à-vis non-NSDAP-controlled publications. Throughout 1933 and the first half of 1934, party agencies pressed for a 'revolutionary' take-over of 'bourgeois' interests, whilst already active in the violent dismantling of socialist and 'Jewish' assets.[45] In spite of Amann's (and, on this occasion, Goebbels's too) efforts to bestow some administrative normativity on the suppression of the left-wing press and the streamlining of the overall publication system in the Third Reich through the statute of the RPK, local party groups appeared to force a typical process of 'radicalisation from below' that – along with a plethora of other activities from 'old fighters' – smeared the regime's image at a time when respectability remained the primary political objective for domestic consolidation.[46] Amann was urging a more 'rationalised' (both financially and organisationally) press structure; yet, the number of local party dailies continued to proliferate throughout 1933–35, increasing patterns of competition not only between NS press and 'bourgeois' publications but crucially amongst party publications too. While this situation was unsatisfactory for both sides – politically and, increasingly, financially – their respective prescriptions pointed to anti-diametrical directions, with Amann pleading for rationalisation and centralisation and party agencies continuing to demand the liquidation of non-party press.

By 1935, the situation in German press had reached a new low ebb, particularly in commercial terms. A drop in readership figures and subscriptions,[47] declining revenues from advertising, increased competition, escalating production costs and the apparent failure of the institutional reform of 1933 to streamline press activities had forced upon the regime authorities an untenable state of affairs. Whatever *ideological* and *institutional* caveats may have existed before in the way of a complete financial and structural re-organisation of German press, the crisis of 1934–35 was predominantly an *economic* affair. Thus, in early 1935, Amann was authorised to proceed with a comprehensive re-organisation project that was destined to change the face of German press for the rest of the NS period, and break traditional patterns of continuity that had existed for many decades or even centuries in the field. The so-called 'Amann Ordinances'[48] of April 1935 constituted an unmistakeable reassertion and manifestation of his dominant position in the administration of the press under the NS regime – or *did they*? If the ordinances were intended – as they claimed – to 'eliminate unhealthy competitive conditions' through a wave of more or less forced mergers and closures, then Amann appeared to successfully halt the process of proliferation that had been under way since January 1933. If, however, rationalisation was a structural and economic decision, there were two further fields of choice that had to accompany this decision: the first was the primary target of removing 'unhealthy competition'; the second was the degree of centralisation and party or regime control that the new status quo would promote. On both counts, Amann's 1935 formula was sharply different to his earlier declarations. The man who had repeatedly stood up for traditional publishers' interests against the radical ambitions of the party apparatus, now appeared willing to pursue a policy that constituted a fundamental assault on their independence and financial concerns. Under the semblance of 'legalism', he forced more than 500 publishing houses to either close down, merge or be absorbed into his own *Eher Verlag*. By 1939, the RPK in association with the *Eher Verlag* controlled more than 150 publishing houses; this figure rose to 550 in 1941 and approached 1000 during the last year of the war.[49] In essence, the Amann ordinances effected a near-complete 'co-ordination' of the non-party press that the local and regional NSDAP agencies had been calling for since the *Machtergreifung*, but the regime had been distinctly unwilling to pursue until early 1935.

At the 1936 Nuremberg Party Rally, Max Amann addressed a large audience of NSDAP members, seizing the opportunity in order to praise the achievements of his 'co-ordination' project in the seventeen months that had passed since the date that his ordinances had come into effect. After making the extraordinary claim that the reformed German press was actually more 'free' and independent than ever before (alluding to the break-up of large publishing trusts and the 'cleansing' of *staatsfeindlich* elements), he produced a list of positive developments since the introduction of the April 1935 legal framework.[50] It is true that both circulation and revenue incomes looked somewhat healthier in the 1936–39 period than in the first three years of NS rule.[51] The claimed improvement, however, was neither impressive nor without its huge long-term cost for the operation of German press. In spite of an orchestrated high-profile campaign to raise the profile of newspapers, promoted by the RMVP in the autumn of 1936, both circulation and, particularly, subscription figures did not show any increase that either Hitler or Goebbels found worth boasting about.[52] Thus, the assessment of the April 1935 ordinances took place on two separate levels, producing contradictory conclusions: whilst on the purely economic level the re-organisation of press concerns through 'cleansing', closures, mergers and take-overs had resulted in a more rational division of labour between national, regional and local press, as well as in an increase in overall revenue, on the political level the indication that readership figures had not recovered alarmed the NS leadership that continued to rely on printed propaganda in order to maintain its ideological hegemony over the masses. Standardisation of content,[53] increasing party encroachment on the press industry, the monotony of material presented, the withdrawal of any critical function from the press and the continuing administrative battle between the various competing NSDAP agencies, were barely conducive to the raising of the press' profile within German society. At the same time, it was ironic that the alleged rationalisation of the press, whilst reducing the number of publications by around 40 per cent, had generated multiple new layers of bureaucracy.[54] So, the extension of the Reich's territory from March 1938 onwards (Anschluß, Sudetenland, Czechoslovakia, Memel) offered mixed prospects. On the one hand, it supplied the German press with new markets that, with minimal administrative re-organisation, could be immediately incorporated into the German press' commercial sphere. On the other hand, the already dysfunctional duplication of competences and jurisdictions inside the pre-1938 Reich was augmented, producing new frictions and overlaps, through its export to the conquered territories.[55]

By the time that the war broke out in Poland, the co-ordination of German press had been largely achieved – faster and more effectively in institutional terms than in any other domain of NS propaganda. The overall number of newspapers within the Reich halved during the 1933–39 period, and again by 1944, in spite of the extension of the Reich's territory and the growth of its target audience.[56] The cumulative effect of the 1933 Enabling Act and the 1935 ordinances resulted in a system of press control by the Amann–Winkler enterprise that amounted to four fifths of all publications in Germany.[57] However, until the last years of the war, press remained a supremely polycratic triangular affair, institutionally dominated by Dietrich, with a tentative stake controlled by the RMVP – that at least prevented its monopolisation by the *Reichspressechef* – and with the dominant presence of Amann in the organisational-financial domain (see Ch. 2). As the war went on, the contraction of the press domain (initially the desired effect of the 'co-ordination' and 'rationalisation' measures of the pre-war years) accelerated – this time due to logistical difficulties and material shortages.[58] The overall number of newspapers had already dropped from almost 4700 in 1933 to less than 2000 before the outbreak of the war; by the end of 1944 it had fallen under 1000.[59] The escalation of the Allied air warfare in 1943–44 proved to be the single most disruptive factor for the functioning of the NS press system (see Ch. 7): the case of Bochum, whose newspapers ceased circulation in the aftermath of the November 1944 air raid, was both indicative of the extent of the problem and suggestive of a wider pattern that affected the whole Reich in the last years of the war.[60]

Broadcasting

Broadcasting occupied an intermediary position between the established medium of press and the new devices of information and leisure that rested on modern technological advances and passive reception. More entrenched and socially widespread than cinema (radio transmissions had started in 1915, with a more systematic approach introduced in 1923[61]), radio was nevertheless still lagging behind newspapers in terms of audience dispersal, variety and sophistication in Germany, prior to Hitler's appointment in January 1933. On the other hand, as a relatively recent technological breakthrough it had not developed a clear physiognomy, combining – often awkwardly – information as an *ersatz*-newspaper and entertainment in lieu of more traditional social activities, such as music and theatre halls.[62] In terms of its communication potential, it was both more versatile than press, capable of reaching audiences across the Reich and beyond, and less flexible, when compared to the diversification of press on the basis of a national, regional and local division of labour. As a device of totalitarian integration and manipulation, broadcasting had significant potential, being far easier to co-ordinate and then regulate, centrally. As a political device of propaganda, it benefited from technological options that enabled it to reach out to a wide range of listener groups, from the *Volksdeutsche* across Europe to foreign audiences (through broadcasting in different languages), and to those traditionally more restricted to the private sphere (such as women). As a medium of information, radio's central or broadly regional programme structure ran the risk of appearing too vague, generic and divorced from the particular local experiences of a population accustomed to the diversification of information represented by the existing diffused press structure.

Thus, the NS regime was faced with both unparalleled opportunities and unique obstacles in its attempt to turn broadcasting into a pivotal extension of its totalitarian project. Radio, unlike the press, could succumb to a centrally-imposed uniformity, but its decidedly decentralised status during the Weimar period necessitated an extremely delicate act involving repatriation of authority from the regional networks back to Berlin and the state. In no other medium of the NS propaganda apparatus was co-ordination and centralisation so closely intertwined and interdependent. During the Weimar Republic, broadcasting had various patrons and agents.[63] The only central regulatory authority, the *Reichsrundfunkgesellschaft* (RRG – Reich Radio Company), was an umbrella organisation, bringing around the same table representatives of the *Reichspost* (which controlled 51 per cent of the company's shares, as well as its technical functions), of the Finance Ministry and of the nine regional broadcasting companies (*Sender*) that operated across the Reich and held the remaining 49 per cent.[64] Understandably, the RRG's loose structure and polycratic composition rendered it barely suitable for promoting the new regime's totalitarian propaganda scheme. Instead, the establishment of the RMVP in March 1933 and of the RKK [which included a separate Radio Chamber – *Reichsrundfunkkammer* (RRK – Reich Radio Chamber)] six months later provided a further administrative layer of control and co-ordination. Goebbels, eager to promote a unitary propaganda vision across all media, ensured that a working division of labour between the RPL, RMVP and the RPK would not result in jurisdictional chaos by always appointing a close aide as the head of all three bodies.[65] After the dissolution of the Reich's previous federal structure, he made clear to the representatives of the regional broadcasting companies that there would be 'no more place for state commissioners and programme advisors; even less so for capital participation of the Länder in the radio companies'; consequently – and in spite of the rather extraordinary resistance of the Bavarian regional station[66] – he replaced all but one of the regional *Intendanten* with his loyalists and demanded from the companies to give up their 49 per cent share in the RRG.[67]

The 'co-ordination' and 'centralisation' of German broadcasting proceeded with the re-organisation of the RRG – a process that started in the summer of 1933 and proceeded cautiously until the outbreak of the war. A new administrative structure was put in place in June that ensured the de facto control of the company by the RMVP. In the appointed board of directors, out of a total of five members, the RMVP nominated three from amongst the directors of the regional companies, with the remaining two posts shared between the *Reichspost* and the Ministry of Finance.[68] Meaningfully, the Ministry of the Interior was no longer represented, in spite of its previously important role in supervising the decentralised structure of broadcasting in co-operation with the Länder, whilst the role of the *Reichspost* was limited to purely technical assistance (the previous post of Radio Commissioner of the *Reichspost* was abolished too).[69] On 8 July 1933, a new charter for the RRG was put into effect, underlining the organisation's responsibility for a genuine NS radio throughout the Reich. The triumph of the RMVP in this process of administrative 'co-ordination' cannot be exaggerated. Goebbels achieved a perfect amalgamation of personnel across the radio division of the ministry, the relevant Chamber of the RKK, the broadcasting division of the RPL and the RRG: Horst Dreßler–Andreß occupied the top position in the first three, whilst the loyal Eugen Hadamowsky moved upwards within the RPL to overall Programme Director (*Reichssendeleiter*) and director (*Hauptgeschäftsführer*) of the RRG.[70]

The second decisive step in the direction of co-ordination/centralisation occurred on 1 April 1934, when it was announced that all regional companies were to be renamed as 'Reichssender'.[71] The change was more symbolic than practical, but it suggested an unequivocal commitment of the NS government to further centralisation and curtailing of the regional companies' freedom in the domain of overall programme and content. The processes of administrative and ideological centralisation were once again intertwined and interdependent. Ever since Chancellor Fritz von Papen had instituted a zone of German-wide broadcasting in 1932, that violated the erstwhile complete independence of the regional companies in terms of programme composition, the trend was decidedly in favour of less local diversification and of increased amounts of 'integration propaganda' for the whole of the 'national community'.[72] Thus, not only political ceremonies but also speeches by high-ranking NS leaders and high-profile entertainment (e.g. concerts) were broadcast across Germany from the regional Sender, thus paving the way for a more effective central management of the content and for a tighter administrative control of the existing structure. Unlike the press – which was designed by the NS authorities as a multi-level operation, extending from the whole country to regions, old Länder and localities – the new radio became a decidedly more centralised enterprise, largely impervious to party involvement on the local level.[73]

More changes were in store, and were implemented in stages. The spring of 1937 was a crucial period of transformation for German broadcasting. Confident in the unopposed reception of his earlier re-organisation project, Goebbels proceeded with both institutional and personnel changes. In early April, Dreßler–Andreß was replaced by Hans Kriegler, ushering in a new era of increased central intervention in the matters of regional broadcasting, whose relative freedom his predecessor had tolerated to an apparently unacceptable extent.[74] Almost concurrently, the new command post of a general radio Intendant was created and awarded to yet another Goebbels loyalist, Heinrich Glasmeier – previously, director of the Cologne regional company. Glasmeier was also appointed general director of the RRG in an attempt to curtail the often disruptive fanaticism, confrontational nature and doubtful organisational skills of Hadamowsky.[75] The new broadcasting structure, which Goebbels introduced as Großdeutsches Rundfunk, was a further indication of the long-term intentions of the RMVP leadership in the direction of achieving a complete subordination of radio to the demands of the central government and the elimination of regional diversification. In fact, it would take another three years to complete this process, under the guise of extraordinary measures necessary for the war effort: in May 1940, the complete unification of the broadcasting companies and the standardisation of the programme across the Reich was achieved (Reichsprogramm der Deutschlandssender). A year later, and after intensifying criticism of the broadcasting content's uniformity and monotony, Goebbels acquiesced in the introduction of a second Reich-wide programme, particularly geared towards entertainment.[76]

By that time, further significant institutional and personnel changes had taken place. Just before the outbreak of the war, the Propaganda minister had replaced Kriegler with Alfred–Ingemar Berndt, whose experience as head of the German Press Division of the RMVP's press section was expected to become of crucial significance during the conduct of the war. Berndt was also to be responsible for all contacts between the RRG and the various Reich-wide news and press agencies, in an attempt to extend the RMVP's authority over the general content of wartime propaganda beyond the strict domain of radio. In the autumn of 1939, Goebbels had for the first time to defend his grip over radio against the ambitious incursions of Ribbentrop's *Auswärtiges Amt* (AA – German Foreign Ministry), whose desire to dominate foreign broadcasting involved a direct jurisdictional conflict with the RMVP (see Ch. 2).[77] The RMVP attempted to counter this move by enhancing its involvement in foreign broadcasts and by issuing a directive that demanded all radio material to be submitted to the ministry for approval.[78] The following year, Goebbels embarked upon a wide re-organisation of the RRG's news section, establishing clear lines of jurisdiction for domestic and foreign radio propaganda within his ministry's division, as well as promoting a better liaison with the *Oberkommando Wehrmacht's* (OKW – Wehrmacht High Command) propaganda companies – Wehrmacht Propaganda [*Propaganda-Kompanien* (PK Troops)].[79] A crucial final step in the direction of total control over the RRG was also taken in early 1940, with the dissolution of the old five-member board structure; the new managing committee would be solely based on personnel from RMVP, with the exclusion of both the *Reichspost* and the Finance Ministry. Berndt, assisted by his deputy, Wolfgang Diewerge, proved instrumental in completing the co-ordination of German broadcasting and entrenching the role of the RMVP at its helm. When he was moved to the commanding post of the ministry's crucial Propaganda Division in September 1941, and was succeeded by his deputy, he considered his work in reorganising broadcasting successfully completed.

Overall, Berndt and Goebbels must have been satisfied with the expansion of the radio's significance and spread within the Reich. Subscription numbers rose almost four-fold between 1933 and 1941 (from 4.5 to over 16 million),[80] with a positive knock-on effect in terms of revenue, as the RRG's budget depended on licence fees. The success of the 'popular radio' (*Volksempfänger*) scheme, introduced in 1933 by Goebbels himself, had paid handsome dividends, elevating the relative significance of broadcasting as a medium of 'integration propaganda' across NS Germany, and strengthening its position vis-à-vis the traditional monopoly of information through press. As the RMVP ensured that the cost of the *Volksempfänger*, starting from the already affordable level of 76DM for the VE301 model in May 1933, be halved by 1938,[81] radio became for the first time a genuinely popular device of information and entertainment, offering opportunities for promoting a strong feeling of belonging to an imaginary national *Gemeinde* across the regions of the *Großdeutsches Reich*.[82] As the success of programmes, such as the 'Wish Concert' (*Wünschkonzert*) would show, a war-weary and increasingly depressed people embraced this opportunity, albeit less as a sign of ideological conformity, than as a response to the effective marketing of radio as a mass entertainment and emotional community-building medium.

There were, however, palpable failures too. In September 1942, the Propaganda minister criticised the lack of efficiency and imagination in the German radio, also divulging his anxiety at the lack of a considerable breakthrough in terms of listeners' endorsement of the programme, in spite of the plethora of changes that had been implemented since the outbreak of the war.[83] After just a year at the helm of the Broadcasting Division of the RMVP, Diewerge had to go. His departure coincided with the return of a talented and reliable old Goebbels ally from the front. Hans Fritzsche, who had served as head of the Press Division's news section and from 1937 as head of the Inland Press Division before resigning in early 1942, took over the political functions of broadcasting with the additional broader remit of a Commissioner for Political Matters.[84] An able journalist and experienced radio commentator, he instilled new life into the medium (after the unfortunate Diewerge spell) and dominated the field until the collapse of the Reich in early May 1945.

Goebbels, however, had already bowed to listeners' demands for a more diverse, entertainment-oriented and less overtly propagandistic broadcasting programme. Thus, while Fritzsche was instrumental in strengthening the authority of political commentary and in revitalising the broadcasting's status as a medium of information and ideological indoctrination, the space and significance allocated to radio entertainment increased steadily during the war years. The 1 : 1 ratio that was the norm during the early years of the NS regime, already changed to 2 : 1 in favour of entertainment by early 1939, had only temporarily stabilised (as a result of the increasing need for military information after September 1939) before reaching 4 : 1 by 1943/44.[85] This significant trend was further bolstered by the appointment of Hans Hinkel as Commissioner for (Radio) Entertainment Matters in February 1942.[86] In fact, Hinkel (already since early 1940, chief executive of the RKK) had been commissioned personally by Goebbels to monitor broadcasting and implement a programme of wide-ranging changes in the autumn of 1941. During the autumn and winter of 1941, he reported frequently to the Propaganda Minister, both with long memoranda and in person, intimating his ideas for a radically new approach, not just to the entertainment aspect of the programme, but also with regard to the whole structure and philosophy of broadcasting in the Third Reich.[87] He criticised the current radio programme as 'boring, dry and humourless' in its attempt to simply emulate the function of a newspaper; instead, he asked for more imaginative editorial skills, more emphasis on entertaining the masses, as well as primary attention to the presentation and layout of the content.[88] Furthermore, he called for more 'passion' in the delivery of the spoken word, primarily through an increased number of speakers and commentators; and for a fundamental change in the choice of musical entertainment provided by the radio[89] – hence his plan for the re-organisation of all music entertainment under specific categories (e.g. 'modern entertainment music', 'dance music', 'cabaret-like', 'suitable for soldiers', 'classical', 'high music' etc.).[90] Therefore, his appointment as Entertainment Commissioner in 1942 constituted both a tangible reward for his preparatory work and a mandate for further far-reaching changes. As a result, the role of Diewerge, as head of the Division until late 1942, was de facto reduced to the field of political information and indoctrination at the same time that the latter had shrank to a level below 20 per cent of the total programme's content. Hinkel and Fritzsche headed the organisational structure of German broadcasting until May 1944, when the former left and afforded Fritzsche the privilege of total control over the Broadcasting Division, with entertainment and political matters reunited in his remit.[91]

Overall, the relative autonomy of the RRG with respect to the RMVP declined sharply during the war years, in line with the general trend towards centralisation. Although the appointment of Berndt in the RRG 'command' post in 1939 appeared to suggest that initially Goebbels preferred the formula of interdependence between the two institutions, his subsequent measures resulted in a virtual absorption of the RRG into the ministry. By 1943, the Hinkel–Fritzsche joint management of the Broadcasting Division, with the extraordinary powers invested in them, had marginalised both Hadamowsky and Glasmeier.[92] With the elimination of these two command posts, a further significant change came about: in the last two years of the war the responsibility for the *Deutschlandssender* programme passed from the RRG directly to the RMVP, removing perhaps the last element of broadcasting's nominal independence from the Propaganda Ministry.

For this broadly effective political functioning of German broadcasting, until the last days of the Reich, Goebbels and his RMVP associates could justly claim most of the credit, as well as accept the responsibility for any shortcoming. However, the absence in the domain of the radio of the sort of open antagonisms and jurisdictional clashes that plagued German press should not conceal a rather high degree of structural interdependence between the two media throughout the NS period. Effectively, when it came to the broad remit of 'political matters' (that is, information), radio depended on roughly the same network of news agencies that also provided material for the newspapers and other Reich publications. With the fusion of Wolff's *Telegraphisches Büro* and Hugenberg's *Telegraphen-Union* into the single body of the *Deutsches Nachrichtenbüro* (DNB – German News Agency) in December 1933, a centralised structure of news dissemination was established.[93] This ensured the consistency and uniformity of information across the board of German media – and there is evidence that the various sections of the RMVP were making efforts to ensure a smooth functioning across the spectrum of propaganda activities.[94] The DNB functioned in principle as the main clearing body for all propaganda material supplied to both press and radio domains. It also included the Wireless News Service [*Drahtlose Dienst* (DD)], which was of crucial significance for the timely dispatch of news. Goebbels had succeeded in transferring the DD from the RRG to the RMVP in May 1933, placing it within the Press Division. This was, however, reversed in 1937/38, when the service was returned to the RRG and became an integral part of the regime's broadcasting network. Here, the jurisdictional lines between press and radio clearly became blurred. In practice, the dependence of the radio network on information provided through the DNB (and later also through the censors of the OKW) meant that, whilst on the organisational and administrative level the RMVP exercised substantial control over broadcasting, the raw material was supplied through a channel that lay outside the strict jurisdictional range of the RMVP. What was even more alarming for the Propaganda minister was the fact that in exceptional circumstances the DNB could bypass the RMVP in communicating 'breaking news'. This happened, for example, on 29 June 1941, with the notorious twelve triumphant 'special announcements' (*Sondermeldungen*) about the breakthrough on the eastern front – a stratagem masterminded and executed by Hitler and his Press Chief, Otto Dietrich to the annoyance of Goebbels (see Ch. 5).

An efficient division of labour between press and radio with regard to political information was never achieved, largely due to the clash between the two *Reichsleiter*, Goebbels and Dietrich: whilst the former saw in broadcasting an opportunity to redress the balance after his failure to infiltrate the press domain, the latter defended with ferocious territoriality his grip over news policy, trying at the same time to counter his opponent's authority over radio and to enhance his own input in the same field (see Ch. 2). It is no coincidence that the Radio Chamber of the PKK was officially dissolved on 28 October 1939 with its functions transferred directly to the RRG.[95] Both, Goebbels and Dreßler–Andreß had envisaged the constitution of an autonomous and self-sufficient broadcasting sphere, encompassing journalists, programme presenters, technical personnel as well as listeners' groups. The reality was quite different, however: not only did the Finance ministry maintain its grip on technical provisions and its representation on the RRG's board, but also the corporate representation of the radio's journalistic staff was placed under the Press Chamber. This situation had clearly left the Radio Chamber, also flanked by the RMVP's Broadcasting Division and the developed RRG structure, without any meaningful remit – thus, its final dissolution surprised or saddened nobody.

Nevertheless, the co-ordination and centralisation of broadcasting reached its intended conclusion during the last years of the war, leaving the RMVP – and Goebbels personally – in a commanding position. In comparison to the chaotic and aggressively polycratic mechanisms of press control, radio remained a largely smooth operation, whereby polyocracy was much more the result of past inheritances and of the proliferation of offices by the RMVP itself, than the legacy of an internecine struggle for jurisdictional control amongst competing agencies. The institutional *Gleichschaltung* of broadcasting proceeded with caution and in stages, substantially accelerated by the circumstances of war. It was facilitated by a successful strategy of infrastructural improvement, technical innovation and a consistent attempt to increase the accessibility of the medium, particularly through the affordable *Volksempfänger*. Success on the organisational and economic level, however, became possible only on the basis of a fundamental concession in terms of content that affected the overall function of the medium in a divergent way to the regime's earlier 'totalitarian' intentions for integration propaganda. The shift towards entertainment, first as a strategy for winning over tired and unimpressed listeners, and then as a conscious means for diversion and escapism from the bleak realities of everyday life and from the depressing military situation, succeeded in boosting the popularity of the medium. But it also revealed a partial abdication on part of the RMVP from its intended ideological function as *political* propaganda channel. As many listeners, increasingly unconvinced by the regime's official information material that was disseminated through both press and the *Deutschlandsender*, turned to foreign stations for an alternative view – in spite of the severe penalties incurred if arrested[96] –, NS broadcasting turned to entertainment as a compensatory factor for sustaining its audience and bolstering their morale (*Stimmung*). The concession was of course onerous for the RMVP, which had increasingly regarded control of radio as a compensation for the loss of influence over the press; but it was one that at least ensured the existence of a popular, open channel of community-building and psychological support.

Overall, the NS regime succeeded admirably in its efforts to bring about a wholesale, swift and enduring 'co-ordination' of the wide domain of propaganda, through a combination of repressive measures and voluntary submission of the organisations themselves, avoiding heavy-handed solutions where possible, showing some modicum of concern for practical/ financial considerations and following a semblance of legality. Negative 'co-ordination' – that is, removal of any *volksfeindlich* influence (socialist/ communist, Jewish) – was the most uncompromising aspect of this process; attacks on the autonomy of other, less ideologically charged interests (e.g. confessional press, independence of regional broadcasting companies) were more veiled and usually justified under the banner of 'rationalisation'.[97] The fact that the strategies and the pace differed from case to case attests to a more nuanced and careful approach to 'co-ordination' that took into account sectional peculiarities and dynamics without losing touch of the wider picture of either ideological *Gleichschaltung* or commercial viability. By the time that the war broke out, much had been achieved in this respect;

what remained was dealt with in a final wave, largely underpinned by the (fundamentally different) circumstances of war, in 1941–42.

However, bringing all aspects and functions of propaganda firmly within the remit of the NS authorities was only one, however, crucial, step; producing a coherent, administratively sound and effective *system* of propaganda was an altogether different matter. Negative 'co-ordination' was only one necessary condition for this, but by no means sufficient. Once within the domain of National Socialism, propaganda activities were caught up in the tangled web of competing jurisdictions, unresolved tensions and personal rivalries that characterised the triangular relation between Hitler, state and party throughout the history of the Third Reich.[98] 'Centralisation' proved a far more complex process, fraught with complications derived from trends that were very much ingrained in the overall functioning of the NS system. To these – and the twisted story of NS propaganda 'centralisation' – we shall turn now.

2
'Polyocracy' versus 'Centralisation': The Multiple 'Networks' of NS Propaganda

Polyocracy and 'charismatic' power in the NS regime

So much has been said in recent decades about the 'polycratic', chaotic, un-bureaucratic and ad hoc nature of the NS regime. This interpretation has had a long academic ancestry dating back to the years of the Second World War. It was Franz Neumann who, in the early 1940s, described the administrative structures and practices of the NS state as a 'behemoth' – a network without unity of purpose or direction:

> I venture to suggest that we are confronted with a form of society in which the ruling groups control the rest of the population directly, without the mediation of that rational though coercive apparatus hitherto known as the state. This new social form is not yet fully realized, but the trend exists which defines the very essence of the regime ... In fact, except for the charismatic power of the Leader, there is no authority that co-ordinates the four powers [party, army, bureaucracy, industry], no place where the compromise between them can be put on a universal valid basis.[1]

Around the same time, Ernst Fraenkel coined the description 'dual state' in order to highlight the deliberate administrative confusion, duplication and overlapping in the structures of NS rule. The complex interweaving of multiple party and state competences, both horizontally (within each group) and vertically (party–state contest for maximum jurisdictional powers), led Fraenkel to a similar conclusion to that of Neumann about the multifaceted nature of decision-making in NS Germany, where traditional bureaucratic expertise was being consistently eroded by the 'charismatic' features of Hitler's leaderships and where the continuity of state structures were constantly subjected to ad hoc law produced in a haphazard manner, in order to accommodate the interests of the various competing groups.[2] For Fraenkel, the NS state was a system in a permanent state of 'crisis', resulting in a (self-) destruction of civil order. Since then, substantial work has been done to shed light on the problematic relation between leadership, state bureaucracy and party elites.[3]

In 1960, Robert Koehl[4] attempted to provide an overall interpretative framework for the absence of a clear bureaucratic structure in the NS regime. His idea focused on the notion of 'neo-feudalism', whereby the un-bureaucratic polyocracy of the NS state depended on a retreat to medieval notions of faith (*Ehre*), commitment (*Gefolgschaft*) and loyalty (*Treue*) that bound together the pandemonium of competing forces, strategies and personal agencies. Koehl found a correlation between the proceeding disintegration of the regime after 1942 and the strengthening of these 'neo-feudal' tendencies:

> [i]n the last years of the Nazi era there is the most striking evolution along feudal lines. Göring, Goebbels, Himmler, and the newcomers, Speer and Bormann, had constructed virtually impregnable appanages. The more dependent Hitler became upon their empires for German victory, the more easily they looted the power of rivals like Rosenberg and Ribbentrop, Sauckel and Keitel. They made their systems independent of the central authorities and even of the Führer's support by absorbing some vehicle of power, usually economic, though Goebbels also used the mass media and Himmler the secret police.

More than three decades later, Ian Kershaw contributed an elaborate model for analysing the way in which disparate forces within the Third Reich (both personal and institutional) became at the same time an extension and a categorical affirmation of Hitler's 'charismatic' authority. His notion of 'working towards the Führer' underlined the exceptional nature of decision-making in NS Germany, whereby an array of diverse – often contrasting or even incongruent – political initiatives emanated, not directly from the leadership, but from individuals or agencies that could successfully claim a derived legitimacy from him.[5] The so-called *Führerprinzip*, as Carl Schmitt had consistently argued, marked the demise of traditional notions of bureaucratic authority and ushered in a new period in which the leader is and acts as the whole national community:

> [o]n this thirtieth of January [1933] ... the Hegelian civil service state of the nineteenth century ... gave way to another state structure. On this day, one can therefore say, Hegel died.[6]

The implication here is that 'charismatic' authority neither can nor seeks to be bureaucratised, instead, the directly derived legitimacy from the 'charismatic' authority of the leader results in a system where every political initiative emanates from, and elaborates upon his singular will. What kept the 'system' together cannot of course be reduced to one factor; but it had little to do with efficiency or rational division of labour. Perhaps the most significant cohesive force was the leader's capacity to forge and maintain – through emotional means – a truly 'charismatic community' (*Gemeinde*) around him.[7] The members of this community, according to Kershaw, influenced as they were by their leader's overall vision and broad guidelines, interpreted his often cryptic will and implemented strategies that, in their opinion, could advance his vision in the most effective and unadulterated form. Thus, a series of political 'laboratories' were established – both within the state structure and as adjuncts to the party – through which prominent members of the charismatic community worked towards fulfilling their impression of their leader's will. In this crucial respect, Kershaw's interpretive model and Koehl's 'neo-feudalist' analysis intersect: the existence of individual power-bases in the institutional structure of NS Germany enabled a concurrent drive to work out different strategies for the realisation of the leader's vision; and the very 'charismatic' nature of Hitler's authority encouraged the de facto institutionalisation and constant – unchecked – expansion of this polycratic structure.

'Working towards the Führer' was not a facile task in itself. Hitler was notoriously vague in his specific political pronouncements and concerned far more with the overall vision than with the fine print. He was also essentially unreliable in his choices, especially when he was performing the supremely 'charismatic' function of institutional *mediation* between competing forces in his 'system'. For some, he deliberately refused to draw definitive administrative lines, lest the margins of his 'charismatic' power should become curtailed; for others this was simply the result of either weakness, confusion or ineptitude.[8] In many cases his verdict had an ad hoc validity, restricted to the case adjudicated; attempts by those involved to project a wider institutional significance to other related realms of jurisdiction were often thwarted by a new Hitlerian mediation to the contrary effect. Performing this role as erratically as he did, ever since January 1933, produced an ever-expanding web of interdependences, duplications and overlaps, which appeared to become even more tangled with every new arbitration. By September 1939, the situation had already spiralled out of control, fuelling new clashes and 'grey zones' of jurisdiction that required urgent attention if the war was to be conducted through a sound system of institutional division of labour. Skirmishes, however, continued unabated and indeed escalated: somewhere in the previous six years there was a Hitler adjudication that one or the other NS figure could invoke to improve his position relative to his internal state or party opponents; the latter would retort with a similar appeal to another, pre-existing settlement for the same reason but to the contrary effect. This, in turn, encouraged an even fiercer competition for authority and jurisdiction amongst the various branches of state and party; and the more secluded

Hitler's position was becoming after 1939 (due to his focus on war) and after 1942 (because of his disillusioned retreat into his inner circle), the more the institutional and personality struggle was turning into an all-out struggle. 'Working *towards* the Führer' was gradually transformed into 'working *in spite of* the Führer'; still in his name, still under his 'charismatic' authority, but largely filling in the gap of his absence, and competing for the prize of his preferred interpretation and for the ensuing rewards.

The role of Goebbels in NS propaganda: power-base and limits

Perhaps no other person apart from Hitler has suffered more from historiographical exaggerations than Goebbels. His role in the development and management of NS propaganda – important though it was – has been distorted almost beyond recognition by postwar attempts to present him as a near-omnipotent tsar of information manipulation and a deviant choreographer of every NS initiative in the realm of news and leisure. Undoubtedly, Goebbels wielded extraordinary power in a domain that held exceptional significance for a system based on 'charismatic' legitimacy in which state and party continued to dovetail until the final days of the regime. Both his loyalty to the Führer and his expertise in communication management were unquestionable. During the last years of the war – and especially after the defeat at Stalingrad in February 1943 – he amassed further extraordinary, if once again ad hoc, powers (Inspector–General for War Damage, Plenipotentiary for Total War, Defender of Berlin) in addition to his generic propaganda remit and his particularly close supervision of film, radio and wider cultural matters. During the victorious phase of the war (1939–42), he was a crucial component of the industry that popularised and communicated triumph to a bewilderingly blasé public opinion. When defeat started to close in on NS Germany, he led the effort for the psychological preparation of German society, ensuring that the 'legacy of 1918' (domestic collapse) would not re-enact itself and once more betray the German effort from within. Partly, because his political and party responsibilities were focused on Berlin, he remained in proximity to Hitler until the very end, at a time where other Führer erstwhile favourites had discredited themselves (e.g. Goering), departed from the capital (e.g. Himmler as war Commander) or simply lost favour (e.g. Speer). During those last months, Goebbels earned a new lease of Hitler's attention and credit, staying with him until the end and emulating his leader's death on 1 May 1945.

Yet, in many ways, this was the meteoric zenith of Goebbels's relationship with his Führer, not its logical culmination. Although safe in both his state and party positions, the Propaganda minister had experienced a virtual rollercoaster of emotions in the previous twelve years. 1933 proved a glorious year from him. He secured unprecedented powers for his RMVP under

Hitler's 13 March decree.[9] As both state minister and leader of the RPL he became responsible for a broad array of matters, ranging from information to party events and from press to entertainment and broad cultural matters. In September, he oversaw the establishment of the RKK as an umbrella organisation for separate 'chambers' in art, film, radio, press, music and theatre.[10] Goebbels maintained a firm grip over state affairs in Berlin, but he also correctly diagnosed his leader's unwillingness to resolve the party–state dualism. He therefore ensured that both his RPL and RMVP empires expanded both horizontally and vertically, in tandem. The party model of *Gau-*, *Kreis-* and *Ort-* division of power (already present of course in the structure of the RPL) was replicated in the case of the RMVP; significantly, local representatives of the RPL also held the same remit as officials of the RMVP and/or the RKK. For example, *Gau-*, *Kreis-* and *Ort-*representatives of the press division of the RPL doubled up as regional/local delegates of the same division of the Propaganda Ministry.[11]

The arduous task of propaganda co-ordination between state and party was performed officially by the *Reichsring für nationalsozialistische Propaganda und Volksaufklärung* – originally created in 1934 to replace the *Konzentration* Office of the RPL and elevated to an autonomous status in May 1941.[12] Its official remit was to manage all national propaganda agencies, crowning the decentralised RPL structure: Ring I encompassed the bulk of party activity in this field, whilst Ring II extended to cover all other organisations operating within the Third Reich.[13] It also supervised the various propaganda 'actions' (*Aktionen*) and, after its institutional elevation in 1941, acted as the clearing house for all propaganda matters, including correspondence and liaison between the various party and state agencies.[14] Goebbels entrusted this crucial position to a close ally, Walter Tießler, and a few weeks before Heß's flight to Scotland, he issued a directive that designated him as his personal liaison (*Verbindungsmann*) with both the RPL and the office of the Führer's Representative.[15] Beyond the *Reichsring*, however, co-ordination was promoted unofficially through the web of personal allegiances through contacts that led back to Goebbels himself. This was, in fact, a mini-'charismatic community' that was meant to be held together by a peculiar 'neo-feudal' network centring on the Propaganda minister and *Reichsleiter*.

The reality was different, however. By the time the war broke out, Goebbels had witnessed his head start in 1933 being constantly eroded through a plethora of organisational amendments, Hitler interventions, hostile bids by his adversaries in both party and government, as well as through his own personal failings. To be sure, his ambitions for clear delineation of the RMVP's vast (and effectively open-ended) remit would have been impossible to realise even in a more orderly, bureaucratic system; but it was a recipe for disaster in the case of the NS polycratic state of affairs and Hitler's 'charismatic' rule. Goebbels's RMVP network had been fortunate to be created in the tabula rasa of the uncertain 1933–34 transition period, as a model for the fusion of party and state jurisdictions, amassing responsibilities in the absence of other credible contenders. When new stars emerged, however, and had to be rewarded institutionally and politically, it started to crumble without the minister possessing the leverage to stave off the stream of incursions. It became clear that the de facto institutional position of the minister did not suffice for maintaining the grip over the RMVP's divisional powers. Radio, press, film, culture, all became individual battlegrounds, necessitating ad hoc strategies in each domain, rather than an overall plan for preserving normative political influence and control.

Goebbels's control over the regime's cultural policy was questioned by equally powerful contenders. Alfred Rosenberg put himself forward as the movement's ideological supremo (also appointed, Commissioner of the Führer for the Supervision of the Entire Intellectual and Doctrinal Training and Education of the NSDAP), even if he effectively discredited himself through a series of unfortunate (and crass) initiatives. Robert Ley fought doggedly for control over the working masses' 'enlightenment' through his powerful DAF and would have wished to inherit the extensive powers of Gregor Strasser prior to 1933 but had also to concede defeat and crucial institutional space to the RMVP.[16] In the field of press, Goebbels had to fight his way amidst Max Amann's almost de facto prestige and the intrigues of the *Reichspressechef* Otto Dietrich, who saw press as his near-exclusive domain. From the autumn of 1937, a new contender had appeared on the scene of the NS neo-feudal map, eager to carve up for himself a new empire: Joachim von Ribbentrop, a champagne-merchant with a dubious reputation in diplomacy (he had served as Ambassador in London) and no real party standing, succeeded Konstantin Freiherr von Neurath in the Foreign Ministry (AA). Ribbentrop, though almost universally detested within the government and the party, had an ace up his sleeve: he was Hitler's personal choice and favourite at the time. At a time that Goebbels's standing with the leadership had sunk to an all-time-low (neither his high-profile affair with the Czech actress, Lida Baarova nor the way in which he masterminded and handled the *Kristallnacht* earned him any favours with Hitler[17]), this meant that no accumulated power could be taken for granted, especially if Ribbentrop decided to plea with Hitler for the extension of his own remit. As the landscape of authority, jurisdiction and personal power kept constantly changing in NS Germany, and as new personal empires were carved out of others' misfortune or injudiciousness, the domain of 'propaganda' also changed shape, becoming an unmistakably polycratic superstructure with regard to both its organisation, its agencies and its output.

When Hitler gave his authorisation for 'Operation White' and ordered the Wehrmacht troops to invade Poland on 1 September 1939, most of the personal 'empires' within the NS regime had already established their legitimacy and power-base. Nominally, Joseph Goebbels occupied the heartland, controlling the RPL, the RMVP and the RKK – whose separate Chambers reported directly to him from 1938 onwards. However, in practice, the domain of 'propaganda' had become overcrowded, inhabited as it was by disparate state and party agencies that continued to 'work towards the Führer'. During the war, new stars complicated the power struggle even further. Heinrich Himmler's amassing of titles and power – in particular his control over domestic affairs as Interior Minister – earned him an oblique state in the propaganda domain. The same was true of Albert Speer who was in charge of armaments and labour/constription matters. Rosenberg at last received a ministerial portfolio for the 'occupied eastern territories'. As for Martin Bormann, as head of the Party Chancellery he came to dominate the party apparatus, whilst in his capacity of Hitler's private secretary he earned for himself the de facto privilege of controlling access to him. With the approach of the war, the institutional role of the OKW in 'propaganda' matters was also enhanced: in April 1939, its traditional office of press officer for military matters (held by Major Hasso von Wedel) was elevated to the status of Division of Wehrmacht Propaganda [*Oberkommando Wehrmacht/ Wehrmacht-Propaganda* (OKW/WPr)] under the control of the Chief of Staff.[18] From September 1939, 'facts' were unfolding on the military front and the OKW was the instigator of the process. Goebbels, however, was anchored in Berlin and so was his political powerhouse, the RMVP. His ministry was the recipient of the OKW communiqué (intimated in person by the OKW–RMVP Liaison Officer), the DNB report and a stream of ad hoc instructions from the Führer Headquarters for press, radio and wider 'propaganda' matters. Dietrich, by contrast, was inside Hitler's inner circle – a position especially valuable in the first four years of the war when the Führer used to travel to the front and be far more involved in the drafting of the final reports to be sent back to Berlin. Furthermore, due to the exceptional significance of foreign policy matters, Ribbentrop too was closer to the leader and so was the leadership of the armed forces, obliged as they were to co-ordinate their strategy on the basis of Hitler's personal whims. This meant that, by the time that Goebbels could nominally exercise his powers over every aspect of the regime's propaganda output, the raw material of information had already been accumulated, manipulated and re-formulated through the intervention of his main adversaries in the party and government.[19] Far from functioning as the command centre of a vast, centralised and co-ordinated information empire, the 'Goebbels network' resembled a weak administrative centre for a spate of semi-independent, uncoordinated and often contradictory propaganda initiatives generated elsewhere. This polycratic structure was a miniature carbon copy of the wider 'neo-feudal' nature of the whole NS system; but whilst the latter worked in theory '*towards* the Führer', the competing 'networks' involved in propaganda worked *regardless* or even *against* the domain's nominal figurehead.

The 'Dietrich network'

If Rosenberg and Ley failed to curb the institutional and political expansion of Goebbels's power, largely because they managed to discredit themselves on a personal level in the eyes of their leader, others experienced notable success. One of them was Otto Dietrich – another *Reichsleiter* (and, in this respect, of the same party currency value with Goebbels) who had been *Reichspressechef* for the NSDAP central press office since August 1931 and de facto Hitler's personal advisor on relevant matters. Technically, a German chancellor was meant to possess the specialised services of the *Pressechef der Reichsregierung* – a position filled by Walther Funk after the NS assumption of power. With the establishment, however, of the RMVP in March 1933, the Chancellor acquired a fully dedicated state institution for the supervision of all propaganda matters, with its press jurisdiction shared between the ministry's division and its RPK organisation. In theory – and according to Goebbels's plans – the RMVP would fuse the functions of the *Pressechef*, as well as of other press-related bodies within the AA and the party's Political Organisation [*Politische Organisation der* NSDAP (PO)] under Hess, thus creating a virtual monopoly over press matters. Hitler, however, took heed of the objections of both Dietrich and the AA: on 23 May 1933, he decided to divide press responsibilities, with the RMVP maintaining its grip over 'propaganda' affairs, Dietrich keeping his *Reichspressechef* post, and Funk maintaining the role of *Pressechef*, now attached to President Hindenburg, whilst also becoming state secretary to the RMVP. With the creation of the Reich Press Chamber (RPK) in September, the kaleidoscope of NS control over press was complete: Goebbels, Dietrich, Funk and now Max Amann (president of the RPK) presided over a muddled organisational structure with uncertain and clearly overlapping normative functions (see Ch. 1). Even worse, both the Party's PO and the AA ensured their right to maintain their press offices with restricted jurisdiction over matters pertaining to their ministerial duties.

Given Funk's nominal press remit, the death of Hindenburg in August 1934 and the merging of the two offices by Hitler did not cause immediate problems, apart from the strengthening of Dietrich's role as *Reichspressechef* to both the chancellor and president – that is, Hitler. However, when in November 1937 the then Finance Minister, Hjalmar Schacht resigned and was replaced by Funk, a new battle began. Goebbels argued in vain that, since the position of the *Pressechef* under Funk had remained effectively vacant, the office should lapse; Dietrich, of course, had serious objections. In an act of mediation that presaged the chaos still to come in subsequent years, Hitler simply duplicated the functions without defining each remit: Dietrich retained his position as *Reichspressechef*, also absorbing the erstwhile functions of the *Pressechef der Reichsregierung* that Funk had allowed to fade, largely in favour of the RMVP![20] In 1938, matters became even more complicated: as a result of another feud between Goebbels and Dietrich over control of the press, Hitler appointed the latter as state secretary to the RMVP, thus inserting him in a subordinate position within the hierarchy of the ministry, whilst allowing him to exercise direct control over the German press through his parallel position as *Reichspressechef*. To make matters worse, three types of hierarchy seemed to clash in the press domain of NS Germany. Goebbels, Dietrich and Amann shared the same party rank, but were inserted at different levels in the state structure: Dietrich was subordinate to Goebbels in the RMVP, as both state secretary and vice-president of the RPK; Amann, as President of the RPK, theoretically took orders from Goebbels and had Dietrich as his assistant; Dietrich, however, held a significant Hitler decree since 28 February 1934 which gave him overall control of the NS press as *Reichspressechef*.[21] The three men were meant to meet and co-ordinate their actions, but Dietrich refused to share his remit, often dealing directly with the RPL press office, whose loyalty to Goebbels depended on who was in charge. Dietrich's control over information dispersal to national, regional and local press originated from a further accumulation of responsibilities in the German News Office (DNB) and as editor of NS-*Korrespondenz*. He thus held a dominant position where it really mattered – that is, where information was produced and then distributed to press and radio networks all over the country.

The 'Dietrich network' expanded between 1933 and 1939 to occupy pivotal positions in both the administration and the party pillars of the network, whilst taking advantage of its figurehead's physical presence next to Hitler and on the front. Dietrich knew that Goebbels's institutional position was too entrenched to be seriously questioned. He therefore began to construct his own 'network' from his traditional strongholds of press and news networks, in tandem with the *Reichspressechef*'s proximity to Hitler, to erode the RMVP's overall competence and to attack other areas of jurisdiction too. During his brief spell on the front in 1941, he ensured the appointment of his trusted deputy Sündermann as liaison with the ministry. It was actually Sündermann who, in November 1940, introduced the *Tagesparolen des Reichspressechefs* for the press – an official summary of the *Reichspressechef*'s directives to the press that was intended to prevent independent instructions from reaching journalists and regional propaganda offices.[22] This constituted a direct assault on Goebbels's capacity for using informal channels of press information to convey guidelines to newspapers, independent of Dietrich's official press conference. In 1941, Dietrich succeeded in removing first Ernst Braeckow (a Goebbels loyalist), who had been one of Dietrich's favourite targets ever since the outbreak of the war (having lost in 1940 his post as Fritzsche's deputy in the Inland Press section after the *Reichspressechef*'s accusations that he had consciously undermined the coverage of his activities), thus further weakening the minister's supervision powers over radio.

Almost a year after the encirclement of the VIth Army in Stalingrad, Rudolf Semmler provided a candid description of the chaos that internecine jurisdictional fights caused in the corridors of the RMVP.[23] Room 24 of the ministry was, in theory, the co-ordinating centre for every press activity throughout the Reich; but the reality was very different – as Dietrich bypassed Goebbels and vice-versa, Ribbentrop and Rosenberg complained, Bormann intervened and the officers of Room 24 had to make choices amongst contradictory instructions. More often than not until Stalingrad, Dietrich's line would prevail to the intense irritation of the Propaganda minister.[24] But, as Semmler pointed out, the result was that a single event could be 'commented upon quite differently by the press [controlled by Dietrich] and by the radio [where Goebbels had far more leeway]'.[25]

Even in the case of the execution of routine information functions, Dietrich had insisted that the daily RMVP Press Conference[26] (which he controlled) and his *Tagesparolen* would set the tone for all media in the Reich. This afforded him a disproportionate degree of influence on broadcasting too, even without technically holding any official relevant position in that domain. This confusing arrangement was sustained until 1942, thanks to the flexibility of Hans Fritzsche, who at the time was in charge of the German Press Division, but had held crucial posts within the DD (as *Hauptschriftleiter*) and had experience as director of the radio's news service.[27] Fritzsche had excelled in serving the two masters concurrently until – as he testified in 1946 at the Nuremberg Trials – he grew weary of Dietrich's interference in propaganda affairs and resigned. When he returned from his brief spell on the front to head the RMVP's Broadcasting Division, the situation tipped in the Propaganda minister's favour, to the intense irritation of Dietrich. But the fact that the *Reichspressechef* could still claim jurisdiction over radio matters through the indirect channel of news policy attests to the legacy of previous developments at a time when Goebbels had lost ground within the NS hierarchy (and inside Hitler's inner circle). Goebbels often vented his frustration or even anger, either through his diary pages or in confidence to his closely associated ministry, but could do very little to alter the makeshift structure of information distribution.

The 'Ribbentrop' network

The 'Ribbentrop network' was also based institutionally in Berlin and, unlike both its Goebbels and Dietrich counterparts, had no real footing in the party structure. However, war (for most NS officials regarded as Ribbentrop's personal enterprise) had enhanced the significance of his ministerial portfolio as well as his direct contact with Hitler himself. Indeed, before he became totally discredited himself during the latter stages of the war, Ribbentrop had successfully repatriated a series of functions from the RMVP, blurred the boundaries with regard to others and thrived on the institutional duplication that Hitler had tolerated or even encouraged. Under Neurath, the AA had gradually lost influence and succumbed to institutional incursions from other government and party bodies – not least the RMVP, which had a clear interest in controlling 'propaganda' functions abroad. During the first months after the establishment of the Propaganda Ministry, Neurath had protested again the usurpation of his office's press and intelligence responsibilities by Goebbels; but the latter's early prestige with Hitler produced the sort of mediation that he desired – the 30 June 1933 decree allowed the RMVP to engage in foreign policy 'propaganda' activities independently from the AA.[28] Even more painfully for Neurath, at a cabinet meeting in May 1933, he had to accept the complete loss of responsibility for a foreign transmission on short-wave to the RMVP.[29]

In 1938–39, however, the situation had changed dramatically. The RMVP's Foreign Press section had remained a small office attached to the overall Press Division, taking the back seat not only to the AA's operations but also to the party's PO under Hess, whose interest in the *Volksdeutsche* (ethnic Germans living abroad) had brought it in direct competition with Ribbentrop's new empire.[30] Now, alarmingly, Ribbentrop ensured that his ministry (rather than the RMVP) held the Conference for Foreign Press, in spite of Goebbels's protests. Taking advantage of Goebbels's isolation in 1938, the press office of the AA, under Paul Schmidt, co-operated with Dietrich in order to dictate policy to the RMVP during the August–September 1938 Czech crisis.[31] Furthermore, given the growing significance of foreign policy in the remaining months until the outbreak of the war, Ribbentrop continued to add insult to injury by using his ministry's Foreign Press Division to issue directives independent of the RMVP.

Then, in May 1939, a new Hitler decree awarded the AA the right to establish its own press division, even if the primary role of the RMVP was also vaguely acknowledged. At the same time, Hitler permitted the creation of a similar division for radio, based in the RRG – that is, at the heart of the RMVP and RRK.[32] The new department was called *Kulturpolitische Abteilung-Rundfunkreferat* (KA-R). What these two initiatives jointly meant became evident in early September, with the campaign against Poland in progress and the Non-Aggression Pact with the Soviet Union firmly in place. A large AA contingency appeared on the doorstep of the RMVP and inserted itself in the ministry's radio and press staff. Claiming direct authorisation from the Führer, Ribbentrop presented to his opponent a decree that allowed the AA to engage in 'propaganda' activities and consolidate its institutional gains of the previous year.[33] This particular incident offers valuable insight into Hitler's own exercise of his 'charismatic' authority and the paralysing effect of this tendency on the whole NS system of decision-making. Two Führer ad hoc rulings on the same jurisdictional dispute in the course of four months produced a spectacular u-turn that not only eroded the RMVP's powers since 1933, but also added a further layer of polycratic confusion to the process of (foreign) propaganda management.[34]

So long as Ribbentrop enjoyed Hitler's favour and Goebbels remained in his Berlin limbo, the AA was in a strong position to consolidate its jurisdictional gains and seek more, either directly from Hitler or – more often – through arbitrary initiatives. In spring 1941, the foreign minister's star continued to shine after the successes in Poland, France and the Balkans. Thus, when it was revealed that the AA had acquired (in co-operation with the OKW) a radio station in occupied Yugoslavia, which it intended to use for foreign 'propaganda' broadcasts to the region, the RMVP hierarchy was mortified. Goebbels saw this initiative – without prior authorisation from either his ministry or Hitler – as a violation of all prior arrangements between the two institutions. Again, there were many issues at stake in this episode: the relative position of the two ministries in the institutional chart of the NS regime; Ribbentrop's growing appetite for cashing in on his prestige with the leadership at the expense of the RMVP; and, perhaps more importantly, the co-operation between AA and OKW that amounted to a total by-passing of the Propaganda Ministry and could set a dangerous precedent with regard to who controlled broadcasting. Goebbels pleaded twice with Hans Lammers – head of the Chancellery – for a Führer clarification, but the response was predictably non-committal, urging the two sides to work out a new compromise solution.[35]

This was the sort of arrangement that Goebbels dreaded in 1941. He was aware of the dynamics that the 'Ribbentrop network' had developed in the previous three years, as a result of its figurehead's favour with Hitler and the significance of foreign policy in NS policy-making at that stage. Besides, the foreign minister was a master of fait accompli. His KA-R initiative rested on a solid authorisation from the leadership, while his newly acquired station (part of an AA registered company called *Deutsche Auslandsrundfunk-Gesellschaft Interradio*) continued to transmit, untouched by intrigue, back in Berlin. Yet, sometime in the summer of 1941, Hitler decided to reward his old companion Rosenberg with an ad hoc portfolio for the eastern occupied territories; with it came a typically vague responsibility for 'propaganda' activities. Thus, the compromise reached between the two ministers in October 1941 resulted from a desire to consolidate the new boundaries of jurisdiction, to ensure at least the management of foreign broadcast (including *Interradio*) as a condominium and to arrest further incursions by the emerging 'Rosenberg network'. It was a typically muddled affair: Ribbentrop's coups were confirmed, as was the RMVP's central overall role in broadcasting in the greater Reich; Ribbentrop added a further piece of legitimacy to his radio business; Goebbels elicited a tentative agreement for joint management of the new structure.[36]

The case of Alfred Rosenberg

The re-emergence of Rosenberg in 1941, after years of oblivion in the institutional desert of the NS regime, was emblematic of the haphazard manner in which fortunes could be won and lost in wartime. After the frustration of his hopes to become foreign minister[37] and to control the domain of party 'cultural affairs' in the early years of NS rule, he continued to publish extensively (books, party magazines and a stream of publications on doctrinal matters directed at local NSDAP offices) and maintained independent institutions [*Dienststelle Rosenberg, Außenpolitisches Amt* (APA)] through which he tried to erode the authority of the RMVP, the AA and Ley's DAF. His 'propaganda' activities were restricted to organising talks or seminars and sending representatives of his agency to address party events. He had clearly lost the game of political influence: against the DAF, which in 1935 absorbed Rosenberg's Theatre-Goers Club and stopped the direct funding of the *Dienststelle Rosenberg* for related activities; against Goebbels's RMVP, as his own agency *NS Kulturgemeinde* never managed to antagonise the RKK or even Goebbels's own ad hoc Reich Culture Senate and all theatre activities became a near-exclusive monopoly of the RKK's (Theatre) Division VI with the new *Theatergesetz* of 1934;[38] and against the AA, especially after Ribbentrop's appointment and ephemeral rise to stardom, which buried Rosenberg's hopes of becoming foreign minister or enhancing the institutional authority of his own APA. He too loathed the new foreign minister and the August 1939 Ribbentrop-Molotov pact offered him a further opportunity to step up his personal attacks on him.[39] In the rush of institutional re-organisation that resulted from the outbreak of the war, Hitler awarded him an ad hoc position as 'Führer's Commissioner for Safeguarding the NS Weltanschauung' – a title that meant nothing in purely political terms, but which afforded Rosenberg a new licence for speaking his mind up. But even on this occasion he typically overstepped his authority, engaging in a pandemonium of declarations of foreign policy matters and forcing the Chancellery to impose on him the condition of prior approval of his activities from the AA.[40]

With the launch of 'Operation Barbarossa' against the Soviet Union in June 1941, Rosenberg (self-proclaimed expert on matters pertaining to Bolshevism and a stubborn supporter of an all-out confrontation with communism) saw in the eastern territories an institutional tabula rasa that suited him perfectly.[41] His appointment as Minister for the Occupied Territories and the right to co-ordinate all 'propaganda' activities in his geographical domain that came with it *could* have constituted the institutional niche through which he would be able to carve out an 'empire' for himself and attack his adversaries. In the NS propaganda 'Behemoth', however, one's enemy's enemy was not automatically considered a friend. The October 1941 compromise agreement between Goebbels and Ribbentrop was evidence of an ad hoc alliance against de-centralisation of 'propaganda' control. Dietrich too saw Rosenberg's appointment as a direct threat to his information and press stronghold; the same may be said to an extent about the OKW leadership, who despised the new minister's fierce independence and tendency to defy patterns of hierarchy. For all of them, Rosenberg was a dangerous and unreliable late-comer in an already overcrowded and tenuously held-together structure. Their worries were perhaps well-founded; yet, they proved exaggerated. For as long as NS Germany controlled large sections of the Soviet territory (i.e., until 1943), he proved a little more than a nuisance, constantly battling about jurisdictional matters with virtually everybody else, intent upon shielding the 'eastern territories' from administrative intervention and erecting his own personal 'empire' there. He failed, however, at producing structures that could de facto antagonise the RMVP and the AA in propaganda activities throughout his domain. By the end of 1943, once again discredited, cut off from Hitler and with most of his erstwhile geographic empire lost to, or threatened by the Red Army, his 'network' had already been reduced to irrelevance.

The rise of Martin Bormann

By contrast, Martin Bormann's authority increased meteorically in the last war years. If Goebbels's ministerial office was just a few yards across the street on Wilhelmstrasse, Bormann found himself at the heart of the official Führer headquarters in Berlin. His organisational talents and ideological fanaticism had propelled him to a pivotal role inside Hitler's 'charismatic' party mechanism; but it was Hess's departure in June 1941 that offered him the ultimate opportunity for political power. His designation as secretary to the Führer (*Sekretär des Führers*) in February 1943 simply confirmed a trend of empowerment vis-à-vis both state and party that was set to continue unabated until the final day of the Third Reich. The 'Bormann network' had an exclusively NSDAP basis but his secretarial functions (even before the award of the official title) had placed him in an institutional position from which he could also command state activities. In fact, as Hitler's inner circle became smaller after 1942 (gradually Dietrich, Ribbentrop and Speer lost favour) and the Führer became increasingly confined to Berlin or Obersalzberg, it was Bormann that came to control access to the Führer. At the same time, as the leader became more and more reclusive, desisting from his earlier wartime involvement in the day-to-day affairs of the state, Bormann was in a position to express 'Hitler's will' and, as we said earlier, to work *for* the Führer *in spite of* him.

The relation between Goebbels and Bormann was emblematic of the unpredictable nature of personal power-bases in the Third Reich. The Propaganda minister, fully aware of Bormann's power derived through his direct access to, and empowerment from Hitler personally, had tried to co-opt him in his fight against other party and state adversaries. In the aftermath of the Stalingrad debacle, he suggested to Hitler the establishment of a committee for the supervision of 'total war'. As this was a concept that he had pioneered and tried to impress upon the leadership, he found it logical to put himself forward for one of the three positions, but he also included both Bormann and Lammers in the proposed triumvirate. Hitler, however, decided to substitute Goebbels with the head of the OKW, Wilhelm Keitel, to the Propaganda minister's utter frustration (see also Ch. 5). More than a year later, on 26 July 1944 – and with the committee having run aground, not least because of Bormann's unwillingness to liaise with the other two members – Goebbels did succeed in claiming exclusively for himself the previously shared responsibility – this time as Plenipotentiary for Total War. Yet, in the following September, he was appalled by a new regulation stating that every RMVP document had to bear Bormann's prior approval and signature.[42] He duly obliged, as he did on a number of other occasions: to override Bormann one needed Hitler's direct authorisation, which in turn was largely controlled by the Führer's secretary himself. Thus, Goebbels accepted that he had to placate him, to show deference to most of his orders and at least try to harness the benefits of a good relation with him in order to weaken the rest of his competitors for power. By going out of his way to appear obliging to the party chancellery's demands (even when they contradicted his own designs)[43] and aligning his own strategy with that of the Führer's secretary, Goebbels achieved an extension of his own power in the last war years. Even when it came to local party interference in propaganda activities, Bormann granted the Propaganda minister's wish that no other agency or official outside the RMVP would have the right to alter official material; in return he elicited a wider acknowledgement from Goebbels that party matters remain the exclusive domain of the Chancellery.[44] By contrast, those who had antagonised Bormann invariably found themselves on the losing side of the battle in the end.[45]

The practicalities of co-ordination between the Goebbels and Bormann 'networks' were managed by a complicated web of intermediaries. The *Reichsring* under Tießler was bestowed with the monumental task of acting as a liaison between the two. At the same time, Goebbels also delegated increased powers to the *Stabsleiter* of the RPL, Eugen Hadamowsky, as his overall representative in the party's propaganda direction and recipient of all information about decisions in individual departments. These changes were re-confirmed in October 1942,[46] but by that time co-ordination had already landed in trouble. In November 1941, Bormann complained that the new head of the RMVP's Propaganda Division, Alfred-Ingemar Berndt, could not be 'competent' to engage in all forms of propaganda, as he apparently did on the basis of the wealth of material that was channelled through his office.[47] Goebbels decided to retaliate, informing Bormann that Berndt was acting perfectly within his jurisdictional domain. He finished his long defence of Berndt (which was also intended as a protection of the RMVP's jurisdictional domain) stating that,

> [i]n spite of these facts [that justify Berndt], I have taken your note as an opportunity to particularly inform one more time the heads of the RMVP's divisions that, before tackling important political tasks or obtaining

reports they should turn to Tießler, so as to keep the Party Chancellery involved or at least informed in every case[48]

Yet, this sort of defiant tone was the exception to the rule. From 1941, until 1943, Tießler received an increasing amount of delicate communication traffic between his RMVP boss and the head of the Party Chancellery. On many occasions, he was obstructed in his duties as liaison between the two institutions by mutual suspicion and unwillingness to co-ordinate their information or activities. Jurisdictional ambiguity had caused a minor incident in the autumn of 1941, when Berndt demanded that all *Gau* opinion reports be sent to his propaganda division by the divisional heads of the RPL; the Party Chancellery quickly reminded the RMVP that such reports could only be transmitted by the Gauleiters to the party.[49] Tießler continued to tread a delicate path between the two institutions and masters, as well as to direct the avalanche of traffic between RMVP and Party Chancellery as effectively as he could. However, he was de facto operating in one of the awkward 'grey zones' of the NS jurisdictional structure and was often reprimanded by Bormann for not conforming to the opaque procedural guidelines of his office. In May 1943, a seemingly minor issue of jurisdiction over 'cultural' broadcasts over the radio provoked a major jurisdictional crisis: Bormann demanded through the *Reichsring* a delineation of authority in this domain, stating clearly that all cultural matters except that of pure administration were decided by the party and not the state institutions (i.e., the RMVP).[50] By that time, Tießler clearly had had enough. In a personal letter to Goebbels he drew attention to a long list of violations of administrative protocol by Hitler's private secretary. After quoting examples of secret reports from the country that were withheld by the Chancellery's officials, he recounted how Bormann referred to him as 'the most fanatical Goebbels-supporter' and concluded that 'in such an atmosphere of mistrust it is impossible for me to work any further'.[51] A few months later, his request to be relieved of his duties and be assigned to a different task was granted.[52]

The case of the 'Bormann network' is indicative of the potential inconsequence between institutional position and political power in the NS system of rule. The blurring of the distinction between party and state did not simply mystify administrative processes and muddle jurisdictions; more significantly, it created parallel hierarchies that intertwined horizontally. The only steadfast anchor in this structure was of course the Führer, in line with the 'charismatic' nature of his authority; yet below this level (a level that in any case operated above and beyond standard norms of decision-making) there was little to provide similar points of stable reference. The firm grounding of Bormann's authority on the basis of exactly this special access to the Führer and his institutional ability (as his personal secretary) to divulge Hitler's wish as his representative or *in spite of* him reflects the most fundamental reason for the RMVP's relative weakness until 1944, at least. Put simply, after a head start in 1933–34, Goebbels had serious and increasing problems in ensuring a direct legitimacy from the Führer for his actions. In fact, the institutional distance between Hitler and Goebbels was constantly expanding until 1943/44, with the strengthening of the authority of the likes of Dietrich, Bormann and Ribbentrop. The nature of the NS regime meant that the diffusion of the 'Führer's wish' from his inner circle outwards and downwards to the rest of the regime and party constructed ad hoc hierarchies and directives that the recipients had to implement without further ado. This is exactly where Bormann's immense power lay – and how it came to represent a major threat to the control exercised by the 'Goebbels network' over propaganda matters.

The 'OKW network'

Against the cumulative (though by no means co-ordinated) attrition of the RMVP's institutional and political position by party agencies, rival ministries and the volatile Hitler's decision, *Führersentscheid*, Goebbels decided to work closely with the OKW in order to partly offset his losses. The significance of the 'OKW network' in the regime's propaganda structure was obviously elevated from 1938 onwards, when a military confrontation became increasingly likely and eventually escalated in an all-out war in Europe. The 'co-ordination' of the armed forces in early 1938 – with the forcible removal of the old leadership under von Blomberg and von Fritsch – had afforded the new OKW leadership direct access to the Führer and a far more prominent position in the NS decision-making process. During the war, the regular *Wehrmachtbericht* (WB – Wehrmacht Communiqué) formed the most authoritative basis for information on the military situation that was to be reported through press and radio, both inside the Reich and abroad. Thus, the Propaganda minister had hastened to agree with the OKW their respective spheres of authority in the production of wartime propaganda as early as the spring of 1938.

The idea for a dedicated team of propagandists in uniforms had been first discussed in the middle of the 1930s, when plans for the re-organisation of the German armed forces were still being discussed in the upper echelons of the NS regime and the military leadership. The issue of providing a framework for effective execution of 'propaganda' activities within the Wehrmacht in the event of war had acquired totemic significance, since it was widely believed that the defeat of 1918 had partly resulted from a wider failure in the propaganda domain. Therefore, earmarked propaganda companies (*Propaganda-Kompanien*, PK) had already been in operation by the time that Germany absorbed the Sudetenland in September 1938. Towards the end of this month the RMVP reached an agreement with the OKW about the guidelines for the conduct of military propaganda in wartime.[53] The members of the PK would be trained soldiers with technical expertise, placed under direct military command, although the RMVP was instrumental in two ways: first, in supplying extra personnel from the different *Gau*, especially when war increased the need for more such units; and, second, in providing operational guidelines for the execution of the PKs's duties, always in co-operation with (and hierarchical deference to) the leadership of the OKW.[54] Finally, in April 1939 the official structure of the OKW Propaganda Division (OKW/WPr) was established, with Hasso von Wedel as its leader, and placed under the overall control of General Alfred Jodl, the Wehrmacht Chief of Operations [*Wehrmacht Führungsstab* (WFSt)]. Its main task was to supervise the array of propaganda activities of the armed forces, ranging from the reporting of word and film footage from the front to influencing the enemy troops. Apart from overseeing the work of the PKs (in the army, air force and navy, as well as the *Waffen-SS* which operated their own specialised units), the OKW/WPr also engaged in the work of 'active propaganda' in the occupied territories, the military censors and the educational activities for the Wehrmacht troops. An array of experts in all areas of propaganda – from film to radio journalism, but also from culture and education – were attached to each division, bringing the total number of OKW/WPr employees to a peak of more than 15,000 in 1942.[55]

The timely delineation of the respective spheres of jurisdiction between OKW and RMVP ensured that the system of co-operation between the two institutions remained largely effective throughout the war. Propaganda material from the PKs would be dispatched to the OKW/WPr main processing centre in Potsdam, where experts and censors would filter it (mainly for security purposes) and then send it to the officials of the RMVP for immediate dissemination. Goebbels ensured that the Wehrmacht received the highly confidential bulletins of his ministry, but he also accepted that the work of the PKs as divisions placed under overall military command was beyond his jurisdictional domain and his power of immediate influence. This was particularly important for the Wochenschau – a device on which the RMVP and Goebbels personally placed the utmost value until the very last days of the Third Reich. In this domain the Propaganda Ministry depended exclusively on the work of the Wehrmacht propaganda division which held a monopoly over supplying the raw visual material directly from the front, and on the military censors who took the final decisions as to which material was appropriate for further propaganda use. He did ensure, however, that reliable officials from the RMVP's divisions worked closely with the OKW/WPr in securing the crucial supply of propaganda material from the front. One of his ministry's officials, Lieutenant-Colonel Hans-Leo Martin, attended the daily Wehrmacht conference, where the first version of the WB was communicated to state and party officials, and reported back to him in the Ministry in Wilhelhstraße.[56]

Himmler and Speer

The zigzag of jurisdictions in the NS propaganda structures was completed by a plethora of more restricted intersections with other 'empires'. Heinrich Himmler's position was exceptionally strong, both in the state (Reichsführer of the *Schutzstaffeln* (SS), Head of the Secret Police, Minister of Interior since 1943) and in the NSDAP [Reichsleiter, head of the SS/SD (*Sicherheitsdienst*)]. His own 'network' produced the famous 'public opinion reports' from the various regions of NS Germany – the indisputably most complete and author- itative resource of this sort whose findings were forwarded to all major party and state institutions. The RPL had its own network of public-opinion gaug- ing (particularly concerned with the impact of propaganda devices on the population), based on the network of regional and local 'propaganda' offices which then reported back to Berlin. However, to the occasional irritation of Goebbels himself, they were no match to its counterpart issued by Himmler's subordinates. In fact, towards the end of the war, the Propaganda minister often reacted angrily to the tone and content of the SS/SD reports which he considered as defeatist and suspicious. Increasingly frequent and explicit references to such taboo issues, such as negative reactions to propaganda campaigns or reporting a general collapse of the *Stimmung* of public opinion, made Goebbels believe that Himmler and his associates were actively engag- ing in a war of attrition. However, the interior minister was far too strong in the NS hierarchy for Goebbels to risk a direct confrontation.

Finally, the 'Goebbels network' was de facto obliged to operate within the context of (increasing) wartime restrictions of personnel and resources. Conscription was of course a problem from the very beginning. But the intensification of the war effort from 1941 onwards, coupled with the appointment of Albert Speer as Minister of Armaments and Munitions[57] and the pressures from the OKW for the extension of call-up, produced further tensions and aggravated the competition for resources. Although Goebbels was initially in favour of Speer's dynamism and appreciated his support for 'total war', the priorities of the two men were rather different: while for Goebbels propaganda output was as instrumental for the war effort as arma- ments production, Speer held a far more technocratic view that relegated the significance of propaganda, especially in the last years of the conflicts. Thus, Goebbels authorised Werner Wächter, chief of propaganda staff and vice- president of the relevant division in the RMVP, to act as his representative and liaison with Speer and Fritz Sauckel, the Reich Defence Commissioner.[58] In fact, from 1943 onwards, Goebbels found himself in a rather paradoxical position vis-à-vis the mobilisation effort spearheaded by Speer and Sauckel. On the one hand, he was as vehement a supporter of 'total war' as the Arms and Munitions minister and the defence commissioner, often pre-empting or exceeding their demands in manpower allocation by drafting large numbers of technical, journalistic and artistic staff. In his capacity as

Reich Commissioner for Total War, Goebbels contributed greatly to the depopulation of the German propaganda and entertainment industries. As the end drew near, he almost gave up on foreign propaganda, permitting the drafting of the last employees in other countries and shutting down offices abroad. He was aware of the impact that his 'total war' measures had on the propaganda network, but he continued to raise the threshold of expectations from his shrinking and demoralised propaganda civilian troops.

On the other hand, he regularly bemoaned the bleeding of propaganda-related staff to the war effort and resented the fact that propaganda had been eclipsed by other priorities during the last years of NS rule. Even after the acceleration of the Reich's mobilisation programme he continued to plan a large-scale recall of a new blood of journalists from the front to spearhead the regime's new radical propaganda ethos. He waged a battle against restrictive allocations of material resources to his ministry's enterprises, such as Agfa film, during the last stages of the war, and won partial but formidable victories (see Ch. 8). A disregard for a rational means–ends assessment underpinned the RMVP's request for army and SS protection of Berlin cinemas during projection times. In the summer of 1944, the Commissioner for Total War, Gauleiter of Berlin and later Commissioner for the city's defence considered wholly justified a sacrifice of military units from the collapsing fronts (especially from the still undecided battle in the west) and a diversion of scarce flak protection from the – otherwise ravaged by air raids – city that he was defending, in order to ensure the safe operation of the remaining cinema premises of the capital. The OKW refused from the beginning; the SS, however, initially agreed, before Himmler personally intervened to put an end to this extraordinary situation. By that time Leopold Gutterer, the RMVP's State Secretary, was planning the extension of the measure to the whole of the city and beyond! Speer and Sauckel in the meantime despaired.

The 'Goebbels network' strikes back: 1943–45

It becomes evident that the various 'networks' within the NS polycratic structure did not fall neatly into the categories of 'state' and 'party'; instead, they intersected, overlapped and often contradicted each other. On many occasions Goebbels deplored the arbitrary and often unpredictable insertion of layers of jurisdictional impediments to his ministry's authority or to his personal access to the Führer. Once he realised that an unimpeded totalitarian control of propaganda was impossible in NS Germany, he became convinced that every single aspect of his domain had to be defended individually, strengthened pre-emptively or reclaimed. What mattered most was control of crucial administrative intersections and, where possible, infiltration of rival institutions. This, rather than an attempt to defend the whole structure on a normative basis, was the only effective device of political empowerment in the polycratic confusion of NS Germany.

The dependence of the 'Goebbels network' on a small number of loyalists or at least trustworthy experts extended over the whole propaganda network. Hans Fritzsche was the sort of skilful but careful operator that was both invaluable to the minister and difficult to be dismissed by his foes. His importance for the Goebbels network cannot be exaggerated, as he was not only trustworthy but capable of carrying out a plethora of crucial assignments within the news, press and radio domains. Walter Tießler, as head of the *Reichsring* and liaison to the Party Chancellery, attempted to promote the RPL/RMVP's interests through careful mediation. Alfred–Ingemar Berndt, whom Goebbels had appointed first to the RRG and in 1939 to the RMVP's Radio Division, proved instrumental in effecting the desired centralisation over broadcasting structures (ch. 1). He resembled Fritzsche and Tiessler in that he could be at the same time responsive to Goebbels's strategies and maintain good relations with his opponents, particularly Dietrich. In recognition of his good services, Goebbels hastened to offer him the commanding post of the Propaganda Division of the ministry, succeeding Braeckow. The Propaganda minister also relied on the good services of Leopold Gutterer who reached the pinnacle of his career within the RMVP network in May 1941 when he became state secretary. An entirely dependable aide, he had been instrumental since 1933 in ensuring the smooth functioning of the ministry as head of both the RMVP's Staff Division and of the section that dealt with the organisation of mass events (*Großveranstaltungen*). In the latter capacity, he also ensured from the very first days of the ministry that a clear delimitation of jurisdictional spheres existed between the RMVP, the RPL as well as an array of other party agencies (including DAF, Rosenberg's *Dienststelle* and Hess' PO) which claimed some degree of involvement in the organisation of party events.

The extent to which the Goebbels network had not just recovered from its 1938–42 setbacks, but achieved a remarkable centralisation of NS propaganda during the last two years of the Third Reich, cannot be exaggerated. Ribbentrop continued to inundate the Propaganda minister with insulting letters spanning ten pages or even more, but the AA's loss of influence and its boss's disgrace meant that Goebbels could afford to file them and take no action.[59] In reality, after an eventful initial period of antagonism between the RMVP's divisions involved in foreign activities and the AA's 'propaganda' offices, there was a trend towards smoother co-operation between the staff of the two institutions. The re-organisation of the RMVP's foreign broadcast under Toni Winkelnkemper entailed a substantial boost to the ministry at the expense of the Foreign Ministry.[60] Otto Dietrich (who retained his position as *Reichspressechef* until early 1945 but had lost the privilege of the immediate contact with Hitler[61]) failed to avert Fritzsche's return to the helm of broadcasting; in the summer of 1944, he even proved unsuccessful in his bid to repatriate the DD to the press domain. Rosenberg's and Ley's attempts to maintain a stake in the propaganda domain were easily brushed aside by

Goebbels. The press never fully succumbed to a Dietrich monopoly – in fact, in 1943 Goebbels himself noted with satisfaction that he had managed to achieve an 'excellent cooperation' with Dietrich;[62] control over news agencies was recovered to an extent that allowed Goebbels relative autonomy in the management of information (in fact, during 1944, the Propaganda minister had insisted that the editors of all news agencies attend his ministerial conference and take instructions directly from him[63]); broadcasting largely remained at the core of the Goebbels network; cinema had never ceased to be its proud monopoly.

Even Bormann had to occasionally bow to the RMVP. Since the beginning of the war, the weekly newsreel copy was edited in Berlin and sent to the Hitler headquarters by Monday for approval. The established routine was that a private screening for Hitler was taking place on Monday evening that offered him the opportunity to make changes; these – bearing the hallmark of Hitler's decision (*Führersentscheid*) – had to be communicated back to the editing offices and be implemented immediately. By the spring of 1944, however, it had become known to the circles of the RMVP that, contrary to his habits during the first three years of the war, Hitler no longer watched the newsreel. In spite of this, a stream of changes continued to pour out of his headquarters bearing the same *Führerentscheid* stamp.[64] Later in the year, there was also a noticeable delay in the communication of the changes, pushing the overall schedule for newsreel production from Monday to Tuesday – and this happened at a time that military setbacks and damage from the Allied air raids had rendered the process of compiling and editing the Wochenschau far more difficult that before. Thus, in December 1944 the head of the RMVP's Film Division, Hinkel, confirmed his suspicion that Hitler was no longer involved in the examination of the weekly newsreel. The case involved the approval of the newsreel for the week of 5 December, which contained a section on the evacuation of the German Alps, as requested by the Luftwaffe. This section had been earmarked for deletion after the screening in the Führer headquarters. When the officials of the RMVP enquired about this, they were informed that Hitler had not taken part in the scrutiny and that the 'decision' emanated from earlier declarations by both Hitler and Dietrich concerning the elimination of material featuring the Alps from the regime's propaganda output. As a result, the RMVP reasserted its authority over the production of the Wochenschau, demanding that all changes be communicated by the previous deadline of Monday evening and – more importantly – that any changes introduced at the Führer headquarter screening could no longer bear the legitimacy of a *Führersentscheid*, given that the Führer himself was no longer participating in the vetting process. This effectively meant that the RMVP was not obliged (as it would have been on the basis of a direct demand from the Führer) to implement the modifications.[65]

In the context of escalating competition for scarce resources that Speer's rationalisation efforts introduced from 1942 onwards, Goebbels had initially failed to achieve an official designation for cinema as 'essential for the war effort' activity; but he had at least elicited a de facto promise that projection premises would be the last 'entertainment' facilities to close down, long after restaurants, music halls or even theatres had been sacrificed for the sake of 'total war'.[66] Luckily for him and his ministry's plans, the resource crisis reached boiling point (in late 1944 and 1945) at a time that his popularity with Hitler had made a dramatic recovery at the expense of Speer, Goering and Ribbentrop. Basking in the glory of the successful financial re-organisation of cinema production in 1941–42, he could now confidently claim that cinema possessed 'the highest political and propaganda significance for the war effort' (*die höchste staatspolitische und propagandistische Bedeutung*) and demand further concessions that ensured the unhindered execution of his overall planning.[67] Therefore, in spite of the Munitions and Armaments ministry's rationalisation plans, Goebbels could use his leverage to elicit crucial concessions in terms of raw material provisions (see Ch. 8).

What was at stake in the last stages of the war had less to do with control of propaganda or 'working towards the Führer'; overall authority over the regime's political direction, winning the war and even Hitler's succession were the far more lucrative rewards by then. From his secure propaganda empire and his new 'total war' power base, Goebbels was clearly vying for total power over party and state against the remaining few – very few – contenders. From 1943 onwards, the RMVP–RPL network was actually becoming the sort of all-encompassing state and party empire that Goebbels had always dreamt of commanding, albeit by then overseeing a crumbling, defeated enterprise. Ideological and political co-ordination of propaganda had proved far easier than its centralisation and effective supervision. Even the latter goal, however, had drawn considerably closer towards the end, even if mainly by default: the Goebbels network was the only propaganda institution that kept functioning literally until the end, adapting in the face of mounting adversity and keeping propaganda noise loud and clear through well-managed channels. Thus, after an impressive, if belated and stillborn, bounce-back during the dying stages of the NS regime, the Propaganda minister had come full circle, albeit through a haphazard, twisted path.

3
The Discourses of NS Propaganda: Long-Term Emplotment and Short-Term Justification

An assessment of NS propaganda in terms of effectiveness depends on a complex process of defining benchmarks – many of which remain essentially relative and perhaps arbitrary. If propaganda assumes a wholly negative connotation (a rather common connotation in the post–1945 period that was not as pronounced during interwar times), indicating a conscious and systematic *distortion* of truth for reasons of political expediency, then its effectiveness can only be gauged in relation to its ability to convince its target audience that the factual gap between truth and 'ersatz' reality does not exist. If, however, propaganda is understood in a more morally and historically neutral context – as a universal factor in political legitimation regardless of regime features – then its primary function is that of a *filter*, intending to sift through factual information and then construct a message based on that manipulated reality that is either more agreeable to its audience or aims to covert it to the regime's rationale (and once again a combination of the two processes is common). The distinction appears subtle but not less significant for that matter. Whilst in the former definition propaganda is believed to fabricate reality as a means of safeguarding and strengthening political control, in the latter case consensus and indoctrination, short-term 'truth' and long-term (wishful) thinking coalesce in order to produce a discourse that is both formative and informative. Thus, the customary identification of propaganda with falsification is misleading and restrictive as a matrix for the understanding of its historical function. No propaganda machinery produces 'truth' or 'lies'; this is a secondary result of the process of filtering the factual raw material, making choices about the content and form of its message, the timing and frequency of its output, the devices and targets of its product. Propaganda is 'truth'; perhaps not 'the whole truth', in most cases not even 'nothing but the truth', but *a truth*, reshaped through the lens of regime intentions and long-term aspirations.[1]

However, there is a further, infinitely more significant function that 'information' performs in this intervening 'filtering' phase. Factual material, even if not distorted or selectively manipulated, does not make much sense beyond its very specific contours of action and (immediate but never conclusive) result. An event is a mere instance – a fragment. The crucial process that invests it with meaning is it particular *emplotment*, its arrangement within a wider discourse of action and intention that links past, present and future in a meaningful, coherent way. This process operates on multiple levels of time, space and ambition. In the particular context of our discussion of NS propaganda in war, a specific battle rests on a situation-specific combination of separate micro-events, but is itself emploted into a more macro-context (of a conflict between states, between ideologies or even a historic crusade with long-term historical significance). This sort of emplotment – by no means a privilege of totalitarian systems of rule (see Introduction) – opens up opportunities for filtering 'events', by organising them into a specific meaningful discourse, of juxtaposing its short-term outcomes to its medium- and long-term significance.

It has been asserted that NS propaganda was substantially more successful in those areas where it activated or responded to deep-seated values of German society, than in those where it sought to establish new 'revolutionary' priorities.[2] For example, a consensus amongst German public opinion with regard to the dismantling of the Versailles Treaty facilitated the enthusiastic endorsement of the regime's 'artichoke' policy (step-by-step revision of the treaty's clauses) from 1936 onwards. Similarly, Germans were more amenable to the anti-Bolshevik message than to the enthusiastically pursued NS project of militarisation and preparation for war – and the exceptionally cool public reaction to the 'success' of the Munich agreement in September 1938 did not go unnoticed by the NS leadership, including Hitler (see Ch. 4). However, propaganda was also education and indoctrination, especially in a system with unbound totalitarian ambitions; it was intended to produce a new consensus of values and not simply to cultivate an existing one without risking incursions in uncharted territories. Rather than being discouraged by the decidedly anti-war stance of the Germans throughout 1938–39, Hitler pressed ahead with his plans, gambling on the regime's propaganda apparatus for ex post facto justification. The challenge for NS propaganda was to 'emplot' a superficially unpopular decision within the matrix of either an existing value consensus or one that it had already started to construct, even if partially or in a tenuous way. Successful propaganda does not always tell its audience what they most want to hear; it also seeks to maximise the appeal of an otherwise unpopular decision by linking it with established aspirations, values and sentiments of the public. To do so, it needs to entertain a sufficient level of legitimacy in the eyes of its audience and to be aware of the specific short-term feelings of its recipients. In other words, when it comes to justifying an unpopular decision, it is essential that a propagandist know whether it is preaching to people who wish to be converted, can be converted, or are unlikely to succumb to particular forms of psychological manipulation.[3]

In this sense, both *long-term emplotment* and *short-term justification* are crucial components of persuasion. Success can be gauged in terms of psychological *integration* – and this integration can be positive (active endorsement of the regime's policy and goals) or negative (a more complex process, whereby the audience eventually subscribes to the goals having first rejected the perceived alternatives), or actually both. But, equally, this integration requires sufficient cohesive matter in both short- and longer-term dimensions. It is not enough for a regime, however popular, to proclaim the relevance of a seemingly disagreeable action to a putative distant utopia; it needs to convince its audience that this connection is evident, that the chosen short-term policy path is the optimal one, and that its expected outcome can contribute to the attainment of the long-term vision. Therefore, three distinct types of discourses interact and dovetail in any propaganda process: two long term (one positive and one negative) and one short term. This triangular scheme constitutes the matrix in which we will discuss the output and reception of NS propaganda during the Second World War.

NS propaganda and long-term positive integration

The NS regime in Germany (in common with all other 'fascist' entities in interwar Europe) possessed a utopian ideological nucleus – the right and duty of the Volk to pursue and fulfil a vision of what constituted the *ideal fatherland*. The particular NS vision of an ideal fatherland consisted of three separate elements. The first (internal) was the *societal*, a discourse of domestic regeneration, unity and stability, based on an integral concept of national community, the marginalisation of the internal 'foes' (*Volksfeinde* – e.g. Jews, socialists, other minority non-conformist groups etc.) and the re-integration of the whole nation in one all-embracing social organism with a single will and conception of national interest. The second (external) aspect was the *territorial*, emanating from an alleged mystic union between the nation and its soil, and aspiring to bring under the control of the rejuvenated nation–state those lands that formed part of an imaginary territorial fatherland. The third (universal) aspect was the *missionary*, referring to the international role that the nation ascribed to itself, its cultural and historic mission vis-à-vis the European civilisation and its place in the new circumstances produced by the regeneration of the national community and its wider consequences.[4]

NS ideology operated on all three levels in an overall organic manner, ensuring the coherence of its message in the short and long term. The centrality of national 'rebirth' (a vision with political, social, economic, moral and cultural connotations)[5] ensured that even unpopular or risky decisions, however abhorrent on their own, could be rationalised as concrete steps towards the direction of this promised rebirth. The overall acceptance on part of the German population of the positive political and moral implications of otherwise unpalatable actions attests to the psychologically integrative power of the 'rebirth' myth in 1930s Germany. In the intervening years between Hitler's appointment as chancellor in January 1933 and the outbreak of the Second World War in September 1939, the NS regime succeeded in manipulating an existing consensus within German society, in order to accommodate its own 'revolutionary' values[6] within what public opinion considered desirable or justifiable course of action. It also achieved some success in extending the contours of such a consensus, thus bridging the initial gap between traditional perceptions of 'rebirth' and the NS's more radical vision. The limits of this process were, of course, apparent: six years were not enough for the completion of the sort of 'total' cultural revolution that the NS regime had actively aspired to. Nevertheless, the psychological infrastructure of a new consensus had already been in place by 1939, through persuasion and coercion, flattery and terror, indoctrination and short-term 'co-ordination' – all in good measure.

The NS regime took active steps in embedding a set of values that it considered as fundamental for the conceptualisation of its long-term utopia. Apart from the myth of 'rebirth', the idea that the German nation constituted a 'community' (*Volksgemeinschaft*), bound by a combination of racial, cultural and historic factors, was of the utmost significance for the pursuit of an 'ideal fatherland'. The discourse of the *Volksgemeinschaft* was the cornerstone of the inclusion–exclusion platform for the construction of a new, organic notion of German identity. It integrated an array of NS ideological beliefs: in the historic and racial superiority of the German–Aryans, in their geographic mission to defend Europe against the hordes of 'Asiatic' invaders, in the brilliance of their cultural output, in their supreme political abilities for leadership etc. Thus, the *Volksgemeinschaft* was at the same time a device for disseminating the elitist discourse on National Socialism with regard to 'pure' Germans *and* the overriding justification for the total 'purification' of the nation from allegedly harmful influences – a sort of reclaiming an ideal sense of community by reversing the process of cultural and 'racial' blending.[7]

A further central long-term ideological theme in NS propaganda was the special significance allotted to Hitler himself, as the utmost incarnation of both NS values and German interest. It is crucial to remember how the impressive (and largely psychological, that is not strictly rational) popularity of Hitler himself proved a more-than-sufficient source of compensation for the notoriety of the 'party', the 'generals' and other largely hated aspects of the regime.[8] The 'Hitler-cult' overpowered individual popular disdain at the 'thuggish' activities of the party mechanism and other institutions or figures that were believed to be outwith the direct control of the leader. The propaganda machinery of the Third Reich proved largely successful in establishing an image of the Führer as above and beyond everyday politics.[9] This image was supported by a discourse that underlined the shift from rational-bureaucratic and institutional to 'charismatic' modes of legitimisation. It rested on the effective cultivation of the idea that the special position of the leader in the

NS system originated from his alleged extraordinary qualities, his capacity for incarnating the collective will of the nation and his unqualified dedication to the national cause. In this sense, Hitler came to represent the vision rather than the actuality of NS politics, and the promise of spiritual salvation and regeneration rather than its interim shortcomings. The perception of Hitler's relative autonomy from the party and the regime (in itself a mirage that had been promoted since the last stages of the *Kampfzeit*) proved extremely convenient for propaganda purposes in two ways: first, by shedding a more positive light on the regime's often mixed political record; and second, by preventing subsequent failures and shortcomings of NS policy from tarnishing the image of the leader, whose halo of flawlessness remained largely untainted until well into the Second World War.[10]

Of course, NS propaganda was largely preaching to an audience that desperately wanted to be converted, even during the crucial period of the regime's domestic consolidation and legitimation (1933–34). Public unease or even anger with certain of the regime's early decisions (e.g. the 1933 boycott of Jewish stores; the *Sturmabteilung* (SA – Storm Division) purge in June 1934; the abortive coup in Austria resulting in the assassination of Chancellor Dollfuß by members of the Austrian NSDAP less than a month later) was evident in a series of contemporary SD and Sopade reports but it appeared to perpetuate the distinction between leader and party/regime, the former still credited with good intentions while the latter held responsible for the failures. From 1935 onwards, the regime's largely successful record in the fields of restoring domestic order, reviving the economy and solving crucial social problems was supplemented by an equally auspicious foreign policy register. By the summer of 1939, Hitler could claim full credit for the re-incorporation of the Saar and the strengthening of Germany's armed forces (1935), the re-militarisation of the Rhineland (1936), the successful union (Anschluß) with Austria (1938) and the fulfilment of the Sudeten Germans' dream of joining the 'fatherland' (1938).[11] Above all, he could boast about what amounted to a virtual demolition of the reviled Versailles arrangement, without having used military might and upsetting peacetime life standards.[12] This was a propaganda opportunity that was not missed by Goebbels in an effort to not only sustain the myth of the leader but also to generate public enthusiasm for the regime itself. In his celebratory speech for Hitler's fiftieth birthday in May 1939, the minister of Popular Enlightenment and Propaganda delivered a tribute to his leader's 'historic genius'. In it, Goebbels presented the successes of the previous years as a virtual *personal* achievement of 'our Führer', emphasising the total identification between him and the 'national community'.[13]

Furthermore, the positive integrative powers of NS propaganda depended heavily on the long-term embedding of the NS period within a special reading of German history – a '*historicisation*' of rebirth under NS rule in the context of alleged historic evidence of German superiority.[14] The decay–regeneration metaphor in NS ideology was of course crucial in the short term, as a device for psychological bolstering of German public opinion after the humiliating reversals epitomised by the Versailles Diktat. This was not, however, the sole or the most significant benchmark for rebirth. Its long-term dimension drew heavily on historic national myths – such as the Teutonic Knights, Frederick the Great, even Bismarck – to establish an open-ended process of reclaiming an allegedly thwarted historic role for the Volk.[15] This aspect of rebirth under NS ideology was at the same time irredentist – in ethnic and territorial terms (union of all Germans – *Gesamtdeutschland*), geopolitical (putting an end to the crippling 'encirclement' of the Reich), racial (establishing a rigid hierarchy of value within Germany and in the rest of Europe), and 'missionary' (fulfilling its destiny vis-à-vis the Volk, Europe and the whole world). History provided the matrix of greatness for envisioning the future, a source of legitimation for National Socialism's increasingly aggressive policies, as well as a reminder to the public of concrete precedents as guarantees for future success.

If until 1938, the focus of the NS discourse of 'mission' was on the protection of the German Volk from the late 1930 – and especially during the war – then there was a palpable shift to a wider perspective that projected the German war effort as a struggle on behalf of 'Europe'. The idea that Germany stood as the guardian of the continent's (allegedly superior) culture, civilisation and history but also as a bulwark to the assault of the 'Jewish–Bolshevik' revolutionary project became ubiquitous in NS propaganda from the summer of 1941 onwards. Under the guise of the Axis alliance and the coalition of forces (Italians, Rumanians, Hungarians, Ukrainians etc.) that participated in 'Operation Barbarossa' the regime was able to present the final assault as an international crusade with a powerful Germany at its helm. From 1941, visual and verbal references to the 'Jewish conspiracy against Europe' remained tied to the 'positive' theme of an alleged German 'crusade' on behalf of the continent.[16] This idea also provided the alibi for justifying the measures that the NS regime introduced later in the direction of mobilising labour across Nazi-occupied Europe and forcefully importing workers into the Reich. Under the slogan 'Europe is working in Germany' (*Europa arbeitet in Deutschland*), the NS authorities presented a glowing picture of working conditions in Germany, claiming not only that the workers showed immense respect and admiration for Hitler, but also that they appreciated the Reich's contribution to the defence and welfare of the whole continent:

> [a] bitter struggle is waged by the Axis powers for the future of our continent. Just as necessity has brought us together in military terms, so too millions of foreign and German workers stand side by side in factories, in farms, or on newly cultivated lands. They fight against the common enemy by using the language of labour ... This demonstrates an enormous dynamics, spearheaded by Germany, that determine the fate of all European nations.[17]

The idea that NS Germany had bequeathed a 'mission' from history on behalf of the whole of Europe was deeply rooted in the movement's worldview (*Weltanschauung*).[18] Its roots lay in a combination of NS fundamental principles: on the one hand, the belief in the alleged superiority (cultural and, in the case of National Socialism, biological too) of the German Volk in contrast to a decadent European 'establishment' (i.e. the 'western powers'); on the other hand, the idea that the benefits of German 'rebirth' under NS had to be exported to the rest of the continent in the context of a 'new order'.[19] In fact, the pseudo-biological foundations of NS ideology facilitated the adoption of the 'European' theme, generating an almost de facto hierarchy of people and a division of labour for a future, reorganised Europe.[20] This 'crusading spirit' had informed the vocabulary of the National Socialism ever since the 1920s, when Alfred Rosenberg (the regime's self-proclaimed chief ideologue) proclaimed an organic, 'volkisch' vision for a future NS Europe.[21] In the following two decades, a stream of publications came to the fore, endeavouring to add historical substance and ideological coherence to an essentially expansionist German plan with evident hegemonic qualities.[22] In fact, as the war approached and especially during the conflict, the 'positive' theme of Europe's *Neugeburt* became inextricably linked to the backbone of NS 'negative' propaganda against the Soviet Union, the western Allies and, of course, the 'international Jewry'. In 1944, Rosenberg again justified the relative loss of conventional freedom under an Axis-occupied Europe by appealing to the idea of a 'deadly threat ... from the forces of darkness, in east and west alike ... against the culture of Europe'; and he concluded,

> [t]herefore there is only one solution for all Germans and all Europeans, who during this hour of destiny fight for their freedom: to reduce to dust all enemies of our venerable, beloved European continent![23]

Undoubtedly, the more NS Germany felt that the tide was turning against it, the more lip-service its ideologues and propagandists felt that they had to pay to the notion of a 'European mission' and to the notion of a 'common destiny' between Germany and the continent (*europäische Schicksalgemeinschaft*).[24] The 'young peoples of Europe' were more and more emphatically juxtaposed to the alleged decadence of 'Americanism', of the convulsive throe of the British empire, of the cultural-biological inferiority of 'Asiatic' Bolshevism and, above all, of the 'international Jewry'.[25] This, however, should not distract from the plethora of NS plans for the reorganisation of the continent that saw the light in the 1930s and during the early stages of the war – that is, *before* defeat forced NS propaganda to resort to the same theme as a means of 'fear' propaganda. Ideas ranged from a wider political re-conceptualisation of the state[26] and the construction of society[27] to fully-fledged visions of economic management (*Großraumwirtschaft*),[28] food and raw material self-sufficiency, currency stability and trade equilibrium.[29]

Apart from Rosenberg's interests generated from his vast remit as minister of the 'eastern occupied territories', most NS leaders paid fulsome tribute to the alleged 'European' dimension of NS policies during the war: Goebbels spoke of the 'liberation of Europe from the chains of plutocratic England', offering instead a 'common basis and a common ideal for the future';[30] Robert Ley – the leader of the DAF – envisioned a politically, culturally and spiritually united 'nations of Europe' under German aegis;[31] the Reich press chief, Otto Dietrich maintained that the German press had a distinct 'European mission' in its efforts to win the hearts of the continent's peoples;[32] Baldur von Schirach – leader of the *Hitlerjugend* (Hitler Youth) – addressed a congress of European youth movements in 1942 and stressed their role for the spiritual regeneration of the whole continent;[33] and even the pre-war Hitler attributed a specific 'European' dimension to his political mission, stressing that,

> the rescue of Europe began at one end of the continent with Mussolini and Fascism. National Socialism continued this rescue in another part of Europe ... [in] brave triumph over the Jewish international attempt to destroy European civilization.[34]

Negative integration: the (powerful) common denominator

However, no identity is the product of integration on the basis of purely positive values. As an inclusion–exclusion process, its building rests on the successful manipulation of carefully drawn dividing lines, of contradistinction and rejection. A lot has been said in historiography about the negative character of fascist ideology, as primarily an *anti-thesis* to existing creeds rather than an autonomous system of values. Following J J Linz's analysis, it is essential to detect in fascism's revolutionary project a synthesis of two interrelated functions: a fundamental rejection of dominant modern ideological systems (such as liberalism and socialism) and a parallel build-up of a novel utopian vision – based on a radical redeployment of modernity[35] – on the ruins of those putatively decadent forces. Thus, whilst negative themes in NS ideology were by no means it raison d'etre or its veneer compensating for an alleged lack of intellectual substance,[36] they did perform a crucial integrative function – as both the psychological nucleus and the last line of fascism's defence against its enemies.

In the NS setting, most of these negative themes corresponded to wider (i.e., not specifically NS) defensive reflexes inherent in German nationalism. Anti-socialism, anti-Semitism, anti-liberalism and anti-internationalism had deep roots within German (and European) society, not least because they could easily be conceptualised as negations of a distinctly German national spirit.[37] In this respect, the NS message of national unity through the persecution of internal and external 'foes' was preaching to an already largely converted audience. But, once again, National Socialism did not exhaust its propaganda energy in simply manipulating pre-existing themes. The negative consensus with regard to the Volk's 'enemies' was significant in the short term for ensuring the popularity of the NS project during its crucial stage of political infancy. However, the regime's leadership exploited this basic consensus, infusing it with distinct NS values. If we take as an example the NS use of the 'anti-Bolshevik' theme, the ingenuity of this scheme becomes apparent. By building on the safe foundations of a very tangible form of anti-socialism (an ideological threat, but also as a national and global danger), the regime could manipulate an established topos of negative psychological integration in order to legitimise novel aspects of its own ideology; for 'anti-Bolshevism' gradually became an infinitely more layered negative term, hosting a concrete geopolitical threat, a racial menace and an internationalist counter-crusade.[38] The notion of a 'Bolshevik–Jewish conspiracy' that increasingly took over the more mundane earlier content of 'anti-Bolshevism' was significantly more than the sum of its constituent parts (Jews, 'Asiatic hordes', socialists); it was a crucial device for the self-legitimation of NS ideology by providing a potent ideological metaphor for what the regime stood for and against – and one that was concrete and instantly recognisable by the majority of the German public opinion.

The ideological cogency of the NS propaganda message depended heavily on the continuity of all themes – both positive and negative. Ideally, propaganda as persuasion and education/indoctrination would have promoted an automatic public identification with the positive themes, thereby producing an instinctive consensus that would depend less and less on negative integration, psychological blackmailing or even brutal coercion. That this had not been achieved by 1939 was indeed a problem for the regime; but the effective manipulation of negative themes had nevertheless promoted a roundabout dynamics of consensus – one that was not enthusiastic or intuitive but no less potent for that matter, if infinitely more fragile. The difference between arriving at a psychological contract with National Socialism and conforming to it through rejection of alternatives or fear was significant; the result less so, at least from a political point of view.

The early common denominator: 'plutocrats' and 'the Jew'

When Germany launched its attack against Poland on 1 September 1939, the NS regime found itself in a rather awkward position. Barely a week earlier the German Foreign Minister, Joachim von Ribbentrop, had concluded a diplomatic coup by signing a treaty of non-aggression with his Soviet counterpart, Viacheslav Molotov, in Moscow. Almost overnight a long-standing, intense reservoir of anti-Bolshevik indoctrination and propaganda had to be sacrificed in favour of a supremely opportunistic geopolitical alliance that startled many – both inside the Reich and across the world. In parallel, the way that the crisis over Poland was handled by the NS authorities – whether out of a 'miscalculation', as A J P Taylor insisted, or out of a genuine disregard for the attitudes of the western powers[39] – resulted in a war for which Germany appeared to hold full moral and political responsibility. By 3 September, Britain and France had brushed aside Hitler's 'peace offer' and declared war on the Third Reich, in accordance with their earlier decision to guarantee Poland's territorial integrity. The military conflict, as the British Prime Minister, Neville Chamberlain stressed, lay squarely with Germany and the Führer:

> [u]p to the very last it would have been quite possible to have arranged a peaceful and honourable settlement between Germany and Poland, but Hitler would not have it ... His action shows convincingly that there is no chance of expecting that this man will ever give up his practice of using force to gain his will. He can only be stopped by force ... [I]t is evil things that we shall be fighting against – brute force, bad faith, injustice, oppression and persecution[40]

Such arguments, as well as the manifested negative feelings of the majority of the German public towards the prospect of war, threw the NS leadership on the defensive (Ch. 4). The need to justify psychologically the decision to risk (and cause) war necessitated a resort to a negative 'anti-western' theme. As a result, attacks on Britain and France served a dual purpose: to supply a positive moral dimension to the German war by presenting it as a struggle of a 'have not' (*Habenicht*) against a 'plutocratic' establishment intent upon stifling any change in Europe; and to displace responsibility for the war by presenting the German *Blitz* as a 'defensive' move, pre-empting the allegedly planned suffocation of the German Volk by the western powers. On numerous occasions throughout 1939–40 Goebbels instructed the German media to stress that responsibility for the conflict – and whatever adverse consequences have arisen out of the hostilities for the civilian population on both sides – lay squarely with the western powers, who – it had to be constantly reminded – in September 1939 had taken the unilateral decision to declare war on the Reich and had repeatedly scorned Germany's 'peace' offers. This sort of justification produced two discourses: one distinctly anti-western, the other focusing on the overriding consideration of 'national interest'. In the autumn edition of the *Illustrierte Beobachter*, Goebbels published a lengthy article titled 'England's Guilt', in which he ran through every single negative propaganda attribute against the west that would permeate NS discourses until the collapse of the regime in 1945. Britain was presented as 'plutocratic', its leadership as a group of 'warmongers', its policy essentially the same as in 1914, and its motives as 'egotistic'. All this was carefully juxtaposed to a 'peaceful' German Reich, locked in a fight to defend 'not only its honour and independence, but also the great social accomplishments it has made through hard and untiring work since 1933'. The moral of the narrative, predictably, revolved around the allocation of responsibility for the war:

> [w]e did not want war. England inflicted it on us. English plutocracy forced it on us. England is responsible for the war, and it will have to pay for it. ... They will one day deal a terrible blow to the capitalist plutocrats who are the cause of their misery.[41]

During this period, NS publications listing the Führer's alleged 'peace' declarations and initiatives became a veritable growth industry inside the Reich, inundating the German population with 'evidence' of the regime's determination to avoid a pan-European conflict. Poland, it was argued, was 'only the alibi for a long-planned war by England'.[42]

Britain in particular was a soft target for NS propaganda. It represented 'plutocracy', an old and rapidly decaying world, a materialistic and egocentric perception of world politics, and an arrogant and decidedly 'anti-German' (*deutschfeindlich*) stance. The theme of 'imperialism' was deployed as an extension of the 'anti-plutocratic' NS discourse against Britain, in an attempt to justify Germany's territorial (and occasionally, colonial too) claims in the 1930s.[43] At the same time, however, a campaign against Britain was the single most significant source of anxiety for the war-weary German public as well as the confirmation of its worst fears since the invasion of Poland. There was a tendency amongst Germans to view the unfolding drama of the conflict in 1939–40 as an unsettling déjà vu, resurrecting the ghost of 1918. In spite of repeated attempts by NS leaders to allay such fears,[44] the extraordinarily frequent occurrence of historical contrasts between the First World War and the NS period in the propaganda output of this period attests to a conscious pre-emptive strategy to assuage such psychologically centrifugal tendencies.

It is interesting to note that, at this initial stage of the war and until the end of 1940, NS propaganda steered its 'anti-plutocratic' animosity towards the British 'ruling clique', in a combination of highly personalised attacks on particularly Chamberlain and Churchill, with more nebulous references to 'Jewish' influences on the country's economic, political and social life.[45] In the context of this campaign, the British elite were represented as an isolated, anachronistic remnant of an old order that stood in the way of the ambitious NS plans for the 'reorganisation' of the continent. In fact, after the evacuation of British forces from continental Europe and the armistice with France, the juxtaposition between an allegedly united Europe, on the one hand, and the British Isles, on the other, assumed the character of a multiple confrontation: historic (the old versus the new Europe), social (the 'gentlemen' versus the people), ideological (the 'liberty' of the 'plutocrats' versus the allegedly genuine freedom pursued through the NS new order), racial (a decaying and declining west versus the Axis alliance of rejuvenated societies and people).[46] In a remarkably candid exposition of the NS project for a new 'European unity', Goebbels presented the conflict between the Reich and Britain in decidedly bipolar terms:

> [w]hat is relevant is that we want to give the millions of Europe a common basis and a common ideal. England has until now resisted this ideal. England has attempted to keep Europe in disorder, since it saw that as the best defence of its island existence. But it is falling under the gigantic blows of our army. Once it falls, we will have the chance to bring peace to Europe.[47]

Behind and beyond Britain, however, NS propaganda detected a more fundamental enemy – 'the Jew' and his alleged 'international conspiracy' (*Weltverschwörung*). Predictably for a movement and a regime that had based a crucial part of its historical raison d'etre on the promise to eliminate Jewish influence on German life, anti-Semitism had provided much of National Socialism's ideological fibre ever since the founding of the NSDAP.[48] From the references in the 1920 'Twenty-Five Point' party programme to the stream of anti-Semitic measures between 1933 and 1939, from the graphic bigotry of Julius Streicher's weekly *Der Stürmer* to Hitler's frequent tirades against the Jews, and from the pseudo-scientific attacks on the alleged biological 'inferiority' of the Jews to the 'spontaneous' violence against the German Jews from 1933 onwards, anti-Semitism provided a powerful common denominator for NS propaganda with a traditionally high level of support amongst the German public.[49] In fact, the Nazis themselves made a very limited conceptual contribution to the foundations of anti-Semitic thought in interwar Germany and Europe; what they did supply, however, was an almost mono-dimensional/mono-causal view of recent historical events (the 1917 Bolshevik revolution in Russia, the defeat in the First World War, the 'stab-in-the-back' myth and the revolution of 1918, the Versailles Treaty, the Weimar Republic, the 1929 economic crisis and so on) as somehow emanating from the workings of 'the Jew'.

Therefore, it was no surprise that the initial anti-western line of NS defence was swiftly complemented by a strong anti-Semitic facet. In a retrospective assessment of this link, Hans Fritzsche included the following reference in his weekly broadcast,

> [i]t is revealed clearly once more that not a system of Government, not a young nationalism, not a new and well applied Socialism brought about this war. The guilty ones are exclusively the Jews and the Plutocrats. ... This clique of Jews and Plutocrats have invested their money in armaments and they had to see to it that they would get their interests and sinking funds; hence they unleashed this war (IMT, Vol. 2, Ch. 14, 1047 Doc. 3064-PS).

At about the same time, the theme of the USA entered the NS propaganda discourse from the backdoor of 'anti-plutocratic' rhetoric. The attitude of the country and the role of President F D Roosevelt personally had caught the attention of the regime's propagandists since the winter of 1939/40 but had produced limited output of a relatively reserved character that was uncharacteristic of the RMVP's overall propaganda idiom or the subsequent stance towards the USA. In fact, the relative dearth of references to the country and its president in the period between the outbreak of the war and February 1941[50] had resulted from a delicate political situation that the NS regime was following closely but with extreme caution, in fear of unfavourable complications. There were in fact many conflicting considerations that underpinned this apparent restraint. On the one hand, the discrepancy between Roosevelt's pro-interventionist stance and the largely anti-war mood of American public opinion[51] entailed a very delicate balancing act on part of Berlin, in the direction of diminishing the stature of the former and encouraging the misgivings of the latter.[52] Beyond the aggressive anti-American rhetoric of many NS leaders, there was a tacit acknowledgement of the complications involved in a military confrontation against the USA. In a conference at the Propaganda Ministry in April 1941 explicit instructions were given to the German press to 'eliminate the hysteria from American public opinion ... [by demonstrating] that we have no need to make such an attack [on the USA]'.[53] A few months later – and with 'Barbarossa' in full swing – the head of the German Press Department of the RMVP, Hans Fritzsche, insisted that the costs (in human and material terms) involved in an operation against the USA clearly outweighed any potential benefits.[54] On the other hand, the growing indications of American aid (moral and material) to Britain provided NS propaganda with opportunities to unmask the president's alleged long-term intentions, incorporating his actions in the wider framework of 'international plutocracy'. For example, in March 1941 Goebbels instructed the German media to give even greater publicity than in the past to the fact that,

> the 7,000 billion credit which the USA is granting Britain is in fact not going to Britain but straight into the pockets of American capitalists. The press must now emphasise that the American people have to raise 7,000 billion which will profit no-one except the big industrialists.[55]

This contradictory stance of NS propaganda vis-à-vis the USA had resulted in a dichotomy between vehement Personal attacks on President Roosevelt and his '*Kriegshetzerclique*', on the one hand, and the war-resistant American public, on the other.[56] The person of the American president had received almost incessant bad coverage by NS propaganda long before the German declaration of war against the USA in December 1941.[57] The refusal of the US official policy to maintain a strict neutrality vis-à-vis the war in Europe, offered NS propaganda further ammunition in its attack against the US establishment, thereby setting the foundations for an amalgamation of the anti-British and the anti-American threads into the 'anti-plutocratic' narrative. The main target was Roosevelt's interventionist policy, his blatant military/ financial and moral support for the British war effort[58] and his allegedly increasing divergence from the mood of the American public opinion. Faced with growing signs of American support for Britain and its allies (including accusations of having dispatched military material to countries fighting against the Axis[59]) and a strengthening of the pro-interventionist tenor of US propaganda, references to America continued to be filtered through the anti-British/'anti-plutocratic' prism, targeting for example Churchill's deliberately exaggerated depiction of his country's military grievances, in order to reinforce Roosevelt's pro-war campaign vis-à-vis a still sceptical American audience.[60]

The tirade did not stop there, however. In line with the NS racialist thinking about an allegedly objective 'hierarchy of races' and the adverse effects of the 'melting pot' process, the USA was depicted as the land of the most devastating experiment in racial miscegenation, resulting in a people without identity, biological quality and spiritual unity.[61] Using arguments deployed in its domestic anti-Semitic campaigns, NS propaganda presented 'Jewish' influence as a hugely disproportionate and destructive factor in modern American life.[62] Roosevelt was the 'pawn' of a barely visible international Jewish stratagem to turn the world's youngest great power into an agent of global chaos.[63] At a time that similar arguments about the alleged connections between the British establishment and 'the Jew' were in wide circulation in the NS propaganda output, the anti-Semitic denominator offered opportunities for a fusion between the anti-British and the anti-US discourses on the basis of an attack on 'world plutocracy' – a fusion that remained loose and oblique in 1939–41 but left the door open for a future recasting of the USA into a lethal enemy of the Reich, of 'Europe' and of the whole world in the event of a globalised conflict.

Anti-Bolshevism

Of course, by the end of June 1941, NS propaganda had infinitely more pressing concerns that temporarily mitigated the strength and volume of its anti-west output: the attack on the Soviet Union re-focused attention on National Socialism's ideological arch-enemy after eighteen months of systematic suppression of anti-Bolshevik arguments in the regime's propaganda discourse. While the anti-British thread continued to operate alongside the main emphasis on the Soviet Union, the USA receded into the background of NS propaganda for a few months. That anti-Bolshevism remained the most appropriate, potent and effective ideological platform for promoting the Volk's most basic form of negative integration was consistent with the fundamental values of the NS Weltanschauung. The stereotypical NS image of 'the Bolshevik' – with all the negative attributes of internationalism, materialism and conspiratorial revolutionary aspirations – intersected with two further NS obsessions: that of the '*Jewish* international conspiracy' and that of the *Russian* (i.e., 'Asiatic', racially inferior and decidedly anti-European) character of the Bolshevik regime. This multiple connection had given rise to an intriguingly layered and composite 'Jewish–Bolshevik' concept by the early 1920s that appeared convincing to a large section of the German population and constituted one of the most crucial aspects of the NSDAP's electoral successes in the 1930–33 period. On a rational level, the NS idea of 'the Bolshevik' was supremely circuitous. Anti-Jewish feeling, strengthened after the 'betrayal of 1918', seemed to foster anti-Bolshevism and vice versa; Bolshevism was at the same time a country-specific force (referring to the Soviet Union) and a generic term (applicable to communists inside Germany and around the world). But these considerations were obviously secondary to the production of a powerful anti-Bolshevik consensus inside the NS movement and popular constituency long before the acquisition of power.[64] Consistently, until the spring of 1939 the NS propaganda discourse vilified Bolshevism in every possible form and direction. In April 1939, Hitler twice referred to it in exactly this circuitous manner,

> I believe that all states will have to face the same problems that we once had to face. State after state will either succumb to the Jewish-Bolshevik pest or will ward it off. We have done so, and we have now erected a national German People's State.[65]
>
> [In the past] Jewish parasites, on the one hand, plundered the nation ruthlessly and, on the other hand, incited the people, reduced as it was to misery. As the misfortune of our nation became the only aim and object of this race, it was possible to breed among the growing army of unemployed suitable elements for the Bolshevik revolution.[66]

In the following months, the initiation of secret negotiations between Berlin and Moscow with the purpose of concluding a bilateral pact of non-aggression resulted in a substantial toning-down of specifically anti-Soviet references in the NS propaganda discourse. With the signing of the Molotov–Ribbentrop pact on 23 August 1939, the theme of 'anti-Bolshevism' disappeared from the regime's vocabulary for a little over two years – that is, until 22 June 1941, when the regime unleashed Operation 'Barbarossa' against the Soviet Union. In the instructions sent to the Reich's Ambassador in Moscow on the event of the invasion, the German Foreign Ministry returned to the pre-1939 theme of the fundamental 'contradiction between National Socialism and Bolshevism', accused the Soviet Union of plotting with Britain and her allies in Europe against Germany and concluded with a strong defence of the Reich's decision to launch a (carefully-presented 'preventive') war against Bolshevism. The official declaration of war put an end to the propaganda anomaly, which had seen the most potent ingredient of negative integration in NS ideology being awkwardly suppressed by the regime's authorities. Now, as Hitler stated in his letter to Mussolini on the eve of the invasion,

> I again feel spiritually free. The partnership with the Soviet Union, in spite of the complete sincerity of the efforts to bring about a final concil-iation, was nevertheless often very irksome to me, for in some way or other it seemed to me to be a break with my whole origin, my concepts, and my former obligations. I am happy now to be relieved of these mental agonies.[67]

This mood of release immediately seized the whole of the German media, resulting in a pandemonium of anti-Bolshevik tirades that were sustained – in different forms and nuances – until the collapse of the regime in the spring of 1945. A few months later, in September, Goebbels himself set the tone for the regime's propaganda discourse vis-à-vis the war in the east:

> Bolshevism is using every available resource to resist annihilation. It is a matter of life or death. Only one of us will survive. One must consider what would have happened if the Führer had not acted to deal with the Soviet danger. Only then can one understand what is at stake. Our soldiers are witnesses to Moscow's plans. They have seen with their own eyes the preparations made for the destruction first of Germany, then of Europe. They also have first hand experience with the Soviet system, and can see the true conditions in the paradise of workers and farmers. ... This is more than a campaign or even a war. It is a historic battle with fate in the broadest sense of the word.[68]

It is interesting to follow the development of the NS anti-Bolshevik discourse during 1941–45 in relation to military developments. Broadly speaking, ref-erences to the Soviet Union remained largely overshadowed by the regime's over-confidence with regard to 'Barbarossa' until the end of 1941, and again in the 1942 spring-to-autumn period of military advances in the east. This explains why, in quantitative terms, the NS propaganda's *negative* output throughout 1941 and 1942 remained focused on the anti-western theme rather than on the 'historic battle' against the Soviet Union.[69] By contrast, after the beginning of 1943 (and coinciding with the Stalingrad debacle, Goebbels's 'total war' speech and the increasingly 'realistic' tone of NS pro-paganda) anti-Bolshevism became the keystone of negative integration within the Reich. Although the NS authorities strove to maintain a balance in their negative references to both the west and the Soviet Union, the latter discourse proved significantly more potent, as evidenced by the attitude of the German population and the Wehrmacht in the last crucial days of April–May 1945. The belief that the Red Army would wreck havoc upon the areas it would occupy formed a powerful common denominator in public perceptions; that the Soviet soldiers would pillage, rape and retaliate, explains why the rump German armies, trapped between the advancing allies from east and west, took great pains to evacuate their troops as well as civilian population to the western zone of occupation.

Of course, this sort of negative rationale seemed totally irrelevant to the NS authorities in 1941 (or even 1942), in the light of the impressive Wehrmacht advances on the eastern front. From the regime's point of view, the successful first phase of the Blitz against the Soviet Union provided the most spectacular opportunity for building a lasting *positive* consensus and allegiance to National Socialism. The alleged collapse of Bolshevism was constantly presented as a cataclysmic turning point in European history – as Julius Streicher wrote in September 1941,

> [t]he end of the battle against the Bolshevist army in the East is German victory and therefore the victory of non-Jewish humanity over the most dangerous instrument of the Jewish world destroyers. The cause of the world's misfortune however will be forever eliminated only when Jewry in its entirety is annihilated.[70]

However, elements of negative propaganda were evident even at this early stage. Both Hitler and Goebbels justified the unforeseen fighting power of the Soviet Union as tangible proof of the 'enemy's preparations against Germany and Europe'. Even on 29 June 1941, the commentary to the Wehrmacht triumphalist communiqués made an oblique reference to the resistance encountered on the eastern front, stating that Stalin had prepared a large army 'exclusively for an attack on Germany'.[71] At the same time, references to the 'barbaric' techniques of the adversary continued to flood the NS propaganda output from the beginning of 'Barbarossa'. Hitler devoted a large part of his 11 December 1941 speech to the Reichstag to offer a synopsis of European history (and of the German contribution to it) in terms of a Manichean struggle between civilisation and barbarism. Although mainly referring to the Middle Ages, the analogy between the then 'terrible stream of barbarous, uncultured hordes sallied forth from the interior of Asia' and the contemporary 'barbaric hordes from the east' was palpable and deliberate.[72] And because images were a far more powerful propaganda weapon than simple words, the regime masterminded a stream of visual demonstrations (ranging from miles of Wochenschau material to poster and leaflet campaigns) to the atrocities of the Red Army, the brutality of its fighting techniques and the viciousness of its retaliation on civilians.

In general terms, NS propaganda thrived on anti-Bolshevism. In 1942, the RMVP organised a large exhibition dedicated to the alleged horrors of

Bolshevism and the nobility of the German campaign in the east. Opening on 9 May in the Berlin Lustgarten with the sarcastic title 'Soviet Paradise' (*Sowjet-Paradies*) and with parallel events in many major German cities, it offered the visitor a historical narrative of 'Jewish–Bolshevik' connivance to dominate the world, starting from Russia and spreading across the continent under the guise of socialism. The exhibition covered a wide range of topics – from the role of the secret police (GPU) to working conditions and living standards – offering a devastatingly grim image of everyday life under the Soviet regime. But, above all, it endeavoured to present the NS war as a crusade of pan-European liberation from the yoke of Bolshevism:

> [h]e who has seen this understands the historic conflict in which we are now engaged, a conflict in which there can be no compromise. There are only two possible outcomes: Either the German people will win and ensure the survival of the world and its culture, or it will perish and all the peoples of the world will fall into the barbarism of the Soviet state that has reduced millions to powerless starving slaves. To stop that from happening, the best elements of Europe are fighting under German leadership at the side of our soldiers to destroy the fateful threat to the life and culture of Europe. Our battle is to free the East, along with its vast and inexhaustible riches and agricultural resources, and to save Europe from the nightmare that has threatened it for millennia.[73]

The predictability of the exhibition's tenor and themes, as well as its ability to synthesise an array of ideas already in circulation ('preventive war' thesis; 'Jewish–Bolshevik conspiracy'; Stalinist 'terror'), ensured its overall success with the German public.[74] During 1942 more than one million people visited the premises (the reduced ticket price of 0.35RM was particularly geared towards maximising visitor numbers), whilst press and radio supplied ample coverage. A short documentary film was also authorised by the RPL and shown in the autumn, featuring ostensibly original depictions from the 'primitive' and 'barbaric' life in the Soviet Union. 'Opinion reports' gathered by either the secret police (SD) or the party's local propaganda offices (*Reichspropagandaämter*, RPA) confirmed that the exhibition had struck the right chord with a German public steeped in almost a decade of almost incessant anti-Bolshevik propaganda and still recovering from the trials of the preceding winter on the eastern front.[75] Goebbels seized the opportunity and fuelled the prevailing atmosphere in an almost self-congratulating article in *Das Reich*:

> [t]he peoples of the Soviet Union live at a level of brutish primitiveness that we can hardly imagine. An exhibition called 'The Soviet Paradise' has recently visited Berlin and other large cities, trying to show the nature of life in the Soviet Union through original materials. Normal and naive

people can hardly believe it. One often saw groups of civilians discussing the matter heatedly, who then had to be told by a few wounded veterans of the Eastern Front that reality in the so-called workers' and peasants' paradise was even worse than what was presented ... None of our soldiers has seen any evidence of an agreement between the theory and practice of Bolshevism. None has returned from the East as a communist. The veil has been removed. Bolshevism is not a danger for us any longer.[76]

The 'Soviet Paradise' rehearsed all positive and negative themes that NS propaganda was running in the first half of 1942. The alleged superiority of National Socialism was accentuated through a direct comparison with a distorted image of Bolshevism. At the same time, heavy psychological investment in the notion of a 'Jewish–Bolshevik conspiracy' helped the regime in two complementary ways – solidifying the *Haltung* of the population vis-à-vis another year of military operations against the Soviet Union and justifying the radicalisation of the policy against the Jews. This combination sheds light on the bizarre story of a sabotage ploy against the exhibition premises, organised by a small underground communist group led by Herbert Baum, which took place in late May. Immediately the regime was mobilised in the direction of 'exposing' the Jewish role (there were many Jews involved in the group) and conveniently authorising a large-scale evacuation action from the capital and other cities of the Reich.[77]

It was the dramatic fate of the VIth Army in Stalingrad that effected a fundamental shift in the regime's propaganda output, in terms of both emphasis and tenor. In the aftermath of the defeat, NS propaganda invested more comprehensively in negative themes of psychological integration. The erosion of NS credibility, including to some extent even the aura of the Führer himself, meant that a direct appeal to long-term NS visions was bound to have minimal effect on a public opinion that was experiencing a growing estrangement from the authorities, regime institutions and personalities. By contrast, negative themes could evoke the same sense of aversion, whilst at the same time making further use of the proximity of the threat to amplify fear as a centripetal force of integration. To use an example, Bolshevism was a distant, vague, though powerful image of menace in 1941, when the war was fought in the faraway steppes of the Ukrainian and Russian landscapes, at the same time that the west appeared all but totally defeated; by 1943–44, however, the alliance between the resurgent Allied forces and the Soviet Union in conjunction with the crushing defeats on the eastern front had brought the spectre of a 'Bolshevisation of Europe' much closer (psychologically as well as geographically) to the 'reality' of the Germans.

In his 'Total War' speech, delivered at the Berlin Sportpalast (see Ch. 6) the Propaganda minister resorted to an unprecedentedly explicit language with reference to the 'Bolshevik menace'. The gist of his passionate sermon was that this was no longer a confident, triumphant war, fought in the remote lands of Asia, but a critical defensive war for the survival of the Reich – and of Europe as a whole. Allusions to apocalyptic scenes of destruction and terror in the event of a Bolshevik victory were by no means a novelty in NS propaganda. This time, however, and in spite of Goebbels's circumlocutions about the 'heroism' and 'sacrifice' of the Wehrmacht soldiers, the tone was decidedly gloomy. The advance of Bolshevism, he argued, resembled a flood which concealed the real face of the enemy – international Jewry – and its intention to 'throw the world into horrible disorder and thus cause the destruction of a thousand-year-old culture, to which it has never contributed'.[78] Perversely, throughout 1943 Goebbels used a series of powerful words to denote the impending danger that were almost verbatim extracted from the regime's own anti-Semitic vocabulary: for example, the Jewish–Bolshevik hordes were presented as 'liquidation squads' (*Liquidationskommandos*); and the war would be transformed into a campaign of 'annihilation' (*Vernichtung*), if the German Volk did not unite in resolute opposition to the enemy.[79] Although references to the 'annihilation' project of the Bolsheviks had been in wide circulation during the second half of 1941, they were mitigated by the confident conviction that such a plan lay in the past and had now been thwarted by another form of 'annihilation' – that of enemy divisions by the Wehrmacht.[80] Now, *Vernichtung* was tangible, painfully relevant to the German Volk, one of only two possible outcomes of this 'race war', in line with Hitler's January 1939 prophesy – either the destruction of Germany or the 'annihilation of the Jewish race in Europe'.[81]

The introduction of 'total war' coincided with the launch of a powerful anti-Bolshevik campaign, targeting both the home front and the soldiers fighting in Russia. The new negative image of 'the Bolshevik–Jew' was a carefully layered psychological construction, intended to incorporate many deep-seated public fears, cliché images of the Soviet Union and basic tenets of NS Weltanschauung. Consciously, Goebbels aimed to frighten the German Volk (and, to some extent, the public opinion in western countries as well) 'to death'.[82] To capitalise on this fear, NS propaganda portrayed the war on the eastern front as an apocalyptic struggle that would decide everything – and irreversibly so: the mere survival of the German Volk itself; the salvation of Europe from 'Asiatic hordes', from 'Mongols and Huns', from the ferment of 'Jewish decomposition'; the continued existence of European culture; the continuation of the Aryan race, and so on. Hitler claimed that the Soviet successes bestowed retrospective justification to the NS strategy. As he underlined in his only major speech of 1943, delivered on the anniversary of the 1923 putsch in November,

[t]oday there is no further need to show how stupid the idea was that Europe might have been protected from Bolshevist Russia by Poland. The widespread belief that it might be possible to appease the Bolshevist colossus by renouncing all thoughts of strength, and that a Europe dedicated to

peace which continued to progressively disarm would have foiled Bolshevist Russia's plans for world conquest, is just as stupid ... Unless this Bolshevistic–Asiatic colossus is finally broken and defeated it will continue to launch its assaults on Europe for a long time to come.[83]

In spite of the depressingly candid reference to the Soviet Union as a 'colossus' (a far cry from the deprecating tenor of 1941 or even early 1942[84]), there was an underlying optimism that the enemy could indeed, and would, be 'broken and defeated'. This belief gradually waned in 1943 after a constant stream of retreats and defeats in the east; the most that the German Volk could hope for, as Goebbels himself acknowledged in June 1943, was a long, difficult campaign that, through the intensification of 'total' measures, would eventually bring victory against Bolshevism.[85]

The construction of a negative mega-narrative: the 'Jewish–Bolshevik–plutocratic alliance'

The declaration of support for the Soviet Union from Britain supplied an opportunity for the conjunction of the anti-western and the emerging anti-Bolshevik discourses of NS propaganda. This opportunity was not missed on the RMVP's chief, who on 26 June, attempted to capitalise on the theme of Bolshevik and 'western' collusion:

Germany was barely able to bring [the war] to a swift conclusion through a large-scale attack against England, because the gigantic Russian troop aggregations tied down so many German troops on our eastern border ... Here met Churchill and Stalin's interests. Both had the wish to prolong the war as much as possible; the former in order to split Europe once more and neutralize once again its political, economic and military strength; the latter, in order to cause a blood-bath and thus make Europe ripe for Bolshevisation.[86]

This short excerpt provides a concise summary of how the regime's emploted Operation 'Barbarossa' in the context of existing propaganda discourses, and employed it as the fundamental cohesive force for a wider synthesis. Ever since the summer of 1940, the Führer had insisted that the non-belligerence of Soviet Union was one of the main reasons as to why Britain continued to fight, obviously in anticipation of Russian help in the near future.[87] Now Goebbels presented the invasion as the culmination of the Reich's defensive (or rather pre-emptive) reaction to its alleged 'encirclement' by hostile superpowers. He also did not dampen down the expectations of the German public for a final settling of accounts with Britain by presenting the war against the Soviet Union as part of the same strategy for fostering Germany's hegemonic position in Europe.

The conjunction of anti-western and anti-Bolshevik themes coincided with the parallel radicalisation of the Final Solution inside the occupied territories of the Reich and a renewed prominence given to the 'anti-Semitic' theme in the discourse of NS propaganda. The emplotment of the war in the context of a decidedly and predominantly *anti-Jewish* campaign, and vice versa, produced a mega-narrative in which Moscow and Bolshevism, London and 'plutocracy', as well as Jewish international interests conspired and combined in a struggle against Germany – and, of course, the 'new order' in Europe.[88] In his October 1941 radio address to the German people, Hitler presented Churchill as the puppet of 'international Jewry', although he was careful enough to revert to the previous distinction between 'plutocratic clique' and the 'British people as a whole [who] do not bear the responsibility [for war]'.[89] As the SD reports in the aftermath of the speech demonstrate, the speech struck the right chord with a German public thirsty for fresh victories and, above all, a double successful strike at both Moscow and London.[90] The mega-narrative was taken up with a vengeance by Goebbels in the summer of 1941, with the 'Jew in the City and the Jew in Kremlin' presented as the single 'schoolmaster' behind both Bolshevism and international capitalism.[91] The result was that, increasingly after the invasion of the Soviet Union, the respective contours of the three primary NS discourses of negative integration became blurred and largely interdependent in NS propaganda output.

The final act in this process of constructing a powerful common denominator of psychological resistance in German society took place in December 1941 with the Japanese attack on Pearl Harbour, the entry of the USA in the conflict and the subsequent declaration of war by Hitler. Now the political and military landscape invited a final synthesis of the anti-Bolshevik, anti-Semitic and anti-plutocratic (USA, Britain) streaks of NS negative propaganda into a vehement campaign of morally discrediting Germany's enemies. For a considerable time Roosevelt had been systematically portrayed not simply as a 'gangster' (a word that was juxtaposed to German and European 'values') at the service of the international 'Jewish conspiracy'; both the American president and the British prime minister had been reduced to mere caricatures of an immoral 'plutocratic' alliance at the mercy of powerful capitalist (therefore by definition, Jewish) interests. The Bolsheviks, on the other hand, were ideologically and politically under the alleged control of the 'terroristic' designs of the Jews, contriving a 'global revolution ... [and] chaos in Germany and Europe'.[92] Now, anti-Semitism offered the cohesive force for the integration of the negative discourses against the Reich's enemies more clearly than ever. Goebbels himself had set the tone in his 'total war' speech at the Berlin Sportpalast the previous February; in early June he used the same location to launch a scathing attack on the allegedly omnipresent Jewish 'threat':

[o]ne looks around in the camp of our enemies: where one looks, Jews and more Jews. Jews behind Roosevelt as his cerebral trust, Jew behind

Churchill, Jews as a malicious agitator and whip in the whole English–American–Soviet press, Jews in the corners of the Kremlin as the real bearers of the Bolshevism. The international Jew is the glue that holds together the hostile coalition. He hits with his world-wide connections the bridges between Moscow, London and Washington. The war derives from him, he wages it from the background, and now he would also like to be his only beneficiary. We face here the most dangerous enemy of the world[93]

In this sense, the process of amalgamating the 'anti-American' theme within the grand 'Jewish–Bolshevik–plutocratic' negative narrative, rested on two parallel ideological associations. The idea of a wider 'Jewish' capitalist conspiracy against Germany and the international order as a whole provided the generic framework in which both the 'Roosevelt clique' in Washington and its Churchill counterpart in London, were articulated as mere pawns of a wider 'Jewish conspiracy' against Germany and the international order as a whole. Then, in the aftermath of the Japanese attack on Pearl Harbor and the German declaration of war against the USA, NS propaganda made a predictably smooth transition to the depiction of America as the latest component in the anti-German coalition. In his lengthy speech to the Reichstag on 11 December 1941, Hitler made ample use of the opportunity of the declaration of war to complete the discursive fusion. Having provided a retrospective of the USA's historically hostile attitude to Germany (with repeated references to the First World War and to Wilson personally), he unleashed a violent diatribe against the American president:

President Roosevelt, lacking ability himself, lends an ear to his brain trust, whose leading men I do not need to mention by name; they are Jews, nothing but Jews. And once again, as in the year 1915, [the USA] will be incited by a Jewish President and his completely Jewish entourage to go to war without any reason or sense whatever, with nations which have never done anything to America, and with people from whom America can never win anything.[94]

For once, Churchill had retreated into the background.[95] But the 'anti-British' discourse, already systematically linked to 'plutocratic' and 'Jewish' themes since the beginning of the conflict in September 1939, needed no further elaboration. The missing link, the role of the USA as the alleged accomplice to the Bolshevik–capitalist conspiracy against the Reich, had at last fallen into place with the declaration of war against the USA.

This said, the military situation in late 1941/early 1942 militated against the complete integration of the negative discourses, thus affording each of them a degree of relative autonomy in the NS propaganda discourse. The reason for this was that Germany was fighting a (still) victorious war in the east, was planning a spectacular Axis bounce-back in north Africa against the British forces, but did not yet have an open front against the USA, with the exception of the surrogate U-boat campaign in the Atlantic. Understandably, with the declaration of war against America, NS propaganda orchestrated a campaign of defamation against the country that reached its peak in the middle of 1942. On 16 December, just five days after Hitler's Reichstag address, Goebbels had given instructions to German propagandists to prepare 'pamphlets ... proving by objective argument that the USA possesses virtually no culture of her own and that her cultural products are essentially derived from European achievements'.[96] Although the RMVP never concealed its intention to bring about a swift overthrow of President Roosevelt, it was quickly acknowledged that this development was highly unlikely to happen, at least in the near future, in spite of the impressive early Japanese successes in the Pacific and east Asia.[97] Thus, the denigration of the USA as the 'destroyer of European civilisation' and 'a land without heart' became a highly popular subject of NS propaganda. Apart from the usual output, primarily by Goebbels and Hitler, a stream of other party 'authorities' rallied to the cause – from the DAF to the RPL.[98] At the same time, the U-boat campaign in the Atlantic provided a respectable supply of propaganda attacks on the USA.[99] In strict consistency with the overall emphasis on the alleged 'defensive' nature of the Reich's military campaigns, the declaration of war against the USA was presented by Hitler as a pre-emptive move 'to avoid every conceivable occasion for a conflict with the USA'.[100] The justificatory subtext was identical to that deployed in September 1939 or June 1941: the Reich was fighting its way out of a planned 'encirclement' by a hostile, conniving powerful coalition of enemies as a 'last resort'.

The signing of the British–Soviet alliance treaty in June 1942 and the wider discussion about the opening of a 'second front' on continental Europe supplied further propaganda ammunition to the construction of the negative mega-narrative, especially since Molotov's visit to the USA for the purpose of signing the alliance was bracketed by three summits between Roosevelt and Hitler – the first in the summer of 1941; the second in June 1942; both to be followed by the Casablanca conference in January 1943.[101] Although NS propaganda had referred to the first two in exceptionally derogatory terms,[102] the increasing signs of Allied military co-ordination at a time of military reverses in north Africa intensified a feeling of insecurity in Berlin. The implications of the emerging anti-fascist coalition's decision to fight the war on the platform of Germany's 'unconditional surrender' and the growing talk of a 'second front' in Europe were certainly not missed on Goebbels[103] who, after the dramatic events at Stalingrad, implemented a wide programme of re-organisation in the structures and content of NS propaganda. Goebbels, however, worked hard to maintain both the integrity of the grand narrative *and* the specific appeal of its components. Although he took the decision to prioritise a vehement anti-Bolshevik campaign in February 1943, at the same time he did not abandon the anti-western thread. Starting with the obvious point that, unlike Britain, the USA did not belong to 'Europe', NS propaganda proceeded to depict US policy as a deliberate ploy against the continent's geopolitical, cultural and economic interests. In the shadow of the successful execution of Operation 'Torch' (Allied landing in north Africa) in early November 1943, Goebbels reacted with an ungainly tirade against American 'world-imperialist' intentions and Roosevelt's 'gangster-like' seizure of European colonies.[104] In parallel, the intensification of Allied air raids over German cities in 1943 (a spin-off from the decisions taken at the Casablanca conference) (see Ch. 7) forced Goebbels to introduce the rather alarmist discourse of 'British-American terror'.[105] In fact, as the devastation caused by the bombing of the Reich escalated during 1943–44, NS propaganda focused its anti-western discourse on the negative outcomes of the air raids for the Reich and 'Europe' alike: on their adverse effect on conditions of living for the civilian population, on the destruction of the 'European' cultural heritage, on the immorality of the Allies' military techniques and devices. By juxtaposing the indiscriminate nature of Allied carpet bombing to an alleged German restraint in the field of attacks on civilian targets (Hitler went as far as claiming that Germany was consciously refraining from bombing civilian populations and cultural locations as a matter of ethical principle[106]), the NS authorities were claiming the moral high ground, presenting the Reich's war as an allegedly noble enterprise geared towards rescuing 'European civilisation' from the onslaught of the Bolshevik–Jewish–plutocratic coalition.[107] Already from the autumn of 1942, the themes of the 'dignity' and the 'nobility' of the struggle that the 'worldwide coalition of the have-nots' is fighting in order 'to get rid of this vilest coalition that the world has ever seen', contrasted starkly to earlier, arrogantly triumphalist and condescending discourses in reference to the west.

Nevertheless, the adoption by NS propaganda of an increasingly vehement anti-Bolshevik stance from 1943 onwards, resulted in a wider long-term transformation of its anti-western discourse, linking a victory of the west with an allegedly catastrophic triumph of Bolshevism (and, of course, the international Jewry). In his 1943 'total war' speech, Goebbels had once again underlined the dignity of the German struggle against the 'Bolshevisation of Europe'. The usual accusations about Britain's and the USA's intentions to hand over Europe to Stalin and thus to destroy the 'Germanic' western civilisation pervaded the bulk of the speech. However, Goebbels went further, striking at the heart of the anti-German coalition:

[w]hat would England and America do if Europe fell into Bolshevism's arms? Will London perhaps persuade Bolshevism to stop at the English Channel? I have already said that Bolshevism has its foreign legions in the form of communist parties in every democratic nation. None of these states can think it is immune to domestic Bolshevism. ... The world no

longer has the choice between falling back into its old fragmentation or accepting a new order for Europe under Axis leadership. The only choice now is between living under Axis protection or in a Bolshevist Europe.[108]

In fact, after the defeat of the VIth Army in Stalingrad, Goebbels had instructed the RMVP authorities to refer to the western powers as 'ancillaries' (*Hillsvölker*) of the Soviet Union – avoiding the more neutral term 'Allied Nations' (*Allierte Nationen*) – and thus to remind the people that 'the collusion between the USA, England and the USSR ... is bound together by the Jews [who] rule everything'.[109] Gradually in the subsequent two years of the conflict anti-Bolshevism would, if not eclipse then, largely absorb the regime's attack on 'western plutocracy', presenting the latter as a – willing or, more often, naive – pawn of the Kremlin. This was the apotheosis of a two-pronged propaganda, for the intended audience was not confined to the boundaries of the Reich. Whilst the NS leadership had every reason to capitalise on the embedded fear of the Soviet Union in German public opinion, this message had international recipients too. By presenting the anti-fascist alliance as essentially a cynical device of a Jewish–Bolshevik plan to dominate 'Europe' (and, through it, the whole world), Goebbels clearly intended to appeal to three audiences: first to the British and American populations, spreading doubts about the sincerity of Stalin's promises and thus weaken the alliance from within; second, to the peoples in Axis-occupied countries, emploting their predicament as a far lesser evil to the prospect of domination by the Soviet Union; and, third, to the populations of neutral countries, in order to generate some sympathy for the alleged nobility and 'missionary' altruism of the German campaign.[110]

Thus, by the spring of 1944, as the expectation of an Allied landing in continental Europe was reaching its climax, anti-western discourses had lost much of its earlier autonomy in the face of an overwhelming propaganda emphasis on the 'Bolshevik menace'. With the opening of the new land front in northern France, NS propaganda could now invoke empirical evidence for its earlier claim that the Reich's two-front struggle was a single historic mission to defend the world from the onslaught of the 'Jewish–Bolshevik' project.[111] This theme was revitalised in the aftermath of the Yalta conference in February 1945 – a meeting that, on the basis of its location and seemingly dominant role of Stalin in the proceedings, appeared to strengthen the NS claim that the Bolsheviks, and not the west, were in charge of the future of the world. But this line of argument went a step further: not only Roosevelt, Churchill and their 'plutocratic cliques', but also Stalin and the Bolsheviks were essentially puppets of a wider, far more lethal 'international Jewish conspiracy'. This was the basis on which the construction of the grand narrative of negative integration was anchored. Anti-semitic propaganda campaigns increased in intensity and volume from 1943 onwards, usually running concurrently with anti-Bolshevik ones but never failing to implicate the western powers in the context of the 'conspiracy' scheme.

The grand narrative of negative integration that NS propaganda deployed in the second half of the war maintained its discursive integrity until the final collapse of the Reich in May 1945; what kept changing was its internal focus and conceptual association of its three components. Even if in terms of coverage, NS propaganda could still combine east and west under the banner of the 'international Jewish conspiracy' against the Reich, the growing emphasis on the Soviet Union as the allegedly uncontested epitome of evil was unmistakeable.[112] The advance of the Red Army eastwards into east Prussia during 1944 provided the regime's propaganda machinery with an opportunity to reinforce the imagery of danger and fear – this time not simply in generic-ideological terms (destruction of European civilisation; German enslavement) but with particular reference to individual suffering and material devastation. The particularly graphic manner in which the NS press publicised images of alleged Soviet savagery against Germans formed part of an attempt to sink public *Stimmung* deeper into a state of primordial fear and thus to indirectly boost its spirit of resistance. Goebbels's carefully chosen circumlocutions about the (far from impeccable) conduct of the Wehrmacht troops on the eastern front in 1941–43 and the regime's policy towards the Jews had served two different purposes: first, to implicate the Germans in the regime's own atrocities and thus bind them to National Socialism's destiny; and, second, to shatter hopes that a conclusion to the war, regardless of the outcome, would bring relief to the Volk.[113] Now, SD and RPA reports commented on the feelings of fear and 'acute danger' experienced by most Germans with regard to the Soviet advances in the east.[114]

It is thus clear that NS propaganda had succeeded in shattering any illusions about the fate of the German Volk in the event of an (increasingly likely) Soviet occupation; but it had failed to replace it with an unequivocal psychological commitment to defend the Reich against the prospect of invasion. In fact, the graphic manner in which Soviet 'atrocities' were portrayed in the German media generated a mixture of fear (which was of course intended), acute pessimism or even fatalism (certainly undesired) and aversion to the techniques employed by the RMVP (again the opposite of what Goebbels had wished). However, with the collapse of the front in early 1945, the regime had simply run out of psychological devices to maintain a basic level of negative public integration. In his last article, the Propaganda minister simply resorted to the most exaggerated reiteration of the apocalyptic imagery that awaited the Germans under Bolshevik rule:

[i]f [the enemy] succeeds, Germany will become a cemetery. Our people will starve and perish, aside from the millions who will be deported to

Siberia as slave labour. In such a situation, any means is justified. We are in a state of national emergency; it is no time to ask what is normally done! Does the enemy worry about that? Where does international law allow for the tens of thousands of German women tortured and raped in the East ...? Will [the Volk] wait until Bolshevist posters appear ordering everyone between fourteen and fifty to show up at a certain spot with clothing and two weeks of food in order to be transported to Siberia?[115]

The same theme was underlined by Hitler himself in his last address to the German people on 24 February 1945:

[s]everal areas in the eastern part of Germany now experience Bolshevism. The crimes committed against our women and children and men by this Jewish plague are the most terrible fate ever conceived by human beings.[116]

By that time there was a further consideration that obliged the NS regime to alter once again its relative emphasis and reinvigorate the 'anti-western' angle of its propaganda output: increasingly in the spring of 1945, it became evident to the regime authorities that the fighting power of the soldier and the resistance mood of the population were diminishing for those areas faced with the prospect of western (as opposed to Soviet) occupation. But the emphasis on anti-Bolshevik 'fear' propaganda had a series of unforeseen complications for the regime. For a start, as the same July 1944 SD report noted, people had come to accept the fact that the danger from the east was 'much more important' than that from the west, even after the Allied invasion of Normandy. This type of mentality was actually opening up a fracture in this narrative that the regime had neither intended nor desired: instead of integrating the Volk on the basis of opposition to *any* form of occupation, it created the impression that the west was a far lesser evil compared to the Bolsheviks. This was the first unambiguous evidence of a tendency that would become much clearer in early 1945, when the German population in the west would in some cases neither resist the onslaught of the western powers nor assist the Wehrmacht soldiers in their defensive struggle.[117] The desperate attempt to shore up the fighting power of the population against the advancing western powers was offset, ironically, by the NS regime's long-term success in fostering a seemingly incontrovertible threshold of negative integration on the basis on anti-Bolshevism. In spite of subsequent efforts by the NS propaganda mechanism to persuade the German population that the occupation of the fatherland – and not the nature of the occupier – should be their ultimate concern, the impression that western soldiers were more 'humane' in comparison to the 'Bolshevik–Mongol' 'bestial hordes' had in fact been unwittingly encouraged by National Socialism – and, for this reason, almost impossible to shake off. In April 1945, Goebbels warned the Germans that,

> [t]he enemy naturally wants to make his battle against the Reich as easy and safe as possible, and hopes to diminish our morale by seductive agitation. That is poison for weak souls. He who falls for it proves he has learned nothing from the war. He thinks it possible to take the easy road, when only the hard path leads to freedom. They are the same doubting souls who have no sense of national honour, and think nothing of living under the clubs of Anglo–American banking Jews, accepting charity from their hands. In other words, they are the rubbish of our nation, who nonetheless give the enemy an entirely false idea of this people.

The main 'enemy' in this context was, of course, the British–American forces, not the Red Army against which Goebbels expected an unmitigated spirit of resistance until the end:

> [t]he German dreamer must wake up if he does not want to lose his freedom and his life. How long will he wait to do what is necessary? Will he wait until Bolshevist posters appear ordering everyone between fourteen and fifty to show up at a certain spot with clothing and two weeks of food in order to be transported to Siberia? Or until the Anglo-American occupation forces ruin our people through starvation and Typhoid Fever? Is that an exaggeration? Not at all! It has become grim reality in the occupied territories in the East and West.[118]

When all positive means of enforcing allegiance to National Socialism per se or convincing people that the war could still be won had been disallowed by reality, the regime could still profit from a deeply embedded fear of the 'Asiatic', 'Jewish' Bolshevism and a basic instinct of *national* self-preservation. This trend was eloquent evidence of the bankruptcy of National Socialism's positive integration project but also of the relative success with which it had handled negative propaganda, as a device for psychological integration. The inability of positive long-term themes to generate enduring support, sustain the population's morale (*Stimmung*) and conduct (*Haltung*) and uphold the regime's psychological hegemony over the Volk necessitated a wider paradigmatic shift in NS propaganda themes and strategy. This shift involved a dual process of readjustment: a move from 'positive' to 'negative' themes of integration; and a need to resort to short-term, ad hoc justificatory arguments as a partial redress for the waning of the more universal themes of NS ideological propaganda. As the critical distance between the two fronts became progressively eroded by the rapid disintegration of the Axis military campaign on all sectors, NS propaganda resorted more and more to 'negative' themes as a psychological corrective to the divergence between rhetoric and truth, perceived and 'ersatz' reality. It also gradually shifted the psychological threshold of defence from National Socialism and its ideology, to the Führer and the safeguarding of 'national existence'. In his last eulogy to his leader Goebbels spoke the truth when he stated that 'Germany is *still* the land of loyalty'[119] – this was a loyalty borne out of despair and the absence of desirable alternatives rather than enthusiasm or self-sacrifice, but it was no less potent for that matter.

4
From 'Short Campaign' to 'Gigantic Confrontation': NS Propaganda and the Justification of War, 1939–41

Justifying 'war', 1939

The decision of the NS leadership to launch war in September 1939 constituted a watershed for the regime's propaganda operation and output. The shift of German foreign policy towards a more ambitious expansionist programme and a more aggressive posture had already become evident to the Germans and the outside world, a year earlier. Even if the forceful annexation of Austria in March (the result of a systematic bullying of the country's government, and of the Austrian chancellor, Kurt von Schuschnigg personally) constituted an outright violation of one of the most fundamental conditions of the Versailles Treaty,[1] international reactions to the coup ranged from indifferent to mildly but passively disapproving. Annexing Austria, however, was one thing; threatening Czechoslovakia was another. The most successful of the successor states to the Habsburg monarchy, integrated into an alliance network sponsored by France, resisting the wider European trend of trading democracy for stability and anti-socialist hysteria, contained a sizeable ethnic German minority (inhabiting the area called Sudetenland, bordering south-eastern Germany), but was otherwise inhabited by an overwhelmingly Slav majority element. In this respect, it lent itself neither to the irredentist theme of NS foreign policy propaganda, nor to the revisionist/anti-Versailles sub-theme.[2]

When, in the summer months of 1938, it became evident that the NS regime was determined to pursue an aggressive 'solution' to the Czech issue, threatening the government in Prague with the prospect of a military invasion, the myth of a responsible Hitlerite revisionism, based on an irredentist vision, was shattered, prompting substantially more active reactions from other European countries.[3] The determination of the appeasers to avoid a military conflagration in central Europe, in conjunction with Mussolini's alarm at the gathering pace of German aggression (a pace that, for logistical, military and economic reasons, he could not follow), produced a channel for a negotiated solution, culminating in the signing of the Munich Pact in September 1938. The settlement salvaged the irredentist credentials of NS foreign policy (only the Sudetenland was ceded to the Reich) whilst upholding a – wounded and, in hindsight, stillborn – Czechoslovak sovereignty over the remaining territory which had been awarded to the state in 1919. The worst appeared to have been averted; but the signs were unmistakeable: NS foreign policy was bent on a territorial vision that was significantly more belligerent and extensive than the condition of peaceful irredentism satisfied at Munich.[4]

The reaction of the German population to the 'Czech crisis' was predictable. Given that most Germans shared the essentially incompatible expectations of annulling the restrictive conditions (territorial and other) of the Versailles Treaty and avoiding another military conflict – especially with the western powers – popular consensus rested on the successful pursuit of *peaceful* revisionism. Thus, expression of enthusiasm for the Anschluß reflected at the same time a restored sense of national pride and adulation for a leader and a regime that had seemingly achieved a pan-German dream so vehemently denied to the country previously without jeopardising the peace.[5] Now, it was different. Even if the Munich agreement had sustained peace, there was a distinct and visible unease about the possible complications that could arise out of an increasingly aggressive NS foreign policy. Hitler himself commented unfavourably on the depressed mood of the German public during the Czech crisis; the regime's public opinion reports confirmed their relief when the conflict was resolved diplomatically. This was the first oblique indication that Hitler had misapprehended the mood and desires of the German Volk: for him the previous consensus of peaceful and effective restoration of Germany's 'pride' involved a stress on the latter quality; for his internal audience it was the former condition that mattered most. This was a discrepancy that did not bode well for the future.

In March 1939, the chronicle of a death foretold for Czechoslovakia came to its conclusions with the (bloodless) invasion and dissolution of the rump state established under the Munich pact.[6] Once again, the condition of 'peace' had not been breached; but the irredentist/revisionist credentials of the NS agenda had been jettisoned irrevocably. This helps us understand the largely different response of the German public. For them, anti-Versailles revisionism, '*Großdeutsche*' irredentism and restoration of national pride were important psychological desiderata; but they did not constitute a psychological carte blanche to the regime, however. The decisive caveat once again lay in the *means* of pursuing the goal; avoiding war was what mattered – and this stipulation was upheld in March 1939 with a campaign that had all the marks of a diplomatic Blitzkrieg.

Of course, the NS regime had to justify its decision – carefully yet rigorously. It had to rationalise not just the 'moral' dimension of the invasion but also its defiance for the agreement at Munich only half a year earlier. The dissolution of the rump Czechoslovak state that had survived the Munich agreement in March 1939 was carefully emploted by NS propaganda as an end and a beginning. On the one hand, this was the triumphant conclusion of a long, painful period of anti-Versailles revisionism that had seen the German Reich humiliated, reduced to an impotent political force, and encircled by a formidable constellation of enemy forces. In April 1939, Hitler retrospectively accused the erstwhile Czechoslovakia of providing 'a bridge to Europe for Bolshevik aggression' – a comment that obviously referred to specifically Soviet intentions.[7] But victory was also a historic moment of re-joining history – a history that had been made by the German 'race' in eastern Europe in the past but had been artificially thwarted by foreign powers of the 'old Europe'. As Goebbels explained it in an article published in the *Völkischer Beobachter* (VB) on 18 March 1939, '[t]he prosperity and economic successes of these peoples and provinces have always been strongest when they were under the protection of the Reich'; now 'the stronger power can afford to be generous and to establish a system that gives justice to both nationalities', restoring rather than destabilising peace and offering protection rather than suppression.[8]

On the other hand, this was a turning point in the sense of a beginning – a new era of 'making history'. In a perfect analogy of rebirth, the 'new forces' of European civilisation had arisen out of the ruins of the decaying old order, not just to claim their allegedly deserved position of dominance but also to 'establish a modern and more dynamic era'.[9] In hindsight, Goebbels's task to promote what had – by the time that the article appeared – proved to be a peaceful campaign without any reaction from the western 'guaranteeing' powers was a facile one. Mixing anti-Versailles rhetoric with irredentist visions of a *Gesamtdeutschland* (the recreation of a large Germanic territorial entity under the control of the Volk) and a discourse that denigrated the moral legitimacy of the successor states created in 1919–20 was calculated to provide an aura of permissibility to any action in that direction. A few days after the march into Czechoslovakia, the city of Memel (a prized item in the list of German irredentism) was peacefully absorbed into the Reich, producing a largely enthusiastic reaction by the German population.[10]

Very soon, however, this much praised process of 'making history' peacefully gave way to military conflict between the Reich and the western powers (September 1939), thus confirming the worst fears of the German population about the adverse consequences of the regime's radicalising attitude. Clearly, the situation that prompted the involvement of Britain and France into the Polish campaign – turning what was most probably intended as a localised campaign into a pan-European conflict[11] – raised the stakes for NS propaganda, threatening what remained a strong but essentially incomplete popular consensus about Hitler's authority and the regime's capacity for representing the Volk's collective interest. Back in February, when German foreign policy was still operating under the cloak of legality (still bound by the conditions of the Munich agreement), Goebbels had disguised a potentially unsettling message under the shroud of peaceful intentions:

> the peoples want the peace. Also the German Volk want it. But it wants in addition something more that the other peoples have possessed for a very long time: the safeguarding of its national life and justice.[12]

Three months later, the regime's definition of this 'protection of national life' became even more blunt in a largely inflammatory speech that the propaganda minister delivered at Danzig – the bone of contention between Germany and Poland, as well as the most potent symbol of the Versailles Diktat for German society. Whilst refraining from any references to a (secretly prepared) aggressive solution, he made clear that,

> you may, German men and women of Danzig confidently look to the future. The National Socialist Reich stands on your side, like you stand on its side ... for Germany is anywhere where Germans stand – thus also with you ... Long live our German Danzig![13]

The '*German* Danzig' theme – both respectably irredentist and clearly alluding to a far more unpalatable for outside countries resurrection of the *Gesamtdeutschland* aggressive vision – had been carefully circulated by NS propaganda since the beginning of May 1939, still in the framework of 'peaceful intentions' but alarmingly juxtaposed to a notion of 'Polish chauvinism' and hostile collusion with the west against the Reich.[14] In recognition of the fact that, after the British–French guarantee of Poland's territorial integrity, the chances of a local 'solution' to the Polish issue escalating into a wider conflict had increased dramatically (in spite of the German Foreign Minister, Joachim von Robbentrop, reassuring everyone in the opposite direction[15]), NS propaganda began a process of an essentially moral justification, intended to override practical public fears about a war. As early as mid-May, Goebbels had provided a series of candid examples as to what this 'chauvinism' meant in practice:

[s]ince 4 May the sales of German newspapers in most Polish cities has been prohibited. In Kattowitz on 5 May in a large newsagent all existing Reich-German newspapers and magazines, altogether 20,000 pieces, were seized and taken away in police motor vehicles. During a nocturnal ceremony on the eve of the Polish national holiday a Polish crowd ... burned a straw doll, which represented the Führer ... This heaviest affront to the German people was celebrated ... A large crowd in Posen shouted heavy

abuse against Germany and sang offensive songs against the Reich and its Leader. On 29 April in Gnesen nine girls from the German community were given prison sentences of two to ten months.[16]

The list of hostile acts against 'ethnic Germans' (*Volksdeutsche*) went on and on, further inflaming the common sensitivity of Germans to the fate of their 'unredeemed' brothers – especially in a state so universally detested as Poland. During the crucial weeks before the launch of the invasion, as the build-up of Wehrmacht forces on the German–Polish frontier intensified without any attempt to conceal it, the German press began an orchestrated campaign against the 'hostile' attitude of Polish authorities vis-à-vis the ethnic German minority residing within its borders. A stream of fresh atrocities were recorded; this time presented as the work of 'organized groups and certain local authorities against the Germans in Poland'. It was asserted that 'a positive man-hunt was in progress against the *Volksdeutschen*, [with] mass arrests ... [and] refugees ... already flocking into German territory'[17] At no point throughout 1939 did NS propaganda disown the theme of Hitler's genuinely peaceful intentions; but the validity of this policy was constantly questioned by underlining its alleged incompatibility with the notion of 'national interest', putatively violated on numerous occasions by the Poles and their western guarantors. During the summer, as the tension was mounting in the German–Polish relations and threatening declarations were exchanged between Berlin, London and Paris, NS propaganda assumed a careful but growing anti-western tenor. The contrast between 'plutocracy' and a German deprived of her rights, of resources and international legitimacy, was calculated to bestow upon the re-awakened German ambition an aura of moral authority, as a necessary corrective to a fundamental historic injustice perpetrated by arrogant and voracious powers.[18] And, in case there would be any doubt about the 'defensive' character of the German decision to invade, a compendium of alleged Polish atrocities against the German minority was published a few months after the attack, with a subsequent (updated) edition in 1940 that put the overall figure of German 'casualties' to more than 50,000.[19]

Thus, by the time that Wehrmacht troops crossed the German–Polish frontier, shattering the last hopes for a peaceful revisionist policy and the avoidance of conflict with the west, the psychological edifice of short-term justification for Operation 'White' had already been dextrously primed by NS propaganda. In an emergency session of the Reichstag held hours after the launch of Operation 'White', Hitler once again rehearsed the main themes of short-term justification for the aggressive solution to the 'Danzig problem': the 'ill-treatment' of ethnic Germans, the 'injustice' of the Versailles system, the defensive nature of this war resulting from alleged Polish provocations ('[t]his night for the first time Polish regular soldiers fired on our own territory. Since 5:45 a.m. we have been returning the fire, and from now on bombs will be met with bombs') and, above all, his peaceful intentions ever since the Czech crisis:

> I attempted to bring about, by the peaceful method of making proposals for revision, an alteration of this intolerable position. It is a lie when the outside world says that we only tried to carry through our revisions by pressure ... But I am wrongly judged if my love of peace and my patience are mistaken for weakness or even cowardice ... I have repeatedly offered friendship and, if necessary, the closest co-operation to Britain, but this cannot be offered from one side only. It must find response on the other side.[20]

From plan to invasion: the campaign against Poland and the first 'triumph'

At least implicit in Hitler's decision to push ahead with the invasion of Poland was the belief or expectation that a swift and impressive victory would allay public fears about the war; and that the destruction of the unpopular Polish state would be hailed as a landmark in the struggle against the Versailles Treaty, supplying tangible proof for the alleged 'regeneration' (*Neugeburt*) of the German volk after almost two decades in the darkness.[21] This message appealed directly to a broader, long-term value consensus amongst German public opinion about revisionism and elevation of the country's international prestige.[22] It is indeed easy to mistake the depressed mood of the German population in September 1939 as evidence of a principled opposition to the use of aggressive techniques for the promotion of otherwise desired goals. It appears, however, that, beyond fears of the fundamental transition from peace to conflict, lay a more layered psychological reality. For this apprehension stemmed from another worry, relating to the attitudes of the western powers, and the prospect of a long drawn-out campaign reminiscent of the First World War (and, crucially, of its devastating outcome for Germany itself in 1918).[23] With the declaration of war on Germany by Britain and France on 3 September came a noticeable depression of public morale inside the Reich, as such fears appeared to be confirmed. However, implicit in this grading of fears was the hope that this would be an easy, short and victorious campaign, followed by a re-establishment of stability in Europe. In this particular respect, Hitler did gamble, but in a significantly more calculated sense than it appeared at first sight. There were few misgivings amongst German society about the actual desirability of, or justification for, the crushing of the neighbouring country; and there were even fewer about the attractions inherent in the restoration of Germany's territorial and political status as the hegemonic force in the continent.[24] Therefore, if fear of war could be alleviated by a *swift* victory with minimal casualties and disruptions for domestic life, this basic consensus could be transformed into enthusiasm and further support for the regime.

That the decision to invade Poland was presented as Hitler's personal enterprise (which it largely was) was a further significant factor in the legitimation of the project. The Führer could simply capitalise on his psychological hegemony over the German Volk – a hegemony that had been constructed on solid grounds since 1933, accentuated through the impressive economic recovery of the mid-1930s and consolidated after the foreign policy successes of the 1936–38 period.[25] Now, for the first time, the Führer was presented by NS propaganda in his capacity as 'warlord'. This was at the same time a gamble and an alleviating technique. While he had nothing to prove with regard to his diplomatic or political talents, his propaganda depiction as a military mastermind involved a new test to his alleged 'genius'. A potential failure would have not only discredited him in this capacity, but would also have critical adverse consequences for his overall standing amongst public opinion. On the other hand, given the immense popularity that Hitler *personally* enjoyed in 1938–39 (as opposed to the persistently low esteem for the party[26]), the particular marketing of his image and his speeches during the campaign provided a psychological buffer zone that somewhat mitigated public anxiety and trepidation.

The personal gamble did pay handsome dividends – in the short-term. Blitzkrieg was the most suitable military method, not only in strategic terms but also in the sense of psychological compensation for the anxious German public. The devastating effectiveness of the Wehrmacht during 'Operation White', the ease with which it overran Polish resistance, the low number of German casualties and the safe 'distance' of the military events from the home front cajoled the Germans into thinking positively about their country's recovery, rebirth and potential.[27] At the same time, the feared response of the western powers to the invasion of Poland was conspicuous in its absence, beyond the official (and nominal) declaration of war. The recovery of public opinion in October 1939 owed its optimism in the belief that the Reich had once again got away with murder and that a long war had been averted – in other words, that a 'short' and 'victorious' campaign was possible.

Hitler's 'peace offer' to the west on 6 October 1939 also struck the right chord with the public,[28] corresponding to the initial propaganda depiction of the attack on Poland as a pre-emptive, defensive and largely reluctant move. The anxiety, however, had been concealed, diluted and partly compensated for – not eliminated. In fact, the real trade-off from a propaganda point of view was between the fear of war and the appeal of victory (*Sieg*). Given that the western declaration of belligerency vis-à-vis Germany had rendered war an immutable reality (and the rejection of Hitler's 'peace' overtures attested to this), the reliance of the regime's propaganda network on the latter became critical. Only victory – even better, triumph – could function as a psychological corrective to apprehension – not simply diverting attention from fears but actively alleviating the sources of public anxiety.

The notion of 'war as a last resort', carefully propagated throughout 1939 by the NS authorities, reflected at the same time an acceptance on part of the regime of the limited 'conquest' of public consciousness and an alternative strategy for fostering it.[29] Using the opportunity of his 1940 New Year speech, Goebbels justified the war as a German *reactive* policy that the Führer endorsed extremely reluctantly in the absence of co-operation from the west. The invasion of Poland, he argued, was 'a war for our national existence' against western plans 'to stifle Germany [and] to destroy the German people'. However, the propaganda opportunities offered by the impressive show of force by the Wehrmacht in the Polish campaign afforded the speech a fair amount of triumphalist realism:

> [t]he following lightning campaign in Poland was unique in all history. On 2 September, the Jablunka Pass was taken. The Polish army in the Corridor was destroyed on 4 September. Bromberg was captured on 6 September. The Westemplatte fell on 7 September. Lodsch was taken on 10 September. The encirclement of Radom was completed on 12 September. 52,000 Poles laid down their weapons ... Brest–Litovsk fell on 17 September ... Over 700,000 Poles were captured. The booty was enormous. Over half a million guns, 16,000 machine guns, 32,000 artillery pieces and over three-and-three-quarter million rounds of artillery munitions fell into our hands.[30]

The campaign against the west: the second 'triumph'

Of course, the crucial test lay ahead – until well into 1940, the western powers had not engaged the Reich on the military field ('phoney war'), thereby nurturing hopes that the situation could somehow stabilise. The inertia that characterised British and French attitudes during this period, however, was in sharp contrast to Hitler's expansive plans. Even since the autumn of 1939, he had been agitating for a swift campaign against France – a plan that was postponed only after military experts convinced him (with notable difficulty) of the complications arising out of weather conditions and the logistical nightmare of re deploying forces from the east to the west in such a short period.[31] This lull, unwanted though it might have been from the NS leadership's point view, provided the regime's propaganda network with an opportunity to prepare public opinion for the impending shattering of illusions. Now that the need for short-term diversion had subsided, after the successful conclusion of 'Operation White', the challenge lay in emploting the campaign in the longer term, especially in view of Hitler's fixed intention to escalate the conflict.[32]

The danger for NS propaganda was that it was endeavouring to alleviate the prevalent mood of war-weariness by promising a swift, victorious *military* campaign. The argument that this would be a short campaign on the basis of Germany's technological, spiritual and moral 'superiority' provided short-term diversion from anti-war feelings, but it also inflated hopes amongst Germans that the amassing of victories would bring the anomalous situation to a swift (and successful) conclusion. By contrast, the regime expected that the 'triumphalism' generated from Wehrmacht's show of force would be translated into a new basis for the positive integration of German public opinion under the long-term vision of 'living-space' (*Lebensraum*) expansion[33] and *total* domination. This psychological discrepancy, latent and barely visible until 1941, did not augur well for the prospects of NS propaganda: consensus seemed to have been reconfigured on the basis of a 'short *and* victorious' war – the two adjectives in order of significance. Its preservation and intensification depended on the regime's ability to guarantee a crucial array of decisive victories that would presage a return to peace in the near future.

Undoubtedly, the impressive show of force in the campaign against the west in May–June 1940 constituted the apogee of the regime's popularity with the masses. In preparation for the assault on the Low Countries and France ('Operation Green'), NS propaganda resorted to the memories of the Versailles negotiations (and the primary role of the French in the Diktat), the dishonourable occupation of the Ruhr in 1923, the exploitation of the Saar until 1935 and the general demeanour of France in promoting the diplomatic encirclement of the Reich (creation of the Little Entente, support for the successor states of the Habsburg Empire against Germany etc.). At the same time, Operation 'Green' was carefully emploted in the wider framework of a reaction to the 'plutocratic war' of the west as a struggle for 'just and durable peace and living space for the German people'[34] – a broad enough framework to presage a similar fate for the British Isles. From the beginning, Goebbels insisted on a careful propaganda strategy that, whilst nurtured the newfound public interest in, and enthusiasm for the war, should avoid 'excessive optimism'.[35] Hans Fritzsche was instructed to supply dispassionate information to the press about victories with the proviso that 'individual successes do not necessarily decide the overall outcome of the operation ... [and that] occasional reverses are unlikely to be entirely avoided'.[36] The seemingly unstoppable advance of the Wehrmacht, however, during May and June effected a lessening of the initial restraint in the tone of NS propaganda and a more blatant triumphalist tone to match the new mood of exaltation amongst Germans. If the victory against Poland had only temporarily alleviated the considerable alarm amongst the population at the prospect of another long drawn-out war with the western powers, the surrender of France and the spectre of Britain's collapse captured the imagination of German society.[37] In the aftermath of the campaign in the west, Goebbels hastened to point out that 'history does not repeat itself', that 1918 had been avenged and that the German people lived in a 'time without precedent' (*Zeit ohne Beispiel*).[38]

Already in the last week of June 1940, the Propaganda minister had instructed the German press and radio to move the focus to the impending attack on 'plutocratic' Britain.[39] The 'great blow against Britain' – which officially began on 12 August 1940 with the 'Eagle' air offensive – was covered ad nauseam in the German media. Special brochures about the air raids against the British capital presented the campaign as an unmitigated triumph:

> [t]he 'sharks' are over London again. Protected by their fighters, the German bombing planes can carry out their attacks unhindered. 7000 meters are between the German airplanes and the burning capital of a dying empire, 7000 meters obscured by rising flames and choking smoke.[40]

The cynicism of the NS propaganda authorities was unequivocally captured in the Ministerial Conference of 7 September 1940, where Goebbels bemoaned the fact that the British air raids over Berlin (25 August, 6 September) 'had not produced the effects which are necessary for us to justify to the world … a massive intensification of our attacks on London'.[41] When this opportunity was provided – after the destructive attacks on Berlin and Hamburg only a few days later – he seized the initiative, justifying the escalation of the Luftwaffe operations as a response to the British 'atrocities'.[42]

Beyond flattery, pride and an intoxicating taste of triumph, however, public enthusiasm continued to originate from the expectation of a *swift victory* – which meant an end to the war. Goebbels himself did not dampen down such hopes, stating that the fate of the thousand-year Reich would be decided 'in these days, weeks and months'.[43] With the Blitz campaign against Britain in full motion in the summer of 1940,[44] the SD reports spoke excitedly about 'an unprecedented solidarity (that) has developed between the front and the domestic population, as well as an unprecedented solidarity amongst the population', in spite of fears about the extension of the conflict and the possible adverse effects of British retaliation.[45] Already, however, in early September the NS authorities had been in possession of a military report stressing that the 'Eagle' offensive would neither bring Britain to her knees nor destroy her fighting power.[46] Therefore, the 'temporary postponement' of the Operation 'Sea Lion' in September (albeit officially announced much later) constituted the first damage-limitation exercise for NS propaganda, not only because premature hopes for a swift British surrender had been belied but also because the propaganda motto of 'fight … until the last foe is conquered' entailed an unwelcome extension of the war beyond 1940.[47] The regime could still capitalise on reports about the devastating effect of the Luftwaffe air warfare on the British Isles and the fact that the British Empire was on the defensive everywhere from the continent to the Atlantic (U-boat campaign[48]) and north Africa. The initial upbeat propaganda tenor, however, was noticeably softened towards the end of October, as Goebbels instructed the German media to emphasise that 'a worldwide empire, such as the British, does not collapse in a matter of weeks'.[49] For the first time since the beginning of the war, NS propaganda had to employ a careful double diversion – diversion from the failure to defeat Britain and from the unwelcome extension of the war into 1941.

Both these objectives contradicted the very foundations of the psychological consensus that NS propaganda had striven to generate and entrench after September 1939. In hindsight, the failure of the Luftwaffe to bring Britain to her knees during the Blitz and the cancellation of the land invasion constituted minor strategic setbacks that did cause a certain degree of alarm amongst German public opinion,[50] but were adequately compensated by a discourse of imminent collapse as a matter of time. This was a war that was conducted in a reassuring distance from the German home front, with limited casualties and other losses against objective hindrances, such as geography and weather conditions. The fact that Britain – or any other power for that matter – could not retaliate in kind produced a buffer zone between the military and the home fronts that NS propaganda could manage with characteristic ease, filtering and emploting information according to short- and long-term designs. In the longer run, however, triumphalism was becoming monotonous, especially since it revolved around the same victories in the absence of more recent achievements. A close look at public opinion reports throughout that period manifests a sort of 'triumph-weariness':[51] given that the public opinion's common denominator remained the expectation of a swift, victorious war, triumph was psychologically important only as the prelude to conclusion, and it was exactly this conclusion that was conspicuously missing.[52]

This complication rendered the task of devising sustainable propaganda strategies for the winter of 1940/41 (the second since the outbreak of the war but the first with 'unfinished' business – campaign against Britain – in the horizon) as particularly important. In early October, the RPL compiled the overall operational plan for the subsequent period until March.[53] With the central slogan 'the victory is with our Führer' the propaganda action was intended to deepen the spirit of community in German society (*Vertiefung der Volksgemeinschaft*) and appeal to a sense of collective pride with regard to the military achievements of the previous year (*Appel an den kämpferischen Stolz und das nationale Selbstvertrauen*). In order to sustain the positive psychological momentum generated from the victories in the west during a difficult period of inactivity and privation, the campaign maintained a focus on Hitler's personality – presented as 'the greatest statesman and military leader of all times' – and on the superiority of the Wehrmacht as guarantee for the final victory. In response to frustrated expectations that the war would be over soon, the campaign also presented the continuation of the conflict into 1941 as the result of the Führer's 'superior' judgement (*Der Führer handelt dann, wenn die Zeit reif ist*). Assisted by co-ordinated film events (including newsreel), posters, brochures and party gatherings across the Reich, the campaign was to purchase invaluable time until the spring thaw allowed the resumption of the offensive and Hitler had made up his mind.

NS policy (and propaganda) at crossroads: Britain or Russia?

Indeed, towards the end of the winter of 1940/41, NS propaganda readjusted its focus in the light of the new military targets decided by Hitler. With the postponement of 'Sea Lion' in the previous autumn and the parallel disintegration of the German–Soviet relations, the future course of German foreign policy entered a phase of decisive reconsideration. Although Hitler had given his first authorisation for 'Barbarossa' in November 1940,[54] his short-term strategic agenda had to take into account a number of other factors – some of which totally exogenous.[55] Perhaps sensing that public opinion was expecting the resumption of the campaign against Britain (directly on the British Isles or indirectly as a blow to the British Empire and its naval power), the Führer appears to have entertained the idea of a 'Mediterranean' front that would result in the ejection of the British presence from the area and the breakdown of communications with the eastern provinces of the empire. Because this scheme presupposed effective control of Gibraltar and a strong Axis presence on both coasts of the Mediterranean, it rested on the co-operation of the still neutral Spain and France, as well as on the success of Italy's military engagements in the Balkans and north Africa. There is evidence showing that Hitler kept his options open in the winter of 1940/41, designating implicitly a deadline for final decision sometime in early spring. In the meantime, operational plans for a possible occupation of Gibraltar ('Felix') had also been authorised and drafted, awaiting the outcome of the diplomatic negotiations between the Reich and the neutral Mediterranean countries.

By the time that the final initiative to convince them had failed (March 1941), the situation in the Mediterranean theatre of the war had changed dramatically. The Italian adventure in Greece had turned sour, whilst the initial modest advances of General Graziani's troops from Libya towards Egypt had been ground to a halt or even partly reversed.[56] Clearly, in these strategic circumstances, no meaningful 'Mediterranean' strategy would have had any chances of success in bringing down British power in the periphery and thus effecting the collapse of the metropolis. However, the breakdown of the Italian military effort in the Balkans was particularly worrying with regard to the planned invasion of the Soviet Union, as well as the control of naval traffic in the eastern Mediterranean sector. Therefore, Hitler's strategy crystallised in early March 1941: a settlement of the situation in the southern Balkans (if need be, through a swift campaign against Yugoslavia and Greece), followed by a massive redeployment of the Wehrmacht's forces along the eastern front for 'Barbarossa', initially scheduled for late May 1941.

From a propaganda point of view, this readjustment amounted to a serious inconvenience. As late as 9 March 1941, Goebbels had confidently predicted the resumption of the offensive against Britain:

[i]t is also high time that London begin to take the hard facts into account. The long winter draws to its end. One does not have three or four months any more, where the illusions are cheap like berries, where one can call the Generals 'Winter' and clouds and revolution as collaborators and omens of coming English victories. The sun shines again, and spring rises to the mountains. Beautiful though it is for us, it means bad weather for English illusion-manufacturers.[57]

Rapid developments, however, in the Balkan front soon eclipsed the discussions about the fate of the operation against the British Isles. On 27 March 1941, a pro-western coup in Belgrade under Stojadinovic replaced the Axis collaborationist government – only days after the country had joined the Tripartite pact – and precipitated the assumption of German military action in the southern Balkans. With the transfer of military forces completed in record time, the Wehrmacht forces launched 'Operation Marita', invading Yugoslavia and – with the support of Bulgaria – attacking Greece in early April.[58] The campaign provided NS propaganda with further opportunities to slander Britain – and this happened a mere six weeks before the launch of the campaign against the Soviet Union. Yet, the unexpected coup d'etat in Yugoslavia and Greece's decision also to resist the German ultimatum presented the NS leadership with the prospect of a difficult (and longer than initially anticipated) engagement in the Balkans. During the secret conference of the RMVP on the day that 'Marita' was launched (6 April 1941) Goebbels noted that,

[i]t would be wise to be prepared from the outset for the operation to be hard and attended by great difficulties, but it will lead to the desired result in six to eight weeks. All in all, we can be very pleased that things have happened the way they have. For, if the stupidity of the Serb government had not given us the opportunity of making a clean sweep in the Balkans now, the latter would have remained the powder-keg of Europe, and Britain ... would always had been in a position to thrust the torch into the hands of a few daring comitadji so that they might once again blow up that powder-keg[59]

So, this more complicated campaign could now be presented as a blessing in disguise and as a crucial extension of the war against Britain and 'those politicians who, against their better judgement and probably bribed, have hurled their country into disaster on Britain's command – the most recent instance being the Yugoslav government'.[60] But the *pièce de résistance* came a few moments later at the conference. In the light of the Soviet Union's signing of a Treaty of Friendship with the new Yugoslav government (a move that was directly antagonising German interests in the region), the Propaganda minister considered it opportune to raise the subject of German–Soviet relations in the candid manner that these secret conferences afforded the participants. Goebbels acknowledged that the subject had 'been under consideration in the responsible quarters, and above all with the Führer himself, for weeks and months'. Although he considered that Stalin would avoid a direct conflict with the Reich over the fate of Serbia, there was a clear indication of a latent change of direction in NS foreign policy when he stated categorically that,

> I may tell you in confidence that probably nothing would suit us better at this moment than Russia's intervention in the present situation. She would suffer a military fiasco in no time at all[61]

Towards the attack on the Soviet Union ('Barbarossa')

The absence of any reference to Bolshevism, Stalin and his empire, even for the purpose of negative integration or diversion from the evident failure of the regime's anti-British strategy, had been conspicuous in the output of NS propaganda for a while – and it remained so until 22 June 1941, that is *after* the start of the war in the east. Preparations for the offensive had to be carried out in utter secrecy so as to maximise the 'surprise' factor of the operation. This consideration was paramount in the strategic planning of Hitler and the Wehrmacht, but it left the RMVP with prohibitively little space for manoeuvre and opinion manipulation. Thus, NS propaganda continued to sing from the same hymn sheet of anti-western diatribe (the 'plutocratic' discourse – see Ch. 3), contributing to a wider diversionary function in the military, strategic and psychological fields. The conclusion of the war in the Balkans with the German occupation of the island of Crete[62] – after a ferocious battle between the Wehrmacht forces and the retreating British troops – offered the RMVP the opportunity to launch another bitter attack on the British and on Churchill personally, emphasising the discrepancy between his earlier comments about his country's determination to defend Crete and his subsequent refusal to accept the German victory in the region as well as the military setback for his forces.[63] Although the time of the invasion of the Soviet Union was drawing near, Goebbels continued to deceive not just public opinion but everyone involved in the dissemination of information. At the beginning of June, he let it be known to press officials that 'the invasion of Britain will start in three, or perhaps, five weeks'.[64]

If 'Operation Marita' in the Balkans provided a welcome diversion from preparations for the assault on the Soviet Union, another – this time unexpected and highly embarrassing for the NS authorities – event monopolised the regime's propaganda energies for most of May 1941. The flight of Hitler's deputy, Rudolf Hess, to Britain, his plane's crash in Scotland and his subsequent arrest by the British generated the sort of publicity that the RMVP could do without. News of Hess's desperate bravado reached Hitler and his entourage on 11 May and resulted in a hasty, injudicious communiqué which stated that the Führer's deputy suffered from a mental illness and was prone to hallucinations. That this communiqué had been drafted and issued by Otto Dietrich (Hitler's chief of press) and Martin Bormann (as Hess's deputy) meant that Goebbels had been sidelined and subsequently confronted with an awkward fait accompli. He was furious with the official justification used in the announcement but ordered his ministerial subordinates to avoid any further references to the affair, focusing instead on 'positive' diversionary themes, such as the successes of the U-boat campaign in the Atlantic and the devastating effect of the Luftwaffe raids over the British Isles.[65] His only input in the handling of the incident was restricted to a subtle change of the justification used – playing down the 'dementia' argument in favour of a more idealistic portrayal of Hess as a person willing to sacrifice himself for the benefit of a German–British understanding that he (like, allegedly, his Führer) so deeply believed in.[66] He refrained from even mentioning the incident in his weekly article in *Das Reich* and instructed instead his trusted associate in the Inland Press Division, Hans Fritzsche, to restate the revised explanation in his regular radio broadcast and advise newspaper editors accordingly. Now, everyone hoped for yet another diversion so that the 'malodorous' Hess affair be banished to oblivion.[67] In the meantime, propaganda efforts would concentrate on providing only a measured response to enemy claims about the incident.

The diversion did come soon enough – on 24 May the much-lauded German battleship Bismarck sank HMS Hood after a long engagement in the Straits of Denmark. The fact that, three days later, it was Bismarck's turn to suffer heavy damages by the British naval forces and eventually go under was of course a serious blow to the NS authorities; but the whole story continued to perform its diversionary role conveniently enough.[68] So did the ongoing battle on the island of Crete throughout May, even if Goebbels exercised restraint over the release of information about the progress of the operation until the situation had been clarified from a military point of view towards the end of the month.[69] At the same time, Goebbels masterminded a counter-campaign to offset the propaganda effect of BBC's 'Victory-campaign'. Already since January 1941, the BBC had urged listeners across NS-occupied Europe to write with chalk the symbol 'V' on every possible building, as a gesture of support for the British war effort against Germany. Although the campaign was initially successful, the Propaganda minister – in association with the Wehrmacht and in spite of the initial opposition of the AA that feared an erosion of its jurisdiction over foreign matters – launched a counterfeit 'V-Aktion', whereby the same symbol was painted on buildings as an indication of support for the Nazis ('V' for the traditional German/Prussian war slogan 'Victoria'). The success of Goebbels's retaliation was such that the BBC was obliged to call off its original campaign before the end of the spring.[70] As a result, by early June a noticeable recovery in the mood of the German population was noted in SD reports. Hess had indeed 'ceased to exist', as Goebbels had hoped for.

And yet German public opinion was indeed expecting that a final confrontation with National Socialism's ideological arch-enemy was a matter of time. The enormous military preparations following 'Marita' on the eastern front, the amassing of troops on the 1939 Polish–Russian frontier and the vocal but toothless – in practical terms – hostility towards Britain could not be concealed from both the German public[71] and foreign observers.[72] The atmosphere of tension was nurtured by both sides: in early June the Russian information agency, TASS had released confidential information describing the German–Soviet relations as strained but subsequently issued a formal apology; on the German side, in spite of the 'silence' of official NS propaganda vis-à-vis the Soviet Union, rumours about an impending conflict in the east had been in circulation at least since early May 1941.[73] At least part of this whisper campaign was either orchestrated or manipulated by the RMVP as an indirect preparation for the looming u-turn.[74] Multiple scenarios about the possible date for the launch of the operation circulated in a seemingly unchecked manner throughout June, reaching a peak around the fourteenth, when there was a widespread impression that a German attack on the Soviet Union was a matter of hours. The deadline came and passed amidst a dearth of official information of the subject. Even Germany's allegedly closest ally, Mussolini, was carefully kept in the dark about the Reich's military preparations and strategic planning.[75] Against the stipulations of the 1939 Pact of Steel, or indeed the Tripartite Pact with Italy and Japan, Hitler consciously refused to divulge any indication of his intentions until after the invasion had started.

In the end, the attack took place – a week later.[76] It was a surprise only where it mattered most – Stalin and the Soviet politico–military leadership were caught unprepared for the enormity of the task facing them, in spite of repeated warnings coming from London and, possibly, Bulgaria.[77] The Germans were in an agitated mood, experiencing a mixture of elation for the possibilities, relief that the period of inaction had come to an end, and fear that the war was taking another unpredictable turn, especially since the western front had not reached a successful (for the Reich) conclusion. Almost overnight the theme of 'anti-Bolshevism' re-entered the core of NS propaganda – surely a more familiar topos of negative integration for public opinion after all those years of anti-communist indoctrination, but one that had to be justified anew in the light of the 1939 alliance (the so-called Molotov–Ribbentrop Non-Aggression Pact). On 26 June 1941, Goebbels referred to the revival of the 'old front' between communism and National

Socialism – a resumption of the same battle that the non-aggression pact had only temporarily halted but that the Soviet leadership allegedly never truly abandoned.[78] This was the final, decisive instalment in the struggle that had started in 1933 inside Germany and now had to be fought for the very soul of Europe, its history and civilisation. Fate and history, the argument continued, had bequeathed to Germany a 'mission' to defend the continent from the cunning Bolshevik designs for a world revolution. But at this point, Goebbels set the tone for the wider framework in which 'Barbarossa' had to be construed, not just as a strategic decision but also as a historic scheme: this German move was a mere response to the consolidation of a 'plutocratic–Bolshevik conspiracy' (*plutokratisch–bolschewistische Komplott*). He continued,

> we see an unholy relationship between plutocracy and bolshevism, which we expected, and we also know only too well from our internal-political struggle in the past to be now surprised about it. [The plutocrats] rightly saw in us the danger of a new, better, more reasonably organised order, in which there was no place for them. They rejected us and fought against us, because we were the bearers of a [superior] moral and *völkisch* social principle, which was ready to destroy their old world.[79]

Just like in September 1939, this new campaign seemed to contradict the overwhelming desire amongst public opinion for the avoidance of war. Once again, the invasion was presented as a pre-emptive defensive move that the Wehrmacht leadership had to undertake in order to avert a Soviet attack on the Reich – planning for which had allegedly already been underway. In terms of long-term emplotment Operation 'Barbarossa' cemented an array of disparate themes in NS propaganda discourse that had previously been either sidelined or invoked in separation from each other. The 'western conspiracy' was now transformed into an unholy alliance of western plutocrats, Bolsheviks and of course Jews – a plot ostensibly geared to eliminating the German Reich from the map of Europe.[80] But this was not a battle simply for the survival of a particular nation; instead, NS Germany was spearheading a historic defence of the *European* heritage and civilisation against the eastern enemy. As Goebbels suggested,

> [t]he gigantic fight of the nine million [soldiers] is about the final decision. It will concern the future fate of Europe. History never saw a military confrontation of such dimensions; in addition, rarely before have questions of such world-wide significance been decided as here. [This war] indeed concerns everything.[81]

The theme of a 'European mission' also re-entered the vocabulary of NS propaganda from the moment that the Soviet Union turned into the chief enemy of the Reich, and it was destined to remain central to NS propaganda in different formats until the end of the war (see Ch. 3). The juxtaposition of the 'Asiatic' qualities of the Russians and the prospect to the vision of a 'European unity' under the aegis of National Socialism lent itself to the sort of historic fundamentalism that Hitler had envisioned for himself and his movement since the 1920s.

The launching of Operation Barbarossa on 22 June 1941 constituted the most emphatic affirmation of Hitler's monopoly of power in foreign policy decision-making. As he stated in his letter to Mussolini on the day of the invasion, this war was a return to his ideological origins and concepts, which at last had set him 'spiritually free'.[82] His decision to abandon the war against Britain and concentrate instead on a new target was criticised by prominent figures in both the military and the diplomatic hierarchy of the NS regime.[83] Only Rosenberg and the SS leadership understood from the first moment the ideological implications of the war and endorsed the effort wholeheartedly.[84] Rosenberg was ecstatic about Operation Barbarossa, regarding it as a return to the ideological core of National Socialism and a historic opportunity to defeat Bolshevism and the Jews, putting behind the unacceptable 'ideological revision' of 1939 (Molotov–Ribbentrop Pact).[85] Himmler was equally jubilant, not only for the significance of the undertaking but also for the opportunities offered to his SS for wider responsibilities and jurisdictions. In 13 March 1941, Hitler personally granted extensive powers to SS units in the NS empire, allowing them 'to act independently and under [Himmler's] responsibility'.[86] Himmler himself could not conceal what was at stake in this operation. In a speech to SS units on the day that Operation Barbarossa was launched, he stressed that this war was the beginning of a fundamental re-organisation of Europe and the whole world.[87] The war of extermination – the 'war within the war' – was about to commence.[88]

5
From Triumph to Disaster: NS Propaganda from the Launch of 'Barbarossa' until Stalingrad

The first stage of 'Barbarossa' (1941)

With the launch of 'Operation Barbarossa', the NS propaganda machinery was presented with an opportunity to put behind both the Hess debacle and the embarrassment caused by the postponement of the operation against the British Isles. The 'surprise' factor – however, so successful in diplomatic and military terms – produced contradictory results inside the Reich. Hitler's decision to impose (for the first time) a block of information for a week after the initial assault afforded time for the regime's propaganda apparatus to adjust to the new political and military landscape, modifying its discourses in order to accommodate the new focus on anti-Bolhevism after almost two years of complete silence on the subject. Yet, the absence of information, in conjunction with the magnitude of the task itself, added to the atmosphere of nervousness.[1] It is no coincidence that Goebbels instructed his press associates to emphasise that the military objective of the operation (total victory against Bolshevism) was not just realisable but attainable within a short period of time.[2] Then, on 29 June – with the German forces having advanced an incredible distance towards Dvinsk, Minsk and Bialystok – the news block was eventually lifted. What followed was a supreme instance of polycratic confusion and lack of internal co-ordination that were endemic in the NS propaganda domain. At the same time that Goebbels counselled restraint with regard to the reporting of the military situation, Hitler and his press chief, Otto Dietrich, bypassed the RMVP and arranged the broadcast of twelve 'Special Announcements' (*Sonderberichte*) over the radio in hourly intervals. Goebbels was furious – not simply because he had seen his authority undercut by the 'Dietrich network' in association with the Führer and the OKW, but mainly because he considered 'highly unfortunate' the abuse of the *Sonderberichte* that he had so meticulously planned in the past as an extraordinary propaganda device.[3]

The triumphalist tenor of reporting continued unabated until the middle of July. From the first week of the month, Hitler had authorised Goebbels to launch a major 'anti-Bolshevik' propaganda campaign. Apart from the grand narrative of 'Jewish–Bolshevik–plutocratic' conspiracy (see Ch. 3), Goebbels instructed his associates to add a positive 'European' spin to the German campaign, presenting it as a historic confrontation for safeguarding the continent's civilisation and history.[4] Extreme care was also taken vis-à-vis the population of the Soviet Union. The RMVP set up a series of clandestine transmitters that attacked Stalin personally but courted the support of the civilians.[5] A special propaganda campaign was launched almost immediately after the first advances of the Wehrmacht, which stressed that the people of the Soviet Union belonged to the 'European race', had fallen prey to a 'Jewish–Bolshevik' slavery and had been fooled by Stalin's pseudo-socialist promises.[6] At the same time, video footage of alleged Soviet atrocities was incorporated into the newsreel, deeply affecting German audiences.[7] To emphasise the distinction between Bolshevism and the eastern populations, special instructions were issued by the RMVP to press and radio authorities that banned the use of the term 'Slav', due to its negative racial connotations.[8]

From 15 July, however, a growing realisation that the initial confident predictions about the Soviet Union's imminent military collapse had been exaggerated confronted NS propaganda with a complex dilemma. On the one hand, it was by then difficult to abandon the initial triumphalist line – largely driven by Dietrich but with crucial input from Hitler himself – without risking either a severe blow to the regime's credibility or indeed a depression of public mood (*Stimmung*). If indeed the fighting and mobilisation potential of the Soviet Union had been underestimated – and this was an admission that was now muttered in the corridors of the RMVP as well as in various circles of the Wehrmacht[9] – then the prospect of prolonging the war into 1942 was extremely difficult to sell to a population that neither desired it nor had been entirely convinced about the unavoidability or necessity of 'Barbarossa' in the first place. On the other hand, continuing to portray the collapse of Bolshevism as imminent was becoming an unsustainable strategy that nurtured unfounded hopes and left German society unprepared for any adverse developments. Goebbels was clearly trapped between the initial optimistic line that was implemented without consultation with his RMVP network and his overall belief in the principle of 'realism'. His subsequent handling of the regime's communication policy with regard to the progress of 'Operation Barbarossa' was largely qualified and compromised by the independent working of other 'networks' inside the state and the NSDAP, over which he had little control at that stage (see Ch 2).

By early August, it was becoming evident in SD 'public opinion' reports that the population's belief in a swift, decisive victory was dwindling.[10] Goebbels – albeit seemingly confident in his belief that 'the Soviets [are] at the end of their military reserves of manpower' – also instructed his RMVP subordinates to take into account the 'stubbornness of Bolshevik resistance' and 'instruct [the people] about the facts'.[11] Yet, ironically, it was the military successes of the Wehrmacht in August and September that made the life of the NS propagandists difficult. A fresh wave of impressive military victories in the centre (Smolensk) and northern (siege of Leningrad) and southern (Kiev) sectors of the front removed many restraints from the Wehrmacht reports (WB)[12] and fuelled yet more over-confident expectations. Behind the scenes the mounting of a final operation against Moscow – generally believed as the decisive step in the direction of bringing the Soviet Union to its knees – was being acrimoniously debated between Hitler and the Wehrmacht leadership. In late August, General Hans Guderian went to see Hitler personally in order to convince him about the need to press on immediately with the advance on Moscow before the arrival of the Russian winter. The Führer, however, wavered; his eventual decision to authorise 'Operation Typhoon' against the Russian capital in late September (with the operations starting almost two weeks later) came only after the first snowstorms.[13]

Hitler spoke in Berlin on 3 October 1941, presenting the Soviet military power as 'broken' and the war in the east as 'decided'.[14] In fact, on 9 October, Dietrich organised a special press conference with the highest possible publicity in order to announce that the military operations in the east were all but finished and that the main task from then onwards was restoring order and implementing plans for the long-term re-organisation of occupied territories.[15] It did not really matter that three weeks earlier Hans Fritzsche had conveyed a very different picture to press representatives, stressing that Soviet reserves in the area surrounding Moscow were 'substantial'.[16] Prominent figures amongst the Wehrmacht leadership (including the commander-in-chief, General Walther Brauchitsch, and the chief of general staff, General Frauz Halder) voiced their protests to Hitler about this new line of reporting but could achieve nothing more than poisoning their relations with the Führer and precipitating the December crisis that led to the dismissal of Brauchitsch and the assumption of the armed forces command by Hitler.[17] But towards the end of October even Goebbels and Fritzsche spoke of the war in the east as practically won.[18]

After the war neither Dietrich nor Fritzsche accepted any responsibility for this phase of the propaganda campaign. Whilst the former put the blame on Hitler personally ('I had no reason to doubt what the war leader and supreme commander told me'[19]), Fritzsche claimed that he was trapped between Goebbels's more cautious line and the official tone of the WB. During his interrogation at Nuremberg, when asked about his own responsibility in the management of the German press during the first stages of 'Barbarossa', he replied that his own address to journalists on 13 October had given a different, if somewhat oblique message:

[t]his speech (13 October) was made in those days of the autumn of 1941 when the Reich Press Chief [Dietrich] had announced that German victory

in the East had been decisive. I had warned the entire German Press about accepting this news without reservations. I did not believe in this decisive victory which supposedly had already taken place. I suggested to all German newspapers to speak about a prolonged duration of the war. In this speech of mine I wanted to decrease the effectiveness of the official victory bulletin.[20]

As the second (and final) phase of the assault on Moscow began in early December, Goebbels criticised the overall propaganda handling of the war in the east. He claimed that the regime 'withheld from [the German people] all unpleasant news' and thus made them 'over-sensitive about any possible temporary reverses'.[21] As early as 4 October, he had also attempted to shift the focus of the debate from *when* to *how* the war would end – thus alluding to the possibility of another winter of war.[22] His article in *Das Reich* with the same theme ('When or how?')[23] appeared on 9 November, at the same time that Hitler was addressing a select party audience for the anniversary of the 1923 putsch.[24] Such coincidence was both unfortunate and indicative of the confusion that inhered in the structures of NS propaganda (see Chs 1 and 2). While Hitler's speech was assuring his audience of the impending victory of the Wehrmacht, Goebbels was reverting to the theme of 'victory at any cost' (and regardless of the time factor) that would become a central tenet of his propaganda in 1942. He was also desperately trying to shift attention from short-term military developments (whether positive or inauspicious) to the larger picture of National Socialism's historic confrontation with the alleged 'Jewish–Bolshevik–plutocratic' conspiracy. This strategy had found supporters – Dr Helmut Friedrichs, Bormann's deputy in the party chancellery, stressed the importance of countering the tendency to view the continuation of the war in 1942 as a failure:

> [w]e have to do everything possible to avoid the impression that the [victorious] end of the war is doubtful. When it comes to a decision for the next 1000 years, it is not so important if [the war] lasts for another year.[25]

The general propaganda guidelines (*Propagandaparolen*[26]) issued immediately afterwards by the Propaganda Division of the ministry stated the obvious – that propaganda was obliged to work within the parameters of Hitler's speech; but it also called for wide publicity to Goebbels's article and demanded the reiteration of both men's arguments without any 'exaggerations'.[27]

At any rate, preparations for the approaching winter had already been in full swing since mid-September. The 'Winter Aid Campaign' (*Winterhilfsspende*) was only the tip of the iceberg, aimed at fostering a sense of solidarity between the military and the domestic fronts at a time of escalating anxiety and geographical distance between the two. Although it should have started early enough to ensure the dispatch of clothing and military material to the front well in advance of the first snowstorms, the early optimism about the conclusion of the war before the end of autumn had also affected the judgement of the OKW command; otherwise, they would not have brushed aside the issue when it was first raised by RMVP officials in late August, claiming that it was both premature and unnecessary to start preparations for yet another winter of war at a time when it could 'cause a shock to the troops as well as to the population at home'.[28] That preparations for the *Winterhilfsspende* turned out to be desperately overdue and insufficient (indications of increasing anxiety were evident in the Ministerial Conference of 18 November 1941, where Goebbels talked of 'some hold-ups due to the transport situation' and instructed his subordinates to avoid references to the campaign at that time[29]) became evident only months later. What is significant here is that, at least from the first week of September, the RMVP was already working on the assumption that the war would most probably not be finished in 1941.

The drafting of various propaganda 'action-plans' for the winter of 1941/42 was well underway in the RMVP and RPL even when Hitler and Dietrich launched their second wave of triumphalism in early October, in the wake of 'Operation Typhoon'. In the rationale for the propaganda action it was stated that,

> [t]he war, against the wishes of the greatest part of the German popula-
> tion, has already lasted two years and we are now facing a third winter of
> war ... It is evident that the coming winter will place upon the Volk more
> sacrifices, restrictions and burdens, without the expectation of any signif-
> icant change in the situation or a counterbalance provided by decisive
> military developments.[30]

Such candid language was of course restricted to internal use; as was the listing of possible factors that would result in further deterioration of public mood, such as the intensification of air raids over German cities, lack of clothing and further restrictions in food rations. The early optimism of the previous months was clearly criticised as an 'undoubted serious error'. When it came to direct communication with the Volk, however, the plan called for a more effective balance between 'openness' (*Öffentlichkeit*) and an uncompromising battle against defeatism or panic-mongering (*unverantwortliche Pessimisten und notorische Schwarzseher*). Particular emphasis was placed on the task of solidifying the psychological links between home and civilian fronts; of reminding the audience that 'since September 1939 Hitler had made numerous new attempts to bring peace to the German people and, when this became impossible [as a result of the western powers' refusal], to conclude the military conflict as soon as possible'; and of making clear to the population that, because Germany 'fights the greatest battle of her history that will decide the fate of the next millennium, there was no possibility of going back now [but] only the choice between victory or collapse'. Comparisons with 1914–18 were allowed in order to demonstrate to the population how much better German society was prepared for this war, how improved the living standards of the civilians were and how many more successes Hitler had achieved in the pre-war period (Rhineland, Austria, Sudetenland, Polish Corridor). Finally, the Propaganda-Plan called for a co-ordinated 'fear' campaign against 'Bolshevik–Jewish' atrocities, painting a bleak future for Europe should the war be lost:

> [d]estruction of all cities and villages, expropriation of each private property, inconceivable blood bath of the population, martyrdom and slaughter of millions, hunger and misery through destruction of the social prosperity, destruction of the supplies and smashing of production, deportation of millions as work slaves to the north Russian and Siberian steppes, forceful re-education of children in a reformatory Bolshevik child camps, elimination of the institution of family, razing of all churches and cultural treasures to the ground.[31]

The main propaganda slogan for the coming winter months was determined in early September – 'Germany's victory, bread and freedom for our Volk and for Europe'.[32] It was reconfirmed a month later, in the light of evidence that the population had started to doubt Hitler's promises or indeed his ability to bring this war to an end. This largely explains why the RMVP and the RPL were insisting that the bulk of the propaganda energies for the coming months be expended on portraying Hitler as the only 'model' for the German people, as the only guarantee of victory against the 'Bolshevik threat' and as an infallible military genius that both Germany and the rest of Europe looked to for the final, allegedly guaranteed victory.

Whilst the bulk of the propaganda output was intended to focus on the ostensible 'Jewish–Bolshevik' collusion, the Plan also called for a ferocious attack on 'world plutocracy' and 'pseudo-democracy'. This angle involved primary Britain and Winston Churchill, but it also made concrete references to the USA and Franklin D Roosevelt (see Ch. 3). Since the summer of 1941, NS propaganda had given full publicity to the publication of the book 'Germany must perish' by the American writer, Theodor Nathan Kaufman. A pamphlet by the leader of the Radio Division of the RMVP, Wolfgang Diewerge, provided propaganda ammunition to the regime claims that the 'Jewish plutocracy' constituted the link between Bolshevism, the western democracies and the (still neutral) USA.[33] Diewerge presented the author of the book as a close political advisor to President Roosevelt (what he calls as the latter's 'Brain Trust'), as 'spokesman of world plutocracy' and instigator of a malicious policy against *all* Germans, geared towards their alleged complete 'annihilation'. Diewerge (and Goebbels who personally supervised the drafting of the pamphlet and allegedly contributed a large section towards the end of the document) timed the launch of his publication to coincide with the meeting between Roosevelt and Churchill aboard the former's yacht in July 1941.

The deterioration of the American–Japanese relations during the summer and autumn of 1941 was greeted with mixed feelings in Berlin. The co-operation of Japan in the Axis, both against the British Empire in the east and in the context of 'Barbarossa', was of crucial significance for the successful conclusion of the war. However, a possible American involvement would only strengthen the British resolve and, potentially, solidify a formidable anti-German coalition. Faced with Roosevelt's pro-intervention stance and being aware that the British propaganda machinery was in full operation in the direction of ensuring the eventual victory of the interventionist line inside the USA, NS propaganda was obliged to tread a delicate path between attacking Roosevelt as a puppet of the 'Jewish–plutocratic alliance' whilst avoiding any direct provocation that could weaken the anti-intervention mood inside the USA. Throughout 1941 this strategy was geared to ensuring that the USA would continue to stay outside the conflict – with or, ideally, without F D Roosevelt at the helm.[34]

The first adversities: Pearl Harbour, 'General Winter' and the extension of the war

By 7 December 1941, this strategy lay in ruins: the Japanese attack on the American naval base of Pearl Harbour in Hawaii had brought the USA into the conflict and boosted the American President's personal fortunes.[35] The German declaration of war against the USA came four days later, accompanied by a long address by Hitler at the Reichstag. With the advance on Moscow in serious trouble due to the advent of winter, and rumours about a crisis in the relations between the NS leadership and the Wehrmacht, the Führer attempted to deflect his audience's attention to, predictably, Roosevelt, Churchill and the international web of 'plutocratic–Jewish conspirators' against the Reich. He provided a lengthy narrative about the allegedly defensive motives of NS foreign policy since 1933, offered an overly optimistic assessment of the progress in the east, repeated his conviction in the historic 'mission' bestowed upon the German Reich and concluded with a scathing attack on the USA and Roosevelt as the arch-representatives of international plutocracy:

> [t]oday I am at the head of the strongest Army in the world, the most gigantic Air Force and of a proud Navy. Behind and around me stands the Party with which I became great and which has become great through me. The enemies I see before me are the same enemies as twenty years ago, but the path along which I look forward cannot be compared with

that on which I look back ... We are allied with strong peoples, who in the same need are faced with the same enemies. The American President and his plutocratic clique have mocked us as the Have-nots; that is true, but the Have-nots will see to it that they are not robbed of the little they have.[36]

At another point in the speech Hitler also provided a first indication of German victims since the commencement of 'Barbarossa'. He reported a total of '162,314 killed, 571,767 wounded and 33,334 missing'.[37] To appreciate the rationale of this apparently 'realistic' admission of difficulties, one simply has to look at the figures that were released by the Wehrmacht and the RMVP with regard to Soviet prisoners of war during the autumn of 1941. By the middle of October, that figure had been raised to more than three million – around 700,000 of whom had purportedly been captured in a single battle around Kiev in late September![38] Of course, the 'distance' between the actual military front and public opinion allowed the regime's propaganda authorities ample space for such a manipulation of numbers. There were, however, growing indications that the credibility of this type of triumphalist discourse was waning – and, with it, the integrity of NS propaganda itself. Until early December 1941, the regime and Wehrmacht talked of 'decisive' victories, of enormous enemy loses and of a certain German victory of gigantic proportions and significance. This emplotment transformed the war in the east into a short-term enterprise, raising the understandable expectation of a rapid victorious conclusion. The more this promised victory was deferred, the more the regime was attempting to compensate with fresh releases of alleged triumphs and excessively high figures of enemy losses.

This was an unsustainable and dangerous strategy that worried Goebbels. It was discussed at the conference of the RMVP on 7 December 1941, with the minister announcing an increasing portion of 'realism' in future reports about the difficulties in the east and the privations that lay ahead for the German people, on the front or at home.[39] A few days later, he was even more revealing about the planned changes in the discourse of official propaganda output. After calling for the abandonment of the previous line of not divulging information about setbacks and difficulties, he concluded that,

> [j]ust as, according to Clausewitz's dictum, a battle without a crisis is no battle but merely an engagement, so, quite naturally, a war without a crisis is no war. It is the task of propaganda, by way of its fundamental attitude, deliberately to make the German people *crisis-proof* (emphasis added).[40]

Premature declarations of total victory and annihilation of the enemy had saturated the NS discourse by October 1941, particularly after the crushing defeat of Marshall Semyon Timoshenko's forces at Viazma and Brjansk.[41]

Towards the end of November, the news that Wehrmacht troops had advanced up to the outskirts of Moscow seemed to uphold the initial impression of imminent victory.[42] Yet, Hitler's speech at the Reichstag on 11 December provided a definite official admission that the conflict could not be concluded within 1941, when he stated that,

> [t]he beginning of winter only will now check this movement; at the beginning of summer it will again no longer be possible to stop the movement.

The steep damage-limitation exercise for the RMVP started with the announcement of the Winter Aid Campaign (*Winterhilfsspende*) in early October – an announcement that displaced public frustration from the prospect of a longer war to the regime's responsibility for not making timely provisions for the soldiers in the battlefield.[43] What would have otherwise been an excellent opportunity to promote the identification between the domestic and the military front had to perform a largely justificatory function, shielding the regime authorities and the High Command from public criticism.[44] By mid-December the tenor of NS propaganda had became noticeably less triumphant, acknowledging the adverse effect of weather conditions and avoiding references to an immediate victory. The Germans had heard the 'weather' argument before (it had been used to justify the cancellation of 'Sea Lion' in September 1940). Given that the campaign against the British Isles had not been resumed in 1941, they had psychologically associated it with an indirect admission of setback. The propaganda appeal to weather conditions in December 1941 was, therefore, a rather familiar and transparent euphemism to blur the disparity between the military situation and the *ersatz* reality that the regime had imprudently fostered in the autumn.[45] In January 1942, with the Winter Aid campaign in full action, news about the Soviet counter-offensives struck a discordant note to earlier German declarations about the enemy's military collapse. Although the eventual stabilisation of the front was widely depicted as proof of the Red Army's inability to undertake serious offensive action after the earlier Wehrmacht victories,[46] Goebbels now spoke openly of a 'steep uphill struggle' (*steile Aufstieg*) that faced the German volk in the future.[47]

It is easy to allocate full responsibility for this debacle to the NS propaganda machinery and even to Goebbels personally. The regime's propaganda supremo had allowed an evidently injudicious and untimely triumphalist discourse to gather its own momentum in the summer and autumn of 1941, even if this was derived and primarily nurtured by Dietrich and perpetuated through widely-read party publications, such as the *Völkischer Beobachter*.[48] The creation of the Ministry for the Occupied Eastern Territories in mid-November appeared to further enforce the belief that the regime's planning had moved from military to postwar considerations. Throughout November, Goebbels kept giving instructions to the press about how to report plans 'for the reconstruction and shaping of the Eastern Areas' in view of the 'new order' established after the impressive German victories.[49] However, Goebbels was only part of a wider network of unwitting distortion of reality that ranged from the Wehrmacht High Command to Hitler himself, who in October had repeatedly and confidently predicted the demise of the Soviet Union during 1941:

> [t]hat I can say now. I say it only today because I can say that this enemy is already broken and will never rise again ...[50] During these three and a half months, my soldiers, the precondition, at least, has been created for a last mighty blow that shall crush this opponent before winter sets in.[51]

A deeply embedded ideological belief in the inherent inferiority of the Slavs and in the allegedly devastating effect of Bolshevism in Russia had fostered an almost de facto conviction amongst population and leaders alike that the Soviet Union would collapse within weeks – like a 'colossus with clay feet', as Goebbels had described it.[52] This was undoubtedly a proof that the mechanisms of indoctrination which the regime had systematically set up since 1933 had made significant inroads into the collective conscience of the German public in some areas at least. Once again, long-term *negative* integration on the basis of an anti-Bolshevik agenda proved largely effective, even at times when *positive* allegiance to, and identification with National Socialism was in short supply. Even after the winter of 1941/42 (which even the regime described in terms of a 'crisis'[53]), the widespread public belief in the superiority of the German armed forces was not seriously questioned – the reluctance to consider the prospect of a serious Soviet counter-attack. But now this belief was mitigated by a growing sense of anxiety. The intensifying resistance of the Red Army soldiers in the east, and especially the activities of the partisan formation during the winter of 1941/42, raised awkward questions about the morale and qualities of the Russians that NS ideology/ propaganda had so meticulously tried to disparage in the past.[54] This was only the foretaste of a much stronger questioning of the NS propaganda's conventional wisdom that would become evident later in the war.

The belief in the superiority of the 'Aryan race' could barely accommodate a tenor of triumphalism vis-à-vis the astounding successes of the Japanese in the Pacific and southern Asia against the Americans during 1942 – successes that entailed a humiliation for another 'white race'.[55] It is indeed ironic that Goebbels hastened to play down the propaganda effect of these victories on the basis that he considered the Japanese reports excessive and unrealistic, not least with regard to their claims about enemy losses![56] There were, however, deeper and more complex reasons for this reticence towards Germany's ally. Japanese successes had come at a time when the NS regime had no comparable achievements of its own to display. At the same time, the impressive performance of the (supposedly racially 'inferior') Japanese underlined the extremely limited contribution to the Axis cause by Fascist Italy – and this was a very difficult task for NS propaganda, given the widespread disdain of the German public opinion towards the Italians and the barely concealed conviction that they were no match (militarily and racially) to the Germans. As a result, throughout 1942 NS propaganda paid particular attention to finding a delicate balance between sustaining the belief in Germany's superiority and making the population mindful of the need to display solidarity vis-à-vis the other partners of the Axis alliance. In a series of *Propagandaparolen*, throughout 1942, it was stressed that Italy and Japan would be presented as the only allies that Germany had in the context of the war of 'Have-Nots' (*Habenichts*) against the 'plutocrats'.[57] The 'racial' dimension of the debate was of course far more acute with regard to the Japanese. 'Racial' references to them in the past had always been couched in pejorative terms, such as 'Asiatic', 'yellow peril'[58] or 'Mongol'. Therefore, the regime authorities emphasised the need to abstain from such terms, as well as to avoid using the juxtaposition of 'Europe-versus-Asia' that had been deployed *ad nauseam* during the first phase of Barbarossa.[59] Japan's impressive successes in the Pacific Ocean during 1942 received considerable coverage in German propaganda, with the emphasis always on the spiritual similarities between the two peoples and the ideological–political affinity between their regimes. The 'racial' complication was usually brushed aside, albeit somewhat awkwardly, by stating that the genetic pool of the Japanese had remained unaltered for almost two millennia, in contrast to that of the Chinese or other 'Asian' people.[60]

The 'year of decision': 1942

With the passing of the 'crisis winter' and the first signs of improvement in the weather situation in the east came renewed expectations for the resumption of the offensive against the Red Army. In mid-February 1942 Goebbels provided a lengthy summary of the developments in the previous year, paying particular attention to the difficulties in the east, which he attributed solely to weather conditions. His prediction for the immediate future was decidedly upbeat:

> [o]ne awaits the next months with fear. If 'General Winter', the avowed ally of the Englishman and Bolsheviks, has indeed worked so badly [for them], what is there to expect from spring and summer, which are well known as more Axis-friendly?[61]

It is interesting that Goebbels avoided giving specific dates for the commencement of the new offensive: 'spring and summer' allowed ample space for strategic manoeuvre, especially in view of the unpredictable Russian weather. Towards the end of March 1942, the Propaganda minister went even further in this cautious approach by prohibiting the use of the phrase 'spring offensive' in the German press and communiqués.[62] At the same time, a fair amount of realism underpinned and qualified his optimistic forecasts. Already since December 1941 plans for a reduction of food rations reflected a general drop in living standards and presaged more difficulties for the future.[63] In spite of optimistic reports in February about a recovery of public morale after a serious slump during the 'crisis winter', Goebbels warned against premature optimism vis-à-vis military developments in north Africa or war aims in the east and insisted on the theme of an 'uphill struggle':

[w]e have still another small piece of difficulty before us, and then things will pick up once again. Thus we want to grit the teeth again and make a courageous step forward. On the summit the[re] lies the large goal[64]

Overall, the period between December 1941 and March 1942 represented a crucial terminus: apart from the Wehrmacht's failure to crush Soviet resistance, the regime's (and, to some extent, Hitler's) military strategy had been exposed to criticism for continuing to engage with new enemies without first having ensured victory on existing fronts.[65] In early 1942, the primary concerns of the population remained focused on the timetable of the campaign; hence the dejected public mood that SD reports recorded during the winter of 1941/42 was linked to the same basic fear – evident since September 1939 – that a swift victory remained unattainable, in spite of the regime's promises to the contrary.[66] However, in the longer term the overwhelming emphasis that NS propaganda had placed on developments in the east during the first months of the campaign had all the makings of a real 'boomerang effect'. The depiction of 'Barbarossa' as the ultimate war against Bolshevism, international Jewry and the 'plutocratic powers' of the west diverted attention from other fronts (north Africa) and developments and established a direct correlation between military outcomes in the east, public morale and the regime's overall credibility. Such a situation could only produce propaganda successes only if the Wehrmacht could regain the initiative and generate new impressive victories. There were still hopes in early 1942 that this would indeed be the case after the previous 'winter crisis'. Whatever was happening on other fronts (north Africa, war against Britain, Pacific war) mattered very little to the population and afforded little breathing space to the NS propaganda system.

Ever since February 1942, Goebbels had been aware of the crucial test of credibility that faced NS propaganda in the coming months. He noted that,

[w]e will have to change our propaganda and policies in the east as already arranged with the Führer. These were hitherto based on the assumption that we would take possession of the east swiftly. This hope has not been realised, however. We ... are therefore compelled to change our slogans and policies fundamentally.[67]

As the Propaganda Plan for the winter of 1941/42 covered the period until March 1942, the RMVP and RPL worked extensively on the formulation of a coherent propaganda strategy for the following spring and summer (period of expected intense military activity). The new campaign used the slogan 'Everything for victory; only victory is significant' – and it is obvious from the wording that the main intention of the NS propaganda authorities was to displace concerns about the duration of the conflict to the magnitude and significance of the expected victory. This allowed a higher-than-usual degree of realism:

> [f]alse optimism is to be avoided. Of course, our complete confidence in victory should be expressed, but no one may be led to hope that final victory can happen without great additional exertions and deprivations, or that the worst is over and that things will be easier from here on. Even if we win major new military successes, citizens should not be led to believe that they can reduce their exertions.[68]

The campaign would end on an optimistic note – victory was certain, due to the spiritual superiority of the German volk and the brilliance of its leadership.

The new attitude of measured 'realism' depended on a delicate balancing act: emphatic presentation of positive news, openness about difficulties, lifting public morale but also dampening down excessive expectations. The restraint of the official propaganda discourse during the spring and the summer of 1942, especially when it came to a short array of impressive victories in the east,[69] manifested a far more cautious approach to the management of victories and anticipations. As early as 2 April, Goebbels instructed the German information network to avoid raising false hopes amongst the public opinion, especially as the weather situation improved in the east and expectations for a renewed offensive were running high.[70] Even the Führer appeared to have heeded the 'lessons' from the winter crisis of 1941/42. In his major speech to the Reichstag on 26 April 1942, he admitted that,

> [a]s regards organization I have taken those measures which are necessary to save our country from a repetition of similar emergencies … From railway entrance to tanks, tractors, platoons and trucks our army in the East will be better equipped for the individual soldier, however, should such severe climate conditions repeat themselves, similar conditions to those of last winter will not arise again as the result of experience and work.[71]

The restraint shown towards the launch of the attack on Sevastopol in early June, the banning of any concrete reference to long-term geographic aims of the summer offensive[72] (e.g. 'Caucasus'[73]) and the cautious line with regard to the battle of Rostov (in many ways a precursor to Stalingrad, in the sense that fierce street fighting made an accurate assessment of the situation impossible)[74] indicated the inroads that Goebbels's line of 'realism' had made into the culture of NS propaganda. Repeatedly, in late spring and in the summer of 1942, Goebbels instructed his subordinates to avoid the mistakes of the previous year. 'No illusions' (*keine Illusionen*) became the basic principle that NS propaganda was meant to uphold throughout the year when faced with exaggerated public expectations for a swift victory or a peace falling short of total victory.[75] Even Hitler's confident prediction that this would be the 'year of decision' (*Jahr der Entscheidung*) resulting in the 'military annihilation of the Soviet Union by the following autumn', came with the caveat that 'it would be wrong to awake the expectation amongst the volk that the war will end during this year'. The same pessimistic impression about the possible continuation of the war into 1943 was restated even more categorically in the instructions issued to party propagandists in August.[76] The timing of this internal admission is even more significant, as by the end of the summer the military situation in the east had improved dramatically; but even after the advances in the southern sector of the front (i.e. towards Stalingrad and Caucasus), Goebbels felt that the German population should be served a diet of restrained optimism and sombre realism.[77] Balance was to be the order of NS propaganda according to Goebbels – neither references to 'year of decision' (which were banned in late May) nor delving into the 'winter crisis' of 1941/42.[78]

Even this seemingly prudent line of information, however, could easily backfire. During the summer of 1942, Goebbels became increasingly worried at reports showing that the coverage of Soviet resistance was getting out of control, raising feelings of admiration amongst Germans.[79] The coverage of the July 1942 summer offensive challenged a series of stereotypes perpetuated by the NS regime: that Russia had been severely weakened by Bolshevism, that the people had been coerced into defending a regime that they detested, that the Slavs were of 'racially inferior' stock.[80] In the second week of July, he held a crucial conference at the RMVP in which he warned that,

> there is the danger that sections of the German public may draw false conclusions from [these reports]. Several reports were psychologically exceedingly dangerous. There was a suggestion in them that the Soviets, too, had ideals which inspired them to fanaticism and heroic resistance so that they would not shrink from any privations or efforts in the war ... This kind of reporting, unless it is opposed, is bound to shake the German people's attitude to Bolshevism and very shortly produce a kind of pro-Bolshevik enthusiasm. National Socialism teaches that Bolshevism must not be seen as an idea but as the excrescence of sub-humanity and criminal Jewish instincts.[81]

And there were further complications for the RMVP strategy. Whilst public *Stimmung* had started showing signs of psychological recovery after a difficult winter and a largely unrewarding spring, the coverage of German victories during the summer offensive – even if deliberately toned down – seemed to resurrect the illusion of a 'short war' that was nearing its successful conclusion.[82] Goebbels's exasperation with the unbridled optimism of some OKW situational reports and press articles was recorded at a conference that took place on 15 August:

> [t]he Minister raises the subject of the powerful mood of optimism in the Reich and in particular refers to various reports by the SD and the Gauleiters which all agree in pointing out that the German people are full of hope of an early end to the war. Even the smallest news items in the press or on the radio serve to strengthen that belief and to make it into a certainty for many people. The Minister says that he has done nothing to nourish such optimism and that he regards it as extremely dangerous.[83]

The turning point: Stalingrad (September 1942–January 1943)

The successes of the Wehrmacht offensive in the east, however, had generated new wild hopes that stretched from the highest echelons of the NS leadership to the majority of civilians. As German troops continued to advance throughout the summer and early autumn of 1942, reaching the outskirts of Stalingrad in August,[84] the city bearing the Soviet leader's name acquired a totemic status, in both NS military planning and propaganda. Goebbels was heartened by the impressive array of victories in the military build-up to the final assault; but he was also aware that this was a project on which Hitler had gambled his political credibility.[85] In this vein, on 18 September 1942, he instructed his subordinates to divert attention from the Stalingrad battle:

> [t]he question about the fall of Stalingrad has been asked amongst the people for some considerable time now, but military progress is not such that a final capture of the city can be expected as yet. For this reason other subjects will now be brought to the fore.[86]

However, triumphalist propaganda came from other sources that the RMVP was still incapable of controlling: Otto Dietrich's premature triumphalism on 15 September, depicting the occupation of the city as a matter of hours, tallied not only with Wehrmacht's similar reporting during that period but also with Hitler's own conviction. In fact, in his address at the opening of the Winter Relief Campaign on 30 September 1942, the Führer was perfectly aware of his Propaganda minister's belated misgivings, as well as the noticeably changing tone of the OKW reports after the difficulties of the campaign. Yet, this did not stop him from contradicting Goebbels's two fundamental stipulations about the coverage of the battle at the Volga – the extensive mention of the subject and the dissemination of a categorically optimistic forecast:

> [t]he occupation of Stalingrad, which will also be carried through, will deepen this gigantic victory and strengthen it, and you can be sure that no human being will drive us out of this place later on.[87]

No wonder then that, according to Hans Fritzsche, Goebbels felt distinctly uncomfortable about the way that the military situation in the east had been communicated to the German public, allegedly even going as far as criticising Hitler for the blunder.[88] However, with regard to the emerging battle for Stalingrad the Propaganda minister too committed serious mistakes that contradicted his new style of information. On 24 August, he referred to the 'favourable development of the military situation at Stalingrad' as a licence to talk more optimistically about the occupation of the city. Twenty days later, he went even further by presenting the final victory at the Volga as 'almost certain'.[89] Against the backdrop of his comments at the RMVP press conference on 12 and 21 September – again warning against excessive optimism –, this uncharacteristic spell of buoyancy appears as a non sequitur. The fact that during the last ten days of the month he was once again exhorting the German press to bring new topics to the fore so as to divert public attention from its apparent psychosis with Stalingrad raises eloquent questions about the minister's own consistency or clarity of vision.

Such was, however, the momentum created in the previous weeks from reports of the rapidly advancing Wehrmacht troops in the east that public expectations could not be diminished by any form of propaganda realism or containment. In fact, the only public disappointment from Hitler's 30 September speech originated from the frustration of the hope that he would announce the capture of Stalingrad.[90] Now, official OKW reports broadcast through the German radio claimed in November that the city had already been taken![91] October and November were indeed 'not easy' months for NS propagandists, as Goebbels himself admitted.[92] His instructions at the Ministerial Conference oscillated between random injections of optimism and fury at the cultivation of illusions. By mid-November – and with the Soviet offensive in full swing – he had effectively run out of positive diversionary themes; in these circumstances, too much 'realism' risked causing an irreversible depression in public morale. Yet, he had no solution to this problem.

The months before the Stalingrad disaster constituted the last, painful stage of a distinct phase in the history of NS propaganda, during which the 'Goebbels network' could not co-ordinate effectively either the output or the strategies involved (see Ch. 2). The war of attrition amongst prominent NS leaders over control of different slices of the information domain left the regime's propaganda functions in a self-destructive disarray. In spite of the RMVP's and the RPL's efforts to co-ordinate activities with coherent 'plans', 'campaigns' and 'actions', the result was often confusion, blunder and reactive damage-limitation. At the same time that many newspapers issued special editions with the breaking news, the radio broadcast noticeably more restrained accounts of the developments in the east. And, whilst at least until mid-October Goebbels appeared reasonably confident about the final victory (even when he urged caution to his subordinates), he was privately anxious to find out what the situation was really like. In late 1942 he asked Fritzsche and Semmler[93] – both had just come back after a period spent in the east – about their impressions. Fritzsche in particular, from his position as regular commentator on the radio, made oblique references to the 'hard times ahead' as early as late November;[94] Goebbels, who was often outraged by his alleged 'pessimism', seemed to share his judgement on that occasion.[95]

But the tragic fate of the VIth Army, encircled since 22 November and desperately running out of both supplies and time,[96] could not be undone by any wishful thinking or propaganda distortion. Hitler's first reaction to the news of the Soviet counter-offensive was to ban any reference to it, but news filtered through on 24 November after a sensational communiqué from the Soviet High Command reported that the German defence line in the southern sector of the front had been comprehensively breached.[97] On his part, Goebbels prohibited press and radio reports from using the adjective 'defensive' with regard to the VIth Army's battle.[98] But the subsequent virtual disappearance of any references to Stalingrad in December and January from the regime's propaganda discourse proved a flawed and heavy-handed response to the deterioration of the military situation and the certainty of the impending crushing defeat. The problem this time – in contrast to the winter of 1941 – lay in the extent of what was being concealed. Back in September, Goebbels had authorised a careful campaign preparing the German public for the eventuality of a failure to capture Stalingrad.[99] Now that this failure was drawing near, however, risking the lives of a whole army group and invaluable military materiel, he too was at a loss. The regime's propaganda authorities placed a protective veil around the battle of Stalingrad, in expectation of a victory – somewhere. Goebbels privately talked of 'crisis days', and this was an understatement: as if developments in the east were not enough, by mid-November the Allied forces had also succeeded in landing on the coast of Morocco and Algeria (Operation 'Torch'), consolidating their recent victories in north Africa.[100] The Propaganda minister kept supporting a diversionary line of silence with regard to Stalingrad at the same time that he castigated the misleading content of the Wehrmacht communiqués with regard to the fall of Tobruk in north Africa. In fact, he seethed against the OKW for delaying the report about this defeat until even the 'last German village had found out the truth' through alternative channels of information (primarily foreign radio programmes).[101] He claimed that, 'after three years of uninterrupted victories, we should not worry about having to tell the German people about a reverse'.[102] He appeared confident that over-all, there was no comparison with the 1918 situation and that Germany would avoid the ferocity of last winter's 'crisis' this time. He even considered it timely to require ample coverage of the 'ferocity and difficulty of the fight-ing' in Stalingrad on 25 November, even if he admitted that preparations for the Winter Aid campaign were – once again – insufficient and overdue.[103] In these circumstances, the reservoir for a successful diversionary propaganda manoeuvre was severely depleted: the (declining) successes of the U-boat war in the Atlantic, the usual caricatures of Churchill and Roosevelt, a new wave of 'anti-plutocratic' propaganda that had been kept in store since the previ-ous May, the usual diet of anti-Semitic propaganda,[104] even the unwelcome news about the British attack on El-Alamein in north Africa (23 October) – anything that did not refer directly to the eastern theatre of war was deployed in a desperate attempt to promote a more global perspective on the conflict.[105] Such a diversion, however, could not work after months of deliberately directing attention to the east and playing up the Stalingrad card. As a series of SD public opinion reports compiled in late November/early December noted, people were concerned about the eastern front; no other news could possibly deflect their attention from Stalingrad.[106]

In the end, the regime had to face the truth – and then confront the public. The staging of the 'Stille Nacht, Heilige Nacht' hoax on 25 December 1942 – an allegedly live broadcast from the Stalingrad front with the German soldiers singing the popular Christmas song – caused a mixture of sadness and unfounded anticipation amongst listeners at home, an anticipation that a 'miracle' could still spare the VIth Army from annihilation. Following a lengthy meeting between Hitler and Goebbels on 13 January, the first oblique admission of the impending defeat crept into the regime's propa-ganda discourse three days later, again through the Wehrmacht commu-niqué, describing the German fighting in Stalingrad as 'defensive'.[107] On the anniversary of the *Machtergreifung*, Goering addressed a large audience of party followers, speaking about the 'sacrifice' of the VIth Army in terms of a historic analogy with Leonidas' three-hundred Spartans at Thermopylae. The Führer, still in his headquarters in the east, refused to confront the public on the anniversary, in spite of the ten-year tradition of addressing personally a large audience in celebration of the *Machtergreifung* in 1933.[108]

Finally, the official declaration that the battle of Stalingrad was over came on 3 February, amidst the sounds of Beethoven's 'Heroica' symphony.[109] The party guidelines to the propagandists emphasised the need to play up the idea of terminal danger from Bolshevism – not just for Germany, but for the whole of Europe and its 'civilisation'.[110] In an emotional article in *Das Reich*, Hans Schwarz van Berk spared no word of praise for the thousands of dead and missing German soldiers, but also for those who survived and continued the struggle for the 'immortal history' of Germany; what they all needed, he maintained, was the home front's unswerving loyalty and commitment.[111] In the regular (classified) instructions to the newspaper and magazine editors across the Reich a similar tone was set with the following description of the battle,[112]

> [t]he heroic battle at Stalingrad has reached its end. This moving event, which casts even the greatest heroic military deeds of the past into the shadows, must be presented by magazines as an example of the highest heroism and complete willingness to sacrifice for the victory of the German people. The word Stalingrad must become a holy symbol for the German people. The immortal heroism of the men of Stalingrad will unleash even more than before the spirit and strength of the German nation, which will ensure the victory it is now even more fanatically determined to win.[113]

It was a well-staged tribute, in spite of the solemnity of the situation and the magnitude of the debacle. But the propaganda transition from impending victory to 'defensive' battle, to 'blow' and finally to the 'heroic conclusion' of the battle and the 'hard lesson'[114] – all within a little over two weeks – caught a disoriented public unprepared for the magnitude of this – real and symbolic – defeat.[115]

6
NS Propaganda and the Loss of the Monopoly of Truth (1943–44)

The Stalingrad aftermath: NS propaganda and 'public opinion'

The claim of the official state discourse to authority and 'truth' is an essential feature of power and legitimacy in all political systems.[1] Similarly, the prestige of a regime depends on the ability of its information network (and propaganda is an integral part of it) to disseminate positive news about its achievements, gloss over the less flattering consequences of its choices and remain rather close-lipped about downright negative developments that might affect its overall image.

Control of the flow of information in NS Germany was not simply a mechanism of rationalising the exercise of power; it was rather part of a crucial parallel process of depoliticising and demobilising German society through ideological conformity whilst maintaining the illusion of popular participation and voluntary plebiscitary approval for the regime.[2] The success of the NS regime in promoting this process through a 'stick-and-carrot' strategy (that is, persuasion *and* coercion) effectively reversed one of the main processes that had been triggered off in the late eighteenth century: the creation of a 'public sphere' (*Öffentlichkeit* qua Jürgen Habermas[3]) in the context of which ideas, decisions and information could be exchanged, discussed and even questioned on a rational and pluralistic basis. The monopolisation of information by NS propaganda resulted in a highly successful dismantling of the German 'public sphere' and an equally impressive colonisation of the collective political imagery of German society – and the exceptions to this (resistance, incidental acts of dissidence etc.) serve as further corroborating evidence of the above process. Such colonisation, disarticulation and then suffocation of the 'public sphere' by NS propaganda inverted the latter's primary historic function – namely, operating as a field of relative resistance to the arbitrary power of state authority and possessing at least a modicum of power to influence it.

Indeed a *partial reconstitution* of a 'public opinion' inside the Reich was already underway from 1942. An increasing number of German civilians responded to NS propaganda with increasing trepidation and disbelief, often resisting its message, or even consciously avoiding its channels of dissemination. In December 1942, an apparent oversight of the censorship system that filtered soldier correspondence addressed to their families and friends back home allowed an embarrassing batch of letters talking in – unacceptable for the regime authorities – the military situation to reach their destination.[4] A few weeks later, SD reports noted that large sections of the population resorted to rumours, underground information and reading between the lines to find out 'the *"truth"* about the situation on the eastern front'.[5]

1942 had already been marked by increasing signs of social unrest – both inside the Reich and in various occupied countries –, widespread defeatism and psychological disaffection with the regime. Notwithstanding the ad nauseam lip-service to the unity of the 'national community'[6] and to the equally shared burden of the war between the domestic and the military front, the depression of living standards (for example, rations had been reduced even further in April 1942)[7] had brought war closer to the civilian population for the first time. Whilst the Wehrmacht forces were still advancing thousands of miles away from the Greater Reich, the effects of the war on the home front had become noticeably more immediate in 1942, and even more so in the following year. This provided the first concrete first-hand experience of a different sort of 'truth' that increasingly contradicted even Hitler's confident prediction that 'whatever fate will bring for us, it will be easier than that what is behind us'.[8]

But in circumstances of effective totalitarian control, emancipation from the psychological control of a still powerful regime was extremely hard. Even before the events at Stalingrad, Goebbels had alluded to the fact that the regime had lost the initiative, if not in military terms then at least from the viewpoint of disseminating information. The Propaganda minister was conscious of the need to maintain the 'noise' levels of information, avoid embarrassing 'silences' and be ahead of events – however adverse or embarrassing these might be. Listening to enemy broadcasts had been criminalised since the first months of the war (see Ch. 1), but in October 1942 the RMVP, realising that many Germans were increasingly turning to foreign stations for information and that enforcing the ban was extremely difficult, publicised a list of individuals who had been sentenced for committing this offence.[9] Bormann's attempt to introduce a 'positive' European dimension to the regime's discourse (see Ch. 3) was particularly intended for audiences outside the Reich – in neutral (Spain, Sweden) or even enemy (Britain) countries – in order to capitalise on the deep-seated distrust of the Stalinist regime and present the campaign in the east as a noble defensive fight for 'European' culture and civilisation.[10] In an attempt to add a practical gloss to the war in the east, Alfred Rosenberg spoke in mid-February about the importance of the German campaign in terms of 'food and raw-material autarchy' for the whole of Europe.[11] Goebbels accepted the value of such 'positive' themes, but he nevertheless stressed that the main focus of propaganda would be on principles ('morality, faith, order, discipline ... for Europe'), and not 'egotistical motives'.[12]

In spite of his own pessimistic assessment of the domestic situation in Germany during 1942, Goebbels persisted in his belief that the regime's propaganda could regain the initiative. In late September 1942, he acknowledged the growing public defiance towards the NS propaganda message – a development that he attributed to the fact that 'its expressions and style have become so worn and shabby that they produce a sense of distaste in the listener or reader'.[13] The shift to a more 'realistic' depiction of the situation, albeit frequently undermined by propaganda blunders, was intended to restore part of the credibility that NS propaganda had squandered through its irresponsible handling of information during 1941. Hans Fritzsche's moving but highly 'realistic' commentary on the conclusion of fighting in Stalingrad, broadcast at 19.45 hr on 3 February 1943, was reported to have struck the right chord with the majority of the population.[14]

Yet the Propaganda minister knew that this in itself was not enough. In this respect, the dramatic developments on the eastern front provided an opportunity for a wider reassessment of the conduct of propaganda. Reclaiming the initiative in psychological terms involved significantly more than a simple combination of negative (e.g. 'fear') and positive propaganda functions. The awkward propaganda silence in the two months before the announcement of the Stalingrad debacle had produced a psychological lacuna at the heart of German society that now threatened the regime's wounded psychological hegemony over the home front. Contrary to the long-term expectations of the NS regime that public allegiance would sooner or later be transformed into an instinctive, unconditional form of loyalty, the RMVP found itself increasingly in conditions of psychological competition against enemy broadcasts and leaflets, rumours, individual testimonies from soldiers and 'first-hand' experience of the war. Such a competition amounted to a direct questioning of the regime's 'monopoly of truth'.

At the first press conference of 1943 – and in the shadow of the impending catastrophe in Stalingrad – Goebbels made a series of significant observations about the future course of NS propaganda. He announced a return to 'a few solid principles' that needed to be invoked 'continually and ceaselessly at every opportunity ... [so as] to hammer them into the consciousness of the people'. From then on the war would be presented as a fundamental struggle 'of life and death' for the German volk, against an increasingly brutal enemy that had brought the forces of National Socialism into a very difficult position. In sharp contrast to earlier declarations (even by Goebbels and Hitler) that this conflict would be inevitably won by the Reich, emphasis would now be placed on the open-ended character of the war:

> *[o]f course we could lose the war* if we did not mobilise all our strengths for the war effort. If on the other hand we mobilise all the forces of the people and apply them correctly, then it may well be the case that Russia will be smashed this summer.[15] (emphasis added)

Clearly, Goebbels was attempting to chart the way for the regime's propaganda bounce-back to coincide with the announcement of the defeat at Stalingrad. His forward planning revealed his determination to intervene in the management of public mood more actively, to increase the 'noise' levels of NS propaganda and to provide a novel overall framework for emploting and contextualising the difficult situation of 1942/43. He was also determined to seize the initiative after the catastrophic handling of recent events by Otto Dietrich and the OKW in order to reclaim a central role in NS propaganda structures. 'Never another "crisis" ' was the slogan that he coined in mid-February in his Ministerial Conferences.[16] He was now ready to seize the political initiative and re-centralise control of propaganda whilst bolstering his standing in the eyes of the Führer. He needed a new platform that would bind propaganda with a more 'positive' pattern of domestic mobilisation in a 'revolutionary direction'.[17] It was this rationale that dictated the switch of propaganda output to *'total war'* in February 1943. This new radical theme, in conjunction with a more effective 'negative' campaign against 'Bolshevism' and 'international Jewry', constituted the two complementary pillars of Goebbels's attempt to alleviate the 'Stalingrad mood'.

Bouncing back after Stalingrad: 'Total war' and 'fear'

The notion of a radicalisation in the domestic mobilisation for war had crept into the official propaganda discourse as early as October 1942.[18] Goebbels's definition of 'total war' was expansive, as befitting the totalitarian aspirations of the NS regime: it signified a struggle that would be waged on every front, foreign and domestic, for the minds and hearts of the people – a carte blanche for the radicalisation of the war effort. What was still a vague and perhaps rhetorical appeal in October, became the primary propaganda escape route out of the ruins of Stalingrad in early 1943.[19] The argument about the necessity of shifting to 'total mobilisation' was introduced systematically by the Propaganda minister on 17 January through his editorial columns in the party's weekly publication, *Das Reich*.[20] Responding to the mounting criticism, primarily from working-class communities, that the burden of war was not shared equitably across German society and that the regime's lip-service to the unity of the 'national community' (*Volksgemeinschaft*) was little more than a rhetorical slogan with little relevance to reality, Goebbels launched a scathing attack on those who still viewed the war as a distant inconvenience:

> [h]ow, for instance, do the hundred thousands diligent men and women of Berlin get around to remaining silent if a few hundred fine people who also happen to reside in Berlin, try to escape from the war by going to the winter health resorts ... ? They are the same people who look at the war not as a fight for our national and individual life, but only as a tiresome interruption of their entertainment. They respect mostly the National–Socialist state only insofar as it provides them with advantages, give highly reluctantly and totally insufficiently to the Winter Aid Campaign, brush aside their communal duties, hold responsible the government even for the weather, the OKW-report bores them, and the[y] listen to the radio only when it plays dance music ... They live almost like in peacetime, while we wage war – indeed for them too.[21]

The editorial blended positive and negative integratory themes in a highly skilful manner. On the one hand, the war against the Soviet Union was presented in the bleakest terms, as a struggle against a brutal regime whose intention was 'the *total annihilation of the German Volk*' (emphasis added). On the other hand, the admission that the resources of the Reich had not been fully exploited or had been misappropriated projected a positive belief that 'total mobilisation' could indeed reverse the situation.[22] In fact, Goebbels craftily connected the success of this mobilisation with the prospect of 'coming quicker to a victorious end' (*Totaler Krieg – kürzester Krieg*) – again an astute association, given the German public's obsession with this theme since September 1939 (see Ch. 4). The overall message of the article, amidst the often bleak depiction of the current situation, remained positively empowering, as if suggesting that victory was in the hands of a united, fully mobilised and committed volk.

By the time that the Propaganda minister addressed a carefully selected, enthusiastic audience in a meticulously choreographed address at the Berlin Sportpalast (18 February 1943), the scene had already been set for the riotous reception of the new message of 'total war'.[23] Goebbels asked for the people's full commitment in total war, their unconditional loyalty to their leader, and painful but vital sacrifices in their everyday lives. He concluded,

> I ask you tenth and last: do you want, as the National Socialistic party program requires it, that in the war equal rights and equal duties predominate, that the Fatherland takes the heavy loads of the war with solidarity on its shoulders and that they are distributed in the same way, whatever the circumstances? I asked you; you gave your answer to me.[24]

In hindsight, this was the beginning of Goebbels's own bounce-back in the power structures of the NS state (see Ch. 2). His rise to undisputed prominence had been confirmed on 30 January 1943, when he gave the customary speech for the anniversary of the *Machtergreifung* in situ Hitler. Since then he had managed to elicit the Führer's unconditional support for all necessary measures in the direction of total mobilisation for war.[25] Now, his speech caught the attention of large sections of the German population, providing much needed psychological support and promise at the time of the gravest (that far) crisis in terms of both military fortunes and domestic morale.[26] His 'total war' was much more than a substandard diversionary trick – although it did perform this function as well, judging from the immediate impact of the Sportpalast speech on public opinion.[27] Instead, it was a carefully pitched concoction of negative sensationalism, raw realism and positive commitment.

Apparently, Hitler was generally pleased with the content of Goebbels's Sportpalast speech but did not like the fact that the 'total war' measures went further than he had personally authorised.[28] Party members – particularly 'old fighters' in the *Gaus* – reacted angrily to what they perceived as Goebbels's attempt to undercut their supreme authority in their regions. To allay their fears and once again flatter their ears the Führer invited Gauleiters to a special event on 24 February – a reminder to the Propaganda minister (who was also Gauleiter of Berlin) of their special position which they occupied in Hitler's state. Goebbels, aware of opposition to his measures from within the party, decided not to attend the meeting.[29] His instructions to his subordinates at the beginning of March showed considerable defiance – in spite of 'resistance', the 'total war' campaign should persevere.[30] But Hitler had already made a point: in the composition of the special committee for Total War he excluded Goebbels in the end, choosing instead the more accommodating solution of a Bormann–Lammers–Keitel triumvirate.[31]

Back on 12 February, the Propaganda minister had announced at the RMVP press conference his intention to launch a vehement anti-Bolshevik campaign through the German media inside the Reich and in the occupied territories.[32] On the face of it, the resort to the well-tried recipe of negative anti-Bolshevik integration (already rehearsed during 1942 with the staging of the 'Soviet Paradise' exhibition – see Ch. 3) contributed nothing new to the long-term discourse of NS propaganda. However, the timing was – and continued to be – highly appropriate. Already in the *Propagandaparolen* of 9 February the launching of the anti-Bolshevik campaign had been linked with the prepared 'total war' platform, which Goebbels had couched in terms of 'hardening measures' (*Verhärtungsmaßnahmen*). By then, the planned Sportpalast speech was only a few days away and the Propaganda minister was eager to 'move on' and refocus the attention to new themes.[33] In the following two weeks the anti-Bolshevik message was being constantly fine-tuned. The new slogan 'Victory or Bolshevik chaos' was unleashed by the RMVP in mid-February and appeared on the front page of almost every single newspaper and magazine, on numerous posters and banners, as well as in two specifically produced pamphlets that inundated bookshops and party offices across the Reich. The campaign endeavoured to cover every possible aspect: the impact of Soviet economic management on agriculture and trade, the housing situation, public health, working conditions, family and youth – all depicted in the bleakest possible way and juxtaposed to the situation in Germany.[34] The campaign also targeted people across Europe with the motto 'Europe wins with Germany or sinks into Bolshevik chaos'. No words of 'fear' were spared in the formulation of the stark message:

> [w]e fight Bolshevism as a destructive Jewish idea that, were it to reach its goal, would bring vast misery and the complete destruction of all cultural values. In short, it would bring chaos ... We are fighting a defensive war for the life and freedom of the German people, and ultimately for the other peoples of Europe as well ... One cannot speak of a transformation or change in Bolshevist practices ... [O]nly the German military is in a position to successfully resist the gigantic Bolshevist war machine ... Neither England nor America, nor any other power, can stop Europe from falling under Bolshevist control if the German military is defeated. They could not stop it, and would also not want to ... The wretched existence of millions of working people in the Soviet Union, the ruthless system of forced labour, and the horrible conditions in the forced labor camps speak clearly and make brutally clear what the fate of our working people would be.

The conclusion was unequivocal: 'this is a fight for life or death; ... we must be just as hard and determined in mobilizing everything for total war'.[35] Authorities were instructed to remind the public about the 'blood bath (caused by Bolshevism) in Spain, Latvia and Bessarabia', as a stark warning about the alleged brutality of Bolshevik occupation methods.[36] The campaign also concentrated on the idea that the war was a 'just' campaign that only Germany could fight on behalf of the whole of Europe against the Soviet threat, calling for the formation of a 'strong anti-Bolshevik European front'.[37]

Nevertheless Goebbels, encouraged by the positive reception of his 'total war' message,[38] continued his two-pronged strategy of optimistic realism with intense anti-Bolshevik alarmism throughout the spring. His utter cynicism is revealed in the instructions that he gave to the German press after the recapture of Rzhev by the Red Army at the beginning of March: not only did he instruct the media to acknowledge the evacuation (albeit presenting it as a planned operation), but he also encouraged them not to deny triumphalist Soviet declarations because they 'support our anti-Bolshevik campaign'.[39] A week later, the German recapture of the city of Kharkov[40] – at last, a victory! – was reported in a noticeably unobtrusive manner, even if Goebbels was on the verge of a perverse despair fearing that the improvement of the situation in the east seriously weakened the impact of both his anti-Bolshevik propaganda and the 'total war' discourse.[41] This explains his angry reaction to the release of a rather jubilant OKW communiqué immediately after the success at Kharkov[42] – the spectre of yet another repetition of the propaganda blunders of 1941 and 1942 was becoming an obsession for him and a constant warning to the German media.

The subversion of the regime's monopoly of truth

The conjuring up of the anti-Bolshevik theme in the context of 'total war' paid handsome dividends. Encouraged by the reported impact of the campaign on German society, the official NS propaganda discourse had been co-ordinated under the banner of negative anti-Soviet and anti-Jewish propaganda. And yet, in spite of the relative success of the 'total war' campaign and of the anti-Semitic, anti-Bolshevik and anti-plutocratic propaganda 'actions' of early 1943 in arresting the disintegration of German domestic morale,[43] Goebbels was in a seriously depressed mode himself by the end of spring. A revealing entry in his diaries evidence exasperation with the fading appeal of NS propaganda, the adverse military situation and the narrowing margins for manoeuvre:

> [s]ometimes I have the feeling that we are not taking the initiative as much as we should in this war. In the past five months, the enemy has assumed the upper hand almost everywhere. They are smashing us in the air war, and have opened severe wounds in the east, they trounced us in North Africa and even the U-boat war is not now bringing the successes which we had expected from it[44]

In the privacy of his own notebook pages the Propaganda minister could afford to be self-critical and at the same time reveal the serious structural deficiencies of the regime that he so loyally served. The anguish recorded in the above excerpt derived from both the factual situation (reverses in every front, intensified aerial bombardment) and the diminishing relevance of his diversionary discourses (e.g. the U-boat campaign, which NS propaganda had virtually exhausted since Stalingrad, in spite of its declining military impact). The enemy had 'assumed the upper hand' and divulged an acute sense of frustration with the inability of the NS regime to control the flow of information, to maintain its monopoly of truth, to manage reality in a way that effectively made the most of whatever successes and lessened the impact of setbacks.

Alarmingly for the NS regime, the critical distance between the military and home fronts was now being constantly eroded by a series of external events on which NS propaganda had little control. The credibility of the regime's official version of the 'truth' (its 'ersatz reality') suffered even further from the gradual emancipation of public opinion from the NS monopoly of information. Soldiers' reports from the front back to their families became a powerful alternative source of information for public. The new strategy of increased *realism* adopted by the RMVP involved a wholesale acknowledgement of the difficulties with which the Wehrmacht troops were faced in the eastern campaign. Thus, such reports (after a rigorous process of censorship) were considered as valuable assets in the preparation of the German population for the difficulties that lay ahead. However, as Goebbels acknowledged in July 1942, soldiers and 'realistic' news reports appeared to nurture a perverse sense of admiration that challenged the official 'truth' about Soviet underdevelopment, moral collapse and political bankruptcy.[45] A similar shift in German perceptions of the Slavs had already been taking place through the first-hand contact with Soviet POWs and Polish labourers in the Reich, again largely casting a doubt on the regime's racial stereotypes.[46] In September 1942, Goebbels registered his anxiety at this situation:

[a]ccording to reports from various parts of the Ruhr, workers from Soviet Russia and our own miners have been talking to each other at work about working conditions. The Russians, on some occasions, have referred to better working conditions in their country and are also talking about the better food which they used to have. The Minister regards such discussions as exceedingly dangerous and asks for suggestions on how this danger can be best countered.[47]

Clearly, increasingly larger sections of the German population were gaining access to alternative channels of information, uncontrollable by NS propaganda and contradictory to its intended message that supplied the raw material for its gradual emancipation from the official version of the 'truth'. In spite of the RMVP's 'hatred' campaign against the British pilots, their Luftwaffe counterparts did not hide their admiration on the basis of their own direct experiences.[48] Increasing contact with workers from Russia, Ukraine and other occupied areas had already challenged the stereotypical negative images that the regime had attempted to cultivate. Instead, a growing number of Germans had started registering their surprise at the workers' demeanour and nature. Alarmingly it was reported that foreign workers were 'sharing the table with German peasants' or that the (German) domestic servants ate together with them and were left with the most difficult tasks in the household. They would 'treat them as equals' and often choose to speak in the workers' language (particularly Polish in the eastern territories) in order to communicate with them.[49] Around the same time the RMVP authorities registered their concern with the conduct of Polish workers and the attitudes of the German population to them, calling for a stricter 'separation' (*Trennung*) between Germans and foreign labour.[50]

Rumours

Yet, the most eloquent evidence of this wider tendency of psychological emancipation came in the form of *rumours*[51] (*Gerüchte*), circulating in parallel to the regime's official propaganda output. The exact origins of those 'whispering campaigns' is difficult to ascertain. Prior to 1942, some of them had been deliberately initiated by the RMVP and party agencies, as a form of indirectly preparing public opinion for developments to come. For example, Goebbels himself appears to have been behind the dissemination of 'unofficial' information about the deterioration of German–Russian relations in early 1941 and an impending military action against the Soviet Union.[52] Only two weeks before the scheduled launch of 'Barbarossa', he had deliberately misled the German media by announcing plans for an alleged attack on Britain as the main strategic priority of the Reich.[53] In an article that he published in the *Völkischer Beobachter* in early June he maintained that the campaign in Crete was a dress-rehearsal for the invasion of the British Isles. That he subsequently organised the withdrawal of every single copy of the publication was calculated to project the impression of a gaffe, thereby focusing more attention on the revelation included in the article.[54] If this trick was perhaps too evident to stop the flow of speculations about the attack on Russia, the RMVP/RPL authorities were more successful in using 'word of mouth' (*Mundpropaganda*) to spread control ideas and rumours. To this effect, every single propaganda 'plan' or 'action' prepared during the war contained lengthy references to the content and timing of *Mundpropaganda*. In the majority of cases, however, rumours emanated either from the anxieties of the Germans themselves (in many cases a psychological doomsday reaction to the absence of 'official' information) or the counter-propaganda of the enemy – or a combination of both. As early as October 1940, immediately after the announcement of the 'postponement' of the attack on the British Isles, stories about an alleged terroristic campaign by the enemy spread panic, particularly in those areas affected by air raids. The anxiety was compounded by rumours of an impending biological attack on German cities.[55]

The volume and 'noise' of the whispering campaigns increased during the first 'crisis winter' of 1941/42, and spiralled out of control in subsequent years. The silence[56] of NS propaganda after the initial triumphalist reports about the advance to Moscow in December 1941 gave rise to two types of rumours. On the one hand, some continued to believe that the Soviet capital was on the verge of being occupied, allegedly 'opening their best bottle of champagne' in celebration;[57] on the other, many started realising that the noticeable toning down of the regime's propaganda output and references to adverse climatic conditions presaged defeat. A year later, with the battle for Stalingrad in full swing, similar tendencies were once again evident – only this time in a far more pronounced way. Nurtured by irresponsible declarations about the allegedly imminent fall of the city (see Ch. 5), during the autumn of 1942 rumours began to circulate maintaining that the campaign was all but finished. As NS propaganda entered yet another period of silence and awkward diversion from developments on the eastern front, such whispering campaigns continued to gather momentum. In December the prevailing public mood of depression and pessimism nurtured new stories (this time not far from the truth) about the VIth Army's desperate position in Stalingrad. By the time that the regime authorities announced the encirclement of the German forces and alluded to the impending catastrophe, many people already seemed convinced that the battle was all but over. Then, in spring 1943 another embarrassing spell of propaganda silence regarding operations in north Africa set off a fresh wave of wild scenarios, this time involving stories about Franco's alleged siding with the western Allies or Rommel's arrest by the British,[58] his departure from the front, his alleged ill health and the certainty of an imminent calamity.[59]

Clearly, there was a psychological pattern behind the appearance of rumours that associated low levels of official propaganda 'noise' with adverse developments and complications which the regime was attempting to hide from the public. The conspicuous absence of Hitler from the public eye nurtured similar rumours about his health (he was believed to be in a sanatorium, having suffered a serious nervous breakdown[60]) or about an alleged coup d'etat inside the party. When the historic northern port city of Lübeck was hit by a destructive air raid in late March 1942, the customary early tendency of NS propaganda to make light of the inflicted damages resulted in a credibility gap that nurtured wild rumours: people talked of more than 7,000 dead and 70,000 injured. Belatedly, the RMVP issued instructions to counter such allegations, correcting the figures to 198 and 680 respectively.[61] Fears about a further escalation of the air raid campaign against German cities encouraged wild reports about a fresh wave of ferocious attacks on areas that had not yet been affected, unless the Reich surrendered.[62] Then, the Propaganda minister's inflammatory references to 'revenge' and 'miracle weapons' in June 1943 produced wild hopes and resulted in a barrage of outrageous rumours (see Ch. 7). Blending delusion with fairly accurate reports about scientific breakthroughs in the field of military technology, many started talking of a new type of bomb with devastating potential, of Luftwaffe planes with revolutionary design and destructive capabilities, as well as of Hitler's reluctant decision to authorise the obliteration of London and other British cities.[63]

The RMVP spent considerable time and energy in either arresting the uncontrollable dynamics of its own whispering campaigns or countering them. Goebbels condemned 'defeatist counter-propaganda' and the irresponsible dissemination of pessimistic rumours[64] for unwittingly fostering the disintegration of public *Stimmung*. In December 1942, Martin Bormann, head of Hitler's chancellery since Rudolf Hess' flight to Scotland, had issued a directive – with the explicit approval of both Hitler and Goebbels – threatening those responsible for the spreading of alarmist reports with severe reprisals.[65] After the Stalingrad debacle the RMVP attempted to conceal from the German media and the people a series of military developments before they had reached unequivocal conclusions. 'Operation Citadel', undertaken early in the summer of 1943, had been kept secret from the public, in fear that it might once again incite illusory expectations and produce a fresh wave of rumours. Judging from previous experience, however, the German public came to interpret (consciously or psychologically) the sudden abandonment of a theme by NS propaganda as an oblique admission of defeat or at least of grave, unforeseen complications; the phrase 'planned evacuation' (increasingly used in 1943/44 in official military reports) as coterminous with reversal and retreat; praises to the 'heroism' and 'loyalty' of the soldiers as a metaphor for impending collapse with heavy losses.[66] The monotonous repetition of the same justification, the same emplotment, the same diversion caused negative reactions amongst the German public that ranged from disbelief to outright mockery. The office of the SD chief, Otto Ohlendorf, had warned about the increasing resistance of the domestic audience to the press and radio output controlled by the regime – a resistance that reached the point of incredulity and conscious evasion in the last two stages of the war.[67] Yet for Goebbels, NS propaganda had become an almost personal enterprise by then. In this respect, his continued irritation with the SD 'public opinion' reports – whose often critical tenor about the effectiveness of propaganda, he considered highly suspicious – can be better understood as a reaction to what he perceived as a *personal* criticism of his primary role in the domain of propaganda and a challenge to his desired total authority.

Enemy counter-propaganda

As if internal disagreements, administrative wrangles and waning impact were not enough, NS propaganda had to deal with another challenge to its 'monopoly of truth'. Information supplied by enemy sources at times of war is a constant concern of all belligerent states, as it is unpredictable, uncontrollable and difficult to arrest – and the NS authorities had resorted extensively to this practice in the first years of the war.[68] Of course, the regime had a de facto advantage compared to its enemies. The totalitarian structures of its information functions, the strict censorship imposed on any form of news, its 'chiliastic' claim to represent the only genuine version of 'truth' – all made the infiltration of German society with counter-propaganda significantly more difficult and (in theory) ineffective than the process of disinformation carried out by the Reich authorities vis-à-vis its opponents.[69] Yet, after the failure of the Luftwaffe to force a British surrender and the abandonment of the invasion plans in the autumn of 1940, British authorities engaged more constructively and systematically with the medium of supplying 'news' directly to the German audience, thereby de facto challenging the NS regime's monopoly of information. By that time official British broadcasts, primarily by the BBC, had already established an enviable reputation for credibility and accuracy, even amongst the Germans.[70] This proved an invaluable long-term investment for, in the aftermath of the first NS propaganda fiascos in 1942, more and more listeners inside the Reich chose to complement their daily diet of NS-controlled information with an increasing dosage of external reports. The more the regime's authorities tightened the loop of legal prohibition and direct terror vis-à-vis those still defying the 1939 ban on listening to foreign broadcasts, the more perversely appealing these became – and this appeal continued to rise as a result of the public opinion's estrangement with the German media.[71]

Apart from exposing the distortion or obstruction of information by the German authorities (such as in the case of the fall of Tobruk in the autumn of 1942), foreign sources undermined Goebbels's more cautious attitude to reporting after Stalingrad. The Propaganda minister repeatedly expressed his scepticism about the motives that induced foreign centres of information to depict their own military fortunes in a bleak, unflattering way, urging his own subordinates to treat such material with restraint and extreme care.[72] His attempt to play down the German success at Kharkov in the spring of 1943 was undermined by the publicisation of the event by foreign media.[73] Undoubtedly, he was meticulously systematic in dealing with enemy counter-propaganda and in deciding which material would be allowed for publication, which would be countered by the NS authorities, which would be commented upon and how, as well as which reports will remained unanswered or concealed. He instructed the RMVP to avoid any comment on enemy reports about the progress of the operations in the east during the spring of 1943 and suppressed the circulation of pessimistic propaganda launched by western media during the 1943 Wehrmacht offensive in the east.[74] But he stepped in to counter popular rumours about the future demeanour of the Bolsheviks in the immediate aftermath of Stalingrad. In order to shatter beliefs that the Bolsheviks 'had changed', that they would 'hang only the Nazis' ('*aufgehängt werden ja nur die Nazis*') and that the Germans treat foreign workers badly with meticulous counter-propaganda, Goebbels launched a concerted counter-propaganda campaign that left no space for illusions, either about the conditions that Germans could expect in the event of a Soviet victory or about the way in which both party and society would be held responsible for the Third Reich's record.[75] He was also extremely eager to deny rumours about impending air raids as they tended to raise public anxiety to paralysing levels and thus affect the morale and attitude of the population.[76]

However, the volatile nature of rumours – and the systematic use of this weapon by the British and the Americans – proved impossible to counter. From the first moment, the RAF organised air campaigns with the sole task of dropping leaflets for the German civilian population. These campaigns intensified after 1941 and, especially, with the entry of the USA into the war.

By 1944, the combined volume of leaflets released by American and British planes over NS-occupied areas had exceeded the 300 million mark (almost half of which fell inside the boundaries of the pre-war Reich).[77] Apart from civilians, the Allied planes started to target soldiers on the frontline, directly firing boxes of printed material on them that was intended to either demoralise them directly or induce them to surrender in return for freedom before facing an allegedly certain death.[78] Such leaflets often sparked off the intended rumours about the enemy and at least raised internal doubts in many soldiers about the prospects and chances of their continuing efforts.

By the time that the leaflet counter-propaganda was reaching its peak, radio broadcasts from enemy sources had already made lasting inroads into the German audience. An increasing number of people defied the wartime legal prohibition and tuned either to official enemy stations (primarily the BBC) or to clandestine programmes – some of which made no secret of its enemy sources but other purporting to be representing German interests and located inside the Reich. The British political warfare executive alone was responsible for an extensive and constantly growing network of such stations across NS-occupied Europe.[79] The issue of reliability was of paramount importance here, because unsolicited and unattributed information suffered from a de facto credibility gap.[80] Therefore, these stations usually mixed accurate, officially endorsed information with unsubstantiated rumours and conscious disinformation.

How many people tuned to every single station at any time, listened to specific broadcasts and internalised specific pieces of 'information' is again impossible to determine. However, there seems to have been an increasing correlation between the false reports provided by at least some of these stations and the rumours that seized German public opinion during the war. For example, the story of an alleged pact between the NS and the British governments about sparing Berlin and London from further bombardment (see above) had fared prominently in the news disseminated by the *Gustav Siegfried Eins* clandestine station.[81] The huge popularity of the station with Germans had resulted from the carefully cultivated impression that it was based in Germany and somehow represented the voice of the traditional German military that had become disaffected with the NS regime. It was perhaps this station, as well as counter-propaganda from other similar sources, that bolstered the impression amongst Germans in December 1941 that the dismissal of General von Brauchitsch from the command of the armed forces (allegedly a resignation on grounds of ill-health) constituted evidence of a serious rift between Hitler and the military. This was a rumour that persisted throughout the winter of 1941/42 and resurfaced many times in subsequent years, in spite of Goebbels's desperate efforts to either suppress or counter it. Other rumours, such as the ones about the spreading of diseases from British forces, the devastation caused by Allied air raids to German cities that the NS regime had allegedly concealed, even those about Hitler's (physical or mental) health, were at least fostered by clandestine radio broadcasts. In this sense, by far the most important contribution of enemy counter-propaganda in general was to find ways of by-passing the totalitarian NS control over information, make inroads into German society and deconstruct the impression that the regime's propaganda represented *the* (or even *a*) truth.

By comparison to the British counter-propaganda, the Soviet output in this field was almost non-existent until the launch of 'Barbarossa' and remained rather limited in influence until after the Stalingrad. This had a lot to do with the general negative impression that most Germans held for the Soviet Union and its leadership – the result of more than two decades of vilification by the west and a few years of steep indoctrination in NS disdain of communism, denigration of the Slavs' 'racial stock' and defamation of Bolshevism. Thus, whilst many Germans felt justified in listening to western broadcasts even from the outset of the war, the majority experienced an instinctive contempt for the Soviet equivalent yield until well into 1942. Although Goebbels's instructions to the German media throughout the summer 1942 offensive and the battle for Stalingrad manifested a growing concern for the potential inroads that the Soviet propaganda was capable of making into German society, it remained a lesser concern, at least in comparison to the British and American counter-information campaigns.

The situation changed dramatically in the spring of 1943. The establishment of the National Committee of Free Germany [*Nationalkomitee Freies Deutschland* (NKFD)] in July succeeded in bringing together a number of exiled former communist leaders from the Reich under the supervision of the Soviet security services.[82] At the same time, the large pool of German prisoners of war provided distinguished figures (amongst them Generals von Seydlitz and, later, the commander of the VIth Army in Stalingrad, von Paulus) to another counter-propaganda institution, the German Officers League [*Bund Deutscher Offiziere* (BDO)], that was set up in September 1943.[83] Independently or in joint enterprises, these two organisations became particularly active in the last two years of the conflict in the direction of appealing directly to the German soldiers, couching their plea in the vocabulary of 'national interest' rather than communist international solidarity. In parallel, NKFD agents inside the Reich played a crucial role in disseminating material intended to challenge the NS regime's monopoly of information, reveal the false promises made to the German people by their leadership in the past and underline the dangers that loomed for Germany if Hitler remained in power and the war continued. Loudspeakers directed at the German troops on the frontline, underground cells operating in tandem with local oppositional groups in different environments (factories, *Volkssturm* groups), clandestine broadcasts and sometimes even direct interferences in the scheduled programme of the German radio – all these methods and activities were systematically employed in the context of a parallel psychological war directed at the increasingly disheartened German people during 1943–45.

It is difficult to underestimate the psychological significance of this cumulative counter-propaganda activity, conducted by both the enemies of the Reich and the small oppositional groups that operated inside the country. One is perfectly justified, however, to ask whether, beyond the psychological gains for the anti-fascist coalition, this sort of activity succeeded in its primary function: to expedite victory, shorten war and weaken the 'staying power' of the enemy. In practical terms, whilst counter-propaganda demolished the NS regime's monopoly of truth and eroded its psychological hegemony over the German volk, it conspicuously failed to induce either the soldiers or the civilians to *act* against their own increasingly unpopular government. This may be construed as evidence that National Socialism had in fact been particularly successful in fostering the forces of *negative integration* within the German collective consciousness. As late as in April 1945, with the final devastating collapse in clear sight, the Wehrmacht or *Volkssturm* fighters remained largely committed to their ascribed tasks[84] – and even when this sense of duty to protect their Vaterland (because it is impossible to detect any widespread eagerness to stand firm guardians of National Socialism in their reactions[85]) diminished in the face of overwhelming enemy forces, it was statistically far more likely to do so against the advancing western forces than the Red Army. As the commander of one of the corps trapped inside the Korsun/Kiev pocket during the winter 1944 Soviet offensive noted in his diary, the NKFD's attempts to convince German soldiers to defect in light of their unequivocally desperate position, were to him incomprehensible – and they must have been to the soldiers too, judging from the conspicuous absence of even a single case of desertion.[86] The NS regime might have lost its potential to generate positive allegiance to its overall vision by 1943, but it certainly had not been shorn of its mechanisms for negative integration and psychological control.

The 'Hitler-cult': staying power and disintegration

With public morale (*Stimmung*) showing no signs of durable recovery in 1943–44 and the party's standing in free fall,[87] the regime's propaganda ammunition appeared ineffectual and depleted. In such grave circumstances only the more systematic management of the 'Hitler-cult' could provide some desperately needed compensation for the failures and blows of the preceding months. Goebbels used the occasion of Hitler's fifty-third birthday in April 1942 to praise his leader's unrivalled qualities in order to divert attention from actual developments in the battlefield to the superiority of the Reich's leadership.[88] Years of highly successful propaganda had transformed the image of the Führer into an emotional superstructure of loyalty that had been on the whole insulated from the everyday regime record, at home or abroad – and Goebbels had sought full credit for this achievement as early as 1941.[89] The peak of the 'Hitler cult' in 1940 – and to some extent in 1941 – was also due to the ability of NS propaganda to credit military victories to Hitler's alleged 'genius' as a political and military leader, thus building on the existing grand narrative of his putative infallibility.[90] Even if this was obviously not possible after 1941, it was still believed by the RMVP that the psychological basis of popular allegiance to the leadership remained largely in place, as a powerful weapon for the recovery of public morale in times of crisis.

Of course, Hitler's image had already come under pressure in the second half of 1941, as a result of both the adverse situation in the east and the complications arising out of the T–4 ('euthanasia') campaign within the Reich. The unprecedented public criticism of the regime (and, implicitly, of its leadership) amongst the Catholic constituency in the summer of 1941 with regard to the disclosure of the systematic extermination of asylum patients underlined the importance of an effective propaganda damage-limitation exercise in order to salvage Hitler's reputation, even at the expense of a policy that had been directly (and secretly) authorised by him almost two years earlier.[91] At the same time, in order to justify the failure of the Blitz in the east, Hitler himself sought recourse to the argument of the generals' 'betrayal'. Press and radio managers were explicitly instructed by Goebbels to avoid excessive triumphalism with regard to the alleged achievements of the Wehrmacht officials in the eastern front, obviously because such a discourse would undermine the efforts to praise Hitler's abilities as a warlord. In public, of course, criticism of the military staff had to be avoided or carefully disguised in order to avoid the impression that the German Volk was being let down by its allegedly superior military leadership. Yet, after the dismissal of General Werner von Brauchitsch and the assumption of supreme command of the Wehrmacht by the Führer in December 1941, it was difficult to continue to shield the NS leadership from criticisms about the slowing down of the advances in Russia and the subsequent failures of the 'winter crisis'. Increasingly after January 1942, NS propaganda combined the discourse of external circumstances ('[last winter was] harder than it has been in central and eastern Europe for the past 140 years'[92]) with the argument about Hitler's achievement of stabilising the front in immensely adverse conditions in order to displace public attention from the shortcomings of the campaign to the allegedly unmitigated power of the Führer's strategic 'genius' (see Ch. 5).

This propaganda strategy of continually shielding the leader from responsibility for failures whilst bestowing upon him full credit for successes was extremely dangerous, especially in the light of the mounting military and domestic problems of 1942–43. Yet, it was clear to the RMVP that loyalty to Hitler remained by far the most potent force of psychological integration at a time when the popularity of the party and the regime as a whole was sinking to an unprecedented low. The German 'home front' appeared to possess a substantially lower threshold of exculpation with regard to the Führer than it did with regard to any other figure or aspect of National Socialism. The deep-seated belief that the leader was unaware of certain (disastrous) decisions taken by the NS authorities was further strengthened during 1942 by the impression that his (justifiable) absence from the Reich and dedication to military matters had permitted other regime or party figures to embark upon extreme or unacceptable policies.[93] Thus, when in his speech to the Reichstag on 26 April 1942 he demanded from the country 'the authority to intervene immediately and take personal charge whenever unconditional attention is not paid to the service of great and vital tasks',[94] there was a widespread sense of public relief, reflecting a still dominant perception that Hitler was the utmost – if not the only – guarantee of success in the war and equality at home.[95] The fact that this decision amounted to a strengthening of the tyrannical and monomaniacal tendencies of the NS system – and the rumours to that effect released by British counter-propaganda in the aftermath of the speech[96] – remained a desperately low priority amongst a war-ravaged population. A few months later, in the end of September, Hitler was in even better form, strengthened by the military successes of the summer 1942 campaigns and still confident that the series of victories constituted an irreversible momentum for the Reich that would ensure the final victory.[97] In spite of their deeply entrenched fears and misgivings about the war, large sections of the German populations still appeared highly receptive to Hitler's propaganda message, at least in psychological terms.

However, there were also alarming signs that even the 'Hitler effect' was being gradually eroded. When the spectre of defeat, or at least the awareness of the hardships of a long drawn-out campaign, cast a grave shadow on the regime's credibility, the worsening military record and the aggravation of domestic problems effected a process of painful deconstruction of the 'Hitler cult'. The nucleus of the 'Hitler-cult' – the psychological power of the Führer's personality – was the regime's last centripetal element to disintegrate, and it wore away much slower than any other aspect, as the instinctive reactions of many Germans to their leader manifested as late as July 1944 – after the abortive assassination attempt (see Ch. 7).[98] But tangible evidence that Hitler had erred or even deceived the Volk gradually exposed him too to criticism about the regime's policies and actions. On the Heroes' Memorial Day (21 March 1943), Hitler resurfaced to give a vehemently anti-Semitic and anti-Bolshevik speech. The speech should have been a crucial boost to public morale, given that it was his first public appearance for four months; but it failed to make a real impact, not just because of his grossly inaccurate figures for the human losses in the war, but mainly because his resort to vague themes (Bolshevist threat, the Jewish conspiracy) were brushed aside by the population as desperate diversions.[99] Very few appeared to have believed his declaration in March 1943 that the number of 'casualties' in the whole war barely exceeded half a million men – in fact, throughout February the RMVP had stubbornly refused to make any announcements about losses during the Stalingrad battle.[100] Goebbels was 'dejected' at the delivery of the speech; Semmler went as far as describing it as 'pathetic'.[101] This was evidence of an extremely dangerous psychological pattern that had appeared for the first time in the aftermath of his September 1942 speech – namely, the public's psychological association of Hitler's speech with the expectation for the announcement of a decisive victory. On both these occasions (on September 1942 and even more so on March 1943) Hitler had very little to announce in this direction, beyond nebulous hopes and unsubstantiated optimism.

In fact, according to an SD report dated January 1943, the public was becoming distrustful of *any* propaganda material, to some extent even if this came from the Führer himself.[102] The realisation that the leader was politically culpable of erroneous judgement proved a much more traumatic conclusion for German society than the (generally assumed) ineptitude of the party or the regime.[103] It was becoming clear that the stereotypical image of the Führer in military uniform studying the map surrounded by his generals, popularised by the wartime newsreel, was no longer such a potent symbolic metaphor for the allegedly assured eventual victory.[104] By early 1944 opinion reports recorded growing references to a 'leadership crisis' (*Fuhrungskrise*) – for sometime a view privately corroborated by Goebbels himself, who did not shy away from implicating Hitler personally in this development.[105] Thus, the attrition of the 'Hitler cult's' psychological power, albeit slower than the collapse of the regime's legitimacy, expedited the process of popular disaffection with the NS management of the national cause and thwarted the regime's effort to use it as a psychological compensation for an increasingly bleak reality, both on the front and inside the Reich.

The withdrawal of Hitler – a new role for Goebbels?

The disintegration of the 'Hitler cult's' charismatic aura could only be aggravated by Hitler's self-imposed withdrawal from the public sphere. Confronted with a widening and essentially unbridgeable gap between his illusory vision and the grim reality, the Führer became more and more reclusive from 1941 onwards and then almost disappeared from the public scene in the last three years of the war. Contrary to the constant advice of his Propaganda minister, he avoided appearing in public or making official announcements, preferring instead the escape and psychological security offered by his Berghof retreat or the illusion of empowerment as warlord at the military headquarters. Apart from the generic psychological weight that he attributed to the Führer's public appearances from a propaganda viewpoint, Goebbels realised that the barrage of distressing news from all fronts and a drop in civilian morale in the spring and summer of 1943 rendered an appearance vital. Yet, Hitler simply prevaricated.[106] Goebbels's dejection is evident in his diary entries of that period;[107] his fear for the long-term consequences of this pattern even more so:

> [l]etters addressed to me from the public] are asking why the Führer does not visit the bombed areas ... and especially why the Führer does not talk to the German people and explain the present situation. I consider it very necessary for the Führer to do this ... One cannot neglect the people for too long ... If the people ever lost their will to resist and their faith in German leadership, the most serious crisis we ever faced would result.[108]

Hitler was in fact sandwiched between two very different strategies concerning the propaganda management of his public image at times of defeat and crisis. Goebbels demanded intensification of his direct communication with the people and continuity in the regime's propaganda strategy. But Hitler was shielded from the hassles of everyday government and decision-making by Martin Bormann – who, after Rudolf Hess' dramatic flight to Scotland in 1941, had assumed the de facto role of Hitler's guardian before his formal appointment as his private secretary (*Sekretär des Führers*) in April 1943. The goal of both strategies was effectively the same: to maintain the elevation of Hitler from the level of politics, to perpetuate his special position and disengage his role from the adverse effects of the regime's policies. Goebbels, however, held a more technical view of propaganda which reversed Hitler's rationale – Hitler *could* compensate for unsuccessful events with his communication becoming more important at times of crisis. By contrast, Bormann's protective attitude to Hitler matched the latter's conviction that his ability to communicate presupposed the regime's capacity for guaranteeing successful outcomes.

The distancing of Hitler from the German people reflected the triumph of the latter strategy, in spite of Goebbels's occasional successes in bringing Hitler out of his voluntary isolation.[109] Evidently, Bormann's approach to his leader's image intended to protect him from the adverse effects of reality whilst maintaining the impression that Hitler was indeed in charge and would soon deliver the appropriate solution to the predicament of the Reich. This strategy, however, could have the exactly opposite effect. On the one hand – as Goebbels himself acknowledged – it could also detach Hitler and his entourage from reality and thus prevent them from reaching accurate conclusions about the worsening military and domestic situation.[110] On the other hand, it could cultivate the impression of a dangerous power vacuum that underlined the failure of their leader and his declining grip on the handling of the regime's fortunes.[111]

Admittedly, however, the 'Hitler cult', though battered by the military defeats of 1943–45 and undermined by the leader's physical withdrawal from the public sphere, still maintained some of its psychological influence on the masses. The 'infallible' leader and 'invincible' warlord of 1941 had become a figure of superlative, even mythological qualities by 1944. But his almost complete withdrawal from 1943 onwards and his conscious evasion of appearing in public confronted Goebbels and the RMVP with a complex challenge: how to justify the Führer's detachment from the people whilst preserving his myth and strengthening the integrative function of his cult. Apart from appearing as the interface between the leader and the people as the former's official spokesperson, the Propaganda minister devised a series of techniques to rationalise Hitler's retreat and recast him as a figure of truly historic significance.[112]

The manipulation of historical analogy offered a further empowering escape to a depressed public. Since the production of the film *Der Größe König* (The Great King) in 1942 (see Ch. 8) a direct parallelism between Hitler and the Prussian king Frederick the Great was systematically disseminated in the regime's propaganda discourse.[113] Hitler clung to this historic parallelism until the very end, carefully extrapolating from the story evidence for the insuperable qualities of the German people that could overcome the numerical and strategic superiority of the enemy.[114] Even Goebbels used the same story to bolster the (sometimes faltering) morale of his leader by reading to him excerpts from Carlyle's history of Frederick the Great.[115] That this was not simply a war for Germany alone but also for the whole of 'Europe', its civilisation and historical legacy, was evident from the analogy with the medieval struggle against Attila the Hun, to which Hitler referred in his last address to the German nation in February 1945.[116] His increasingly frequent references to 'divine providence', his reminder to the people that his prophetic declarations in the past had been corroborated by subsequent events and his claim that he stood as the guardian of history – the history of the German nation and of the 'civilised' world in general – as very few others had done before him, attested to the transformation of his (self-) image into a transcendental symbol of historic destiny. In the last months – and in spite of ephemeral rushes of groundless optimism – he appeared to seek refuge in another historical analogy with a bleaker message: as he stressed to Martin Bormann,

> [t]hink of Leonidas and his three hundred Spartans. In any case it does not suit our style to allow ourselves to be slaughtered like sheep. They may exterminate us, but they will not be able to lead us to slaughter.[117]

At a time that the imagery of the 'Hitler cult' lapsed into a lethargic state, Goebbels strove to sustain the strength of the psychological pact between people and the Führer. His role changed dramatically after 1941: instead of being the legitimator of Hitler's policies and projector of his cult, now he was forced to actively devise his image, and to act as a constant reminder of an 'ideal Hitler' that no longer existed. Since his landmark 'Total War' speech in February 1943, the Propaganda minister had expended considerable time and effort to restore an instinctive form of public allegiance to the Führer and enforce the idea that he alone represented the common destiny (*Schicksal*) of the German Volk. Apart from maintaining the established pattern of his regular public engagements (the series of yearly speeches on the eve of the Führer's birthday, his weekly editorial in *Das Reich*, his New Year proclamations), he also became the most visible figure of the NS hierarchy, both on the national and the regional/local level of propaganda conduct.[118] He continued to tour the Reich as devastating Allied air raids intensified during 1942–43, extending beyond the initial focus on the Ruhr–Hamburg axis to Berlin, Frankfurt and other, previously less targeted areas, believing that '[t]he population must in no circumstances be given the impression that the Party is not equal to the tasks imposed by such heavy air raids'.[119] His visit to Cologne immediately after the devastating air raid in July 1943 was received enthusiastically from the population.[120] But he also endeavoured to reclaim the propaganda vacuum that had been created by Hitler's absence from the public scene by stressing the latter's exhaustive dedication to the conduct of the war ('the Führer is totally absorbed in his work during the war'[121]) and by defending the regime's more modest tenor after Stalingrad ('[t]he German government always has a good reason for its silence'[122]).

The rise of Goebbels in the public sphere in the last years of the war was largely the effect of a reactive effort to fill in the psychological fissure created by Hitler's self-imposed seclusion. In the end, however – and in spite of his frenetic activity and determination to sustain the regime's propaganda noise – he could offer no adequate psychological counterweight to the waning of the 'Hitler cult' and to the wider withdrawal of the leader's figure into a mythical, elusive realm of existence. His personal standing was essentially linked to that of the regime/party and not of his Führer. Furthermore, his credibility as propaganda manager had suffered a series of blows in previous years that had seriously weakened his appeal to the public, giving rise to a series of jokes about his tendency to over-promise and miserably under-deliver.[123] To make things worse, he was largely mistrusted or even loathed by powerful party factions, who resented his renewed bid for power and his expanding power base within the NS administrative chaos in the last two years of the war.[124]

By contrast, and in spite of his ever-increasing detachment and his degenerating health, Hitler remained an extremely potent communicator until the bitter end. Even his 1 January 1945 address to the German people was 'extraordinarily well received', causing widespread 'joy' amongst the listeners. Apparently, even after such 'a long period of silence', a short speech by the Führer was enough to 'make all rumours and doubts disappear with a bang'. As reports noted, the content mattered little; it was the mere fact that Hitler had spoken again directly to the people that could still generate an 'unprecedented joyful mood' (*feierliche Stimmung*).[125] Although for a long time he had been talking about the 'ultimate sacrifice', even in the bleakest hours of the Reich towards the end of April 1945, he was desperately clinging to the hope of one victory. On 20–21 April he ordered a last-ditch concerted move of all remaining forces under the command of SS Obergruppenführer, Felix Steiner, in order to repel the Red Army forces that were in the outskirts of Berlin. When, however, confirmation that the counter-offensive had never taken place reached the bunker the next afternoon, Hitler unleashed his last diatribe against almost everyone outside his own 'inner circle'. The explicit content of his monologue encapsulated all the themes of his private discourses since 1943: the 'betrayal' of the generals, the 'deception' of his advisors, the cowardice of the people and of the whole world.[126] A profound sense of futility for his own struggle was made even more devastating by what he now openly described as 'a nation so inconstant, so erratic', a nation that he would have needed another 'twenty years' to shape effectively and imbue with unwavering NS values.[127]

7
The Winding Road to Defeat: The Propaganda of Diversion and Negative Integration

NS propaganda from consensus to negative integration

As the Third Reich was entering its own Decameron of total collapse in the end of April 1945, Goebbels's speech on Hitler's fifty-sixth birthday articulated the familiar core themes, if in a gloomier overall tone: Germany, 'the most shining culture', would lead 'Europe and the civilised world' against the 'forces of hate and destruction'; the Führer is fighting a war of 'divine providence'; the national community 'will not desert its Führer or the Führer desert his people'; the 'perverse coalition of plutocracy and Bolshevism' – a coalition that would drown 'humanity in a sea of blood and tears' – 'is collapsing'.[1] Such continuity of discourse patterns, however, conceals the fundamental revision of the overall objectives pursued by NS propaganda in the last three years of the war. The last phase (spring 1943–spring 1945) was marked by a dual switch: from 'positive' to 'negative' integration themes (see Ch. 3); and from long-term generic to short-term situation-specific discourses, dictated by external, uncontrollable developments in the military domain. Whilst short-term justification and diversion served the purpose of propping up the population's *Stimmung* in the face of mounting adversities, 'negative' grand narratives (see Ch. 3) were directed at the *Haltung* (overall demeanour), ensuring that the Germans would fight until the end – not necessarily enthusiastically or as an act of devotion to National Socialism per se, but at least as a defensive reaction to what they perceived as infinitely worse and discredited alternatives.

The transformation of NS propaganda into a mechanism of fostering *negative* integration amongst the German population had tremendous repercussions for the articulation of its core ideological themes. As Goebbels had repeatedly stressed, propaganda should always perform a synchronised function of diminishing and reinforcing anxiety amongst the population.[2]

With the reversal of fortunes in the military field and the disintegration of public morale after 1942, it became crucial for the task of public negative integration to promote a mobilising explicit but not paralysing imagery of 'anxiety'. In the short term, however, the need to justify failures or displace apprehension resulted in a series of ad hoc discourses that attempted to lift the morale and recapture the attention of the population. Things could have turned out differently for the regime had Stalingrad and the new 'crisis winter' of 1942/43 been followed by yet another summer offensive with impressive (rather than ephemeral) gains, as had been the case in 1942 and was indeed widely anticipated in the first half of 1943.[3] Goebbels was perfectly aware of the desperate need for 'a victory somewhere';[4] instead, a constant stream of setbacks forced the regime to operate largely on a day-to-day basis defined by enemy advances and German retreats rather than the desired other way round.

In search for 'victory'

The responses to the post-Stalingrad array of calamities indicate the extent to which NS propaganda had been forced on the defensive and largely lost the initiative. Perhaps the only relatively positive short-term diversion that it could still muster in 1943 was the U-boat campaign in the Atlantic. During the period of 'silence' about the Stalingrad battle, Hitler had proudly declared that until the final months of 1942 the U-boat fleet had sunk more than twice as much enemy ship capacity than in the whole of the First World War – and it seems that the public found some consolation in these news amidst an atmosphere of general gloom about the eastern and the African fronts.[5] Figures still looked impressive on paper – as Rudolf Scharping claimed in his weekly radio commentary, the destruction of the equivalent of 12 million tonnes of shipping that the German U-boats inflicted on the Allies in 1942 represented a 'higher tonnage figure than what the USA and England could build during the same year'.[6] 1942, however, was different from 1943. Already, by the time that Scharping was playing the U-boat card as diversion, he must have been aware of the diminishing effectiveness of the campaign and the consequent drop in tonnage figures. The more careful Hans Fritzsche often alluded to this gradual change (and, significantly, he demonstrated an increasing reluctance to invoke the submarine theme in his radio commentaries during 1943), resorting instead to vague predictions for the future: that, as Goebbels himself had claimed, 'Britain will be brought to her knees as a result of the German U-boats' and that 'the destruction of (enemy) tonnage is twice as high as in the previous world war'.[7] In his second Berlin Sportpalast speech in June 1943 Goebbels resorted to the same tested imagery of an unbeatable U-boat fleet wrecking havoc throughout the Atlantic. In spite of confidential alarming indications that the submarine fleet effectiveness had passed its peak by that time, the Propaganda minister performed a delicate balancing act:

> [t]he English are using the air war against us. We are using submarines against them. The results of the air war are more visible, but the submarine campaign is more important to the war in the long run, since its wounds are deeper. Through May of this year, 26.5 million BRT of enemy shipping have been sunk by the German navy and Luftwaffe. The significance of that figure is clear when one remembers that German submarine warfare nearly brought England to the ground in 1917 and 1918 while sinking only about 12 million BRT.[8]

The plausibility and psychological power of this claim lay in a meticulous long-term marketing of the U-boat product by NS propaganda. Associated with images of high modernity, German technological superiority and strategic excellence, the U-boat theme had received a spectacular makeover with the promotion of Karl Dönitz to the position of grand admiral in 1943. That German public opinion was still clutching to the hope that submarine warfare would make a significant impact on the conduct of the war is evident by SD reports during the spring and summer of 1943.[9] NS propaganda chose not to spare any words with regard to the damaging effect of the intensifying Allied air raids over the Reich; but, as Goebbels clearly asserted in his speech quoted above, the 'terror air attacks' and the U-boat campaign were linked, the latter as the allegedly most effective retaliation for the former. Fritzsche went even further, claiming that the intensification of the British and American air attacks was a desperate attempt to compensate for the failure of the Soviet land operations in the east.[10] But a dissection of Goebbels's subsequent speeches reveals a carefully disguised realisation that the war in the Atlantic was not going according to plan anymore. In July, he wrote that,

> [a]lso what concerns the air- and the U-boat war, restraint in the news policy at this moment is the uppermost consideration. It needs no stressing that, as far as German warfare is concerned, everything possible is done *to make us active* again on these both theatres of war. If nothing is said publicly about these matters, then there is a good reason for it; however, it does not mean that we would have nothing to say about it. We do not speak about it, so as not to allow the enemy to appraise the coming developments. Nevertheless, nobody should believe that only the government did not know what today every child knows.[11] (emphasis added)

In spite of encouraging comments during the first half of 1943, the much anticipated U-boat autumn offensive never materialised; instead, a depressing awareness that the American and British convoys had found ways to deal with the threat of submarine warfare had seized German public opinion long before the regime was forced to tone down its triumphalist diversionary use of the U-boat theme.[12]

The worsening of the military situation from 1943 onwards forced the regime to make constant use of short-term diversionary propaganda. In April the discovery of a mass grave near Katyn in Poland, where the bodies of thousands of murdered Polish officers had been buried, provided him with an excellent opportunity to maintain the noise of his anti-Bolshevik campaign.[13] At the beginning of May, he attempted to capitalise on this evidence of Bolshevik 'brutality' and to give a new lease of life to his anti-Soviet propaganda campaign:

> [t]he fact that a member from the opposing alliance [the Soviets] takes away 12,000 officers, the blossom of his army, and shoots them in the neck, in the forest of Katyn appears not be a suitable situation to cause a deeper tear to the coalition of our adversaries; it is looked merely upon as a small accident which does no harm to [their] common love. Those in the Kremlin do not show the slightest inclination to blush in the face of such accusations; on the contrary, they turn the tables and take up swiftly and deceitfully the role of the accuser.[14]

The discovery of the Katyn mass graves in April was greeted with a mixture of enthusiasm and relief by NS propagandists, as it offered a perfect distraction from the imminent loss of North Africa whilst being perfectly aligned with the 1943 anti-Bolshevik campaign.[15] But Goebbels bemoaned the timid exploitation of this propaganda opportunity by the regime's media. Contrary to his earlier optimistic expectations that Katyn would be paraded by German media for weeks, the story ran aground within a few days, disappearing into the inside pages of newspapers and sidelined in radio commentaries. Irritatingly, the military censors exercised their primary powers in the production of the newsreel by removing footage concerning the discovery of the Katyn mass graves from the final version of the Wochenschau, fearing that such images would upset the families of soldiers. Goebbels privately vented his frustration at what he considered as a waste of an excellent propaganda opportunity but had to acquiesce.[16] This was yet another cautionary tale of the limits of centralisation in the NS propaganda domain, even at a time that the 'Goebbels network' had recovered much of its previously lost ground and no longer faced any real internal competition.

By May, things had taken a bad turn once again: the long-anticipated loss of Tunis (and, with it, of the whole of North Africa) threatened to generate a 'second Stalingrad' mood, in spite of Goebbels's explicit ban on making this sort of linguistic parallelism in the German media. The regime's handling of this new crisis was relatively effective and timely. The replacement of General Rommel with Hans–Jürgen von Arnim in March was intended to shield the former's standing with the German Volk and send the first veiled signs to public opinion that this had become a 'battle over [already] lost possessions'.[17] To counter these psychological tendencies on 13 May, Goebbels outlined the regime's propaganda strategy, aimed at both providing short-term relief and a more positive long-term message. Rather like in the case of Stalingrad, the Propaganda minister praised the 'sacrifice' and 'heroism' of the Axis troops, fighting a brave war against numerically superior enemy forces. However, instead of reiterating the same hollow eulogy on gallantry and valour that had accompanied the announcement of the VIth Army's destruction, he emploted this new sacrifice in a far more positive way: by allowing crucial time for the completion of the continental defence shield ('Fortress Europe') the Wehrmacht had thwarted the Allied plans for a 'second front' in Europe (a direct reference to the Roosevelt–Churchill communiqué in Casablanca a few months earlier). As Goebbels himself stressed, 'Tunis was just a minor skirmish' compared to what awaited the enemy if an Allied invasion of Europe was attempted.[18]

The hollowness of these claims became evident only a few weeks later with the Allied landing on Sicily in June 1943. The initial tenor of NS propaganda was once again defiant, largely fuelled by exaggerated OKW reports and the intervention of the Reich press chief, Otto Dietrich. Soon, however, the failure of Italian defences proved highly embarrassing for the authorities in Berlin, especially after all the propaganda efforts that they had expended in buttressing the wounded prestige of Fascist Italy in the eyes of the German population after the evacuation of north Africa. Clearly the failure of the Italian defences in Pantelleria (the first target of the Allied invasion; 'a small Italian island off the north African coast', as Fritzsche presented it in an attempt to play down the strategic significance of its capture by the enemy[19]) was awkward enough, especially since the Wehrmacht reports had taken up Mussolini's guarantees about the island's alleged impregnability at face value. Throughout July there were upbeat reports about an alleged 'stabilisation' of the front in Sicily, where German forces were reported to have inflicted serious casualties on Allied troops.[20] In August, however, an equally embarrassing propaganda U-turn was deemed necessary in the light of the evacuation of all Axis troops from Sicily. This development came at the worst possible time for NS propaganda authorities, who were intent on diverting attention from operations in the east and choosing instead to focus attention of the Sicilian front. The loss of Sicily was presented in terms of a clever strategic ploy, orchestrated by General Hans–Valentin Hube with a dexterity that surpassed – as was argued – the clearing of the British troops in Dunkirk three years earlier.[21] What was even more awkward for the regime's propagandists was the attempt to justify the evacuation in the light of previous comments about defending 'Fortress Europe'.

Goebbels showed little inclination to conceal the gravity of the situation, given the superiority of enemy forces in south Italy. He did not spare any words in outlining to the German people how 'decisive' this phase of the war actually was, in light of the constant reverses in the east and in the south.[22] However, neither he, nor anyone in the regime's leadership had expected the dramatic developments surrounding Italy in July–August 1943. The collapse of the Mussolini regime after the dramatic Fascist Grand Council meeting of 24/25 July, the subsequent arrest of the Duce and his replacement by Marshall Pietro Badoglio surpassed even the most pessimistic predictions of the NS leadership.[23] For the best part of two months, NS propaganda fell into an embarrassing silence about the events in Italy, eloquently reflecting the state of disarray that Mussolini's fall had caused in Berlin. Apart from issuing a rather laconic communiqué attributing the removal of the Duce from power to ill health, and a reiteration of Badoglio's initial pledge to honour his commitment to Italy's Axis partner, there was a virtual lacuna in the regime's propaganda output that nurtured rumours and depressed public mood even further.[24] Fritzsche made a brief reference to the situation in late July and then simply reiterated his boss's blanket justification – that the situation was in a constant flux and, therefore, any predictions would be irresponsible.[25] Many Germans openly spoke of 'betrayal' long before Goebbels used the word (in mid-September) and noted how the instability of Italian Fascism compared unfavourably to the alleged solidity and efficacy of National Socialism.[26]

That the Italians as people and the Fascist regime (excluding to an extent Mussolini) were denigrated by the German population was nothing new; ever since the Duce's abortive Balkan and north African expeditions in 1940/41[27] there had been a widespread mistrust, or even derision, of the Italian people. Many had also blamed the Italian troops' low fighting power for the adverse developments in north Africa in early 1943. Even during the fight over Sicily, NS propaganda had attempted to shore up a modicum of sympathy for the Italians, for example, by presenting their soldiers as 'bravely fighting alongside their German colleagues'.[28] Distrust towards the Italians, however, ran much deeper than the regime's propaganda could ever reach. Very few people believed Badoglio's assurances that he would continue to fight the Axis war; Italy's final 'betrayal' was considered an irreversible certainty for the near future. The gap caused by the regime's propaganda deficit nurtured apocalyptic scenarios shared by many Germans: that the Italian front would collapse instantly, that the Allies would proceed to the Alps and from there wreck havoc on south Germany, that the endless Soviet reserves would annihilate the Wehrmacht, and so on.[29]

In the end, with Badoglio's announcement of the Italian armistice on 8 September and his duplicity fully exposed, the regime decided to seize the initiative and provide its own assessment of the Italian situation. By that time, Mussolini had also been rescued from his Alpine confinement place by an astonishingly courageous SS commando operation headed by Otto Skorzeny. As the dust had finally settled on the Italian political landscape, Goebbels devoted his editorial in the 19 September *Das Reich* issue to a concerted damage-limitation exercise – not only with regard to the dramatic developments in Italy but also about the NS regime's embarrassing silence on this matter in the preceding weeks. The tenor of the message was predictably defiant: the 'Badoglio-clique' were little more than a gang of 'traitors', not to be confused with the alleged genuine commitment of the Italian people to the Axis cause; this unfortunate event would not weaken but strengthen German resolve to fight and win; and, above all, the timely German intervention spared the lives of thousands of Axis troops that would have otherwise been condemned to 'annihilation'. As for the regime's 'silence' in previous weeks, Goebbels invoked once again the principle of responsible information that could not have been sustained in the confusion that followed the 24/25 July Grand Council meeting:

> [t]he fact that there can be no reference to this [the collapse of the Fascist regime] needs probably of no further justification. It would have been possible naturally in the uncertain week – just like in any other – to speak to the general public, and just in this case there would be even more to be said about the problems of the war and the international political situation than on any other occasion. But concern for our national interests sealed our lips. What we could say, we did not want to say, and what we wanted to say, we could not say.[30]

The theme of 'betrayal' that saturated the Propaganda minister's article supplied an excellent opportunity for a significantly broader long-term emplotment of the events. Thus, the RVMP orchestrated a gigantic propaganda campaign against the new Italian regime, depicting the Badoglio 'traitor-clique' (*Verräterklique*) as mere pawns of the wider 'Jewish, Freemason and plutocratic' conspiracy against Germany.[31] The fate of the Italian people under the new regime was painted in the darkest possible colours, in an attempt to generate some sympathy for Germany's Axis ally and, perhaps more importantly, for the Italian workers who had been transferred to the Reich.[32] It was too late, however. The loss of any respect or even sympathy for the Italian people inside Germany led to a stream of derogatory comments about them in the German media throughout the following months. Hitler himself tried to arrest this trend; in one of his rare appearances in 1943 at the twentieth anniversary of the November 1923 putsch, he spoke passionately about the contribution of the Duce to the cause of regenerating Italy and Europe as a whole:

> I am happy that we have at least succeeded in freeing from the clutches of the most pitiful creatures of this otherwise so powerful era the man who himself has done everything, both to make his people great, strong and happy, and to allow it to participate in a historical conflict which will ultimately decide the fate and the culture of this continent.[33]

Whilst launching a bitter diatribe against the 'Badoglio–Savoy betrayal', Hitler was extremely sensitive to arresting the anti-Italian tendencies in NS propaganda and popular feeling. That he eventually failed to do so is indicated by the fact that in March 1944 he authorised Martin Bormann to prohibit any criticism of Italy in the German media or popular talk;[34] and even this proved insufficient to stop the public from denigrating the contribution of the Italians to the military and industrial effort of the Reich, going as far as saying that 'the Italians [workers] are not worth their food'.[35] But, overall, concerns about developments in Italy petered out rather swiftly by the end of 1943, overshadowed by other, significantly more serious and relevant – to the Germans – military developments. The further deterioration of the Wehrmacht's position on the eastern front, in conjunction with the intensification and geographic extension of Allied air raids over the Reich, reduced Italy to a distant, almost extraneous issue for the overwhelming majority of the Germans, in spite of the regime's effort to evince a sense of optimism about the apparent (yet short-lived) stabilisation of the front in the Italian peninsula. In this respect, the events surrounding Mussolini's removal from power and Badoglio's armistice proved little more than a temporary diversion from other, far more persistent and solemn propaganda matters.

Allied 'terror attacks' and 'retaliation' (*Vergeltung*)

By far the most serious concern for the civilian population – and challenge to the regime's efforts to sustain its '*ersatz* reality' – came from the direct experience of war that the German population was subjected to through the (escalating) Allied bombardment. The intensification of Allied air warfare on the Reich during 1942 and the inability of German air defences to counter the threat exposed the German population to a direct experience of war and became a crucial determinant of public *Stimmung* that the regime could not control. The initially limited and irregular nature of Allied bombardment created the conviction in the NS leadership that the military and propaganda threat should be neither concealed from the public nor exaggerated.[36] However, by the spring of 1942 it was clear that the air raids were becoming more consistent and destructive. Thus the regime employed a series of discourses to provide psychological support for the victims of the bombardments, ranging from promises of increased airplane production[37] to praise for the steadfast perseverance of the German population in the affected areas[38] and castigation of British/American 'barbarism'.[39]

April 1942 saw the first major Allied air raids in north Germany. The towns of Lübeck and Rostock suffered extensive damage from incendiary and explosive bombs – not only to their military installations (Heinkel airplane construction plant in Rostock) but also to a series of historic buildings of the medieval centre.[40] The initially exaggerated reports of the British press and the BBC about casualty figures filtered through Germany, echoed in rumours that were in wide circulation through April and May (see Ch. 5). In spite of a short respite in early May, Allied air warfare was resumed with terrible severity towards the end of the month.[41] On 30 May, it was the turn of Cologne to suffer the most massive and devastating air raid up to that point; when the thousand Allied planes left, almost 45,000 were homeless and a large part of the city centre lay in ruins.[42] Immediately after the attack, the RMVP authorised the publication of an account of the British 'terror attacks', paying tribute to the determination of the affected populations – and to that of Cologne in particular – to bring life back to normality and to rebuild their destroyed cities.[43]

By the summer of 1942, the fate of Lübeck, Rostock and Cologne was rapidly becoming a rather common experience in a constantly growing number of German cities.[44] The general propaganda response to this reality was characterised by realism (in acknowledging the consequences on civilian population and cities) and caution (in avoiding either exaggeration or embellishment of the situation). Repeatedly, Goebbels criticised the OKW communiqués for not doing justice to the havoc caused by aerial bombardments and for the resilient attitude of the local populations.[45] He was particularly candid when describing the devastating effect of these campaigns on everyday civilian life and praised the Volk for its resolute spirit.[46] He also hastened to manipulate the genuine public shock in the aftermath of raids in historic locations (such as Lübeck) or heavily populated areas to accuse the 'plutocratic powers' of the west for immorality and for wrecking havoc in the context of an unashamedly 'brutalising' campaign against civilians and areas of world-heritage status:

> [i]t is in the nature of terror, however, that it can be only encouraged and strengthened by terror. Terror and counterterror alike cause victims, but they stand in no relation to the victims which will result if one bends to terror. Violence only gives way only to more violence. This is most elementary of all laws of life. If we use the same method in response to the British brutalising methods, we only act according to this law. So a person sensitive to culture – and we reckon ourselves as belonging to this type, slowly becoming extinct in the world – may lament the loss of time-honoured historical monuments and art monuments not only in Lübeck, Rostock and Cologne, but also in Bath, York and Canterbury; yet the blame is not on our shoulders but on those of that nefarious criminal who stands presently at the head of the British empire [Churchill].[47]

In hindsight, the long-term implications of this 'new method' of warfare (as Hitler described it in September 1942) for domestic morale could not be – and indeed were not – fully appreciated by the NS leadership until well into 1943.[48] In May 1942 – that is after the first German cities had experienced a foretaste of the disaster to come from the air – Goebbels maintained a defiant tone in his regular press conferences, stating that the raids 'do not impress us in the least and that every single attempt will cost the British heavy losses'.[49] It was only in the following autumn that the long-term dangers of this intensifying Allied campaign started to dawn on the Propaganda minister. On the one hand, absolute control over the flow of information could no longer be sustained, given that people in the bombed areas had *direct* experience of the gap between the regime's *ersatz* reality and the Reich's worsening fortunes in the war. Over the following two years the intensity of air warfare would be internalised by the public opinion as a far more reliable representation of 'truth' than the NS propaganda reports and the reassurances of the leadership.[50] Given the increasing psychological correlation of domestic morale with the intensity of Allied bombing,[51] the regime's efforts to arrest or even reverse public pessimism and anxiety would prove to be an essentially impossible task, so long as the Luftwaffe was incapable of defending the skies of Germany. On the other hand, the initial heavy concentration of Allied bombardment on specific areas of the Reich (mainly the strip between Cologne, the Ruhrgebiet and up to Hamburg) meant that the different sections of 'national community' were exposed to fundamentally divergent everyday war experiences. The gradual loss of such an element of uniformity eroded the internal coherence of the domestic front and undermined the regime's efforts to sustain the homogeneity of its message to the public. NS propaganda had no other means of responding to this divergence of experience than to resort to a diversification of its own discourse, depending on the audience.

Yet this was a classic no-win situation for NS propagandists. Avoiding excessive reporting in case this caused unwarranted alarm in other, not yet affected, areas could be regarded as insensitivity: this is exactly what happened in the case of Essen after the January 1943 air raid when new reports described the damages as 'slight' instead of the more fitting adjective 'serious';[52] and again in July 1944 when the OKW reports made no reference to the severe damage inflicted on Neustadt.[53] In those cases, where the regime's authorities acknowledged the extent of the destruction, the result was a depression of civilian morale and an escalating anxiety about the military fortunes of the Reich (the widespread rumours circulating across Germany in 1943–44 about the likelihood or the results of air raids attest to this). Furthermore, the selective Allied targeting caused bitterness to the affected population towards those still spared from this experience. For example, whilst demanding utmost realism in the coverage of the bombing campaigns in Rostock in April, and in Cologne and the Ruhr in the following months, Goebbels realised that the mere accident of Berlin having suffered no major air raid until then was breeding resentment amongst the population of the affected areas and nurturing rumours about an alleged German–British agreement with regard to sparing London and Berlin.[54] In this respect, it comes as no surprise that, when eventually Berlin was hit by a strong Allied air raid in November 1943, there was at least a sense of perverse relief in the RMVP at the way in which the extension of the Allied targets had re-united the civilian population through the grim experience of destruction.[55]

Still, Goebbels was determined to put up a good propaganda fight. He called for a fundamental reassessment of the official attitude to air raids, retaking the initiative in shaping public perceptions of the situation and avoiding the constant repetition of the same justifications and accusation (e.g. cultural destruction).[56] Then, in the shadow of new devastating air raids (e.g. Munich and the Ruhr area[57]) and of numerous reports recording the damaging effect of the intensifying air warfare on the home front[58], the Propaganda minister delivered his second Berlin Sportpalast speech on 5 June 1943. After praising the 'hard-tested' German Volk for its 'unprecedented heroism', he delivered an unambiguous promise to his rapturous audience:

> [w]e know that there is only one effective way to answer the British–American terror: counter-terror (*Gegenterror*). The entire German Volk is filled with one thought: to repay like with like ... Each English voice today that regards the bombing war against German women, old people and children as a humane or even Christian method to defeat the German people will give us welcome grounds one day for our response to these crimes. The British people have no reason to rejoice. They will have to pay for the actions of their leaders.[59]

In the same speech, Goebbels acknowledged the psychological significance of 'an eye-for-an-eye retaliation' (*'Gleiches mit Gleichem zu vergelten'*). The 'hour of revenge' (*Vergeltung*) – Goebbels personally promised – would come in the near future. Appealing directly to an instinctive sense of hatred and help-lessness that had seized the German population in the affected areas, the Propaganda minister promised to his audience that the enemy would suffer untold misery when the time of 'revenge' comes:

> [t]he enem,y can turn our homes into rubble; the hearts of the people are filled with hatred, but they cannot burn. One day the hour of repayment will come [*Loud applause*], and – in recognition of the heroism proven today – after the war there will be a sacred duty for the whole people to rebuild their towns and homes even more nicely than before.[60]

This acknowledgement of the 'longing for revenge' – as the RMVP's coordinator of publicity for *Vergeltung*, Schwarz van Berk described it in *Das Reich* a month later – and the clear pledge to deliver it in the near future, struck the right chord with the German civilian population.[61] Privately, Goebbels did not hide his admiration for the way in which Churchill had dealt with the Luftwaffe Blitz against the British Isles in the summer of 1940.[62] Whilst continuing to attribute full responsibility for the destructive air warfare to the British prime minister[63], he was at last acknowledging both the gravity of the situation for the Reich (in July, after a terrible raid against Hamburg,[64] he maintained that 'the enemy air offensive is entering a new and decisive phase'[65]) and the urgent psychological need for reassuring propaganda counter-measures.

The pledge for a terrible 'counter-attack' (*Gegenangriff*) continued to fare prominently in the Propaganda minister's public speeches in the following months. Two weeks after his June Sportpalast speech, he toured bombed areas in the Ruhr, stressing defiantly that 'we will break terror with counter-terror'.[66] In August he even went as far as declaring that,

> [a]t a later date we will have the additional [technical and organisational] means for a massive counter-attack. Until then we will have to put up with [the 'terror campaigns'].[67]

Was this new campaign, however, another case of too-little-too-late for NS propaganda? It is obvious that, by the time Goebbels effected this dramatic change in his attitude towards Allied air raids, the regime's 'monopoly of truth' had suffered a severe blow from which it would be extremely hard to recover. Personal civilian experience of the devastating effects of Allied bombardment and of the striking inability of German air defences to limit its impact had a cumulative disruptive effect on civilian life and cultivated the impression that the home front had been left totally defenceless. Reports from the affected areas underlined the rapid deterioration of public mood and the collapse of the regime's credibility.[68] The only encouraging sign for the NS authorities was the fact that the adverse impact on the *Stimmung* did not translate into a similar erosion of the public's *Haltung* – that is, of their overall conduct and determination to fight back. Always alert to the significance of the distinction between the two, Goebbels showered the affected populations with praise. When he addressed a 20,000-strong audience in the ravaged city of Dortmund in June 1943, he honoured the population for their determination to resist; in return he received a rapturous applause. He had every reason to be pleased with his strategy of visiting the bomb-affected areas; even more so since, as he wrote in his diary,

> one cannot simply speak of good *Haltung* [in Dortmund]. Here is evidence of *Stimmung* generated from the *Haltung* … I have never experienced a more enthusiastic gathering in Westfalen than this one![69]

Even as late as November 1944, the RPA authorities were reporting how the war-ravaged population of Bochum managed to clear the city's centre from the rubble left behind by the Allied air raid within an incredible twelve hours! The report also noted with satisfaction that the majority of the inhabitants, when faced with defeatist comments ('Why rebuild? By the time your house is ready, the war will be lost'), reacted angrily and defiantly. The irony about the *Vergeltung* discourse lay in its surprising success as a propaganda device at an extremely difficult time of military reverses and increasing material destruction in the Reich. There is no evidence that Goebbels himself had initially intended it to become one of the most systematic campaigns that the regime waged in order to restore confidence amongst the population. The timing of launching the 'retaliation' theme rather points to a short-term, reflexive technique aiming to deflect attention from the intensifying air raids in the first half of 1943. It was only well within the summer of 1943 that both Hitler and his Propaganda minister appreciated its positive psychological effect and chose to sustain its momentum, in spite of discouraging reports from the regime's military experts and uncertainty as to whether a meaningful retaliatory campaign could indeed be waged in the near future.[70]

Progressively, *Vergeltung* became associated with the mirage of 'miracle weapons' (*Wunderwaffen*)[71] and the apocalyptic vision of unmatched destruction inflicted upon the enemy. This displacement of attention away from everyday military reverses to the sphere of 'miracle' proved effective in the short term, as public opinion reports recorded a noticeable improvement in morale amongst both the civilian population and the soldiers on the front.[72] The decision to name the new weapons using the letter 'V' and a number (V–1, V–2 etc.) was taken in order to impress upon the audience that *Vergeltung* was the primary motivation behind their development – and that their destructive potential was open-ended, escalating to unimaginable levels in the future.[73]

But, as summer and autumn passed without anything to report, the civilian population – especially in the areas mostly affected by air raids – began to despair and then become exasperated at what they perceived as a 'war of nerves of [German] propaganda against its own audience'.[74] Technical problems, coupled with constant harassment by enemy planes and damages caused to the launch sites in northern France,[75] resulted in a continuous rescheduling of the first counter-attack, however hard the RMVP was endeavouring to make it coincide with one of the regime's special dates (8/9 November, New Year, 30 January, Hitler's birthday). Goebbels endeavoured to maintain the propaganda noise about the 'wonder weapons' throughout autumn, though in a noticeably more restrained and vague manner.[76] Faced with derisory comments by the British and US media, the Propaganda minister decided to reply with renewed promises that 'one day ... England will know the reality'.[77] But that 'one day' remained anchored in an uncertain future, making people even more nervous and distrustful of Germany's overall capacity to face the enemy air campaign.[78] In December, SD reports underlined the adverse effect of a further delay in delivering the long-awaited *Vergeltung*, predicting that in the contrary event 'a catastrophic effect on public *Stimmung* and *Haltung*' should be expected.[79]

Now even Goebbels realised the need to tone down references to 'retaliation': in January 1944, he banned concrete references to the term in the press and radio broadcasts. He briefly revived the theme in March, talking of a 'not too distant time' for the decisive turning-point.[80] The home front received such comments with increasing scepticism;[81] but as the prospect of an Allied invasion in Europe (see below) gradually captured the imagination of the public in the spring and early summer of 1944, resulting in a psychological correlation between the invasion per se and the launch of the V weapons, the German public engaged in a new round of wishful thinking about the *Vergeltung* and the 'wonder weapons' that went even far beyond the intentions of official propaganda.[82]

Goebbels was aware that this was the regime's last-ditch opportunity to recreate a new *ersatz* reality of an allegedly 'decisive' (*kriegsentscheidend*) campaign fought away from the losing battles in the east and away from the battered home front. The delay, however, in launching the 'wonder weapons' undermined further his credibility, heavily invested since mid-1943 in the success of 'retaliation'.[83] In anticipation of the V–1 launch, the NS leadership attempted to sustain the public's attention to the *Vergeltung* theme by authorising a wave of conventional air raids across the Channel in the first three months of 1944.[84] In presenting this so-called baby Blitz as mere scene-setting for the allegedly impending decisive blow, Goebbels justified the postponement of 'revenge' by claiming that,

> [u]ntil now we have refrained from replying to [the enemy's] boastful accounts of the air war ... There will be enough time for that when we stand equal again. The jubilation in London will be more modest after a relentless German answer, which will once again permit a factual discussion. Even today the Luftwaffe is responding with gradually growing massive counter-attacks, but these are only a forestaste of what is still to come.[85]

This was the sort of message that a volatile German public still wanted to hear in 1944. As the SD public opinion reports show, the hope for a devastating retaliatory attack, however vague and uncertain, formed the backbone of public psychological resilience in late 1943/early 1944, at a time of dramatic reverses on all fronts. Such disproportionate anticipation for what was otherwise a far-from-systematic programme of new weapons' production, constantly postponed and fraught by technical problems and logistical hindrances, was useful as a diversionary tool and psychological buttress in the short term, but dangerous in the longer term if the NS regime failed to approximate such expectations. Indeed, by late spring 1944 delays in the launch of the *Wunderwaffen* – a whole year after it had been promised to the German people – had transformed initial hopes into once again dejection about the prospects of the Reich's ability to counter the Allied air raids.

So, when the first launch of V–1 rockets finally took place – conveniently less than a week after the allied landing in Normandy, in spite of a short delay[86] – Goebbels was both elated and apprehensive. NS propaganda had exaggerated the power of the rockets, claiming that the new weapon was capable of wrecking untold havoc on British cities in a significantly more economical way than air raids. Now, according to an article appearing in *Das Reich*, the Allies had their own devastating 'second front', more deadly than an air raid and more potent in terms of psychological demoralisation of the enemy. This launch, the newspaper concluded, was a testimony to 'German genius' and hard work, as well as a moral vindication for all those Germans who had lost family and friends under the ruins of bombed cities.[87] However, Goebbels himself knew that the results of the V–1 launch could not match the expectations nurtured in the past twelve months, let alone meet the wildly blown-up hopes of the population.[88] NS propaganda had promised that the effects of V–1 would not be restricted to the devastation brought upon British cities, but would also result in a lessening of Allied air raids over the Reich. In fact, the opposite proved to be the case: after an initial transient period of enthusiasm the impression was that, contrary to the NS propaganda's initial jubilant reports, neither the Luftwaffe nor the 'miracle weapons' were capable of staging the devastating retaliation originally promised. This could be empirically validated through the experience of enemy air raids that became more frequent and destructive than ever before. In the absence of tangible evidence about the impact of the V–1 rockets, the German population interpreted the intensifying Allied air raids as proof that the first weapon had failed to deliver.[89] The RPL opinion reports in the summer of 1944 noted rising public misgivings about the prospect of a V–1 devastating retaliatory attack on the British Isles. In spite of the graphic journalistic descriptions of the alleged effect of the first attacks[90], the population could not but notice the total absence of visual evidence, as well as the growing restraint in the reporting of the V–1 attacks in the German media during July.[91]

Yet, the *Vergeltung* rhetoric, fuelled by the deliberately extreme coverage of the alleged brutality of enemy attacks on Germany, was the best that the RMVP could afford in 1944 at a time of military collapse. New hopes were now placed on the planned V–2 weapons that would make the long-awaited difference.[92] Such hollow anticipations were not dispelled by the regime as they served a crucial psychological function of propping up public *Stimmung* at a very difficult juncture for the Reich. During the summer and autumn of 1944, all reports agreed on one psychological observation: the V–2 theme continued to buttress the population's morale, even if this meant that the majority of Germans were convinced that 'only the new weapons can have a decisive impact on the war effort'.[93] The launch of the first V–2 attacks in early September 1944 was received with an outcry of enthusiasm that lasted until the end of autumn. In November, an RPL opinion report noted that,

> undoubtedly the operation of V-2 has contributed to the elevation of the mood. [The people] recognize that we seem to have now arrived at a

turning point in which our new weapons come into the picture; they recognize that we do not stand defenseless anymore, but that we are capable of repaying the opponent in kind (*Gleiches mit Gleichem*).[94]

By the end of the year, however, and in the absence of any evidence that the much-awaited new weapons would indeed have a decisive impact on the enemy's ability to attack Germany or invade the Reich from the west, the V–2 theme started to fade out, causing a fresh, very serious slump in the Volk's morale.[95] The V–3 project was soon abandoned and references to *Vergeltung* died away. By that time, the home front had other, more pressing matters to deal with, as the western Allies and the Red Army launched their final attack on the Reich itself.

The eastern front: defeat, 'shortening of the front' and 'planned evacuation'

In his November 1943 address to party comrades, Hitler provided an overview of the grim situation that faced the Reich. He was rather plain-spoken about current and future dangers but not without an almost metaphysical sense of optimism. In a pattern that would be repeated with nauseating frequency in the final two years of the campaign, the Führer resorted to the most basic form of long-term emplotment:

> this National Socialist state, by a series of powerful blows unrivalled in history, has destroyed the ring which encircled it, and by the heroism of its soldiers has at almost everywhere moved the front lines considerably more than 1000 kilometers from the frontiers of the Reich. Our enemies have become modest. What they call victories today, are what in our case they used to describe as totally unimportant operations.[96]

The speech was well-received, resulting in a significant – if temporary – improvement of the population's *Stimmung*.[97] Certainly his references to 'retaliation' struck the right chord with the public. Whatever sort and degree of comfort, however, the German public opinion could draw from the fanciful claim that, in spite of all reverses and defeats, the war was still being fought in distant lands can be gauged by the less enthusiastic reactions in bomb-affected areas. Hitler was stating a rather obvious propaganda truth here: so long as the war could be kept away from the German borders, the regime could still enjoy the privilege of manipulating this 'distance' and thus compensating for the effects of air warfare against the Reich. With regard to the military situation, his message was mixed: whilst the front in Italy had been successfully stabilised at a significantly more southern location than the Allies had hoped for, '[t]he battle in the East is the most difficult which the German People have ever had to bear'.

In justifying the noticeable drop in the effectiveness of the German military's performance in 1943, Hitler adhered to the Goebbelian line of 'military tactics', stating that this was due to 'sober calculation' rather than weakness. A few months later the Propaganda minister explained the overall framework of NS propaganda for the year 1944 to the German media by invoking the same principle of strategic 'elasticity'. He insisted that the situation was not as grim as it might have appeared at first glance. Appealing to a wider perspective on the military conflict, he stressed that the Wehrmacht was still fighting well into its own impressive territorial gains from earlier campaigns. He refused to sanction the concepts of either 'retreat' or 'setback' with regard to developments in the east, in spite of the fact that the Red Army's 1943 second offensive had resulted in losses of territory and strategic locations for the German forces, without any sign of potential stabilisation. For him, all this amounted to a 'shortening of the front', reminiscent of the retrenchment that had followed the advance on Moscow in the winter of 1941 – and had led to the effective entrenchment of the defensive line.[98] The idea that Germany had still not fulfilled its potential and had not mobilised the totality of its material, military and spiritual forces offered an oblique opportunity for a more positive long-term message. As late as September 1944, Goebbels insisted that,

[o]ur people's total war effort has found and is finding ways to transform national strength into genuine war potential, and has already produced astonishing results. We are thus building operative reserves that will be of decisive importance for the coming decisions in both the military and the economic sectors. It will not be long before we stop living from hand to mouth in both sectors, but are once again in a position to operate according to a broad plan.[99]

The 'home front', however, was becoming increasingly resistant to the vagueness of such claims and promises. Propaganda diversionary discourses were rapidly losing their ability to displace anxiety – or convince for that matter. The reverses in the east could barely be disguised as calculated exercises; one by one, the locations of the impressive 1941–42 victories disappeared from the OKW communiqués, threatening to transform the German campaign in the east from a massive territorial gain into a painful deficit. By the time that the Soviet 1943 summer offensive started (in August) the OKW situation reports had become rather vague about the actual situation on the eastern front, avoiding the tendency to territorialise the battle (references to exact locations were increasingly scarce). The evacuation of Orel on 4 August was couched in the alarmingly familiar euphemistic language of a 'mavoeuvre' that had allegedly arrested the advance of the Soviet troops.[100] The final loss of Kharkov in late August 1943 was presented yet again as a tactical move that thwarted the Soviet and English strategy of bringing Germany to her knees.[101]

In early September 1943, the regime prepared for the fourth anniversary of the outbreak of the war and the beginning of the fifth year of hostilities. Carefully worded instructions were issued to the press and radio in order to give an upbeat twist to propaganda output. There was, of course, no point delving into the discussion about the expected duration of the war itself; what mattered most was to present even the current state of the confrontation as a still favourable one. History proved an invaluable reservoir of flattery for the civilian population:

> [w]hat we face today has been faced by very many previous generations before us. Today, German cities and homesteads lay in ashes, but in the past, too, German cities and villages have been destroyed. We are not the only ones who have had to bear these things. Our fathers and forefathers had to fight the same battles. They were victorious, and built a new and richer life from the ruins.

The suggestion that 'this is the decisive stage of the war' sounded hollow to a population that had heard 1941 and 1942 being described as 'year(s) of decision'. Yet, the stark imagery of Bolshevik 'terror', coupled with the depiction of the struggle as 'a test of character for the [superior] resolve of the German Volk' and the suggestion that only through a 'moral collapse' of the home front would a defeat of Germany be possible, were calculated to appeal to a fundamentally different public mindset. Nothing was lost, it was confidently argued; 'our lines are not in Flanders, but on the Atlantic. Our lines are not in Minsk, but at Leningrad, Orel and Kharkov'.[102] On 18 October, the German Volk was reminded of the anniversary of Gneisenau's victory against Napoleon;[103] barely a month later the regime's propaganda commemorated the twenty-fifth anniversary of the 1918 collapse. The cumulative message to the public was clear – 'this was an attack on German hearts' that the people could withstand, as they had done in the glorious days of Prussia; there would be no other 1918.[104]

The German military collapse continued unabated, however. By November 1943 the Red Army had crossed the obstacle of river Dnieper, leaving NS propaganda with nothing better than to resort to a monotonous repetition of the 'planned evacuation' theme. German casualties for the year approached one million; the remaining strength of the Axis divisions in the east barely exceeded the two-million mark. In December, Crimea was lost and the Soviet troops launched a new offensive in Ukraine; in early January, they had advanced within a few miles from the 1939 Polish border; even in the northern sector (Leningrad) where the Wehrmacht had fared much better than the other two during 1943, the final countdown had started. Contrary to the wishful thinking of Hitler that the campaign could still be switched from a desperately defensive one to an offensive (a belief that led to the re-designation of the formations' names on the basis of Ukrainian locations that they were supposed to re-conquer[105]), by early spring 1944 Red Army forces had found themselves within miles from the 1941 German–Soviet frontier.

Bearing all these highly dramatic developments in the military field, it is indeed difficult to comprehend Goebbels's rather defiant mood towards the end of 1943. In his diaries he noted that '[o]ur Volk is presently in a splendid frame of mind'.[106] However, the Propaganda minister was not totally divorced from reality. Although there were alarming SD reports that the public mistrusted – or even disparaged – the regime's and the OKW's use of language with regard to developments in the east, the main pillars of propaganda diversion seemed to be working rather adequately, strengthening the resolve of the civilians and preventing a serious further depression of the domestic *Stimmung*. Goebbels's strategy was two-fold: extreme negative integration and displacement of attention away from the east. The former strategy soon enveloped the theme of 'war criminals'[107] – a discourse introduced by the Allies against the NS leadership but which the RMVP hijacked and applied to their 'terror campaigns'. In his editorial for the new-year (1944) issue of *Das Reich*, Goebbels launched a scathing attack on the methods used by the American and British forces, stating that their ultimate goal was 'to hang not only the German leadership, but the entire German people'.[108] And he continued,

[t]he enemy has committed every conceivable crime against humanity, culture and civilization. They are in fact so spiritually corrupt as to boast about it in public. They plunder honest and decent nations to fill the pockets of their own money barons. They let millions go hungry and hundreds of thousands starve to reduce them to political inactivity. They murder huge numbers of women and children, hoping through their unbelievable barbarism to weaken the will and destroy the confidence of their husbands and fathers. They bomb and burn more than two millennia of Europe's cultural treasures ... Who has the right to speak of war crimes and historical justice, the enemy or we?[109]

This strategy of displacement of public anger was layered and all-embracing. Goebbels's renewed negative propaganda campaign against the Reich's enemies might have started as a diversion from the failure of his own exaggerated 'retaliation' promises (long overdue by late 1943/early 1944), but soon developed its own momentum. The juxtaposition of Allied 'terror' to the resilience of the German population in the ruthlessly targeted cities cast the regime and its people as morally superior to their enemies, with significantly higher spiritual values and superb buoyancy in the face of adversity. When Berlin finally became the target of a systematic bombing campaign in late 1943/early 1944,[110] Goebbels encouraged its citizens to combine '[h]ard and conscientious work join[ed] with passionate fanaticism and bitter rage [in order] to achieve ever new major accomplishments'.[111] The 'rage' was intended to be directed against the enemy in every possible way: against its leadership, its people (in spite of the survival of conventional feelings of sympathy for civilians, and women/children in particular, the hardening effect of the war had largely overwhelmed them in favour of a 'counter-terror' revenge mentality), its pilots (in early 1944 Goebbels urged the population to lynch those captured![112]), its soldiers.[113]

This reminder about who was allegedly responsible for the war was crucial in 1943–44, in order to counter an alarmingly increasing tendency amongst the Germans to put blame on the NS regime for the conflict and the misfor-tunes that followed it. The gamble did pay off: SD reports stressed a sense of 'extreme hatred' directed at those responsible for the 'bomb-terror'.[114] However, Goebbels went even further, once again inverting his own earlier comments about the relation between government and people. While in the first victorious stage of the war he had employed a careful distinction between 'plutocratic cliques' and 'common people', in September 1943 he angrily dismissed similar talk with regard to the Reich:

[i]t is an old trick of political warfare to separate the people from its government, in order to make the former leaderless and defenseless. This trick would be – if it ever succeeded with us – the only means with which the opponent could overcome us. Whoever falls for this enemy stratagem, is either a fool or a traitor.

This was, he repeated, a struggle for the survival of everything 'German' – not of a generation, not of a regime or a party, but of a centuries-old country and civilisation:

[t]he goal [of our enemies] is to eradicate every possibility of [future] life and development for our Volk. If they succeeded in attaining this goal, today's generation would have gambled away everything that countless generations of Germans in a millennium-long struggle of existence have achieved before us.[115]

By attributing a wider historical–cultural significance to this increasingly desperate campaign, Goebbels was also ensuring that the fighting spirit of the population did not depend on their support for or disdain for National Socialism per se or its government. The recourse to the idea of the '*Vaterland*' and '*Volksgemeinschaft*' had of course been previously employed within the context of National Socialism's own vision (see Ch. 3), but the waning appeal of the latter – in association with Allied claims that they were fight-ing only against the NS party and regime[116] – necessitated a wider perspec-tive. In May 1944, the Propaganda minister stressed that,

[w]e must defend our very life, for the enemy is attacking not simply the party or the Wehrmacht or the industry or the state, but directs his attack at us as a people.[117]

Diverting attention from the east ... and the west

As the need for diverting attention from the reverses in the east intensified, the regime simply exploited opportunities offered by external factors. Both Hitler's and Goebbels's main speeches on 8 November 1943 made scant references to the eastern front, engaging instead ad nauseam with the military situation in Italy and the alleged 'barbarism' of the western forces.[118] The impact of Hitler's speech was notable in this direction: in spite of the overwhelming sense of fear and despair that had seized public opinion in early autumn, there was now the impression that 'the situation in the east was not so critical as the people had believed earlier', otherwise the Führer would not have made the trip back to Munich to deliver the speech![119] A few days later, the conference between Roosevelt, Stalin and Churchill at Teheran provided further opportunities for diversionary negative integration: by restating their commitment to the opening of a continental 'second front' against Germany and discussing the postwar fate of the Reich, the east–west allies supplied NS propaganda with further opportunities for expanding its 'moral' discourse.[120] The Allied commitment to the 'unconditional surrender of Germany' in particular served NS 'fear' propaganda extremely well: by presenting the Allies' uncompromising stance as both a ploy to 'annihilate' the Reich and to advance the 'Jewish–Bolshevik' goal of world domination,[121] the RMVP succeeded in turning it into evidence for credibility of its own 'negative' propaganda and thus into a powerful device of integration inside the Reich.

In the aftermath of the conference, NS propaganda launched a campaign with regard to the planned Allied invasion in continental Europe – a campaign that maintained its momentum until the actual date of the operation, more than seven months later. The effort to divert attention from yet another 'crisis winter' in the east was obvious – perhaps a bit too obvious for some who remained bewildered by the fact that the whole issue had been completely sidelined in the regime's propaganda output. Increasingly the impending invasion was internalised by the German population as a sort of terminus for the launch of the 'retaliatory' measures, promised so long ago and categorically restated in December 1943. Although an increasing number of Germans had clearly started to mistrust the regime's repeated claims, considering them as mere 'propaganda manoeuvre'[122], hopes persisted and indeed were revived in connection with the 'invasion' theme.[123]

The volatility of German public opinion during the winter and spring of 1944 renders any generalisation misleading. The rather surprising confidence of December 1943 that things would improve in the east soon gave way to extreme fear and anxiety by February 1944, following the dramatic reverses in Crimea and Ukraine.[124] Yet, at the beginning of April, there was still the hope (largely irrational, given that the SD reports confirmed the view that the German population was aware of the adverse situation on all fronts) that things 'would work out in our favour'.[125] Be that out of a 'defeatist' expectation that the invasion would bring about the rapid collapse of the Reich and thus the desired peace or out of a hope that 'retaliation' and 'wonder weapons' were spared for the invading armies, the bulk of the Germans experienced a sort of feverish expectation with regard to the invasion towards the end of spring.[126] In fact, the longer the build-up to the invasion was lasting, the more the *Stimmung* inside the Reich was displaying signs of an optimistic outlook and strengthening morale. The SD report for the beginning of May showed that the 'Stalingrad mood' that had been detected in 1943 had vanished, giving way to a confident prediction that the time of retribution and enemy defeat was drawing near.[127] Goebbels's boastful claims that the Reich had prepared for any eventuality, Hitler's own pledge that the 'retaliation' against Britain would start sometime in mid-June[128] and the deployment by NS propaganda of Rommel's figure – this time in charge of the defence of the northern continental coast against invasion – appeared to have paid off.

The build-up to the invasion was long – in fact, a bit too long for NS propaganda to sustain without being once again criticised for repetitiveness and monotony.[129] Although until April propaganda output engaged almost interminably with the prospect of an Allied 'attack on Europe' in the most defiant tone possible ('they only have to come and you will see what aces we have to play', claimed Dietrich), in late May Goebbels urged press and radio authorities to refrain from using the term 'invasion'.[130] Having used developments in the west as a diversionary theme from the disintegration of the eastern front, the new challenge for NS propaganda was now three-fold: to sustain the overall improvement in public morale that had been noted in the spring of 1944 after the low ebb of 1943; to continue cultivating a more global perspective on war that would not be affected by day-to-day developments that were bound to have an adverse psychological effect; and to appeal to the population's will to resist the enemy at all cost now that the enemy was closing in on the old Reich itself. SD opinion reports were encouraging, showing that the majority of the people had been largely convinced by the idea of the 'Atlantic Wall' of defence (allegedly impregnable[131]) and the preparedness of the Wehrmacht forces to deal successfully with a continental landing.[132] Goebbels, who back in January had predicted that the invasion would take place 'in ninety days'[133] or otherwise fail, now waited, hoping that the time was working against the enemy. 'Let them come', he wrote defiantly in his diary.[134]

And come they did. The 'invasion' finally took place on the morning of 6 June.[135] For the last time, the atmosphere inside the Reich reminded people of 'earlier times', that is of the first period of enthusiasm and wild anticipation.[136] The actual situation, however, that NS propaganda was managing was rapidly turning against it: in spite of the boastful claims made by the German media in the aftermath of the invasion (confident predictions that the Wehrmacht would 'throw the enemy into the Channel' and 'repeat the story of Gallipoli'[137]), the Allied forces succeeded in entrenching their positions and in further subverting the fighting power of the Wehrmacht and Luftwaffe.[138] Goebbels concealed neither the magnitude of the struggle nor the numerical superiority of the adversary from his audience. Almost two weeks after the launch of the invasion, he was full of reassurances in his weekly *Das Reich* editorial, pointing to the 'gigantic losses' of the enemy and the indescribable heroism of the Wehrmacht soldiers. The tenor, however, of the article was cautious and restrained, stressing that the most difficult battle lay ahead. He refused to give 'the public a clear and accurate picture of the military situation in the West at present', resorting instead to trademark negative themes, such as 'international plutocracy' and 'Jewish interests', which he presented as the real winners of the situation in Europe. The best he could offer to a news-thirsty public opinion was the reassurance that 'its fate and life are in good hands'.[139] Such diffidence from the man who had confidently predicted the defeat of the enemy in the event of an Allied invasion was disconcerting.

The German population remained mesmerised by the combination of the 'decisive battle' (a reference that, incidentally, Goebbels had attempted to ban in early 1944) in the west and the prospect of the 'miracle weapons' until early July. The evacuation of Rome by Axis troops in early June (a development that had predated the invasion) received scant treatment in the German media and even less attention by the public;[140] nor did the defeat of the German troops in Montecassino in the south bother anyone very much – after all, NS propaganda had expended considerable energy in presenting the Italian front as 'a military sideshow':

[t]hey do not see central Italy as the place where real operational decisions will occur. The public does not know where the real main defensive line in Italy is, the line that defends areas important for the whole war effort, but it is clear that this line does not run through Gaeta and Cassino ... The goal [of our enemies] is to make a main battle front out of a sideshow. They want Germany to fight in central Italy not with its left hand, but with a major portion of its strength. The dedision as to the outcome of the war will be made elsewhere this summer.[141]

Of course, the timing of the Allied invasion acted as the perfect diversionary device from the rapid disintegration of the Italian front.[142] Even Hitler himself had attempted to emplot the loss of the Italian capital within the context of the alleged rapidly approaching 'annihilation' of the enemy on the continent.[143] The evacuation of Rome was also to be reported as a tactical manoeuvre for which the Allies 'have paid a huge price in blood without any strategically important gains, and now must supply a city of two million people'.[144] This act of playing down the military consequences of the retreat in Italy seemed to coincide with a wider transformation in the attitude of the

German public opinion that was now becoming apparent. The invasion of continental Europe, in association with the Allied 'terror air attacks', had forced German citizens to focus more clearly on those aspects of the war that had a direct bearing on their lives, abandoning the wider conception of the conflict as a historic struggle carried out on multiple fronts. The NS media attempted to give a positive spin to General Kesserling's decision to declare Rome an 'open city' and give it up without a fight in order to salvage its cultural masterpieces. In contrast to the devastation wrought upon the German cities, the Germans 'did not loot Rome or burn it down or use it as a defensive fortification', as the Allied forces would allegedly have done. The message was clear: a culturally superior people had refused to match the brutality of the enemy, opting instead for 'a sacrifice, and one of the hardest that the German leadership has made during this war'. To be sure, German public opinion was definitely not impressed by the argument: feelings of bitterness at the rescue of Rome when German cities were still been reduced to rubble, as well as a fresh wave of anti-Italian feeling, were evident in the June SD reports.[145] The Italian front, however, did not matter in the face of the grave situation in the Reich's western neighbourhood.[146]

By mid-July 1944 the 'invasion' spell on German public opinion had faded away, exposing the population to the harsh realities of collapse on all fronts.[147] However, in spite of the crude awakening to the success of the invasion and the deterioration of the military situation in the south and the east (with a new Soviet summer offensive now widely anticipated), the German civilian front remained generally calm and self-controlled. Criticism of the OKW for their strategy in the areas of Cherbourg and Caen (which had by then been lost) was vehement but reflected little panic. Of course, the rapid disintegration of Wehrmacht defences in France raised awkward questions about the alleged impenetrable 'Atlantic Wall' and the overall credibility of the regime's information supply.[148] Nevertheless, there was no immediate collapse of morale in the aftermath of the revelation that the Wehrmacht was retreating from strongholds in Normandy; instead, many still believed that the situation *could* be reversed.[149] Only the situation in the east – until then shrouded in a vague, diversionary language in the absence (or careful concealment by NS propaganda) of major setbacks – attracted fresh attention and produced anxiety, especially after the 'evacuation' of a place like Grozdo (July 1944) that was situated very close to the old (east Prussian) borders of the Reich.[150]

At exactly this point, the assassination attempt against Hitler on 20 July 1944 gave the regime and its propagandists a further lease of life, not only in terms of short-term diversion but also in strengthening the appeal of its major asset – Hitler himself. That the action itself was far from popular is indicated by the absence of any positive public responses to the plot: having recovered from the initial 'shock',[151] the overwhelming majority of Germans reacted in a way that went beyond the most optimistic expectations of the regime's officials, registering their unswerving loyalty to the Führer and condemning unequivocally the conspirators.[152] Goebbels perhaps suspected that even this impressive recovery in domestic morale and allegiance to Hitler was not sustainable in the longer (or even medium) term in the absence of military successes. His strategy, therefore, was two-fold. On the one hand, he ensured that more effective conditions for the conduct of war be established in the aftermath of the 20 July 'shock'. In yet another attempt to revive the fortunes of his flagging 'total war' campaign, he won the battle over other regime agencies for control over the war effort by being appointed by Hitler as Reich Plenipotentiary for the Mobilisation of Total War.[153] On 6 August 1944, he announced the stepping up of the 'total war' effort, urging Germans to lead a 'Spartan lifestyle', 'to toss overboard all the old comforts and conveniences ... [and] see the war as our first priority'.[154] On the other hand, he did his utmost to maintain the diversionary effect of the plot for as long as possible. The plot itself, the way it was carried out and the nature of the people involved in it offered further opportunities for a more effective long-term emplotment of the 20 July events. Goebbels delved into the 'aristocratic' character of the conspirators, presenting them as the pawns of international 'plutocracy' representing foreign interests and conniving against the whole German Volk.[155] Public opinion had already obliged: numerous reports in the aftermath of the assassination attempt confirmed the view that many Volksgenossen felt 'betrayed' by certain circles, even within the Wehrmacht, that had deceived the Führer and sabotaged the overall German war effort.[156]

This sort of displacement of responsibility was exactly what Goebbels and the NS leadership had wished for. Anything from the retreat in the east to the death (now considered by some as 'assassination') of leading Nazis – such as Fritz Todt – to the 20 July plot were widely attributed to the scheming of a small conspiratorial clique inside the Reich.[157] Having spoken ad nauseam about the moral and political implications of the 20 July plot to an audience of faithful Gauleiter at Posen in August, Goebbels gave another long speech at Cologne in October that resembled a seminar in historical indoctrination.[158] It was a relentless morale-boosting exercise, steeped in historical analogy and derived from wishful thinking: the Seven Years War and Frederick the Great were compared to the current military situation and Hitler; the 'capitulation' of 1918 and the conventional 'stab-at-the-back' theme with the 20 July plot and the conspirators' 'betrayal'; and the ups and downs of the NS period with the wild ebb and flow that had characterised the whole Prussian history. The determination to fight, to 'use *every* opportunity', to defend 'to the end' the fatherland evinced a renewed sense of defiance and almost transcendental optimism.[159] Once again, 'fate' and 'providence' fared prominently in the speech, developing the theme that Hitler himself had introduced with fervour in his address to the German people immediately after the July assassination attempt.[160]

However, behind the façade of bravado, Goebbels carefully disguised a further message to his audience. He urged them not to expect 'miracles' but simply to fight on. The (ephemeral, as it turned out) revival of the U-boat campaign in the Atlantic in the autumn of 1944 was an encouraging sign that the regime's promise for new, technologically superior submarines was on its way to fulfilment. At the same time, unchecked wishful thinking about the alleged power of V–2 rockets sustained a popular mood of wild anticipation about 'retaliation'. Goebbels's quandary could not have been more painful at this point. The recovery of public morale throughout 1944, in spite of the dire military situation, depended crucially on the regime's ability to maintain a high level of expectation, even if this involved talk of a 'miracle'. But Goebbels was also aware of the limited likelihood of the timely introduction of these 'miracle' weapons or of their overall military effectiveness.[161] The message in his October speech at Cologne should, therefore, be regarded as a conscious attempt to prepare public opinion for the eventual failure of '*Vergeltung*' and to dampen down further expectations before the actual dearth of Nazi alternative solutions was fully exposed.

In the longer term too, the upturn in public *Stimmung* in the aftermath of the assassination attack against Hitler came at a price for the regime's overall propaganda credibility, for the 'betrayal' argument, so carefully constructed on the ruins of Wehrmacht's prestige and independence, soon gave rise to awkward questions about Hitler's own judgement. People could not resist the temptation to draw an analogy with the events surrounding Mussolini's removal from power a year earlier, identifying a common theme in the Duce's and Hitler's reliance on allegedly scheming and inept agents for the realisation of their respective 'revolutions'.[162] The prestige of the armed forces' leadership (consistently, if indirectly, undermined since 1941 in order to bolster Hitler's own talent as supreme commander) reached its lowest ebb. But soon the German public also started questioning vocally Hitler's ostensible 'genius', reaching the conclusion that he had either allowed himself to be deceived by his subordinates or that he had consciously lied to the population.[163] Did this mean that all previous assurances about Germany's 'final victory' were part of that large-scale deception? In spite of Goebbels's (often ridiculed) reassurances in August 1944 to the contrary[164], more and more Germans were convinced about it *and* willing to register their criticisms in a substantially more open manner.[165]

Preparing for the final showdown

It becomes clear that the Propaganda minister – by then enjoying a virtual institutional monopoly over the regime's information network (see Chs 1–2) and 'total war' effort[166] – had already started preparing for the final decisive confrontation. Propping up the morale of the population and the troops constituted the top priority for the regime's propaganda efforts. The RMVP continued (and in some cases intensified) its radio propaganda 'noise', in spite of the material destruction caused by Allied bombardment and the gradual dismemberment of the Reich as a result of the parallel enemy advances from east and west. It also ensured that the newspaper, *Heimat und Front* was delivered to the troops as an antidote to the enemy counter-propaganda with constant leaflet dropping and radio broadcasts. Negative psychological integration was indeed crucial, given the decline of positive allegiance to the regime amongst soldiers and civilians towards the end of 1944. This is why anti-Bolshevism (see Ch. 3) had already taken the concrete form of 'atrocity propaganda', based on the (exaggerated or not) depiction of the Red Army's conduct in the occupied eastern provinces of the Reich. As early as October 1944 the advance of the Red Army into East Prussia was reported through the most graphic stories of murder, slaughter and destruction.[167] In his customary address to the German people on the anniversary of the *Machtergreifung* on 30 January 1945, Hitler emphasised that the German soldiers in the east defended not just the Reich and the Volk but the whole of Europe against the advancing 'Asiatic hurricane [that] exterminates hundreds of thousands in the villages and market places'. The combined imagery of 'eastern barbarism', 'Jewish' hatred and 'plutocratic' future exploitation was carefully juxtaposed to the confident belief in a final, historic victory:

> [w]e shall overcome this calamity, too, and this fight, too, will not be won by central Asia but by Europe; and at its head will be the nation that has represented Europe against the East for 1,500 years and shall represent it for all times: our Greater German Reich, the German nation.[168]

Goebbels's management of this 'atrocity propaganda' against the Red Army won him the plaudits of Hitler in one of their last meetings in March 1945.[169] It was a campaign that did not aim for subtlety or sophistication but for achieving the maximum degree of psychological terrorisation – and, with it, the strengthening of the civilians' and soldiers' fighting power in the east. From the pages of *Der Stürmer* Julius Streicher carried the message to the extremes – a predictable upshot given the newspaper's excessive coverage of stories pertaining to 'Jewish Bolshevism' ever since its first publication in 1923. In late February 1945 Streicher published an article in which he used distorted excerpts from the Bible to maximise public anxiety about the advancing Red Army troops:

> [j]ust as the Jewish leader Moses ordered his forces to do to the conquered peoples thousands of years ago, so today the Red soldiers under the command of Jewry behave today wherever they reach through treachery or force: men are murdered or shipped abroad as slaves, women and girls are raped and defiled![170]

Goebbels too resorted to the tested recipe of virulent anti-Semitism. In his 21 January editorial in *Das Reich*, he attempted to resurrect Hitler's January 1939 trite 'prophesy' about the 'annihilation' of international Jewry in the event of a war. The message was still rather optimistic, predicting the eventual collapse of the Jewish 'international plot' against Europe. However, the Propaganda minister added a further dimension to his message: although NS Germany had 'broken completely [her enemies'] power' inside the Reich, they had regrouped in other countries and were now launching their campaign of hate. There had been a widespread impression amongst Germans that the Jews would take revenge on the German Reich for all the suffering that (justifiably or not – here opinions diverged) they had endured. Goebbels's increasing (and deliberate) openness with regard to the regime's attitude to Jews and Slavs in the past forced many Germans to conclude that the reversal of the Reich's fortunes in the war constituted a sort of deserved retribution:

> [t]wo workers are ... in agreement that we ourselves are to blame for this war because we treated the Jews so badly. We need not be surprised if they now do the same to us.[171]

References to the notion of a 'Jewish revenge' were officially banned by the authorities, in an attempt to arrest the growing tendency amongst Germans to see their predicament as a metaphysical retribution for the treatment that they had inflicted (or allowed to be inflicted) on the Jews.[172] Nevertheless, Goebbels kept the spotlight on the 'fear' element by portraying the situation in stark 'either–or' colours: this final assault on Germany, he warned in January 1945, would spare no-one.[173]

Further opportunities for negative propaganda were in ample supply during the last nine months of the war. Every conference between the western Allies and the Soviet Union supplied further ammunition to the regime with regard to the argument that this had become a struggle for national survival – now it was the time of the Roosevelt–Churchill Quebec conference (September 1944)[174]. In early autumn 1944 a draft for the (still under discussion) Morgenthau Plan was leaked to the press. Apart from reiterating the, by then conventional, Allied arguments about the Reich's 'unconditional surrender', the plan reflected a conscious decision to de-industrialise Germany, divide its territories and place its overall political and economic life under strict foreign tutelage. What was even more shocking to the Germans was the extent to which the envisaged postwar German territory would shrink, even compared to Churchill's 1943 plan. Goebbels seized the opportunity for both defamation of the 'plutocracies' and scare-mongering inside the Reich. He derided the Morgenthau plan as a project aimed to force the German Volk to give up its industrial might and 'cultivate potatoes'.[175] Morgenthau himself was disparaged as yet another 'Jew' in the plutocratic clique[176]; the plan was a disaster worse than the Versailles Diktat twenty-five years earlier.[177] Apocalyptic scenarios for the eventuality of defeat were paraded: about the future of Germany as an occupied sub-state 'until the year 2000', about the territory's splitting up into small units that would later be diluted in a 'federal Europe' (a development that was portrayed as a return to the pre-1648 fragmentation of the German states), about the transport of 'five to six million Germans to the Soviet Union [as slave labour]', about the Allies' deliberate decision to inflict on the Reich conditions of economic dislocation in an alleged spiteful revenge.[178] Then came the Yalta conference (February 1945) with the implicit Allied acknowledgement of Soviet interests in the continent, as well as the first official plans for the future shape of occupied Germany. The Propaganda minister once again saw immense opportunities for negative psychological integration behind the bleak message from the summit: He orchestrated another campaign, steeped in the customary anti-Semitic references, but with the added threat of 'mass deportations', permanent foreign occupation and plundering of the Reich.[179] The more the advancing troops of the western forces and the Soviet Union marched into German territory, the more news about atrocities in the east or food shortages and economic dislocation in the west were circulating, and the more NS propaganda retreated into short-term diversionary themes that aimed at what Goebbels repeatedly called 'resistance at any price'.[180]

In the end, he was right – the Germans did resist; the regime had the doubtful privilege of scripting its own death. In fact, the general *Stimmung* of the civilian population during the autumn of 1944 and the ensuing winter remained in a noticeably better shape than it had been a year before. After the July 20 assassination attack – and in spite of a constant stream of bad news from Italy (rapidly retreating northwards), Hungary/Romania (seeking separate peace), France (fall of Paris, rout of Wehrmacht forces) and, of course, the east (Red Army crossing into East Prussia) – there were even a few occasions for 'positive' propaganda. The temporary failure of the Red Army offensive in the area around Goldap and Gumbinnen in East Prussia (which the German IVth Army recaptured in early November before finally retreating in early 1945) saturated the Reich's remaining newspapers' pages for days.[181] Then came the introduction of a new wave of 'total war' measures, spearheaded by the Propaganda minister in his new capacity of Plenipotentiary for Total War (*Reichsbevollmächtiger für den totalen Krieg*). These, as RPL reports demonstrated, proved exceptionally popular with a civilian population still eager to believe that the war was not lost, even if they raised awkward questions about previous declarations regarding the Reich's preparedness to fight against the enemy.[182] Furthermore, the introduction of the *Volkssturm* ('people's army' made up of civilians between the age of sixteen and sixty) in early November provided a point of psychological rallying for the civilian population. This was genuinely a Goebbels project – and one that corresponded to his fresh instructions to cover truth in a 'poetic' manner ('calling imagination ... to complete facts'[183]) – that was taken up with rather striking enthusiasm by party authorities across the (remaining) Reich, generating a wave of public enthusiasm, evident in the high number of volunteers.[184]

Finally, towards the end of 1944 Hitler devoted himself almost entirely to the preparation of what proved to be the Third Reich's last offensive action – this time in the Ardennes area on the western front.[185] It was a daring operation, involving a massive transfer of human and material resources from the east and depending on the condition that bad weather would pin down enemy planes. The attack was launched on 16 December and took the US forces by total surprise. Back in Berlin Goebbels had ensured that there would be a total ban on any kind of reporting in press and radio alike; the fact that he succeeded this time, in spite of Hitler's desire to issue a short statement and Dietrich's unbridled foreboding, was evidence of his strengthened position and prestige.[186] For a few days it seemed that that the Germans had achieved their strategic target of throwing the Allied forces back, allowing the NS leadership to entertain the illusory hope of a 'second Dunkirk'. A wave of jubilation in the western territories of the Reich was reported almost immediately.[187] But just before Christmas the improved weather allowed the resumption of air raids and halted the offensive action. Goebbels continued to emit a careful optimism, authorising the press to cover the early successes of the attack and praise the alleged genius of the Führer.[188] By that time, however, it was obvious to him that the situation was beyond repair. With the Ardennes offensive called off in early January and the resumption of the Red Army attack in the Vistula area to the east, any propaganda reassurance appeared more hollow than ever to a demoralised population.

What was also becoming clear was the fragmentation and atomisation of 'public opinion', as each part of the remaining Reich was subjected to totally different experiences and enemies.[189] Alarming reports from the west spoke of 'civilians greeting the American soldiers with white flags' (even in the Propaganda minister's home town!) or demanding 'peace at any price'[190], of soldiers unable to 'make a stance somewhere' and of demoralised communities in the east paralysed from the fear of Soviet retribution. The long-term effect of anti-Bolshevik atrocity propaganda had found its way into the collective consciousness of the inhabitants in the east, rendering the prospect of a capitulation unfathomable. The breakdown, however, of confidence in the ability of the Wehrmacht to arrest the enemy advances resulted in a growing wave of refugees towards the west. Goebbels intervened once again to mobilise more civilian forces and to ban 'defeatist' references from the press (for example, he banned the use of the verb '*durchhalten*' – hold out – from the propaganda vocabulary); but he also knew that there could be no real regrouping without a glimmer of victory somewhere. He remained hopeful, like Hitler did, that such a victory was still possible: the campaign in Hungary started with Goebbels unable to conceal his anticipation;

Hitler was still expecting a stabilisation of the front in the west – first on the Rhine, then in Saar, finally west of Berlin. Frustratingly for them, it all came to nothing.

For a while Goebbels attempted a positive line of propaganda through the limited successes of the new breed of U-boats in the Atlantic;[191] he even used the metaphor of the 'marathon-runner' in order to convey the image of an enemy who had accelerated too quickly and was now running out of steam.[192] In November 1943 Hitler had predicted that '[e]very new landing will force [our enemies] to tie up more and more shipping. It will fragment our enemies' forces and provide new opportunities for us to use our weaponry.' A few months later he claimed that 'the closer the enemy comes to the realisation of its goal [destruction of Germany], the weaker its coalition will become'. Apart from the nominal belief that victory would still be possible somehow, the NS leadership had largely given up hopes for a dramatic military reversal in their favour. Only the prospect of the enemy coalition's collapse and the regrouping of 'Europe' in a crusade against Bolshevism could provide a droplet of optimism and encouragement to an otherwise desolate public opinion. But even this was considered highly unlikely – even by Goebbels himself.

Perversely, the death of the US President F D Roosevelt on 12 April appeared momentarily to confirm this desperate hope about a miraculous turnaround in the military field that the NS leadership had nurtured. In his last eulogy to his leader on the latter's fifty-sixth birthday, Goebbels predicted the collapse of the 'Jewish–plutocratic–Bolshevik' coalition now that '[f]ate has taken the head of the enemy conspiracy [Roosevelt]'. The article was imbued with a perverse mixture of scare-mongering and sanguinity: on the one hand, the prospect of a Bolshevik victory that would bring communism to the 'coast of the Atlantic' and would sooner rather than later 'reward Britain for its betrayal'; on the other hand, the confident belief in a last-minute Germany victory that would result in the recovery of the Reich, the revival of Germany and Europe as a whole:

[w]ithin a few years after the war, Germany will flourish as never before. Its ruined landscapes and provinces will be filled with new, more beautiful cities and villages in which happy people dwell. All of Europe will share in this prosperity. We will again be friends of all peoples of good will, and will work together with them to repair the grave wounds that scar the face of our noble continent. Our daily bread will grow on rich fields of grain, stilling the hunger of the millions who today suffer and starve ... The underworld will not rule this part of the world, rather order, peace and prosperity.[193]

The Propaganda minister's swansong came at a time when Hitler was still clinging to the hope that the hastily regrouped Wehrmacht forces around the besieged capital of the Reich would succeed in repelling the adversary and turning the war tide. His decision to stay in Berlin with his Führer came a few days after he had cleared off his desk at the RMVP, gathered his staff and spoke to them about their place in history before releasing them.[194] He had praised the virtue of loyalty and had asked the German Volk to sustain it; but he was the only old fighter that stayed with his Führer till the end – first Goering and then Himmler had 'betrayed' their leader at the eleventh hour. Although he continued to remind the Germans that the final outcome of the struggle 'depends on us alone', he had also placed his hopes on the allegedly 'superior qualities' of the Reich's leadership, stressing that,

> God will throw Lucifer back into the abyss even as he stands before the gates of power over all the peoples. A man of truly timeless greatness, of unique courage, of a steadfastness that elevates the hearts of some and shakes those of others, will be his tool.

By the time that the Soviet troops waved the red flag from the dome of the destroyed Reichstag building, there was no NS propaganda and no leader to idolise or defend. Having given up illusions that it could still foster a positive sense of loyalty to the system, NS propaganda at least made the timely correction in the direction of shoring up resistance against effectively discredited alternatives. That it did so fairly convincingly, that it defended a threshold of 'fear' and 'resistance' in the east and hostile apathy in the west (the instances of 'white flags' were not widespread enough to be considered the norm of public attitude to the – western – enemy) must have been a consolation of sorts for the Propaganda minister before committing suicide with his family in the Berlin bunker on 1 May 1945. He had wished that the Germans would not offer their adversaries 'a cheap victory'[195] – and they duly obliged.

8
Cinema and Totalitarian Propaganda: 'Information' and 'Leisure' in NS Germany, 1939–45

The cinema of the NS period continues to be a fiercely debated topic, occupying an ambiguous terrain between the conventional categories of 'information' and 'entertainment', between tendencies already activated during the Weimar period and NS intentions, between active propaganda and diversion, as well as between the requirements of a political-ideological and a financial enterprise. How useful all these distinctions are remains a moot point, as the ongoing debate on the artistic merits of Leni Riefenstahl's films has shown. In all, the cinema of the NS period displayed a remarkable diversification of themes, approaches and techniques that helped it to avoid a definitive categorisation as either 'art' *or* 'propaganda', information *or* entertainment, ideology *or* culture. Its variety of genres and blurring (either deliberate or inadvertent) of the distinctions between 'reality', ideological projection, entertainment and didactic manipulation has puzzled analysts ever since the 1940s, starting with the first authoritative study of NS cinema by Siegfried Kracauer.[1] For example, is a seemingly unpolitical comedy an innocent, value-free pursuit of pure entertainment? Does a newsreel simply depict reality or align facts to an ideologico-political project? Is the use of historical inference in film purely didactic or consciously manipulative?[2] Is a self-styled 'documentary' more or less political/ideological when it claims to rest on factual (visual and textual) evidence? Invocation and integration of 'facts' does not necessarily amount to a depiction of 'reality', in the same way that the fictional does not automatically purport to be unreal; factual 'evidence' and depicted 'reality' can easily be aesthetically and emotionally entertaining, whilst spectacle can be viciously political, enforcing and sustaining long-term patterns of 'cultural hegemony'.[3] The film-as-message reflects choices of forms and content, and rests on inclusions and omissions which are never totally involuntary or totally conscious. In this respect too, cinema under National Socialism was not so different from other contemporary (or even subsequent) national cinema productions; nor was it fundamentally different to other mass media (such as radio) in its blurring of the boundaries between information and entertainment, the 'political' and the 'cultural'.

However, NS cinema was indeed exceptional in at least one sense compared to other mass media: its particularism derived from its different social significance and function.[4] In generic terms, cinema was by far the most 'modern' medium of interaction between state, mass society as *Volksgemeinschaft* and the individual. As a product, a film was transmitted as such to a potentially open-ended audience, levelling out the social, geographic and political attributes of each spectator. In fact, it involved two different kinds of audience: one, like national broadcasting and newspapers, that amounted to the imaginary 'national community', bound together through the concurrent transmission of the same message; and another, more restricted but potent, through the physical coexistence of the spectators inside a hall, far more closely bound by the forces of mass psychology. Furthermore, cinema depended on the choice of the individual to become a spectator and thus to step out of their 'private' sphere and into the domain of socialisation. Broadcasting and newspaper-reading were de facto private – individual or involving a familiar audience – activities that had been integrated into a daily routine. Going to the cinema, however, was a pastime, an ad hoc leisure activity, carrying with it more complex expectations. As a result, its penetration inside the public body depended not just on infrastructural expansion (and this trend, spectacularly promoted by the NS authorities, had already been in motion since the 1920s) but also on a far more deliberate audience choice that was always transient and could easily be reversed in the future.

Beyond these more nuanced differences, there was a practical one that set cinema aside from the other media of propaganda: it was expensive and technically demanding. In other words, it required long preparation, substantial investments in resources and time, specific expertise and a more complex system of distribution. These attributes rendered it far less vulnerable to spontaneous improvisation by NS authorities, far less appealing or accessible to party involvement, more concentrated structurally and far more expensive. This explains why the domain of cinema remained firmly and unequivocally under the grip of the RMVP – and of Goebbels personally – throughout the twelve years of NS rule, without the sort of competition witnessed in the case of press and even broadcasting [See Ch. 1].[5] Faced with an ambivalent picture of opportunities and risks, Goebbels embraced the former, managing the film industry as a crucial device for cultural and political hegemony not only within the Reich but also in the conquered territories.[6] In the context of this strategy, financial security, infrastructural expansion and intensification of production were far more important than a heavy-handed nationalisation and political co-ordination – and this in itself set the treatment of film by the NS regime apart from its attitude to other media.

By the time that Hitler came to power, film production and content had already been largely defined and dominated by Hollywood. It was popular American films that had shaped the expectations of audiences across the globe, established an indirect form of aesthetical hegemony and determined norms for the various genres. This process of conditioning carried two implications for the NS managers of German cinema. Given the element of spectator choice outlined above, they had to win over the masses to their own brand of cinematic spectacle, construct *ersatz*-symbols and –stars, and emulate without plagiarising. The 'right wing', ultra-nationalist tendencies in the last years of Weimar cinema[7] had produced films that bridged the ideological and aesthetical gap between a Hollywood-inspired and an alleged NS artefact.[8] The shift of production to expensive big-budget productions, visually spectacular films saturated with easily identifiable faces and names attests to a process of adaptation of NS cinema to pre-existing norms rather than the opposite. The regime authorities experimented with every available form – from documentary (e.g. with scientific and environmental subjects) and crudely propagandistic films (e.g. *Hitlerjugend Quex*[9]) to history dramas (e.g. *Bismarck, Ohm Krüger, Kolberg*) and 'light' comedies or romantic dramas (e.g. *Hab' mich lieb, Wir tanzen um die Welt, Karneval der Liebe, Die Frau meiner Träume*);[10] but it meaningfully refused to view the politically-laden ones as an unbending priority and discard others simply because of their ideological flimsiness. Furthermore, when it came to the quest for foreign domination and appeal to non-German audiences, NS authorities applied rigorous market criteria to the selection and distribution (if not, partly, production too) of their films to audiences abroad. Goebbels was personally convinced that inference and indirect cultural hegemony were far more valuable assets than the saturation of the marketplace with contrived, forceful political indoctrination.[11] It was a seemingly 'light' blockbuster, *Münchhausen*, that was chosen to celebrate the twenty-fifth anniversary of the largest German film studio – Ufa (*Universum Film* AG) in 1942; and it was *Kolberg*, the most expensive and spectacular history drama ever produced in Germany, that was selected as National Socialism's cinematic swansong in 1945, even if it was never widely shown in the end.

The result of all these tendencies and decisions was that NS cinema embraced a wide repertoire of themes, forms and visual representations that almost always maintained a dialectical relation to entertainment and indoctrination, information and leisure, art and politics, private and public, and to 'reality' and 'fiction'. In this context, totalitarianism referred neither to the sort of ideological co-ordination and structural centralisation witnessed in the domains of press and radio, nor to a process of forcefully penetrating society as a whole through specific genres. Instead, the cinema of the NS period aspired to be a totalitarian device in two different ways: first, by aligning existing audience expectations and habits to an *indirect* propagation of its own ideological and cultural agenda; and, second, by distorting the reality–fiction/politics–art dualism and generating a single domain, where subtle nuances pre-dominated, often unbeknownst to the audience. During the war years, when 'integration propaganda' became far more crucial for the Third Reich's military effort and the home front's 'staying power' (see Introduction),[12] NS cinema grew in popularity because it succeeded by and large in saturating the market with products that spanned the whole information–leisure spectrum. It constantly took stock of spectators' responses (through the various 'public opinion' reports that regularly reached the RMVP) and constantly reconsidered its priorities through the lens of its audience's changing expectations. As a result, NS cinema successfully addressed the audience's dual need to know more about the military effort and at the same time escape from the everyday privations of war.

A definite categorisation of film production in wartime Germany appears impossible, as different criteria (e.g. gfiction, reference to past or present, etc.) produce different lists. For the purpose of our analysis, we will divide the bulk of film production in the 1939–45 period into five broad genres on the basis of the strength of their claim to transmit, represent, infer or avoid an alleged 'reality' – starting with the strongest: newsreel (Wochenschau); films based on contemporary footage, emploting that 'reality' into a coherent documentary narrative; historical films that suggested a bridging of the gap between past and present;[13] films that aligned a seemingly 'neutral' or fictional theme to contemporary social or political debates;[14] and, finally, films that were perceived as ostensibly 'light' entertainment, usually with themes that remained confined to the private sphere. If the first two categories appear less problematic in their intended and perceived (propaganda) functions,[15] the remaining three present overlaps and nuances that are sometimes difficult to negotiate: for example, many 'historical' films were timed to coincide with relevant political and social developments; 'light' entertainment could also be rooted in history and vice versa. But all categories defied the standard interpretation of information/propaganda-versus-entertainment.

The Wochenschau (newsreel)

Newsreel (Wochenschau) appeared in Germany just before the end of the nineteenth century. It was Oskar Meßter, an affluent Prussian nationalist film enthusiast, who in 1897 produced a first short film about the Brandenburg Gate. Almost immediately after the beginning of the First World War, he spearheaded the attempt to create a more elaborate network for the production of 'moving image' newsreel for the information of the German people about military and other issues. In 1917 the *Bild- und Filmamt* was created in order to systematise the production of such short films for propaganda purposes; and Meßter ensured that earmarked military units (both land troops and air force crews) were equipped with cameras to perform a crucial dual task: to supply the military with sensitive information about the conduct of the war (including reconnaissance photos and espionage) and to turn this material (after censorship) into newsreel for the population. As the German High Command was becoming increasingly convinced of the political expediency of propaganda in the last two years of the war,[16] the significance of the newsreel was also elevated, not just for the obvious purpose of propaganda but also as a commercial enterprise with a lucrative market abroad.

The next significant breakthrough in the history of the German Wochenschau came in September 1930 with the production of the first sound newsreel by the film-giant Ufa. By that time Ufa (which had been founded in December 1917) enjoyed a dominant position – both commercially and in terms of prestige – not just within Germany but also on a European scale, second only to Hollywood. It had been rescued financially by American studios in 1925 (through the so-called 'Parufamet' contract, signed with Metro and Paramount) but after the collapse of the deal in 1927, it had once again come under full German ownership through its acquisition by Alfred Hugenberg's Deulig company.[17] In 1925 Ufa had produced its first newsreel having merged the existing operations of the Decla and Meßter studios. Its own version (*Ufa Tonwoche*) was one of the four newsreel editions: Deulig (part of the Ufa–Hugenberg empire) carried on producing its own, Bavaria/Tobis supplied another, whilst the German company of the US giant Fox was also active in the growing market of Wochenschau.

This seeming pluralism continued until 1940 but after the creation of the RMVP in 1933, every aspect of newsreel production and distribution gradually came under the control of the regime. As early as May 1935, Goebbels had spoken of his desire to see the running of the Wochenschau as a centralised enterprise, firmly under the control of the state.[18] The caution, however, with which the RMVP approached the project of nationalising the overall German film industry in the 1930s did not make allowances for such heavy-handed measures; instead, the amalgamation of the four versions of the weekly newsreel came about in November 1940 as an almost logical extension of the indirect takeover of film studios under the guise of Winkler's *Cautio Treuhand GmbH* since 1935–37. In 1936 Eberhard Fangauf, an RMVP expert of film technology, was authorised to explore the optimal way in which the newsreel could come under the direct control of the ministry. The earlier (1935) decision to allocate responsibility for final editing to the German News Agency [*Deutsche Nachrichtenbüro* (DNB)] was an unsatisfactory transitional measure, as the DNB lay in a disputed jurisdictional area between the RMVP and Dietrich's network of news control (see Chs 1–2). As a result, the first crucial step towards the centralisation of the Wochenschau was taken early in 1938 with the creation of a supervisory office for newsreel production (*Deutsche Wochenschauzentrale*), headed by the new head of the RMVP's film division, Fritz Hippler. This paved the way for the two last steps: first, in autumn 1939, the distribution of only one version of newsreel used by the other existing companies; and, finally, in November 1940, the official merger of the four companies into an official state enterprise, produced under the aegis of the new *Deutsche Wochenschau GmbH* (DW).[19] This step, in conjunction with the exceptionally high interest shown by Goebbels personally and the primary role of the Wehrmacht's Propaganda Troops (*Propaganda-Kompanien, PK*) and of the censors of the OKW, transformed newsreel into a de facto state-controlled affair. But Goebbels's decision to amalgamate all aspects of film production in the Reich into the (by 1942 nationalised) Ufa was particularly significant not just for domestic audiences but also for international customers, who had been the recipients of the special version of newsreel produced by Ufa since 1925 (*Ufa-Auslandstonwoche*). This perpetuated the illusion of the newsreel's commercial and political independence from exclusive state control.[20]

As expected, the outbreak of the Second World War elevated the propaganda significance of the newsreel. The length of each copy increased from the prewar average of 300 to 370 metres in 1939/40 (roughly ten minutes) and reached its peak during 1941 with around 1000 metres (the Wochenschau – about the attack on France – marked a record of 1200 metres, or forty minutes). At the same time, the expansion of the cinema infrastructure across the Reich (and, from 1938, in the occupied territories as well) facilitated the wider distribution of the newsreel but caused another problem: with roughly 400 copies made every week and more than 5000 cinema premises, the average distribution cycle of any single Wochenschau in the countryside often exceeded two or even three months.[21] Given that, since 1938 Goebbels had decreed that every feature show should be prefaced by the Wochenschau, distribution pressures caused further delays which could no longer be tolerated after the invasion of Poland. As Hippler himself had noted, the newsreel was far more than a routine function of the state's information network:

> [o]n this occasion it is not about 'objective' reporting but, in the knowledge that we are right, about cultivating an optimistic propaganda, confident in victory, as well as, of course, strengthening the potential of the German Volk for mental fight. Speakers and language, text and music must adhere to this line.[22]

Therefore, in order to facilitate the timely reporting of military news to an information-greedy public, the RMVP authorised and funded the increase of available copies from the pre-war 700 to 1500 in the summer of 1940, and finally to 2000 or sometimes more from 1943 onwards.[23] As a result, both the attendance figures and the popularity of the newsreel increased dramatically with the onset of war, drawing record audiences throughout 1941.[24] The RMVP's confidence in the popularity of the newsreel was underlined by Goebbels's decision in March 1941 to allow a short interlude between the show of the Wochenschau and the feature film.[25] This decision was later complemented by another; this time ordering the closure of doors during the show of the newsreel, in order to ensure that those arriving late would not obstruct the show by entering during projection.

At the peak of the German military fortunes in 1940–42, the newsreel became a veritable growth industry. The growing popular demand for footage from the front was regarded as an opportunity for forging a closer psychological link between home and military fronts, as well as between the individual and the overall *national* effort. In 1941 Johannes Eckhardt confirmed this development:

> [w]e notice with pleasure that the wish becomes bigger and bigger to see faces in close-ups in the German newsreel in order to be able to observe these pictures for as long as possible. This wish testifies to the need to get closer to the person whom the picture shows; to grasp him emotionally and thus to fathom the secret of his personality.[26]

Demand, therefore, put pressure on the RMVP and the OKW to expand the PK and ensure the supply of more raw film in order to meet the target of expanding the length and availability of the newsreel. By early 1943 the number of those working in the PK had exceeded 200.[27] This meant that the available weekly footage before editing had also increased dramatically, resulting in newsreels that acknowledged ten or sometimes fifteen cameramen.[28] Practically, the amount of raw film needed to support this parallel expansion of length, copies and versions (through the proliferation of the *Auslandstonwoche*) rose exponentially, reaching a record two million metres in 1943.[29]

The popularity of the Wochenschau, however, followed the fortunes of the German military campaign. After the peak of 1941/42, the reversal of the situation on the front rendered the job of the DW far more complicated in terms of maintaining the triumphalist character of the previous three years, bolstering the enthusiasm of the audience and attracting the interest of the population. During the last two months of the Stalingrad campaign, the newsreel attempted a clumsy diversionary move by removing all references to the battle and baffling its audiences even after the official declaration about the defeat of the VIth Army with its refusal to acknowledge the disaster.[30] As a result, its popularity started to plummet from 1942 to 1943 onwards, with reported cases of audiences parodying its content, whistling and clapping during the projection or even deliberately staying outside the cinema during the newsreel show.[31] This shifting attitude necessitated the implementation of a coercive measure by Goebbels: in 1941 the Propaganda minister ordered that the theatre doors remain locked from the start of the newsreel until the end of the feature film, thus prohibiting those who made use of the previous five-minute interlude to skip the Wochenschau.[32]

But, coercion aside, there was little that the regime's authorities could do to restore the credibility of the newsreel other than maintain its constancy and safeguard its display in tandem with the – still very popular – film productions. The changing realities of the war, both on the front and inside the Reich, convinced the OKW authorities that a new approach was necessary. On the one hand, it was becoming obvious that the narrative of impressive victories which had been sustained between 1939 and early 1942 was no longer tenable. For example, the prior emphasis on using maps, location-specific footage and a wealth of topographical information in order to highlight the speed and extent of German advances had become a liability at a time of retreat or at best stabilisation. In May 1944 – when the collapse of the eastern front had started to appear as irreversible – the head of the RMVP Film division, Hans Hinkel, convinced Goebbels that the customary map of Russia that used to appear in earlier Wochenschau had to be sacrificed as 'it bears no relevance to the current military situation'.[33] On the other hand, the increasing exposure of the civilian population to the devastating effects of war (e.g. through Allied air bombing campaigns) forced the OKW in 1943 to issue new guidelines to its PK crews, stating that the reporters had to be very careful with the use of film and always bear in mind that their work would be seen by millions, thus emphasising the need to avoid any material that could distress the latter.[34]

Clearly, the NS regime was unwilling to abandon its erstwhile most successful medium of public information; and its efforts, as well as its responsiveness to the changing circumstances of war, paid off to an extent. Part of this success had to do with the fact that, unlike press or radio, the Wochenschau remained inside the realm of the RMVP's control throughout the war and thus allowed the ministry's authorities to achieve an optimal level of co-ordination between wider propaganda campaigns and specific newsreel content. In the autumn of 1944, for example, Goebbels managed to give the widest possible publicity to the launch of the *Volkssturm* (see Ch. 7) through an admirably synchronised campaign across the board of propaganda media.[35] Every new theme or discourse, and every new emphasis of the regime's propaganda was echoed in the choice of themes for the weekly newsreel presentation, ensuring maximum exposure and consistency. In fact, in spite of a growing problem of credibility, public opinion reports as late as the summer of 1944 emphasised that the Wochenschau remained relatively 'well-received' (*gut aufgenommen*) by the audiences.[36] There were, of course, increasingly vocal criticisms by members of the public and the regime authorities alike: some criticised the abstract character of themes and the avoidance of offering a clear picture of the military situation, the noticeable retreat of Hitler from the limelight, the over-burdening of the edition with 'scientific' themes,[37] the repetition of similar 'social' themes (e.g. soldier life in Russia) and the gradual restriction of the newsreel's variety.[38] Occasionally, even Goebbels's tight grip on the medium could not offer guarantees against potential slip-ups: on numerous occasions during 1944, the Wochenschau contained images from the effect of Allied air raids on Berlin which the Propaganda minister found truly unacceptable.[39] The Propaganda minister was determined, however, not to give up: during 1944 he tightened the process even further, appointing a special *Hauptschriftleiter der deutschen Wochenschau* who would participate in the ministerial conference and be solely responsible to the RMVP and the OKW.[40] And it was a testament to the commitment of the PK, of the officials in the OKW and the RMVP, as well as of Goebbels's personal investment in the Wochenschau, that its production continued until only a few weeks before capitulation and that the extensive supply network across the Reich was maintained against all odds until the very end.

The extent to which the mere survival of a regular Wochenschau in late 1944–early 1945 was an achievement in itself is highlighted by the mounting technical and logistical problems facing production during that period. Already in July 1944 Hinkel wrote to the secretary of the RMVP portraying a bleak situation for the Wochenschau in the light of anticipated reduction by at least one-third of raw film allocation. Although the worst-case scenario that Hinkel had outlined (a 45 per cent reduction to 770,000 metres, meaning one newsreel of less than twenty minutes every fortnight!) was averted due to the extraordinary allocation of extra raw film by the state and the use of the RKK reserves, the determination of the RMVP to maintain the frequency and the volume of the product resulted in drastic cuts in its length to around twelve minutes or 400 metres.[41] The situation, however, reached break point in the winter of 1944/45. A new wave of drastic cuts in raw film and coal allocation cast an even graver shadow on the whole system of Wochenschau production. During 1944, production had concentrated in the more secure facilities in and around Berlin (Tempelhof, Kraußenstraße, Neubabelsberg and Buchholz). But the intensification of land and air warfare around the German capital during the last months of the war caused extensive damage to the last available producing facilities at a time when necessary repairs were almost impossible to carry out. In a confidential report compiled by the DW for Goebbels in January 1945 (and therefore had no reason to gloss over the situation) it was noted that the weekly newsreel production was at severe risk: coal in the copying facilities sufficed for four more days, film quotas were declining or withheld due to transport difficulties (enough for only two further weeks of newsreel) and the dispatch of newsreel copies was hampered by the interruption of normal networks of distribution.[42] Hinkel (head of the Film Division) wondered whether in these circumstances the Wochenschau had to be reduced to a bimonthly edition.[43] On this occasion the RMVP's Film Section ensured within a few days the provision of 1.2 million metres of raw film from the OKW reserves and the allocation of extra coal;[44] it was thus possible to avert planned interruptions of the power supply or the exhaustion of the coal and film reserves.[45] There was, however, no normativity in these arrangements. Similar, but more severe, shortages continued to be reported to the Film Division of the ministry, each requiring new ad hoc arrangements that had to be negotiated with increasingly reluctant and under-resourced state agencies, dipping deeper and deeper into their reserves. Wochenschau 755/10, released towards the end of March with a total length of just eleven minutes, was destined to be the swansong of NS newsreel production. Amongst its ten short items it featured a scene where Hitler awards Iron Cross medals to members of the *Hitlerjugend* in what was also his last public and celluloid appearance. It was a fitting epilogue: the contrast to the almost weekly appearance of a confident, defiant and triumphant warlord who had dominated the Wochenschau during the first three years of the war could not have been starker.

Documentary as reality

In the first years of the war, the newsreel industry accumulated an amazing wealth of material that depicted the triumph of the Wehrmacht forces in all theatres of war. Recognising that even the initially apathetic German public had developed into a greedy consumer of such triumphalist images and demanded even more, the RMVP authorities developed new ideas for the exploitation of the material that had been edited out of the final newsreel products. As a result, a series of documentary-style films were produced through co-operation between the OKW, the DW and the RMVP. These included three feature-length military epics about the early NS campaigns against Poland (*Feldzug in Polen*, 1939; *Feuertaufe*, 1940) and against the West (*Sieg im Westen*, 1940), as well as a plethora of other, generally shorter propaganda films usually produced by *Ufa-Sonderproduktion* but with financial help from the RMVP or other state/party agencies (e.g. *Kosakenlied* and *Russen flüchten vor den Bolschewisten*, both 1944). This category also comprised some further feature-length films, such as the feature-long anti-Semitic film *Der ewige Jude* (1940) that used documentary-style footage and techniques in order to invest its defamatory political agenda with an aura of alleged historical accuracy; and *Verräter vor dem Volksgericht* (1944), chronicling the trial and execution of the 20 July 1944 conspirators against Hitler. Finally, there was a number of films that attempted to combine a fictional story with documentary material, such as *U-Boote Westwärts* and *Kampfgeschwader Lützow* (both 1941).

It was exactly this claim to objectivity through the use of documentary techniques that provided the common thread that ran through the diverse films of this category. The deliberate use of the documentary genre by the NS authorities as a window to an allegedly objective reality, immortalised through the insider's angle of the PK camera crews and – again ostensibly – eliminating the distorting influence of fictional story-telling, was intended to raise the stakes of historical objectivity and thus introduce a sharp distinction between the real and the fictional. It is interesting at this point to compare *Der ewige Jude* with the other major anti-Semitic film of the NS period, again released in 1940, *Jud Süß*. Whilst the former purported to depict the life, historical trajectory, culture and collective rituals of the Jews in an allegedly matter-of-fact manner, the latter bridged the gap between reality and fiction by re-working a real-life story set in eighteenth-century Stuttgart in a melodramatic form. In spite of this fundamental distinction in self-classification, both films were awarded the same certificates (*Prädikate*) as politically and artistically 'particularly worthy' and 'worthy for the youth' (*Jugendwert*), although *Der ewige Jude* had to be released in a second version – excluding the final, extremely graphic scene of ritual sacrifice – in order to make this suitable for a female and youth audience. Though each film represented a different genre and occupied divergent positions on the reality–fiction axis, they were largely intended and viewed as complementary, not least because of their almost concurrent release.[46]

Audience responses, however, varied greatly: it appears that the far more graphic and shocking treatment of the topic in *Der ewige Jude* to an extent recoiled, with the SD opinion reports stressing that the less blatant approach of *Jud Süß* proved far more acceptable to the general public.[47] Interestingly, this sort of audience response reveals an interesting bridging by the viewers of the genre distinction, perceiving the two films as similar in function and message.[48] Thus, the public responded favourably to film's intention to draw indirect analogies between the eighteenth and the twentieth centuries, perceiving history as a continuum and the story-line to be sufficiently 'real'; by contrast, they found the other film's claim to objectivity and contemporaneity both superfluous and exaggerated. Of course, it did not help *Der ewige Jude* that it was released immediately after the huge success of *Jud Süß*: the same audience showed signs of weariness and saturation after their second exposure to the same general theme. However, it is noteworthy that the public chose to attribute a high degree of realism to a 'period drama' whilst largely rejecting the crude realism of the allegedly purer realism of the documentary re-working of the same theme.[49]

The audience reaction to the two major anti-Semitic films serves to illustrate a wider tendency in the history of NS cinema – namely, the resistance to the overly didactic and blatantly ideological use of the film medium. Earlier films, such as *Hans Westmar* and *SA-Mann Brand*, (both released during the first year of NS rule) largely failed to capture the audience's imagination. They certainly must have convinced Goebbels that allusion and entertainment could prove far more effective propaganda tools than heavy-handed attempts at barefaced indoctrination.[50] The screening of *Hans Westmar* to a select Hitler Youth audience in 1942 illustrated to the RMVP authorities that even ideologically primed sections of the audience showed little enthusiasm for crude attempts at indoctrination. Although it was suggested at the time that the original 1933 film be transformed into a documentary, Goebbels eventually designated the film as unsuitable for wartime audiences.[51] Only *SA-Mann Brand* was rescued from oblivion, enjoying a new general release for party members in 1942 as the closest equivalent to providing an epic version of the NSDAP's own Horst Wessel 'martyr' on celluloid.[52] In November 1944 the rerun of 'national films' that was authorised in the aftermath of the Volkssturm's oath ceremony contained no full-length documentary or early propaganda film and was heavily biased towards the period genre; only *U-Boote Westwärts* and *Stukas* (1941) were represented in the list as examples of a mixed documentary–fictional genre.[53] As Goebbels himself had stressed in his speech to the Reich Film Guild, cinema should be primarily viewed as entertainment with a didactic purpose rather than the other way round.[54]

It was exactly this ratio of entertainment to ideology, as well as the correspondence between content and context, that held the secret to commercial success and audience approval in wartime Germany. The three 1940 newsreel-based documentaries about the campaigns in Poland and the west proved extremely popular because they appealed to a public steeped in triumphalist propaganda, secure in its knowledge of confirmed German strength and seeking to allay its initial fears about the war through basking in the visual representation of German military superiority.[55] *Feldzug in Polen* celebrated the first tangible show of the Wehrmacht's potential. The RMVP and the OKW intended it as a testimony to the success of the German Blitzkrieg, which took 'just three weeks to restore order and peace in eastern Europe and to guarantee the security of the Reich's eastern borders'.[56] *Feuertaufe*, albeit based on similar newsreel footage and largely authorised by the Luftwaffe as a way to redress the balance in the coverage of army and air force, came at an auspicious moment when audience interest was still high and the popularity of newsreel material continued to increase.[57] But it was the third instalment in this series of documentaries – *Sieg im Westen*, released in 1941 – that perfected the visual/narrative techniques and proved by far the most sensational. Part of this appeal had to do with the theme of the film (a highly praised military campaign that allegedly highlighted the German military and strategic superiority, as well as Hitler's 'genius' as war leader). A further bonus lay in the excellent quality of the newsreel footage, chosen and edited carefully from literally millions of raw film metres shot by the OKW–PK crews during the campaign. The film's main asset, however, lay in its skilful combination of highly entertaining visual material with a narrative retrospective of German history that had correctly diagnosed the mood of the contemporary German and spoke to them directly in terms that they understood and appreciated. Thus, the first part of the film is dedicated to a panorama of German history (particularly since Versailles but also stretching as far back as 1648 and reaching until the invasion of Poland) presenting the war as a last-ditch defensive move by the NS regime against an alleged international alliance against the Reich. Distilling the complexities of the preceding three decades down to a Mannichaean struggle between good and evil, the film avoided extensive scenes of destruction in favour of a more humane depiction of the idealised German soldier.[58] The connections forged between the First World War heroes, Hindenburg and Ludendorff, on the one hand, and Hitler, on the other, were used to emphasise the continuities in the German efforts to secure its own position in an otherwise allegedly hostile continent. Whilst realistic and anchored in an ostensibly direct depiction of 'reality', *Sieg im Westen* pitched itself perfectly vis-à-vis a public that rejoiced at German victories, was intoxicated by the Wehrmacht's show of strength but continued to be averse to the prospect of a long war and its brutalising effect on civilian society.

Ironically, neither Goebbels nor the majority of the party liked the film. Many raised questions about its certificate status as 'politically and artistically particularly worthy', particularly since it was based overwhelmingly on previously shot newsreel footage.[59] Yet, the audience's enthusiastic reception showed that distinctions between reality and entertainment in cinema could be skilfully negotiated by the filmmakers and received favourably by the audience. In other words, it was the entertaining aspect of the depicted 'reality' that guaranteed the commercial success and appeal of *Sieg im Westen* and *Feldzug in Polen*. Perhaps Siegfried Kracauer's designation of NS films as 'totalitarian panoramas, connecting the march of time with the march of ideas'[60] overstated the ideological commitment of the audiences to the alluded 'totalitarian' political framework of NS cinema: the public appreciated the 'reality' of a victorious war as partly an exhilarating piece of entertainment unfolding in front of their eyes with the added aura of allegedly accurate representation through newsreel footage. The same audience showed a similar degree of flexibility in internalising fictional or historical themes as allegories of contemporary reality.[61] Entertainment mattered as the gateway to any subsequent psychological associations, deductions and generalisations. This is where the crude and exaggerated realism of *Der ewige Jude* had clearly failed.

This said, the regime's propaganda intentions had vastly changed between 1940 and the last two years of the war. By 1943–44 defeat and desolation necessitated a different approach, where the careful trading of fear through the – more popular then ever – medium of film could succeed where once *Der ewige Jude* had gone amiss. In 1943–44 *Ufa-Sonderproduktion* released a series of short 'educational' films (*Kulturfilme*) with a blatantly negative message. The titles were suggestive of their intended function: *Russians flee before the Bolsheviks* (*Russen flüchten vor den Bolschewisten*, 1944), *The Misery of Children in the Soviet Union* (*Kinderelend in Sowjetrußland*, 1944). Unpleasant though the exaggerated depiction of a lethal enemy might have been for the audiences, the industry of fear served a clear function in enforcing a threshold of negative integration in the face of the advancing Red Army.[62] The change in the tone and content of this category of films could not have been starker to the earlier years of the war: whilst in 1941 the production programme of Tobis contained a wealth of 'positive' propaganda short films on themes such as the alleged German roots of Alsace (*Schönes Deutsches Elsass*,

Straßburg) and Flanders (*Flanders germanisches Gesicht*), the similarities between Croat and German rural culture (*Kroatische Bauernleben*) and the (once again) German roots of baroque architecture in Prague (*Prager Barock*),[63] the last wave of short films were intended to strengthen the resolve of the population to resist. Even Alfred Rosenberg's efforts to get involved in the production of educational films, flatly rejected in 1942 by the RMVP, were reconsidered and eventually supported – both technically and financially – in 1944.[64] The use of documentary techniques in the production of all these late NS films was intended to shock, not to placate or soothe the audience. Similarly, *Verräter vor dem Volksgericht* was produced with both a public and party audience in mind, emphasising in the harshest and most graphic possible terms the vehemence of reprisals against those accused of conspiracy against Hitler and the regime after the assassination attempt of 20 July 1944[65] – and it is not coincidental that Goebbels insisted that the film be shown to a large gathering of Gauleiters in the autumn of 1944.[66]

The historical film as contemporary narrative

The sharp reduction in the number of documentary full-length films from 1941 onwards did not mean that the RMVP authorities abandoned the claim to the depiction of an alleged 'reality' – either historical or contemporary, ideally both – or that they attributed to the medium a substantially more escapist, diversionary function. The long saga of the documentary production *Hitlers Sieg, Freiheit Europas* in 1942–43 acted as an eloquent cautionary tale, not just in terms of the difficulties involved in pitching such a project correctly (avoiding either an off-putting realism or an overly didactic, unspectacular presentation of reality) but also with regard to the importance of the timing factor. In fact, this film was produced during a period that witnessed the gradual change of the Reich's military fortunes. Starting in 1941, it was reviewed in January 1942 and was deemed unsuitable without a series of script changes. When, more than a year later, it was once again reviewed, the RMVP authorities decided to reject it on the basis that it was out of date with military and political developments, paying what was considered as 'insufficient attention' to themes such as the alleged danger of Bolshevism and the role of international Jewry.[67] By that time of course the overall popularity of the Wochenschau and, generally, of documentary-style films had suffered from the absence of 'good news' from the military front. The lesson, however, from the almost concurrent production of *Jud Süß* and *Der ewige Jude* in 1941 had already illustrated to the RMVP authorities that there was another, far more effective as it turned out, path to the alignment of film entertainment with contemporary propaganda discourses.

The so-called historical film had a long lineage in German and indeed European cinema before the Nazis came to power. The category included two main types of film: first, those that depicted actual historical personalities and events, thus claiming to offer a dramatisation of an otherwise allegedly accurate representation of historical 'reality'; and, second, those that placed (semi-) fictional story-lines in a time/place framework that purported to have captured the factual essence of the represented historical setting. It is obvious that the former type was in a position to raise a far stronger claim to 'accuracy', thus blurring the genre distinctions between documentary, educational and entertainment film. Nevertheless, this did not prevent film-makers from engaging with the latter type to seek a validation of the 'reality' of their own vision by claiming that the representation of the historical background was achieved with the utmost attention to the alleged truth. Eric Rentschler has observed that in the overwhelming majority of cases NS cinema avoided blatantly contemporary settings for its films, opting instead for either unspecific or historical backgrounds; it then invited the audience to engage in multiple processes of association with the present, drawing analogies and eliciting a moral substance that was decidedly aligned to wider socio-political narratives of their contemporary milieu.[68] The process of de-fictionalising the (semi-) fictional and turning subjective story-telling into a deciphered allegory of complex contemporary issues – in other words, of jumping from 'representation' to an alleged objective 'reality' – depended on prior public exposure to such issues. In this respect, the success of the 'historical film' required a converted audience, or at least one that wished to be converted.[69] Thus, the vivid reactions of the public to the stereotypically negative depiction of 'the Jew' as sly, hypocritical, deceitful and morally repugnant in *Jud Süß* pointed to the success of a long lineage of NS anti-Semitic propaganda that had allowed the collective cinematic crowd to perform the transcendence of the film's historical setting and relive the depicted story as diachronic 'truth' with contemporary relevance.[70]

Overall, the 'historical film' cut across conventional dichotomies of reality-versus-fiction, past-versus-present and propaganda-versus-entertainment. It too became a veritable growth market in NS Germany, but acquired a particular significance during the war years precisely because of this versatility of its character and open-ended opportunities for supporting wider propaganda discourses. 'Timeliness', as Jacques Ellul had stressed,[71] was of crucial significance in the process of audience identification with the story and its diachronic moral dimensions, as well as with the *dramatis personae*. The increasing input of the RMVP authorities in the commission of specific films during the war years reflected their intention to sustain public exposure to the same general themes that formed the backbone of contemporary propaganda campaigns. In this sense, the intended manipulative effect of mass entertainment rested on a series of choices made by various agents in the production process: selection of theme and background of the story; of directors and actors; of financing decisions; of shooting and editing techniques; and of distribution aspects. Whilst it would be impossible to claim that the propagandist (e.g. the RMVP authorities) was in a position to intervene crucially in all these areas, political input was pivotal in all but one of them.[72] Whilst Goebbels and the RMVP film authorities could influence the framework of production and its practical aspects, primary aesthetic accountability lay with the artists themselves; on this level, the interventions of the RMVP were restricted to subsequent review and revision, as well as to a final verdict as to whether, when and where the film would be released. The propagandist depended on the artists for the realisation of the intended vision; the latter relied on the former for the initial and final authorisation but also worked on general pre-production instructions in an attempt to anticipate Goebbels's expectations. The result was a confluence of visions – in the overwhelming majority of cases, compatible and complementary – in the context of a joint authorship.

Perhaps no other 'historical film' epitomises this compound process better than the 'swansong' of NS cinema, *Kolberg* (1945).[73] Goebbels's crucial role in commissioning the film in the first place has been widely acknowledged; the same applies to the RMVP's explicit commitment to meet any level of expenditure, to assist crucially in the actual shooting, the subsequent timely editing of the film and its widest possible distribution (including a deliberate decision to parachute the first copy to the besieged city of La Rochelle in France in time for the twelfth anniversary of the NS *Machtergreifung*).[74] The idea for a film on the story of the Prussian city of Kolberg's resistance to the advancing Napoleonic armies in early nineteenth century dated back to the early years of the war. However, the emphatic resuscitation and prioritisation of the project in mid-1943 betrayed the sort of deliberate narrative alignment of the regime's official propaganda with the exploitation of cinema entertainment as a device of psychological 'integration'. Goebbels commissioned Veit Harlan to direct the film as an allegory of the power of domestic loyalty and unity in the face of extreme adversity.[75] In spite of logistical and financial difficulties, shooting started in the actual location of the city in East Prussia for the most expensive Ufa production ever. The figures surrounding the production of *Kolberg* are extraordinary even without any other contextual information: shot in expensive Agfacolor film with more than 3000 metres and 110 minutes length, production costs reached a staggering 8.5 million RM. The RMVP had made clear that the unconditional co-operation of all state and Wehrmacht agencies was anticipated;[76] and they duly obliged, providing the director with almost 180,000 soldiers at a time when the Soviet troops were about to cross into East Prussia. The schedule involved a painstaking process of editing at the Ufa studios of Neubabelsberg, Berlin at a time that the city stood on the verge of paralysis as a result of air raids and any type of resource was scarce. Given that almost all production facilities in Berlin (as well as elsewhere) had already suffered considerable damage during 1944, whilst in December copying at the Afifa premises had been severely disrupted, it is indeed astonishing that the Neubabelsberg Ufa studio continued to produce and edit films until well into the spring of 1945![77]

By early autumn 1944 *Kolberg* appeared in Ufa's progress report as having entered the last stages of production, with an anticipated release date of 1 November 1944.[78] However, Goebbels's intention to review the film and make any necessary changes, as well as the expressed desire to produce as many copies as possible of this 'politically especially significant' film, dictated a series of postponements, first until December and then for another six weeks,[79] thus bringing the date of release well into January 1945. Having reviewed his ministerial copy, Goebbels expressed his overall excitement but demanded some changes, mostly to do with textual references but also with regard to some visual aspects (e.g. shortening of the destruction scenes in favour of developing the personality of the main characters).[80] The film opened officially in Berlin on 30 January 1945, having been lavished with every possible 'certificate', including the highest distinction of 'Film of the Nation'.[81]

After the war Harlan attempted to recast himself as the reluctant executor of a putative Goebbels vision for *Kolberg*.[82] He claimed that the early interventionist stance of the Propaganda minister in the framing of the story-line was emblematic of his obsessive interest in the film at the expense of the director's own creative sovereignty.[83] However, between the decision on the script in 1943 and the review of the ministerial copy in November 1944, Harlan imbued the film with his own cinematic vision; and it was his crucial input in this field, quite like Riefenstahl's similar contribution to the visual eloquence of *Triumph des Willens* less than a decade earlier, that lies at the heart of a discussion about authorship on the art-propaganda nexus.[84]

The sort of conjunction of political (propaganda) and aesthetic visions witnessed in the case of *Kolberg* constituted the culmination of a trend that had seen the 'Goebbels network' taking a keen interest in the production of films with a historical content, whilst maintaining an overall supervisory role of the entire film production during the war.[85] In this respect, the genre of 'historical film' in NS Germany cannot be seen as independent from the wider exigencies of 'integration propaganda', both in positive and negative terms. *Kolberg* offered a eulogy to the heroism and loyalty of the city's inhabitants in the nineteenth century – even to the point of distorting the facts of the story in presenting the resistance as successful – as a thinly veiled incitement to contemporary Germans to stay united; but it also juxtaposed the image of the courageous German to the negative stereotype of the French – conceited, aloof, cynical, occasionally inhuman. The 'other' was the indisputable co-star in every 'historical film'. In fact, it was *through the 'other'* that the alleged moral superiority of the Germans could be conceptualised and validated: in *Das Herz der Königin* (1940), *Ohm Krüger* (1941) and *Carl Peters* (1941) it was the British; in *Der Große König* (1942) – the second biopic based on the life of King Friedrich the Great after *Fredericus* (1936) – it was again the French; in *Jud Süß* and *Die Rotschilds* it was international Jewry; in

GPU (1942) it was the Bolsheviks. Negative incarnations of the 'other' invariably featured in every German wartime historical film, even if it was only for a cameo appearance: in *Die Entlaßung* (1942) – the second biopic on the life of Chancellor Bismarck, chronicling the events that led to his dismissal – the character of the assassin was purported to be of English descent. But even in those films with a far less obvious attribution of specific identity to negative characters, allusions to negative stereotypes were intended to be easily detected. For example, *Paracelsus* (1943) cast its main figure of the sixteenth-century unconventional physician in contrast to Pfefferkorn – a scheming, cynical merchant who was willing to sacrifice the common interest (defence against the plague) for the goal of making more money, thus opposing Paracelsus's idea of sealing off the city.[86] In presenting Pfefferkorn as the caricature of the rich, unscrupulous trader with no loyalties or interest in anything beyond his individual profit, the film drew from the vast pool of anti-Semitic inferences in order to accentuate the positive qualities of Paracelsus himself. Thus, in all historical films produced under National Socialism the functions of celebrating an alleged German genius and of denigrating evil in the form of Germany's enemies were inextricably tied, the latter crucially validating and accentuating the former.

Timeliness was, of course, a huge risk when it came to films, particularly since the whole process from commissioning to release and distribution of the final product could take years. By the summer of 1939 there were a series of historical films in various stages of preparation. Whilst relations with the western powers had noticeably deteriorated since 1938 and had therefore allowed this to be factored in the new productions, very few people (even within the hierarchy of the NSDAP or the regime) could have entertained the idea of a military alliance with the Soviet Union. When this became a reality with the signing of the Molotov–Ribbentrop pact on 23/24 August 1939, the German studios had already been busy producing films with a clear anti-Bolshevik content. Some of these, such as *Legion Condor* – a Spanish Civil War epic – and *GUR* were only months away from general release. The new political reality, however, imposed an opportunistic ban on all such films. One of them, a full-length documentary on the contribution of German volunteers in Spain with a blatant anti-Soviet tenor (*Im Kampfgegen den Weltfeind: Deutsche Freiwillige in Spanien*), had to be immediately withdrawn altogether from cinema halls.[87] Indeed, anti-Bolshevik films had to wait until after June 1941 (Operation Barbarossa) in order to reach again the general public as part of an orchestrated anti-Soviet propaganda campaign.

Even the mere change from peace to wartime imposed restrictions and fundamental changes on the production plans of the German film studios. A new emphasis on propaganda shorts-films, *Kulturfilme* and deliberately diversionary entertainment necessitated a wider revisiting of the long-term production plans. At the same time, the increasing tendency of the RMVP to commission films with specific content (and the historical film was constantly on the top of the RMVP officials' preference list) restricted the studios' room for manoeuvre in terms of forward planning. Even if the international context did not change after 1941, thereby averting a repetition of the 1939 situation with the war and the alliance with the Soviet Union, it was always hard to predict the outcome of particular campaigns or the actual parameters of the military or civilian situation. *Paracelsus* turned out to be a commercial disaster; other films, including *Kolberg*, had to be revised in textual and visual terms alike, in order to avoid upsetting the civilian audience at a time of increasingly harsh conditions of everyday life caused by material restrictions and the intensifying Allied air campaign.

This unpredictability explains why the RMVP authorities expended so much energy, often to the vexation of the artistic management of a film, in terms of ensuring an optimal level of integration between the film and the wider context of contemporary propaganda. Clearly, the sort of biopics that flooded the market during the Second World War had been carefully chosen to enforce public loyalty to the allegedly extraordinary qualities of the Hitler's leadership.[88] Between 1940 and 1941 a stream of historical/biopic films with an anti-British content flooded the market, meticulously integrated in the wider propaganda patterns dictated by Germany's campaigns against the west and Operation Sea Lion. The struggle of Irish independence against the British was captured in *Der Fuchs von Glevarnon* (1940) and *Mein Leben für Irland* (1941), whilst a similar heroic depiction of the Scottish struggle against English domination informed *Das Herz der Königin* (1940), based on the life (and decapitation) of Mary Stuart, Queen of Scots. In addition, two more expensive productions, *Carl Peters* (1941) and *Ohm Krüger* (1941), exemplified the use of the colonial theme in order to discredit British 'plutocratic' and 'imperialist' leadership (see Ch. 3). Both films contained a two-pronged attack: against the allegedly inhuman behaviour of the British colonialists conduct in Africa; and against their cynical plot to thwart the ambitions of 'proletarian' nations (*Habenichts*) to maintain and expand their territorial resources. In *Ohm Krüger* the ostensible moral superiority of the Boer's fight to save Transvaal (and of Krüger as their leader) was juxtaposed to the depravity of Cecil Rhodes, Queen Victoria and of the Prince of Wales, whose main concerns were either purely materialistic (the discovery of gold in Transvaal) or crudely geopolitical.[89] In his deathbed in Switzerland the defeated, broken Krüger concluded the film with an attempt to set the film's historical theme in a contemporary setting:

[t]his is how the British overpowered and degraded my people ... [B]ut one day a greater nation will rise to crush Britain ... Only then will the world be a better place to live in.

A similar pattern of forced historical analogy, suited to the contemporary setting of NS foreign policy and the accompanying propaganda, was offered in the last scenes of *Carl Peters*. Again, a defeated visionary of extraordinary qualities, a leader presented as being far ahead of his time, prophesied that his vision will be taken up in the future and brought to fruition.[90] But the moral saga of this film was far more ambiguous here, for it was not just the British but also the timidity of the German parliamentary system that had thwarted the dynamism of the Volk. Here, the anti-British theme was smoothly collated with another major propaganda discursive pattern – that of critically assessing the mistakes of the Second (Wilhelminian) German Reich, culminating in the First World War.[91] This consideration makes the ambiguity of these two films – they showed defeats and not victories – far more intelligible: by emploting historical fragments into a wider project of fulfilling Germany's ambitions that allowed comparisons between past and present, the whole history of the German nation was presented as a moral saga geared towards a final vindication in spite of temporary setbacks. This analogy worked well on two crucial psychological levels: first, in presenting the present fight as a morally validated crusade for avenging past injustices; and second, in convincing people that even short-term defeats in the current war could not reverse the march of history towards the final German victory.

The superiority of the contemporary German leadership, exemplified by the allegedly extraordinary qualities of the Führer, was the theme of another two major biopics of the early war years, based on the life of the same historical personality – Otto Bismarck. *Bismarck* (1940) and *Die Entlaßung* (1942) offered a dramatisation of two critical fragments in the history of the First Reich. The first portrayed the Iron Chancellor as a man contemptuous of parliamentary diletantism and willing to stake everything in order to achieve his vision of German unification. At a significant juncture the film showed him arguing his case in favour of making a diplomatic and military volte-face by turning against the Habsburg Empire as a necessary precondition for the accomplishment of his long-term unification policy. The analogy of this decision with the signing of the Molotov–Ribbentrop pact in August 1939 was intentional, if relatively understated,[92] at least when compared to other more blatant attempts at drawing comparisons with the contemporary diplomatic situation found in other films. *Die Entlaßung*, released almost two years later and at a time that the military-diplomatic situation had dramatically changed, was a far more solemn affair, depicting the last years of Bismarck's political life leading to his eventual dismissal by the young King Wilhelm II. The ambiguity of the theme – like *Ohm Krüger*, ending with the sight of a defeated genius – was intended to be fully compensated by Bismarck's final uttering:

> Princes come and go, people die, but the nation is eternal ... What must remain is the Reich; if the people and the Reich become one, then the Reich too will be eternal ... My work is done. It was just a beginning. Who will complete it?[93]

Faced with such a blatantly rhetorical question, a well-trained audience drew the intended analogy with Hitler. Yet, by 1942 the Reich was once again trapped in a two-front war, just like Bismarck's criticised successors had done after his dismissal by failing to renew the alliance with Russia. Goebbels was indeed sceptical about alternative readings of the film and authorised a test screening to a select audience of party members and experts. The results were inconclusive, with reactions ranging from enthusiasm to trepidation to full negativity.[94] Amongst the varied criticisms, there were some common threads: bad timing after the failure to end the war against the Soviet Union in 1942 and the general public anxiety about the two-front war; shallow depiction of history; putting the blame for the First World War on Germany's flawed foreign policy and not on its enemies; and insufficient attention to the subversive role of the Jews. One comment in particular reflected eloquently the unforeseen complications of using history as a moral saga with contemporary relevance: as one member of the audience stated, the idea that genius can indeed be defeated by 'petty political intrigue' cast in doubt the propaganda discourse that Hitler's superiority alone would guarantee the final victory.[95] However, in the end the Propaganda minister put his own doubts aside and gave the film its widest possible distribution in September 1942.[96] Rosenberg's attempt to use Bormann in order to attack the film and its preferential status in terms of *Prädikate* (which, in his opinion, were not warranted by the film's quality)[97] was easily brushed aside once it became obvious that Hitler himself liked the film.[98]

There were no such misgivings amongst the NS nomenclatura with regard to the other major 1942 biopic, *Der Große König*.[99] Crowning a long line of films on the life of Frederick the Great going back to 1922 (*Fridericus Rex*), this was a complex film with a host of discursive patterns that could neatly accommodate the regime's contemporary propaganda themes. The image of a lone king, fighting against all odds, betrayed by his closest associates but steadfast in his belief that his instinct was guiding him in the right direction, constituted perhaps the most deliberate historical analogy with Hitler's leadership. Cunning planning and coincidence conspired to render the film politically expedient in a host of meaningful ways. Since December 1941 Hitler had restructured the Wehrmacht High Command and taken over the leadership of the armed forces in the face of growing opposition from generals.[100] He had also become far more reclusive, absorbed in the business of military planning and avoiding his erstwhile public appearances. The film focused heavily on Frederick's clash with the Prussian army leadership in a way that made direct parallels with the OKW unmistakeable. Goebbels himself made no secret of the deliberate character of this analogy when he spoke in his diary of the film's castigation of the generals' 'defeatism'.[101]

But the portrayal of a leader isolating himself from unwise counsel, fighting alone on the strength of his conviction and eventually winning a stupendous victory was useful for the recasting of the 'Hitler myth' by the RMVP in the second half of the war. Unlike Bismarck, Frederick was a figure staring at a crushing defeat and reigning over a crumbling empire. From 1942 onwards Hitler too started to lose his earlier aura of invincibility and infallibility (see Ch 6). With this film the regime planned not just to eulogise its leadership and draw historical parallels with prominent predecessors, and to present its own campaign as the conclusion of a long-term historical epic for the unification of the German Volk, but – as Goebbels noted – also to strengthen the resistance of the people vis-à-vis the privations of war and solidify its rapport with Hitler even in the latter's growing absence.[102] The peculiarly prophetic assassination sub-plot of the film, in which the king survives and then thanks 'Providence' for this (just like Hitler did in the aftermath of the 20 July 1944 explosion), gave a new lease of life to *Der Große König* in 1944–45, when the newly appointed head of the RMVP's Film Division, Fritz Hippler, decided to relaunch films of political value (see above).[103] But, overall, this was the kind of historical film that the regime authorities always wanted to produce: positive ending; depiction of a leader blessed with almost superhuman qualities but troubled by the sheer magnitude of his historic responsibility; a people eventually determined to fight; an aggressive, unscrupulous enemy; and ample opportunities for clear but not overly didactic historical analogies with the present.[104]

Timing, therefore, mattered, both for the regime that commissioned the films and for the audience that eventually decided their commercial and political fortune. Goebbels proved supremely responsive to the signals sent from the cinema halls through the various public opinion reports. The failure of *GPU* – primarily attributed to the blatant didactic caricaturing of the Russians and Germans alike – put a premature end to commissioned full-length anti-Bolshevik productions, channelling instead the needs of anti-Soviet propaganda to press, radio and shorter documentary or *Kulturfilme*. Openly anti-British films peaked in 1940–41 and – with the exception of the unimpressive and unsuccessful *Titanic* (1943) – all but disappeared from the list of big productions. *Geheimakten W.B.I* (1942) was a biopic presenting the life of Wilhelm Bauer who designed the first modern submarine, made to coincide with the peak of the U-Boot campaign in the Atlantic at a time that the RMVP was making the most propaganda currency out of this theme, for self-congratulation and diversion purposes alike.[105] A similar fate marked the brief appearance of the anti-Semitic film, from the lighter comedies of 1939 (e.g. *Leinen aus Irland*) to the 1940–41 trilogy featuring *Die Rotschilds, Jud Süß* and *Der ewige Jude*. As the case of the latter film showed to the Propaganda Minister, audiences appreciated and responded to allusions to the contemporaneity of the historical in the context of an otherwise entertaining, subtle and not heavy-handed or overly moralising story-line. In fact, the most successful 'intrapolations' were often those that were suggested as secondary aspects, enforcing rather than instructing or introducing stereotypes: the English assassin of Bismarck in *Die Entlaßung*, the Jewish shopkeeper

Salomonsson in *Heimkehr* (1941), Napoleon and the French generals in *Kolberg*, the amoral and cynical Rhodes in *Ohm Krüger*, the particular portrayal of Bismarck, Krüger and Frederick the Great suggestive of continuity with Hitler, and the decadent English 'plutocracy' in *Die Rotschilds*. With the sole exception of *Jud Süß*, the most effective negative portrayal of 'the Jew' was supplied by films in which the main story-line was not anti-Semitic or had been carefully dovetailed with a wider attack on western 'plutocracy' (see Ch. 3). In *Die Rotschilds* the notion of a Jewish conspiracy is depicted in tandem with the wider degeneration of western liberalism that had allegedly sold itself to the materialistic and rootless Jew to the point that it had been taken over by it. Even in *Heimkehr* the predicament of the *Volksdeutsche* under the Poles implicated the Jews as the main instigators of anti-German violence. Thus the film indirectly presented the war against Poland as a 'defensive' move of the Reich against not just its eastern neighbours but also against the emerging unholy international alliance against it.[106]

The historical film production under the Third Reich fulfilled Goebbels's intention to blur the distinction between 'art' and 'politics', with varying degrees of success. Quite like propaganda itself, it proved far more effective when it enforced already prevalent stereotypes and avoided the trap of turning cinema entertainment into a vehicle of blatant ideological indoctrination. In fact, the cinema halls fulfilled a crucial dual role, wholly intended by the RMVP: a space of mass diversion and a laboratory for indirectly testing or enforcing wider propaganda campaigns or themes. The exercise of primary control over cinema by the Goebbels network is better understood in this context rather than in terms of unabashed 'totalitarian' domination. It was not the grand NS ideological narrative but a series of sub-themes – most of them old and tested, sometimes new and experimental – featured against an otherwise innocuous background that informed the best-received and most commercially successful films.[107] In this respect, the shift towards 'lighter' entertainment in 1943–44 constituted far less of a concession to audience pressure or a sacrifice for the NS propagandist than has been widely assumed; for the nature of the film medium was porous enough to allow for the penetration of such indirect sub-themes even when neither the setting nor the moral of the story lent themselves to grand statements of the whole NS ideological package.

Commercial and politically valuable?
The 'entertainment film' and NS propaganda

Throughout the years of NS rule but more significantly during the sensitive war period both the RMVP and the RPL managed a large body of correspondence relating to every aspect of the regime's film policy (critique, production, distribution etc.).[108] The particular attention shown by the RMVP authorities to the 'state-commissioned' films (*Staatsauftragsfilme*) was understandable given Goebbels's intention to use historical films as both devices of 'making politics' and *Durchhaltefilme* (namely films combining rich visual entertainment and political messages intended to bolster the staying power of the German population at a time of increasing adversities and privations). But meticulous attention to the political, social and cultural implications of the seemingly more innocuous 'entertainment' films betrayed a subset of motives that throws heuristic distinction between 'politics' and 'entertainment' into serious doubt. In fact, the complexity of the background to the production, distribution and monitoring of 'entertainment' films was emblematic of the disparate considerations invested in the overall management of German film industry during the war years. Diversion, political integration propaganda, social penetration and perpetuation of 'cultural hegemony', and commercial investment – all these factors were equally significant benchmarks of success. The 'orchestra principle' – followed by Goebbels in the management of the propaganda apparatus – allowed for different porous combinations and degrees of intention, not an incontrovertible division of labour. Gerd Albrecht's calculation that the number of 'purely political' propaganda films produced under the Third Reich amounted to less that one-seventh of the overall corpus of movies[109] obscures a far wider common deliberation that underpinned every regime intervention in film production: to expand or at least maintain its audience by appealing to a kaleidoscope of tastes, psychological needs and aesthetic expectations. In this context, shifts in production patterns and ratios disclosed the ever-changing diagnosis of the RMVP authorities as to what type(s) of film could promote the wider goal of audience expansion or retention in the particular short-term circumstances of the military campaign. The prioritisation of the documentary genre in 1939–40, the intensification of spectacular historical films in 1941–42 and the subsequent shift to 'entertainment' films (*Unterhaltungsfilme*) were examples of tweaking the relative composition of the cinema 'orchestra', on the basis of 'public opinion' feedback. They represented *relative* shifts of quantity and not fundamental shifts in the propaganda paradigm.

The constant reports that was channelled back to the RMVP from as varied sources as the SD, the RPA, the Gauleiters themselves and party figures facilitated a largely effective fine-tuning process. Throughout 1943, reports from all over the Reich kept flooding the RMVP that exuded a scepticism about the potential of the so-called 'political film' to penetrate an audience so accustomed to the association of cinema with light entertainment and escapism. By that time, of course, the initially extremely popular Wochenschau had fallen into disrepute in spite of the RMVP's efforts to align it to every cinema activity. But even when it came to expensively produced 'historical' films, neither audience figures nor reactions during and after the screening were encouraging. The Gauleiter of Sachsen stated the obvious when he pointed out that audiences in his *Gau* preferred romantic comedies and dramas to historical or political films. He noted that spectators appeared unmoved by the significance of the represented events and portrayed characters, noting with scepticism that the audience's interaction with political films showed a low degree of appreciation and understanding.[110] This, again, was simply one manifestation of a broader problem that the RMVP authorities had to address, namely working out an effective balance between entertainment, information and 'enlightenment' that ensured the popularity of the medium, maintained its audience base but at the same time enhanced the overall propaganda effect of its message.

Unlike most in the NSDAP, Goebbels had understood the dual function that cinema could perform (entertainment *and* indoctrination). More crucially, he appreciated how the two were interdependent – especially how 'light entertainment' was used to enforce cultural hegemony, to placate an audience base that would subsequently be exposed to more 'political' products and to provide short-term diversion when reality contradicted the regime's discourse. To the constant accusations from party officials (such as Rosenberg) that cinema was underexploited as a 'political propaganda tool' (*zu wenig im Dienste der politischen Propaganda steht*[111]), Goebbels responded defiantly by increasing the share of 'light' entertainment in the Reich's overall film production. In 1942 he spoke of an 80–20 ratio and stressed the significance of 'art providing relaxation' at a time of increasing war-induced privations for the population.[112] He also personally denied Rosenberg's *Dienststelle* the opportunity to make a series of didactic ideological films in 1942[113] and fended off party attempts to infiltrate the film censorship system and the award of *Prädikate*.[114] On these occasions, the Propaganda minister was promoting a different understanding of how entertainment and indoctrination, when carefully balanced and used in a mutually complementary manner, could promote 'total' ideological, cultural and political goals far more effectively than a heavy-handed 'educational' cinema could ever do.

An interesting example of this tendency related to the RMVP's efforts to ensure a degree of diversification and flexibility in the distribution of film repertoire across the Greater Reich. As mentioned before, cinema as propaganda medium differed from either press or radio in the 'total' nature of its end-product: a film or newsreel was produced and released for a massive audience with a far smaller margin for adaptation to specific geographic and social attributes of its intended audience. With the extension of the German territory from 1938 onwards – but particularly during the war, when population groups of different ethnic, religious and cultural character were incorporated into the Reich, most of them in the occupied territories – the diversity of the spectators' everyday experience, expectations and sensibilities presented the RMVP authorities with a side effect of their totalitarian project: whilst the single film artefact promoted a single world-view and was thus supremely suitable for enforcing a 'cultural hegemony', its suitability for specific groups could no longer be taken for granted.

This, however, does not mean that the RMVP authorities gave up the efforts to mediate in the distribution network and thus mitigate the inflexibility of the medium in this domain. Already in December 1942, Goebbels had asked for a more effective differentiation between the repertoire shown in urban cinemas and that destined for provincial facilities, even within the Old Reich. This distinction between 'city' and 'province' appears to have troubled the RMVP authorities even with regard to a 'light' musical production such as Paul Martin's wartime *Maske in Blau*. The film, released without any censorship problems in 1942, came to the attention of Goebbels and Walter Tießler – head of the *Reichsring* (see Ch. 2) – who debated the suitability of the film for general release in May/June 1943. In spite of Tiessler's strong objections to both its general artistic value and its appropriateness for the sensibilities of a non-urban audience (the story involved a talented female dancer who is lured from the province into the Berlin dance scene by a composer, in spite of her father's objections), Goebbels stated the well-received entertainment character of the film and did not intervene on this occasion in the distribution process.[115]

When it came, however, to potentially sensitive political matters or social issues the Propaganda minister displayed a willingness to issue directives that banned films from specific areas. The release of Veit Harlan's *Die Goldene Stadt* in erstwhile Czechoslovakia provoked an angry reaction from the Gauleiter of Sudetenland, who wrote to the RMVP and openly challenged the *Prädikat* 'especially artistically worthwhile' (*künstlerisch besonders wertvoll*) that the film had been awarded. The Gauleiter noted that the film's depiction of Czech people as 'cunning and sly' could aggravate the already troubled relations of NS authorities with the local population.[116] As a result, Tießler wrote to the ministry's Film Division and asked that *Die Goldene Stadt* be banned from the Protectorate of Bohemia and Moravia with immediate effect.[117] Sometimes, restrictions in distribution were pre-emptive. *Wien 1910*, a semi-historical film about the rise of political anti-Semitism in pre-WWI Austrian capital directed by E W Emo, was banned from both Austria and the Protectorate by Goebbels personally – and this after the minister had demanded a series of modifications in the script.[118] Cultural differences between the citizens of the Old Reich and the populations that resided in the newly absorbed or occupied territories demanded further sacrifices and imposed new restrictions on production and distribution alike. Films produced with a German audience in mind (particularly historical or political) could be inappropriate for, or inaccessible to foreign spectators; by the same token, films produced elsewhere (e.g., Fascist Italy) often presented the same difficulties for the German audiences.[119]

If, as conventional distinctions between 'propaganda' and 'entertainment' would suggest, *Unterhaltungsfilme* bore far less of the ideological burden than the more overtly political/documentary/historical films, how are we then to understand either the kind of feedback from the SD and the RPA or the willingness of the RMVP authorities to take remedial action? The story of *Große Freiheit N. 7* (1944) was emblematic of Goebbels's far-from-indifferent attitude to entertainment films. Produced amidst mounting problems caused by air raids in a race against time, forced to relocate from Berlin to Prague due to the damage caused to the Tempelhof Terra facilities, the film also suffered from the Propaganda minister's last-minute 'improvement' diet that delayed its eventual release by more than five months. Even when the film premiered in Prague, the RMVP eventually decreed that it was unsuitable for general release within the old Reich, in spite of its spiralling production cost (shot in Agfacolor and with expensive actors, such as Ilse Werner and Hans Albers).[120] The Propaganda minister was so annoyed with the ostensible indecency of the main female character (even if she commits suicide in the first scene, again in a perfectly redemptive pattern of ethical rehabilitation) that he had taken the decision to ban the film even before he surveyed the ministerial copy! In spite of the desperate pleas of the Ufa management to Goebbels to autho-rise the general release of the film in view of both its enormous cost and the anticipated box-office revenue, he based his decision to thwart the film's distribution within the old Reich on political rather than aesthetic grounds.[121]

In the 1943 general production report of the nationalised Ufa, a series of demanded (from above) alterations relating to entertainment films appeared in the margins, equally substantive as those accompanying historical pro-ductions such as *Die Entlaßung* that featured in the same list.[122] These com-ments involved minor interventions: removal of the 'Hitler salute' (*Meine Freundin Josephine*); the marriage of a German soldier with a Flemish and not French girl (*Schicksal im Osten*); the removal of a direct reference to religious and church matters (*Das letzte Abenteuer, Bis ins 4.Glied*). A similar story involved Rolf Hansen's expensive 'entertainment' film *Die Große Liebe* (1942). The film's spectacular box office success (more than 18 million tick-ets sold) had a lot to do with the appearance of the extremely popular actress Zara Leander; but it was also well-liked for its music and the romantic aspect of a love affair between a soldier on leave and a local singer.[123] This did not stop a high-level NSDAP officer in Leipzig from writing a letter to the Race Political Office (*Rassenpolitisches Amt*), complaining that the film's portrayal of a love affair of a German with a Danish girl could send the wrong message to a city with a sizeable population of foreign workers![124] In 1941, the depic-tion of a marriage between a German girl and an Italian in *Ins blaue Leben* provoked a similar censure from local party authorities in Magdeburg, which the Party Chancellery appeared to condone.[125] Even *Annellie* (1941), one of the most highly praised earlier entertainment films, received its own share of criticism by local party authorities in a party report from Danzig. The same report also stressed the need to avoid showing films in which people speak with southern dialects in eastern Reich provinces![126]

Could it be that even entertainment films were far from the innocuous, propaganda-free material that some accounts of NS cinema had suggested?

Crucially, the most commercially successful films ever produced under the Third Reich were indeed popular *Unterhaltungsfilme*, such as the *Wünschkonzert*[127] and *Die Große Liebe* (both reaching audience figures well in excess of 25 million RM and generating substantial net profits). Such power over the audience – that is, over society as whole – was tempting, especially at a time that other, more traditional means of propaganda penetration were already suffering from a crippling fascination deficit. Commercial success meant not just much-needed revenue at a time of financial hardship and mounting production difficulties, but also social and cultural influence.

If we consider a 'propaganda' film as a coherent, rigid narrative of grand ideological proportions, then no *Unterhaltungsfilm* could possibly fulfil this goal, and nor was it intended to do so by producers and regime supervisors alike. If, however, we substitute ideological coherence (which, in any case, was often problematic even in the far more politically charged historical films) with the more timid objective of enforcing and perpetuating patterns of social and ethical conformity, then entertainment films remained supremely 'political'. It would be misleading to award exceptional or unique status to the use of entertainment in the Third Reich: cultural hegemony through art and entertainment has been identified as a rather commonplace function in democratic, authoritarian and totalitarian societies alike.[128] Nor was the intervention of regime authorities in film production *during wartime* an exclusively anomaly of Hitler's regime.[129] What remained highly particular to NS Germany was the degree of attention afforded by the RMVP and particularly by Goebbels's personally to film production, as well as the wider ideological and cultural background that turned the seemingly innocuous entertainment film into a crucial instrument of the propaganda 'orchestra principle'. It might be tempting to overstep Goebbels' input in this process, but the Propaganda minister oversaw a system of production that was 'working towards him', in many cases almost by default.

Equally, it would be misleading to exaggerate the effectiveness of this supervisory role exercised by the RMVP: there were numerous instances of failure in the overall censorship process, of squandering of resources and spectacular u-turns. At exactly this point, commercial considerations seemed to subside in favour of more specific political, social and cultural caveats. Film under the Third Reich proved to be invaluable, successful and unpredictable, all alike. Assuming a status of full regime control over content and production would be as deceptive as a sharp separation of motives behind the making of documentary, educational, historical and entertainment films; and the latter were perceived almost as 'real' and 'contemporary' as the rest. The process of drawing analogies was always in effect amongst the audience, unpredictable and – at least partly – autonomous from any regime intentions. In this respect, the RMVP's intervention (anticipatory or ex post facto) was a pre-emptive attempt to turn film themes into politically congruent and desirable allusions whilst arresting other, unwanted inferences.

Managing German cinema, 1939–45

Largely untroubled by the customary internecine battle that raged in other spheres of his ministry's jurisdiction, and having established an efficient understanding with those that mattered for the film industry, Goebbels entrenched and bolstered his commanding role within the film industry during the war years. He was aided in his efforts by a natural expansion of the medium's popularity and infrastructure that had been taking place since the end of the First World War. From 1918 to 1929 the number of available movie theatres across the Reich rose by two-thirds, reaching around 5500 by early 1930s. An even more impressive upward trend was evident in the sale of tickets, from around 250 million per year in early 1920s to 350 million in 1929 and more than 400 million in 1937.[130] Within the first decade of NS rule attendance figures per person grew at least two-fold in the major urban centres, sometimes (as in the case of Karlsruhe and Lübeck[131]) three-fold.[132] Yet, even these impressive figures obscure an even more striking geographic extension of German cinema's catchment area: whilst in the early 1930s it was fairly rare to find a cinema theatre in towns with a population smaller than 20,000, by 1942–43 the building of new premises across the province,[133] the conversion of existing facilities (temporary or permanent) into projection locations, the party's active involvement in organising regular screenings of 'educational' value (e.g. the DAF's *Kraft durch Freude* scheme, *Hitlerjugend* events etc.) and the investment in mobile projection units that toured the countryside, all contributed to a far wider penetration of German society by cinema.[134] By late 1942 the nationalised German film industry had reached a peak that seemed unimaginable a decade earlier. Cinema facilities had expanded exponentially, reaching the figure of 8334 across the whole territory controlled by the Reich. The establishment of the *Deutsche Filmtheater-Gesellschaft* (DFT) as a party umbrella organisation for the management of cinema distribution and projection across the Reich introduced yet another layer of covert state/party monopoly in a crucial domain of film policy. Income from ticket sales reached one billion RM in the same year, while profits for the new Ufi climbed to 1.7 million DM.[135] Throughout the Reich, Ufi controlled nearly an undisputable lion's share – 160 cinema theatres with a seating capacity of over 160,000. Whoever remained out of the company's network was doomed to distribution ostracism![136]

Goebbels had demanded a total wartime production figure of 100 German films per year – by all accounts a highly ambitious level, given the increasing demands of the military situation in terms of material and human resources. However, the two stages of the industry's re-organisation from the mid-1930s to 1942 bore fruits: by 1939 domestic production reached a peak of 110 films, while the ratio of German to foreign films halved (from 10:6 to 10:3).[137] By 1943 the number of performances per year had climbed from its 10,000 pre-war figure to a staggering 43,000.[138] The Propaganda minister must have felt personally vindicated with his project of stealth nationalisation when, in late 1941, he noted in his diary,

> [m]ovie production is flourishing almost unbelievably despite the war. What a good idea of mine it was to have taken possession of the films on behalf of the Reich several years ago! It would be terrible if the high profits now being earned by the motion-picture industry were to flow into private hands[139]

Things started to go downhill for German cinema, however, after the peak of 1941–42. Already since 1940, there had been alarming indications with regard to the capacity of a film industry operating in the context of an escalating war to meet ambitious production quotas. The RMVP's insistence on exceeding 100 German films per year had been achieved in the 1937–39 period but remained unreachable afterwards. By 1942 production had sunk to well below 52 – only slightly recovering to 74 in 1943 and then steadily declining in 1944–45.[140] What was even more alarming was that these figures were achieved with most German studios working at full capacity or even stretching beyond their available means to meet the increasing number of state-commissioned productions. For example, a relatively small (if profitable) Ufi-controlled peripheral studio in Austria, *Wien-Film*, was at a time engaged in the production of twelve different films when its nominally allocated quota by the RMVP was closer to half that figure.[141] In spite of considerable RMVP optimism that overall production could still be elevated to the desired 'hundred films' level, particularly through decentralising production to occupied territories and increasing the market share of foreign films,[142] the war had started to take its toll on German cinema even before military developments had forced the RMVP to fight for its sheer, day-to-day viability. By late 1944 the word 'difficulties' (*Schwierigkeiten*) accompanied every official report as an explanation for the failure to meet quotas and the overall deteriorating situation. Shortage of Agfa (raw) film had become an acute problem by the autumn of 1944, due to loss of territory and damage to producing facilities due to air raids alike.[143] In November 1944 the main supplier (*Reichsstelle Chemie*) warned that the monthly provision of film had to be reduced from 12 million to 7 million metres: the Reichsfilmkammer (Reich Film Chamber) RFK – had to sacrifice almost 2.5 million metres, whilst film for export purposes would be slashed by two-thirds and the OKW quota by 75%.[144] For a moment even newsreel production was endangered, in spite of the significance attached to it by the RMVP, the OKW and the party.

This crisis could only deepen. The devastation wrought on the Reich by the intensifying Allied air raids also affected the cinema infrastructure. The number of facilities for projection fell from the 1942 peak of 8334 to 6500 in spring 1943; more than 230 cinemas had been totally destroyed by the summer of 1943 and more were to be razed to the ground or simply lost (due to military retreats) in the last two years. Consequently, serious flaws in the distribution network were exposed, especially after January 1942 when the *Deutsche Filmvetriebs GmbH* was established as a centralised agency for film programming and supply. For example, following the severe air raid on Lübeck in October 1942 the only Ufi-controlled cinema was destroyed and the citizens were left with the only alternative of an independently-owned facility that received only old films.[145] It is indeed incredible that the Ufi network was in a position to compensate for its losses until late 1944, through either the opening of new facilities or the conversion of all premises into projection rooms. From September 1944 all theatres, concert halls and night clubs (but not cinemas!) were shut down, allowing the RMVP to reuse spaces for regular film shows. As a result, the serious slump in seats witnessed in 1943 was reversed, albeit not fully compensated for; in the autumn of 1944 Lübeck got an extra 1015 seats, Breslau 1043 and Halle almost 1100.[146] In Berlin alone a similar recovery was noted with satisfaction by the RMVP officials: whilst seats nearly halved between 1943 and 1944, by January 1945 they had climbed up to 32,000 – less than 20 per cent lower than the peak 1943 figure![147]

The twin problems of devastation of premises, on the one hand, and spectators' fear about their safety during air raids, on the other, had been noted by the new leader of the RMVP's Film Division and *Reichsfilmintendant*, Hans Hinkel in a report submitted to Goebbels in late April 1944: attendance figures for 1944 showed the first recorded decrease after a decade of spectacular rise, particularly in the large communities (over 50,000, inhabitants) that were mostly affected by air attacks.[148] This is why Hinkel campaigned vigorously for the extension of his 'People's Cinema' scheme,[149] identifying new empty venues across the Reich and ensuring that cinema-going would be built into the routine of communities affected by war and air raids. Already in the end of 1943, a confidential report lauded the efforts of certain Gauleiters to build small projection rooms inside new bunkers, thus partly compensating for damage to facilities and maintaining the contact of their *Gau* population with the regime's film production.[150] Furthermore, mobile projection units continued to tour provincial Germany, providing cinema entertainment and 'education' in the context of party-organised events.[151] Given that the Allied air warfare against the Reich showed no signs of abating in 1944, the report underlined the need to extend this provision to all new bunkers built, in conjunction with a redoubling of the efforts to ensure continual supply of film products across Germany.

Clearly, the nationalised German film industry was struggling in 1944–45, after a period of overall impressive growth. In the extraordinary circumstances of military collapse, it was becoming obvious that the RMVP could no longer run a financially successful film enterprise, continue to produce many new films, ensure its widest distribution *and* operate in the cost-saving mode imposed by 'total war' or actual material shortages. Goebbels had made many choices with regard to German cinema ever since 1933; a decade later he had to make a final one; and it was a choice fully consistent with his intention to maintain his ministry's propaganda 'noise' until the very end, to safeguard its channels of communication with the public and preserve a semblance of normality against all odds. As the Reich's situation on both the military and the domestic fields deteriorated dramatically after 1942, the need to bolster the staying power of soldiers and civilians alike acquired an increasingly higher priority than considerations of profit. The extraordinary allocation of raw film and other essential resources for the sustenance of the whole production and distribution network in 1944–45 suggested a growing priority to film output per se, regardless of those commercial considerations that had played a role until 1942. Otherwise, it is extremely hard to comprehend the decision to produce two absurdly expensive, full-length Ufa films (both in lavish 35 mm Agfacolour!) in the last months of the Reich's existence in spite of the extremely limited opportunities for distribution and profit: apart from Kolberg, *Die Opfergang*, again directed by Veit Harlan, premiered in a war-ravaged Hamburg on 8 December 1944 and three weeks later in Berlin. Its length was ninety-eight minutes and it received the high *Prädikat* designation of 'especially artistically worthy'.[152]

In the autumn of 1944 the Ufi officials started preparing the production plan for 1945 as if nothing had changed. In his report to Goebbels, Hinkel offered a detailed overview of the industry's status in October: seven films in the final stages of production (including *Kolberg*), two more undergoing last-minute revisions, seven more in editing, four in preparation and a further eight in preparation for 1945.[153] A month later Agnar Hölaas announced the final decisions about planning for the following year: against all odds, about thirty films had been planned, most of them assigned to Ufa's Berlin facilities.[154] More than just an attempt at wishful thinking, the resolve of the German film industry in the final months of the Third Reich reveals a conscious decision on part of the RMVP to spare state-sponsored film production from the otherwise ruthless cost-cutting measures necessitated by the dearth of raw materials and by military collapse. One could possibly read in the diversion of invaluable military and financial resources away from the front and to the production of a historical epic such as *Kolberg* an array of different motives: an escapist detachment from reality, a realisation that the war on the military front had been lost, a transcendental belief in the power of cinema, an exorcism of an adverse reality, and maybe Goebbels's obsession with leaving a lasting *personal* monument to history – echoing Joachim Fest's judgment of the Propaganda minister as a 'propagandist for himself'.[155] Be that as it may – and there are perhaps elements of truth in all these interpretations – NS cinema remained until the very end a realm of unbound artistic, aesthetic and political reverie for the Propaganda minister, a medium of his personal vision as well as an autonomous goal in itself, increasingly diverging from the everyday demands of popular propaganda and projecting an ideal scenario for the regime, for NS Germany and for the *Volksgemeinschaft* in blatant defiance of reality.

Conclusions: Legitimising the Impossible?

The final act of NS propaganda outlived Hitler and Goebbels. On 1 May 1945, with both of them dead and their bodies burnt as requested, Admiral Karl Dönitz – as the Führer's designated successor – announced to the Germans that Hitler had died whilst 'fighting heroically' to defend the city of Berlin. The Third Reich, Dönitz continued, would continue to fight on, honouring its founder's legacy and 'mission' to defend Germany and Europe from Bolshevism. By that time of course the conflict had been decided – and the German public knew very well that such declarations were a hollow bravado just before the end. On 8 May 1945, Dönitz signed the 'unconditional surrender' of NS Germany.

The cataclysmic collapse of National Socialism during those last days of April–May 1945 was indeed striking; but the fact that the regime's propaganda network continued to operate in spite of the colossal material, logistical and psychological disruption that it had suffered almost unremittingly since the beginning of 1943 was in some respects even more remarkable. With the exception of Hitler's withdrawal from the limelight, the backbone of NS propaganda's routine remained largely intact until the very end; and so did its totalitarian aspirations vis-à-vis of controlling the population, notwithstanding the gradual disintegration of its psychological hegemony and the disaggregation of its target audience. The heavy investment in 'negative' integratory themes and short-term diversion did not of course aspire to strengthen the 'positive' strands of public allegiance to the regime, nor did it result in sustaining an optimistic outlook of everyday life (*Stimmung*); yet, it did make sure nevertheless that an absolute minimum of fighting and 'staying power' (*Haltung*) would persist – and even outlive the Führer himself. This transformation in the regime's propaganda themes, discourses and overall message in the last two years of the conflict encapsulated both the spectacular failures and the enduring successes of the NS grip over German society.

In the end, notwithstanding the sophistication of its technological, political/ideological and psychological apparatus, NS propaganda was overpowered by an empirical reality that it had sought to administer and exorcise but whose outcome was decided on a terrain that it could not influence in any significant way. It is, of course, crucial to note that the seeds of its disintegration lay in the very recipe of its success until the first months of 'Operation Barbarossa' in 1941. The extremely high stakes behind the carefully choreographed idolisation of Hitler, the promotion of a discourse centring on his alleged 'infallibility', and the unmanageable triumphalism of its early wartime rhetoric were transformed into major liabilities once the regime's military campaign first stopped producing victories and then was confronted by a stream of crushing setbacks. Hitler's increasing aloofness, the betrayal of his promise that the war would be a short, victorious campaign, and the contradiction of the regime's official 'reality' by first-hand experience disempowered and debilitated the mechanisms of NS legitimation. At the same time, the demobilised and depoliticised German population reclaimed a small but crucial part of their autonomy in thinking and acting independent of the regime's will or exhortation. This amounted to the gradual reconstitution of a sort of autonomous 'public sphere' in the widening lacunae that the NS propaganda had failed to saturate with its official discourse, vision and authority. Once the regime had been deprived of its uncontested monopoly of supplying 'truth' and once its 'ersatz reality' started contradicting the empirical experience of the German population, a dormant civil society with independent powers of shaping opinion began to reassert itself timidly, in gradual open nonconformity to the NS regime's official propaganda message.

The extent to which NS Germany developed into a paralysingly *polycratic* structure during the war cannot be exaggerated. In his postwar memoirs, Hitler's own Chief of Press, Otto Dietrich (and, as we saw, a prominent agent of polycratic disorder himself) described the situation as 'the greatest confusion that has ever existed in a civilised state'.[1] Neo-feudal 'networks' of de facto authority entered into a ferocious jurisdictional battle that was never contained or resolved in a rational-bureaucratic manner. Instead, formal power-bases, rooted in state or party agencies (or often in a mixture thereof), competed for overall power, specific jurisdictions, as well as for the Führer's favour. This latter factor, pivotal in a system geared towards a 'charismatic' model of leadership, proved Goebbels's blessing and nemesis alike. From 1928, he had exploited this same resource against other party contenders, capitalising heavily on Hitler's support in order to erect a massive party and then state personal empire in the domain of propaganda. From there, he extended his grip over even wider secondary fields, such as culture, education and foreign information activities, largely at the expense of other institutions and individuals. The creation of the 'Goebbels network' was predicated on two interrelated premises: first, to enforce an effective 'coordination' (*Gleichschaltung* – that is, nazification) of propaganda as a whole and of its information and entertainment networks separately; and, second, to streamline, centralise and direct the state and party propaganda apparatus in its expanding functions and scope. His stranglehold, however, proved tentative and porous in the process. From the middle of 1934 and more so in the 1937–42 period, the hard political currency of Hitler's favour largely eluded Goebbels. In fact, had Hitler been less disinclined towards punishing his associates who appeared to have failed him or become less useful than others, he could have dealt with him more harshly. He did not, in the same way that he did not relieve Goering of his powers over the Luftwaffe even when his failure became critical for the whole of Germany's war effort. But these were barren and frustrating years for the Propaganda minister, as he witnessed his authority over crucial areas of the NS propaganda domain wither away to the benefit and delight of the likes of Otto Dietrich, Joachim von Ribbentrop, Albert Speer and Martin Bormann.

The result was that Goebbels and his 'network' never managed the bulk of information relating to propaganda; never exercised *full* control over the formulation of the propaganda message; never enjoyed the privilege of planning propaganda campaigns with the total apparatus of resources at their disposal and under their effective control; and never operated in an empty field without internal – and often fierce – competition. Channels of information-gathering frequently bypassed the RMVP, sometimes were deflected from within the ministry (by people who were technically Goebbels's subordinates and responsible to him) or released when it was already too late to control the flow of information. Furthermore, even when the minister was in a position to work out a propaganda strategy, this had to be often negotiated with parallel efforts of other agencies that antagonised any notion of RMVP monopoly over communication. This development was the result of Hitler's own defiance of normative notions of jurisdictional division of power that rendered the institutional position of his ministers and officials incidental and changeable on an ad hoc basis. But it was also the result of a peculiar state–party dualism, which saw both systems expand and overlap in a largely uncoordinated manner from 1933 onwards. That Goebbels held the leadership of both the RMVP (state) and RPL (party) propaganda head-institutions was reassuring but not sufficient to guarantee uniform strategies, precisely because of the existence of overlapping zigzag networks that transgressed state–party or institutional lines of jurisdiction. Lastly, the Propaganda minister did not fully or always control the devices of propaganda dissemination (the instruments of his 'orchestra') and was not in a position to promote integrated strategies through effective, harmonious deployment of all available assets; nor was he in a position to control all exercises of 'public opinion' monitoring: whilst the RMVP had its own network of data gathering in this field, so did the Ministry of the Interior and – informally – the Party Chancellery (directly from the Gaus), whose information reached the Propaganda ministry in a selective and already mediated way.

Goebbels had to wait until 1942–43 to see his fortunes turn around dramatically. This was largely the result of Hitler's disillusionment with erstwhile favourites and of his retreat from the limelight. Even then, however, Goebbels still had to wage battles to repatriate jurisdictions and powers from other personal 'networks'. Ironically, the pinnacle of his power came in the last months of the war, when almost everything had been lost but when he enjoyed at last Hitler's full favour. His perseverance during the difficult inter-regnum was eventually – if belatedly – rewarded. The trajectory of the 'Goebbels network' from early ascendancy and empowerment to its struggle for defend-ing its grip over propaganda and to its final – pyrrhic – victory encapsulated a wider battle between discordant visions that was emblematic of the overall function of the NS system of rule: a battle between centralisation and 'co-ordination' versus polycratic erosion, duplication and jurisdictional elasticity. Whilst Goebbels achieved a rapid coordination of state and private activities in his wide domain, he faced immense problems in translating this into a totalitarian structure under his undisputed command. Thus, Goebbels turned propaganda into an evolving 'totalitarian' device of NS legitimation, but then saw it fall prey to a paralysing polycratic zigzag that he could not control. His efforts to reclaim the role of central command had less to do with enhancing the quality of the regime's propaganda output as such; it was primarily a weapon in the context of an internecine battle for relative power gains in Hitler's 'charismatic' regime that had rendered centralisation a chimera and nurtured a constant war of personal fiefdoms inside it until the very end.

In this respect, it is tempting to view the output of NS propaganda as a *cumulative* result – the sum of discourses articulated by different bodies – negotiated between mutually suspicious agents and, more often than not, transmitted without any prior overall consensus. Especially until early 1943 each 'network' had given up the illusion of internal 'totalitarian' co-ordination and centralisation, manufacturing propaganda for its own sake and at the expense of its rival(s), with which it was supposed to co-operate. The dearth of normative procedures and fixed hierarchies, particularly in the field of press and, to an extent, in broadcasting too, engendered opportunities for input and jurisdictional inflation. Sometimes this depended on proximity to the source of information or on closeness to Hitler himself; on many occasions it was simply a matter of timing – who could get the information first and be the quickest in mobilising their resources. The final product may have always been underpinned by broadly similar long-term political objec-tives (victory of the regime; military success; strengthening of the national community) and themes of negative integration (crushing of the 'enemy', inside and beyond the Reich). The constant competition, however, inside the ranks of state and party, as well as the different degrees of interference into specific propaganda activities by rival agencies and personalities, defied normativity and produced often unpredictable results. This situation gener-ated constant tensions on the level of information management that fre-quently gave rise to divergent forms of 'official' output; it was indeed an 'orchestra', but one whose members often followed different maestros and tempos, read from different sheets and produced dissonant noises. From an external point of view, the NS propaganda message appeared essentially consistent and uniform; just below the surface, however, a fierce battle raged for the ownership and handling of the specific content.

In the Introduction, I attempted to determine the benchmarks for assessing the effectiveness of propaganda. A large share of responsibility for the distorting exaggerations surrounding the study of NS propaganda has originated from an analytical culture of 'particularism' with which postwar research has approached almost everything that has to do with National Socialism, including its propaganda apparatus, the alleged 'genius' of Goebbels, the 'totalitarian' control of media, the receptiveness of the German public and the co-relation between indoctrination and fanatical fighting power. It might be reassuring for us to 'demonise' the record and fetishise the alleged departure of National Socialism from a 'western norm'; it might be equally comforting to draw definitive distinctions between totalitarian 'propaganda' and information on the one hand, and information/persuasion in democratic societies on the other. There was indeed a lot that set Hitler's regime apart from its western counterparts and from our structures of power nowadays. This does not justify, however, a retreat to a paradigm of 'exceptionalism' when we refer to the former. NS propaganda (its totalitarian aspirations included) operated firmly inside the framework of modernity, even if it was one that the western world was thankfully unwilling to accept. In his final comments at the Nuremberg Trials, Albert Speer provided a stark warning about the destructive potential inherent in modern civilisation, if left unchecked without a wider moral framework of self-restraint and respect for individualism.[2] NS Germany sought to radicalise and not foil modernity, and to re-found and recast it on the basis of fanatical ideological principles of collective action that overshadowed other considerations and jettisoned conventional safeguards. This was a fundamental departure from 'western norms' – but one that was largely based on excess and unacceptable distortion; not paradigmatic uniqueness.[3]

Instead, NS propaganda operated structurally within the broad logic of legitimising the exercise of power and eliciting consensus that characterises the functioning of every modern political system. It collected news, formulated headlines, made choices about the most effective timing and devices (media, campaigns, grand narratives) for the dissemination of its message and constantly monitored the effects of its operation. It operated on two dimensions of time: short-term (responding to external developments, explaining and justifying specific incidents) and long-term (piecing together events and then emploting them in a context of shared values through which its audience understood the complex reality). As stressed earlier, effective propaganda at any given moment derives from a combination of both these dimensions: convincing, authoritative communication per se and an equally persuasive alignment of short-term reality with cultivated, widely shared beliefs and attitudes amongst its target audience. Such propaganda may help the soldier on the front to fight more fanatically or to resist the temptation to give up in the face of overwhelming adversity; but it cannot win wars decided on predominantly military and logistical grounds. It may assist the population to maintain its composure and perseverance, even when confronted with immense tests and privations; but it cannot 'brain-wash' a complex modern society in the course of little over than a decade, if at all. It may change gradually the perceptions of its audience; but it cannot do this without a degree of consensus or without partial failures. It may enhance the legitimacy of a regime and the appeal of a favourable 'truth' or mitigate the adverse psychological effects of 'bad news', intervening in the process of perceiving reality; but it cannot change the course of events or cancel out the effects of external developments. It may be successfully centralised in political-administrative terms by one agency or even one person (even if, as we saw, this was not exactly the case in NS Germany); but it cannot be conducted single-handedly by one agent of however exceptional qualities. NS propaganda, like the personality of Hitler and the alleged exceptionalism of the whole political record of the regime that he headed until its collapse, is in desperate need of de-escalation. This by no means involves 'normalisation', 'trivialisation' or the sort of historiographical 'revisionism' that has been rightly censured in scholarly, political and moral terms alike. It does suggest, however, a wholesale reassessment of what NS propaganda could objectively achieve and did achieve; of what it could not possibly perform and indeed did not; but, perhaps more significantly, of what constitutes 'propaganda' (allowing for distinctions between regime types, historical periods and personal qualities; but not overstating them) and how it is bound by a plethora of external forces and agencies that it nominally manages but cannot fully command in the first place.

Perhaps Hitler's consistent presence in the public sphere (as Goebbels continued to request) could have mitigated or slowed down the process of both the disintegration of the NS propaganda's effectiveness and the emancipation of a 'public sphere'. Or maybe a more centralised and normative approach to decision-making could have generated a more coherent and orderly system, thus rescuing NS propaganda from many of its mistakes in the 1941–45 period. But it has to be emphasised that the task of the NS propaganda machine had become virtually impossible after 1942–43. It had succeeded in averting the possibility of another '1918' in terms of a collapse of the 'domestic front': an increasingly fatalistic German population remained sufficiently demobilised and accepted that its fate had become tied to the cardiogram of the regime and of the Führer personally in the absence of more promising alternatives. And perhaps the success of NS propaganda lay in exactly discrediting these alternatives and in effectively identifying the imagery of 'national interest' with the regime and its 'charismatic' figure-head, even when disaster and collapse appeared as certainties. Beyond that, there was indeed little that could have been done: the collapse of the regime lay in direct correlation to the worsening of its military fortunes after 1941 and, in particular, to the direct, painful manner in which hardship was felt by Germans as part of their everyday experience in 1942–45.

Notes

Introduction: 'Totalitarianism', Propaganda, War and the Third Reich

1. J Ellul, *The Technological Society* (New York: Vintage Books, 1964), 21–2; cf. J Ellul, *Propaganda: The Formation of Men's Attitudes* (New York: Knopf, 1971).
2. J Wright, *Terrorist Propaganda* (New York: St Martin's, 1990), 70–1; D McQuail, *Mass Communication Theory: An Introduction* (London/Beverly Hills/New Delhi: Sage, 2003, 4th ed.), 99 ff; K Robins, F Webster, M Pickering, 'Propaganda, information and social control', in J Hawthorn (ed.), *Propaganda, Persuasion and Polemic* (London: Edward Arnold, 1987, 2nd ed.), 2–4.
3. B Ginsberg, *The Captive Public. How Mass Opinion Promotes State Power* (New York: Basoc Books, 1986); W Kornhauser, 'Mass society', *International Encyclopedia of the Social Sciences* (New York: Macmillan, 1968); W Kornhauser, *The Politics of Mass Society* (New York: Free Press, 1959); McQuail, *Mass Communication Theory*, 91–2.
4. BA, NS 18/349, 39–40 (Tiessler, Vorlage: Filme Beurteilung, no date); 347, 39 (Party Chancellery, Report from Magdeburg-Anhalt, 9.12.1941). See in general, J A C Brown, *Techniques of Persuasion. From Propaganda to Brainwashing* (Baltimore: Penguin, 1963), 308 ff.
5. L W Doob, *Public Opinion and Propaganda* (New York: Henry Holt and Co, 1948), 131–9; G S Jowett, V O'Donnell, *Propaganda and Persuasion* (Newbury Park/ London/New Delhi: Sage, 1992), 15–16.
6. Jowett and O'Donnell, *Propaganda and Persuasion*, 187 ff. The two films are discussed in ch. 8.
7. H C Triandis, *Interpersonal Behavior* (Monterey: Brooks/Cole, 1977), ch. 3; Ellul, *Propaganda*, 35–7.
8. The use of the term 'revolution' in a fascist context has caused a lot of controversy. The traditional perception of 'revolution' as a positive, emancipatory break is, of course, non-applicable in this context. However, a growing number of scholars in the fray of fascist studies detect a clear 'revolutionary' (i.e., radical) core in fascist ideology. See the interesting discussion hosted in *Erwägen, Wissen, Ethik*, 15/3 (2004); in particular, the three articles by R D Griffin: 'Fascism's new faces (and new facelessness) in the "post-fascist" epoch', 287–301; 'Da capo, con meno brio: towards a more useful conceptualization of generic fascism', 361–77; 'Grey cats, blue cows, and wide awake groundhogs: notes towards the development of a "deliberative ethos" in fascist studies', 429–41.
9. Jowett and O'Donnell, *Propaganda and Persuasion*, 122–54; D J Bern, *Beliefs, Attitudes and Human Affairs* (Belmont: Brooks/Cole, 1970).
10. See, for example, J Goebbels, 'Stimmung und Haltung', *Das Reich*, 4.11.1943.
11. Cf. I Kershaw, 'How effective was Nazi propaganda?', in D Welch (ed.), *Nazi Propaganda: The Power and the Limitations* (London: Croom Helm, 1983), 180–205.
12. I Ajzen, M Fishbein, *Understanding Attitudes and Predicting Social Behavior* (Englewood Cliffs: Prentice–Hall, 1980).
13. C I Hovland, I L Janis, H H Kelly, *Communication and Persuasion. Psychological Studies of Opinion Change* (New Haven: Yale University Press, 1953); R J Boster,

P Mongeau, 'Fear-arousing persuasive messages', in R N Bostrum and N H Westley (eds), *Communication Yearbook 8* (Beverly Hills, CA: Sage, 1984), 330–75.

14. Ellul, *Propaganda*, 58–60.
15. R E Herzstein, *The War that Hitler Won: Goebbels and the Nazi Media Campaign* (New York: Paragon, 1987).
16. D Lerner, 'Effective propaganda: conditions and evaluation', in D Lerner (ed.), *Propaganda in War and Crisis. Materials for American Policy* (New York: Stewart, 1951), 344–54.
17. M Balfour, *Propaganda in War 1939–1945: Organisation, Policies and Publics in Britain and Germany* (London: Routledge, 1979).
18. D Roberts, *The Poverty of Great Politics. Understanding the Totalitarian Moment* (London: Routledge, 2006).
19. C J Friedrich, Z K Brzezinski, *Totalitarian Dictatorship and Autocracy* (New York/Washington/London: Praeger, 1965), 21–6.
20. On the similarities and differences in the use of propaganda between 'totalitarian' and 'democratic' states see T H Qualter, *Opinion Control in the Democracies* (New York: St Martin's Press, 1985); Jowett and O'Donnell, *Propaganda and Persuasion*, 25–7; Robins, Webster and Pickering, *Propaganda, Persuasion and Polemic*, 6–7, 14 ff.
21. For a discussion of this see I Kershaw, *The Nazi Dictatorship. Problems and Perspectives of Interpretation* (London: Edward Arnold, 1995, 4th ed.), ch. 4; P Diehl–Thiele, *Partei und Staat im Dritten Reich. Untersuchung zum Verhältnis von NSDAP und allgemeiner innerer Staatsverwaltung, 1933–1945* (Munich: CH Beck Verlag, 1971), ch. 2.
22. K Lang, 'Communication research: origins and developments', in G Gerbner, W Schramm, T L Worth, and L Gross (eds), *International Encyclopedia of Communications* (New York: Oxford University Press, 1989), 469–74.
23. D Marvick (ed.), *Harold D Lasswell on Political Sociology* (Chicago/London: The University of Chicago Press, 1977), ch. 10.
24. R Semmler, *Goebbels: The Man Next to Hitler* (London: Westhouse, 1947), 3.3.1943, 72–3.
25. E K Bramsted, *Goebbels and National Socialist Propaganda 1925–1945* (East Lansing: Michigan State University Press, 1965), 253.
26. McQuail, *Mass Communication Theory*, 82; Ellul, *Propaganda*, 57–8.
27. *Aufklärungs- und Redner-Informationsmaterial der Reichspropagandaleitung der NSDAP*, 11 (1939), 31–41; cf. International Military Tribunal (IMT): 15.1.1946, 266 ff; Vol. XVII, 27.7.1946, 155 ff (Hans Fritzsche interrogation).
28. IMT, Vol. 17, Session 166 (28.6.1946), 273–4.
29. Jowett and O'Donnell, *Propaganda and Persuasion*, 32–3.
30. Robins, Webster and Pickering, *Propaganda, Persuasion and Polemic*, 5 ff; B Taithe, T Thornton, 'Propaganda: a misnomer of rhetoric and persuasion?', in B Taithe, T Thornton (eds), *Propaganda. Political Rhetoric and Identity, 1300–2000* (Stroud: Sutton Publishing, 1999), 1–24.
31. Jowett and O'Donnell, *Propaganda and Persuasion*, 80 ff.
32. Jowett and O'Donnell, *Propaganda and Persuasion*, 212 ff.
33. For example, I Kershaw, *Popular Opinion and Political Dissent in the Third Reich: Bavaria, 1933–45* (Oxford: Clarendon, 1983); I Kershaw, *The Hitler-Myth. Image and Reality in the Third Reich* (Oxford/New York: Oxford University Press, 1989); M G Steinert, *Hitler's War and the Germans: Public Mood and Attitude During the Second World War* (Athens, OH: Ohio University Press, 1977).
34. Ellul, *Propaganda*, 17–20.

1   Propaganda, 'Co-ordination' and 'Centralisation': The Goebbels Network in Search of a Total Empire

1. K D Bracher, *Die nationalsozialistische Machtergreifung* (Cologne, 1960); M Broszat, *The Hitler State: The Foundation and Development of the Third Reich* (London: Longman, 1981).
2. R Griffin, *The Nature of Fascism* (London/New York: Routledge, 1994), 47 ff.
3. H Arendt, *The Origins of Totalitarianism* (New York: Meridian Books, 1958); C J Friedrich, 'The unique character of totalitarian society', in C J Friedrich (ed.) *Totalitarianism* (New York: Grosset & Dunlap, 1954), 47–60; C J Friedrich, Z K Brzezinski, *Totalitarian Dictatorship and Autocracy* (Cambridge, MA: Harvard University Press, 1956), 15–26; cf. K D Bracher, *Totalitarismus und Faschismus. Eine wissenschaftliche und politische Begriffskontroverse* (Munich/Vienna: IZG, 1980).
4. M Mann, 'The contradictions of continuous revolution', and H Mommsen, 'Working towards the "Führer": reflections on the nature of the Hitler dictatorship', both in I Kershaw, M Lewin (eds), *Stalinism and Nazism* (Cambridge: Cambridge University Press, 1997), 135–57 and 75–87 respectively; A Kallis, ' "Fascism", "para-fascism" and "fascistization": on the similarities of three conceptual categories', *European History Quarterly*, 33/2 (2003), 219–49; Griffin, *The Nature of Fascism*, 26–55; R Eatwell, 'Towards a new model of generic fascism', *Journal of Theoretical Politics*, 2 (1992), 161–94. On Weber's theory of 'ideal-types' see L A Coser, *The Sociology of Max Weber* (New York: Vintage Books, 1977), 223 ff.
5. See, for example, A Lyttelton, 'Fascism in Italy: the second wave', *Journal of Contemporary History*, 1 (1966), 75–100.
6. D Welch, *Propaganda and the German Cinema, 1933–1945* (London/New York: IB Tauris, 2001, rev. ed.), 7–9.
7. Goebbels's speech is featured in C Belling, *Der Film in Staat und Partei* (Berlin, 1936), 28–30.
8. D Welch, *Propaganda and the German Cinema*, 10–12.
9. I Hoffman, *The Triumph of Propaganda – Film and National Socialism 1933–1945* (Providence/Oxford: Berghahn Books, 1996), ch. 4.
10. On the creation of SPIO see M Behn, 'Gleichschritt in die "neue Zeit". Filmpolitik zwischen SPIO und NS', in H–M Bock, M Töteberg (eds), *Das Ufa-Buch* (Frankfurt: Zweitausendeins, 1992), 341–69.
11. G Albrecht, *Nationalsozialistische Filmpolitik. Eine soziologische Untersuchung über die Spielfilme des Dritten Reichs* (Stuttgart: Ferdinand Enke, 1969), 12 ff.
12. Welch, *Propaganda and the German Cinema*, 8–10.
13. Reichsgesetzblatt (RGB), 1934, I, 95.
14. J Wulf, *Theater und Film im Dritten Reich* (Gütersloh: Sigbert Mohn Verlag, 1964), 275–6.
15. Welch, *Propaganda and the German Cinema*, 14–15.
16. P M Taylor, *Munitions of the Mind. A History of Propaganda from the Ancient World to the Present Era* (Manchester: Manchester University Press, 2003, 3rd ed.), 1–18; Albrecht, *Nationalsozialistische Filmpolitik*.
17. E Rentschler, *The Ministry of Illusion. Nazi Cinema and Its Afterlife* (Cambridge, MA/London: Harvard University Press, 1996), 43 ff; K Witte, 'Film im Nationalsozialismus', Wolfgang Jacobsen (ed.), *Geschichte des deutschen Films* (Stuttgart/Weimar: J B Metzler 1993), 119–70; Hoffman, *The Triumph of Propaganda*, 96 ff.

18. RGB, I, 694–5.
19. For this reading of National Socialism as a 'neo-feudal' system of rule see R Koehl, 'Feudal aspects of National Socialism', *American Political Science Review*, Vol. LVI/4 (1960): 921–33.
20. Wulf, *Theater und Film im Dritten Reich*, 271.
21. See, for example, the September 1933 law that banned Jewish artists and writers from the Reich's cultural production [R Hilberg, *The Destruction of the European Jews* (London: W H Allen, 1961), 7 ff].
22. For figures on film production under the Third Reich see Welch, *Propaganda and the German Cinema*, 20 ff.
23. Welch, *Propaganda and the German Cinema*, 23–5; F Moeller, *Der Filmminister. Goebbels und der Film im Dritten Reich* (Berlin: Henschel Verlag, 1998), ch. 2.
24. See, in general, C Quanz, *Der Film als Propagandainstrument Joseph Goebbels* (Cologne: Teiresias, 2000).
25. A Kallis, 'The "regime model" of fascism: a typology', *European History Quarterly*, 30/1 (2000), 77–104.
26. R Taylor, *Film Propaganda: Soviet Russia and Nazi Germany* (London/New York: I B Tauris, 1998), 242–8; cf. Albrecht, *Nationalsozialistische Filmpolitik*, 478–9 (speech to the RFK, February 1941).
27. M S Phillips, 'The Nazi control of the German film industry', *Journal of European Studies*, 1/1 (1971), 37–68; G Schoenberner, 'Ideologie und Propaganda im NS-Film: Von der Eroberung der Studios zur Manipulation ihrer Produkte', in U Jung (ed.), *Der deutsche Film. Aspekte seiner Geschichte von den Anfängen bis zu Gegenwart* (Trier: Wissenschaftlicher Verlag, 1993), 91–110.
28. Welch, *Propaganda and the German Cinema*, 25–6.
29. M Geyer, 'Restorative elites, German society and the Nazi pursuit of goals', in R Bessel (ed.), *Fascist Italy and Nazi Germany. Comparisons and Contrasts* (Cambridge: Cambridge University Press, 1996), 139–40.
30. In general, see Welch, *Propaganda and the German Cinema*, 23–7; Roel vande Winkel, 'Nazi newsreels in Europe?', 1939–1945: the many faces of Ufa's foreign weekly newsreel (Auslandstonwoche) versus German's weekly newsreel (Deutsche Wochenschau), *Historical Journal of Film, Radio and Television*, 24 (2004), 5–34; M Töteberg, 'Unter den Brücken. Kino und Film im Totalen Krieg', in M Töteberg and H–M Bock (eds), *Das UFA-Buch* (Frankfurt: Zweitausendeins, 1992), 466–8.
31. A variety of Italian official reports from the 1936–43 period documents the increasing competition between the two regimes [*Archivio Centrale dello Stato*, Ministero di Cultura Popolare, Gabinetto, 'Cinematografia' (folders 235, 339)]; cf. Welch, *Propaganda and the German Cinema*, 26 ff.
32. On the relation between National Socialism and modernity see J Herf, *Reactionary Modernism: Technology, Culture and Politics in Weimar and the Third Reich* (Cambridge: Cambridge University Press, 1984), chs 2–6; Roberts, *The Poverty of Great Politics*.
33. O J Hale, *The Captive Press in the Third Reich* (Princeton, NJ: Princeton University Press, 1973), 127 ff; in general see N Frei, 'Nationalsozialistische Presse und Propaganda', in M Broszat und H Möller (eds), *Das Dritte Reich. Herrschaftsstruktur und Geschichte* (Munich: Beck Verlag, 1986), 152–75.
34. K D Abel, *Presselenkung im NS-Staat. Eine Studie zur Geschichte der Publizistik in der nationalsozialistischen Zeit* (Berlin: Colloquium Verlag, 1990), 5–10; K Koszyk, *Deutsche Presse, 1914–1945*, Part III (Berlin: Colloquium, 1972), 387–9.

35. C Larson, 'The German Press Chamber', *Public Opinion Quarterly*, 9 (October 1937), 53–70; Kiefer Alexander, 'Government control of publishing in Germany', *Political Science Quarterly*, 57 (1938): 80–8.
36. This measure was accompanied by the announcement of the 'cleansing' of the profession from 'Jews'. See W Hagemann, *Publizistik im Dritten Reich. Ein Beitrag zur Methode der Massenführung* (Hamburg: Hansischer Gildenverlag, 1948), 39; Hale, *The Captive Press in the Third Reich*, 76 ff; J Wulf, *Presse und Funk im Dritten Reich. Eine Dokumentation* (Reinbek: Rowohlt, 1966), 137 ff.
37. N Frei and J Schmitz, *Journalismus im Dritten Reich* (Munich: Beck, 1999, 3rd ed.), 22–6.
38. M Amann, Interview Notes at Nuremberg (22.8.1945), in *Spruchkammer München*, I, file for Max Amann.
39. Abel, *Presselenkung im NS-Staat*, 29–37.
40. Ellul, *Propaganda*, 12–13; Rentschler, *The Ministry of Illusion*, ch. 1; Taylor, *Film Propaganda*, 144–5.
41. Quoted in *Zeitungsverlag*, 18.3.1933, 1.
42. For an analysis of the law see H Schmidt–Leonhardt, *Das Schriftleitergesetz* (Berlin, 1944), 34 ff; and Abel, *Presselenkung im NS-Staat*.
43. Koszyk, *Deutsche Presse*, 367 ff.
44. F Schmidt, *Presse in Fessel. Das Zeitungsmonopol im Dritten Reich* (Berlin: Verlag Archiv und Kartei, 1947), 84 ff.
45. Hale, *The Captive Press in the Third Reich*, ch. 4; cf. *Zeitungsverlag*, 21.10.1933, 1.
46. Cf. M Mann, *Fascists* (Cambridge: Cambridge University Press, 2004), ch. 1.
47. Hale, *The Captive Press in the Third Reich*, 231 ff.
48. *Handbuch der deutschen Tagespresse*, 1937, 394–9.
49. Koszyk, *Deutsche Presse*, 370 ff.
50. M Amann, Address to the Party Rally at Nuremberg, published in *Der Parteitag der Ehre vom 8. bis 14. September 1936. Offizieller Bericht über den Verlauf des Reichsparteitages mit sämtlichen Kongreßreden* (Munich: Zentralverlag der NSDAP, 1936), 212–24.
51. Hale, *The Captive Press in the Third Reich*, 136; Frei, *Das Dritte Reich*, 170 ff.
52. Cf. Hitler's speech at the Reichstag (20.2.1938), in M Domarus, *Hitler: Reden and Proklamationen*, I, 864–9, where he did not enter into a discussion of the impact of the regime's press policy on the political dailies' circulation.
53. Cf. R Rienhardt, 'Vertraune, Eigenarbeit, Entfaltungsfreiheit', *Zeitungs–Verlag*, 9.10.1937, 3.
54. Hale, *The Captive Press in the Third Reich*, 236 ff.
55. See, in general, Frei and Schmitz, *Journalismus im Dritten Reich*; Hale, *The Captive Press in the Third Reich*, 255–64.
56. D Kohlmann–Viand, *NS-Pressepolitik im Zweiten Weltkrieg. Die 'Vertraulichen Informationen' als Mittel der Presselenkung* (Munich: Saur, 1991), 199.
57. W Hagemann, *Publizistik im Dritten Reich*, 40 ff; P Longerich, 'Nationalsozialistische Propaganda', in K D Bracher, M Funke, H–A Jacobsen (eds), *Deutschland 1933–1945. Neue Studien zur nationalsozialistischen Herrschaft* (Düsseldorf: Droste-Verlag, 1992), 291–314.
58. Koszyk, *Deutsche Presse*, 425–43.
59. Kohlmann–Viand, *NS – Pressepolitik im Zweiten Weltkrieg*, 139–40.
60. BA, R 55/602, 142 (Bericht, RPA Westfalen-Süd to RMVP, 14.11.1944).
61. Jowett and O'Donnell, *Propaganda and Persuasion*, 101 ff.
62. On the history and evolution of broadcasting in Germany see H–W Stuiber, *Medien in Deutschland*, Vol. 2: *Rundfunk*, Part I (Konstanz: UVK-Medien, 1998),

133–83; K C Führer, 'Auf dem Weg zur "Massenkultur"'. Kino und Rundfunk in der Weimarer Republik', *Historische Zeitschrift* 262 (1996), 739–81.

63. I Schneider, *Radio-Kultur in der Weimarer Republik. Eine Dokumentation* (Tübingen: Gunter Narr Verlag, 1984); P Dahl, *Radio. Sozialgeschichte des Rundfunks für Sender und Empfänger* (Reinbek: Freies Sender Kombinat/AG Radio, 1983).

64. Stuiber, *Medien in Deutschland*, 51–9; A Diller, *Rundfunkpolitik im Dritten Reich*, (München: DTV, 1980), 134–42.

65. Stuiber, *Medien in Deutschland*, 163 ff; Diller, *Rundfunkpolitik im Dritten Reich*, 88 ff.

66. BA, R 43/11, 1149 (Goebbels to Esser, 21.10.1933).

67. W Schütte, *Regionalität und Föderalismus im Rundfunk. Die geschichtliche Entwicklung in Deutschland 1923–1945* (Frankfurt: 1971), 34–78; Diller, *Rundfunkpolitik im Dritten Reich*, 112 ff.

68. H J P Bergmeier, R E Lotz, *Hitler's Airwaves: The Inside Story of Nazi Radio Broadcasting and Propaganda Swing* (New Haven, CT: Yale University Press, 1997), ch. 1; Diller, *Rundfunkpolitik im Dritten Reich*, 161–8.

69. H Pohle, *Der Rundfunk als Instrument der Politik. Zur Geschichte des deutschen Rundfunks von 1923/38* (Hamburg: Eigenverlag, 1955), 187–9.

70. Stuiber, *Medien in Deutschland*, 163–4.

71. W Lerg, R Steininger (eds), *Rundfunk und Politik 1923–1973. Beiträge zur Rundfunkforschung* (Berlin: Spiess, 1975), 161–2.

72. W B Lerg, *Rundfunkpolitik in der Weimarer Republik* (Munich: DTV, 1980), 460 ff.

73. See, in general, Stuiber, *Medien in Deutschland*, 157–61; D Rimmele, 'Anspruch und Realität nationalsozialistischer Rundfunkarbeit vor 1933 in Hamburg', in W Lerg and R Steininger, *Rundfunk und Politik 1923–1973*, 135–57; Diller, *Rundfunkpolitik im Dritten Reich*, 84–93.

74. Bergmeier and Lodz, *Hitler's Airwaves*, 11; Pohle, *Der Rundfunk als Instrument der Politik*, 214 ff.

75. Stuiber, *Medien in Deutschland*, 167; K Dussel, *Deutsche Rundfunkgeschichte. Eine Einführung* (Konstanz: UVK–Medien, 1999), 88 ff; M A Doherty, *Nazi Wireless Propaganda: Lord Haw–Haw and British Public Opinion in the Second World War* (Edinburgh: Edinburgh University Press, 2000), 4.

76. Bergmeier and Lodz, *Hitler's Airwaves*, 14.

77. Balfour, *Propaganda in War 1939–1945*, 103 ff.

78. Bergmeier and Lodz, *Hitler's Airwaves*, 19; E Kordt, *Nicht aus den Akten ...* (Stuttgart: Union Deutsche Verlagsgesellschaft: 1950), 320 ff.

79. BA, R 55/537, 19–20 (Leiter Rundfunk to Fritzsche, 12.1.1943). See also ch. 2.

80. Pohle, *Der Rundfunk als Instrument der Politik*, 272; K Scheel, *Krieg über Ätherwellen. NS-Rundfunk und Monopole 1933–1945* (Berlin: Deutscher Verlag der Wissenschaften, 1970).

81. Stuiber, *Medien in Deutschland*, 59–65; G Goebel, 'Der Deutsche Rundfunk ...', *Archiv für das Post- und Fernmeldewesen*, 6 (1950), 353–53, here 409 ff.

82. M Pater, 'Rundfunkangebote', in I Marßolek, A von Saldern (eds), *Radio im Nationalsozialismus. Zwischen Lenkung und Ablenkung, Zuhören und Gehörtwerden*, Vol. 1 (Tübingen: Diskord, 1998), 129–242.

83. W A Boelcke (ed.), *The Secret Conferences of Dr Goebbels. The Nazi Propaganda War, 1939–43* (New York/NY: E P Dutton & Co, 1970), 27.9.1942, 280–1.

84. Diller, *Rundfunkpolitik im Dritten Reich*, 369–70.

85. N Drechsler, 'Die Funktion der Musik im deutschen Rundfunk 1933–1945', *Musikwissenschaftliche Studien*, 1988; Pohle, *Der Rundfunk als Instrument der Politik*, 329; W Klingler, *Nationalsozialistische Rundfunkpolitik 1942–1945. Organisation, Programm und die Hörer* (Dissertation: Mannheim, 1983).

86. Diller, *Rundfunkpolitik im Dritten Reich*, 358 ff.
87. BA, R 55/1254, 1–22 (Hinkel to Goebbels, October–November 1941); 23 (Goebbels to Hinkel, 7.11.1941); 36 (Hinkel to Goebbels, 16.12.1941). Two main meetings took place in order to discuss Hinkel's report: one on 23.12. 1942 [BA, R 55/1254, 35] and the other on 5.2.1942 [BA, R 55/1254, 37].
88. BA, R 55/1254, 38–41 (Hinkel's final report to Goebbels, February 1942).
89. BA, R 55/1254, 42–4 (Hinkel to Goebbels, 12.2.1942).
90. BA, R 55/559, 540–3 (*Abgrenzung der Aufgabengebiete der musikalischen Programmgruppen*).
91. IMT, Vol. 6, Doc. 3469-PS, 174 ff (Fritzsche affidavit, 7.1.1946).
92. Diller, *Rundfunkpolitik im Dritten Reich*, 355–6.
93. Frei and Schmitz, *Journalismus im Dritten Reich*, 33 ff.
94. See, for example, the agreement for co-ordination between the Foreign News Section and the Radio Section of the RMVP through the creation of the *Zentrales Information- und Nachrichtenbeuro* in BA, R 55/537, 42.
95. Scheel, *Krieg über Ätherwellen*, 316 ff; Wulf, *Presse und Funk im Dritten Reich*, 315–7 (Rundschreiben 39/39, RKK, 4.11.1939).
96. 'Der Rundfunkerlaß des Ministerrats', *Die schöne Rundfunkzeitschift*, 17.9.1939, in Wulf, *Presse und Funk im Dritten Reich*, 378–9; cf Schütte, *Regionalität und Föderalismus im Rundfunk*, 178–9.
97. Koszyk, *Deutsche Presse*, 389–408.
98. U von Hehl, *Nationalsozialistische Herrschaft* (Munich: R Oldenbourg Verlag, 1996), 60–65; cf. K Hildebrand, 'Nationalsozialismus oder Hitlerismus?', in M Bosch (ed.), *Persönlichkeit und Struktur in der Geschichte* (Düsseldorf: Droste, 1977), 55–61; A Kallis, *Fascist Ideology. Territory and Expansionism in Italy and Germany, 1919–1945* (London: Routledge, 2000), ch. 3.

2 'Polyocracy' versus 'Centralisation': The Multiple 'Networks' of NS Propaganda

1. F Neumann, *Behemoth: The Structure and Practice of National Socialism* (London: Victor Gollancz, 1944), 381–4.
2. E Fraenkel, *The Dual. State* (New York: Octagon Books, 1969); G Sørensen, 'The dual state and fascism', *Totalitarian Movements and Political Religions*, 2 (2001), 25–40.
3. For example, J Caplan, *Government without Administration. State and Civil Service, in Weimar and Nazi Germany* (Oxford: Clarendon Press, 1988), 321–81 (esp. 331–2); and J Caplan, 'National Socialism and the Theory of the State', in T Childers, J Caplan (eds), *Reevaluating the Third Reich* (New York/London: Holmes & Meier, 1993), 98–102. In general, see Kershaw, *The Nazi Dictatorship*.
4. Koehl, *American Political Science Review*, 927.
5. I Kershaw, ' "Working Towards the Führer": reflections on the nature of the Hitler Dictatorship', in I Kershaw, M Lewin (eds), *Stalinism and Nazism: Dictatorships in Comparison* (Cambridge: Cambridge University Press, 1997), 88–107; T Kirk, A McElligott (eds), *Working towards the Führer: Essays in Honour of Sir Ian Kershaw* (Manchester: Manchester University Press, 2004).
6. C Schmitt, *Staat, Bewegung und Volk. Die Dreigliederung der politischen Einheit* (Hamburg: Hanseatische Verlagsanstalt, 1934), 31 ff.

7. Kershaw, *The Nazi Dictatorship*, 187–95. On Weber's notion of 'charismatic' legitimation see M Weber, 'Politics as vocation', in Gerth H and C Wright Mills (ed.), *Max Weber: Essays in Sociology* (New York: Oxford University Press, 1985); M R Lepsius, 'Charismatic leadership: Max Weber's model and its applicability to the rule of Hitler', in C F Graumann and S Moscovici (eds), *Changing Conceptions of Political Leadership* (New York: Springer–Verlag, 1986).
8. Kershaw, *The Nazi Dictatorship*, 69–92.
9. IMT, 2315/2319-PS; Diller, *Rundfunkpolitik im Dritten Reich*, 77–84.
10. RGB, 1933, I, 661; Diller, *Rundfunkpolitik im Dritten Reich*, 154–9; Abel, *Presselenkung im NS-Staat*, 3 ff.
11. Z A B Zeman, *Nazi Propaganda*, reprinted in R Jackall (ed.), *Propaganda* (New York: New York University Press, 1995), 178–9.
12. BA, NS 18/1390, 46 (Goebbels to RPL, 21.4.1941).
13. BA, NS 18/1229, 1 (3.2.1944).
14. J Blumberg, 'Die Entwicklung des Amtes des Reichspropagandaleiters bis zur Machtübernahme', BA, Berlin.
15. BA, NS 18/1390 (Goebbels to RPL, 21.4.1941).
16. Herzstein, *The War that Hitler Won*, 155 ff.
17. O Dietrich, *The Hitler I Knew* (London: Methuen and Co, 1957), 238.
18. O Dietrich, *12 Jahre mit Hitler* (Munich: Atlas–Verlag, 1955), 154; Martin H-L, *Unser Mann bei Goebbels. Verbindungsoffizier des Oberkommandos der Wehrmacht beim Reichspropagandaminister 1940–1944* (Neckargemünd: Scharnhorst Buchkameradschaft 1973), 22 ff; Balfour, *Propaganda in War 1939–1945*, 105.
19. A Uzulis, *Nachrichtenagenturen im Nationalsozialismus. Propagandainstrumente und Mittel der Presselenkung* (Frankfurt: P. Lang, 1995), 313, 356–7.
20. Dietrich, *The Hitler I Knew*, 237 ff.
21. Abel, *Presselenkung im NS-Staat*, 7 ff.
22. Abel, *Presselenkung im NS-Staat*, 51 ff; Balfour, *Propaganda in War, 1939–1945*, 106–7.
23. Semmler, *Goebbels*, 24.11.1943, 111–13.
24. Cf. Semmler, *Goebbels*, 13.3.1943, 74.
25. Cf. IMT, Vol. 19, 328 ff (Hans Fritzsche case, 24.7.1946).
26. H W Flannery, *Assignment to Berlin* (London: The Right Book Club, 1943), 31–4.
27. BA, R 55/1254, 39 (Fritzsche to Dietrich, 21.8.1944).
28. Bergmeier and Lotz, *Hitler's Airwaves*, 179.
29. ADAP, C, 1, II 480 (Cabinet meeting on 24.5.1933).
30. Heß could also rely on the *Foreign Organisation* (*Auslandsorganisation*, AA) and on the earmarked *Volksdeutscherrat* which he had established in 1933 to the exasperation of the AA.
31. Herzstein, *The War that Hitler Won: Goebbels and the Nazi Media Campaign*, 173 ff.
32. Bergmeier and Lotz, *Hitler's Airwaves*, 178 ff; E Kordt, *Nicht aus den Akten ...*, 320 ff; Balfour, *Propaganda in War 1939–1945*, 103.
33. *Documents on German Foreign Policy* (DGFP), D, 8, 30 (8.9.1939); Diller, *Rundfunkpolitik im Dritten Reich*, 316–34.
34. Boelcke, *Die Macht des Radios*, 87–8.
35. Bergmeier and Lotz, *Hitler's Airwaves*, 186–9.
36. Bergmeier and Lotz, *Hitler's Airwaves*, 190–1; Diller, *Rundfunkpolitik im Dritten Reich*, 326–9; Boelcke, *Die Macht des Radios*, 95–7.
37. M Hauner, 'The professionals and the amateurs in National Socialist foreign policy: revolution and subversion in the Islamic and Indian world', in G Hirschfeld,

L Kettenacker (eds), *Der 'Führerstaat'. Mythos und Realität* (Stuttgart: Kett–Cotta, 1981), 316 ff; H–A Jacobsen, *Nationalsozialistische Außenpolitik 1933–1945* (Frankfurt: Alfred Metzner Verlag, 1968), 90–160; W Michalka, *Ribbentrop und die deutsche Weltpolitik 1933–1940. Außenpolitische Konzeptionen und Entscheidungsprozeße im Dritten Reich* (Munich: Wilhelm Fink Verlag, 1980).

38. Wulf, *Theater und Film im Dritten Reich*, 121–3.
39. H G Seraphin, *Das Politische Tagesbuch Alfred Rosenbergs 1934/5 und 1939/40* (Göttingen, Berlin and Frankfurt, 1956), 22/25.8.1939; R Cecil, *The Myth of the Master Race. Alfred Rosenberg and Nazi Ideology* (London: Bratsford, 1972), 179 ff.
40. Balfour, *Propaganda in War 1939–1945*, 166–7.
41. Seraphin, *Das Politische Tagesbuch Alfred Rosenbergs 1934/5 und 1939/40*, 29.5/21.6.1941; Cecil, *The Myth of the Master Race*, 187 ff.
42. D Orlow, *The History of the Nazi Party, 1919–1945*, Vol. II: 1933–1945 (Pittsburgh: Pittsburgh University Press, 1973), 470.
43. See, for example, Semmler, *Goebbels*, 20.11.1943, where he expresses the view that '[Goebbels] admits to his intimates his weakness in relation with Bormann [and] ... is frightened of him [Bormann]'.
44. Herzstein, *The War that Hitler Won: Goebbels and the Nazi Media Campaign*, 150–1.
45. Balfour, *Propaganda in War 1939–1945*, 151–3; Herzstein, *The War that Hitler Won: Goebbels and the Nazi Media Campaign*, 237–8.
46. BA, NS 18/1403 (Goebbels to Gutterer, 7.10.1942); cf. BA, NS 18/1403 (Hadamowsky to RMVP departments, 2.1.1942).
47. BA, NS 18/1403 (Bormann to Goebbels, 20.11.1941).
48. BA, NS 18/1403 (Goebbels to Bormann, 3.11.1941).
49. BA, NS 18/1403 (Berndt to RPL, 19.9.1941; and Friedrichs to RMVP, 29.9.1941).
50. BA, NS 18/1403 (Hauptamt Reichsring to Hadamowsky, 6.5.1943).
51. BA, NS 18/1403 (Tießler to Goebbels, 19.4.1943).
52. BA, NS 18/1403 (Goebbels to Bormann, May 1943).
53. O Buchbender, *Das tönende Erz: Deutsche Propaganda gegen die Rote Armee im Zweiten Weltkrieg* (Stuttgart: Seewald, 1978), 17–19.
54. Herzstein, *The War that Hitler Won: Goebbels and the Nazi Media Campaign*, 228 ff.
55. H von Wedel, *Die Propagandatruppen der deutschen Wehrmacht* (Neckargemünd: Scharnhorst Buchkameradschaft, 1962).
56. Martin, *Unser Mann bei Goebbels*, 22–40.
57. R–D Müller, 'Albert Speer und die Rüstungspolitik im Totalen Krieg', *Das Deutsche Reich und des Zweite Weltkrieg (DRZW)*, Vol. 5/2: *Organisation und Mobilisierung des deutschen Machtbereichs, Zweiter Halbband: Kriegsverwaltung, Wirtschaft und personelle Ressourcen 1942–1944/45* (Stuttgart: Deutsche Verlags-Anstalt, 1989), 545–693.
58. BA, NS 18/1390 (Goebbels to RPL, 3.1943).
59. See for example, Semmler, *Goebbels*, 20.2/2.3.1943, 70–2.
60. Diller, *Rundfunkpolitik im Dritten Reich*, 304 ff.
61. Koszyk, *Deutsche Presse*, 127 ff; Dietrich, *The Hitler I Knew*, 101–2.
62. *Goebbels Diary*, 13.4.1943.
63. Abel, *Presselenkung im NS-Staat*, 56–7.
64. Herzstein, *The War that Hitler Won: Goebbels and the Nazi Media Campaign*, 226–7.
65. BA, R 55/663, 92 (Reichsfilmintendant to Goebbels, 7.12.1944).
66. Herzstein, *The War that Hitler Won: Goebbels and the Nazi Media Campaign*, 269 ff.
67. BA, NS 18/282, 1–2 (Goebbels to Bormann, 21.11.41).

3 The Discourses of NS Propaganda: Long-Term Emplotment and Short-Term Justification

1. Jowett and O'Donnell, *Propaganda and Persuasion*, 14–15; Taithe and Thornton, *Propaganda. Political Rhetoric and Identity*, 16 ff.
2. I Kershaw, 'How Effective was Nazi Propaganda?', in D Welch (ed.), *Nazi Propaganda: The Power and the Limitations* (London: Croom Helm, 1983), 180–205.
3. Taithe and Thornton, *Propaganda. Political Rhetoric and Identity*, 3–4; McQuail, *Mass Communication Theory*, 66–9.
4. Kallis, *Fascist Ideology*, ch. 2; A Kallis, 'To expand or not to expand? Territory, generic fascism and the quest for an "ideal fatherland" ', *Journal of Contemporary History*, 38 (2003): 238–60.
5. Griffin, *The Nature of Fascism*, chs 1–2.
6. R Griffin, 'Revolution from the right: fascism', in D Parker (ed.), *Revolutions and the Revolutionary Tradition in the West 1560–1991* (London: Routledge, 2000), 185–201. On the use of the term 'revolution' in the context of fascism see Introduction, note 8; and, for an interesting discussion on the subject, R Griffin, 'Fascism is more than reaction', *Searchlight*, 27/4 (1999): 24–6.
7. D Welch, 'Manufacturing a Consensus: Nazi Propaganda and the Building of a National Community (Volksgemeinschaft)', *Contemporary European History*, 2 (1993); W Struve, *Elites against Democracy: Leadership Ideals in Bourgeois Political Thought in Germany, 1890–1933* (Princeton, NJ: Princeton University Press, 1973); Kallis, *Fascist Ideology*, ch. 2; M Hauner, 'A German Racial Revolution?', *Journal of Contemporary History*, 19 (1984): 671–90.
8. For example, J P Faye, *Langages totalitaires. Critique de la raison/ l'économie narrative* (Paris: Hermann, 1972), 407 ff; and J B Thompson, *Studies in the Theory of Ideology* (London: Polity, 1984), 211–27, for an analysis of this dualism between party and leader.
9. Kallis, *Fascist Ideology*, ch. 3; cf. R Eatwell, 'On defining the "fascist minimum": the centrality of ideology', *Journal of Political Ideologies*, 1 (1996), 303–19; Noel O'Sullivan, *Fascism* (London: Dent 1983), 134 ff.
10. J Nyomarkay, *Charisma and Factionalism in the Nazi Party* (Minneapolis: University of Minnesota Press, 1967), esp. ch. 6; K Hildebrand, 'Monokratie oder Polykratie?', in G Hirschfeld, L Kettenacker (eds), *Der 'Führerstaat'. Mythos und Realität. Studien zur Struktur und Politik des Dritten Reiches* (Stuttgart: Klett–Cotta, 1981), 73–96; K D Bracher, 'The Role of Hitler: Perspectives of Interpretation', in W Laqueur (ed.), *Fascism: A Reader's Guide* (Harmondsworth: Penguin, 1979), 211–55. See also, later ch. 6.
11. W Wette, 'Ideologien, Propaganda und Innenpolitik als Voraussetzungen der Kriegspolitik des Dritten Reiches', *DRZW*, Vol. 1: *Kriegsbeginn und Kriegsziele* (Stuttgart: Deutsche Verlags-Anstalt, 1979), 603–64.
12. I Kershaw, *The Hitler-Myth*, 124–32.
13. J Goebbels, 'Unser Hitler', April 1939, in his *Die Zeit ohne Beispiel* (Munich: Zentralverlag der NSDAP, 1941).
14. Griffin, *The Nature of Fascism*, chs 2 and 4.
15. L Birken, *Hitler as Philosophe. Remnants of the Enlightenment in National Socialism* (Westport, CT/London: Praeger, 1995), ch. 5; H D Andrews, 'Hitler and Bismarck: a history', *German Studies Review*, 14 (1991): 511–32.
16. See for example, 'Juden-Komplott gegen Europa', Plakat campaign, July 1941.

17. F Didier, *Europa arbeitet in Deutschland. Sauckel mobilisiert die Leistungsreserven* (Munich: Zentralverlag der NSDAP, 1943), 4.

18. See in general R Griffin, 'Europe for the Europeans: the fascist vision for the new Europe', Humanities Research Centre Occasional Papers, 1 (1994).

19. F A Six, 'Das Reich und die Grundlegung Europas', F A Six (ed.), *Jahrbuch der Weltpolitik 1942* (Berlin: Junker und Dünnhaupt, 1942), 13–36. In general, see J K Hönsch, 'Nationalsozialistische Europapläne im zweiten Weltkrieg', in R G Plaschka, H Haselsteiner, A M Drabek, B Zaar (eds), *Mitteleuropa-Konzeptionen in der ersten Hälfte des 20. Jahrhunderts* (Vienna: Verlag der österreichischen Akademie der Wissenschaften, 1995), 307–25.

20. A Kallis, 'Race, "value" and the hierarchy of human life: ideological and structural determinants of national socialist policy-making', *Journal of Genocide Research*, 7 (2005): 5–30.

21. See, for example, A Rosenberg, *Der völkische Staatsgedanke: Überlieferung und Neugeburt* (Munich: Deutschvölkische Buchhandlung, 1924); cf. A Rosenberg, *Neugeburt Europas als werdende Geschichte* (Halle: Max Niemeyer, 1939).

22. For example, 'Der Sieg im Osten ist Europas Sieg', *Berlin Rom Tokio. Monatsschrift für die Vertiefung der kulturellen Beziehungen der Völker des weltpolitischen Dreiecks*, 9 (1941), 2–4.

23. A Rosenberg, *Deutsche und europäische Geistesfreiheit [Rede auf einer Weltanschauliche Feierstunde der NSDAP in Prag 16.1.1944]* (Munich: Zentralverlag der NSDAP, 1944).

24. F Steive, 'Deutschland und Europa im Laufe der Geschichte', in *Europa. Handbuch der politischen, wirtschaftlichen und kulturellen Entwicklung des neuen Europa*, ed. by Deutsches Institut für Außenpolitische Forschung (Leipzig: Helingsche Verlagsanstalt, 1943), 19–27; cf. BA: R 55/524, 197; R 55/525, 33.

25. See, for example, 'Amerika als Zerrbild europäischer Lebensordnung', *Schulungs-Unterlage No. 19* (Der Reichsorganisationsleitung der NSDAP, Munich: Hauptschulungsamt, 1942).

26. K R Ganzer, 'Das Reich als Europäische Ordnungsmacht' (1941), in S Hagen, U P Ina (eds), *Europäische Geschichte. Quellen und Materialien* (Munich: Bayrischer Schulbuch Verlag, 1994), 383–5; K Mergerle, 'Eine bessere Weltordnung', in *Berlin Rom Tokio. Monatsschrift für die Vertiefung der kulturellen Beziehungen der Völker des weltpolitischen Dreiecks*, 7 (1939): 2–4.

27. W Daitz, 'Die Erneuerung des Reiches und die Wiedergeburt Europas aus dem Lebensgesetz der europäischen Völkerfamilie' (1942), in W Daitz, *Der Weg zur Volkswirtschaft, Großraumwirtschaft und Großraumpolitik* (Dresden: Zentralforschungsinstitut für Nationale Wirtschaftsordnung und Großraumwirtschaft, 1943), III, 77–94.

28. W Daitz, 'Die Grundlagen europäischer Marktordnung' (1941), in Daitz, *Der Weg zur Volkswirtschaft, Großraumwirtschaft und Großraumpolitik*, III, 123–7; W Daitz, 'Großraumwirtschaft' (1938), in *Der Weg zur Volkswirtschaft, Großraumwirtschaft und Großraumpolitik*, II, 24–30.

29. For Rosenberg's plans for 'foodstuff self-sufficiency', see later, ch. 5. For plans for commercial and financial reorganisation see, amongst others, W Funk, 'Der wirtschaftliche Aufbau Europas', in *Europa. Handbuch der politischen, Wirtschaftlichen und Kulturellen Entwicklung des neuen Europa*, edited by *Deutsches Institut für Außenpolitische Forschung* (Leipzig: Helingsche Verlagsanstalt, 1943), 87–93; A S Milward, *The German Economy at War* (London: The Athalone Press, 1965), 192–4; A S Milward, 'The Reichsmark Bloc and the International Economy'

in H W Koch (ed.), *Aspects of the Third Reich* (New York: St. Martin's, 1985), 331–59.

30. J Goebbels, 'Das kommende Europa', Speech to Czech artists and journalists, 11.9.1940, in his *Die Zeit ohne Beispiel*, 314–23.

31. R Ley, *Internationaler Völkerbrei oder Vereinigte National-Staaten Europas?* (Berlin: Verlag der DAF, 1943).

32. O Dietrich, 'Rede zur europäischen Verantwortung der Presse' (1942), in *Europa – Handbuch*, 258–9.

33. Von Schirach B, Speech at the European Youth Congress in Vienna (1942), in W Lipgens (ed.), *Documents on the history of European integration*, Vol. I: *Continental plans for European Union 1939–1945* (Berlin: De Gruyter, 1985), 102–3.

34. Hitler, Address to the Reichstag, 30.1.1939, in N H Baynes (ed.), *The Speeches of Adolf Hitler*, Vol. I (London: Oxford University Press, 1942), 737–41; cf. Hitler's 28.4.1939 Address to the Reichstag, in Baynes, *The Speeches of Adolf Hitler*, 774 ff.

35. Roberts, *The Poverty of Great Politics*.

36. G Allardyce, 'What Fascism is not: thoughts on the deflation of a concept', *American Historical Review*, 84 (1979): 367–88.

37. M Mann, *Fascists* (Cambridge: Cambridge University Press, 2004), chs 1–2.

38. Birken, *Hitler as Philosophe*, chs 6–7; E Nolte, *Das Europäische Bürgerkrieg, 1917–1945. Nationalsozialismus und Bolschewismus* (Berlin: Propyläen, 1987); G Eley, 'What produces Fascism: pre-industrial traditions or the crisis of the capitalist state', *Politics and Society*, 12 (1983): 76–82.

39. A J P Taylor, *The Origins of the Second World War* (London: Hamish Hamilton, 1961), 69 f; Kallis, *Fascist Ideology*, ch. 6.

40. N Chamberlain, Radio Address to the British People, 3.9.1939, in D Dutton, *Neville Chamberlain* (London: Arnold; New York: Oxford University Press, 2001), 139 ff.

41. J Goebbels, 'Englands Schuld', *Illustrierter Beobachter*, Sondernummer 'Englands Schuld', 14, available at the German Propaganda Archive: http://www.calvin.edu/cas/gpa (translation by Randall Bytwerk). Future references to the site will be to the GPA.

42. *Aufklärungs- and Redner-Informationsmaterial der RPL des NSDAP*, 11 (1939): 37–40.

43. For example J Goebbels, 'Wirtschaft und Krieg, Rede zur Eröffnung der Leipziger Frühjahrsmesse', 3.3.1940, in his *Die Zeit ohne Beispiel*, 274–5.

44. See, for example Goebbels, 'Zeit ohne Beispiel', 26.5.1940, in his *Die Zeit ohne Beispiel*, 289–95, in which he stressed that 'in 1914 Germany was, in psychological terms, on the defensive ... [now] Germany is clearly on the offensive'.

45. Goebbels, 'England und seine Plutokraten', 5.1.1941, in his *Die Zeit ohne Beispiel*, 359 ff. See also W L Shirer, *Berlin Diary. The Journal of a Foreign Correspondent, 1934–1941* (London: Hamish Hamilton, 1942), 23.9.1940, 400–3.

46. A Rosenberg: 'Die Überwindung des Gentlemen', VB, 30.6.1940; 'Die neue Sprache Europas', VB, 16.6.1940; 'Freimaurerverbote', VB, 11.8.1940; J Goebbels, 'Was denkt sich Churchill eigentlich?', 28.12.1940, in his *Die Zeit ohne Beispiel*, 347 ff.

47. J Goebbels, 'Das kommende Europa. Rede an die tschechischen Kulturschaffenden und Journalisten', *Die Zeit ohne Beispiel*, 323, available at GPA (translation by Randall Bytwerk).

48. W Meyer zu Uptrup, *Kampf gegen die 'jüdische Weltverschwörung'; Propaganda und Antisemitismus der Nationalsozialisten 1919 bis 1945* (Berlin: Metropol Verlag, 2003).

49. D J Goldhagen, *Hitler's Willing Executioners. Ordinary Germans and the Holocaust* (London: Abacus 1997), esp. 77–90.

50. During the first half of 1939, derogatory references to the USA abounded in Nazi propaganda: see, for example, Hitler's long response to F D Roosevelt's message delivered on 28 April 1939, in M Domarus, *Hitler: Reden und Proklamationen*, Vol. II: *Untergang (1939–1945)* (Würzburg: Schmidt, 1963), 975 ff; Goebbels, 'Wer will den Krieg?', l.4.1939, in his *Die Zeit ohne Beispiel*, 90 ff.

51. W A Williams, 'The legend of isolationism in the 1920s', in Williams, The *Tragedy of American Diplomacy* (New York: Dell, 1962), 104–59; M Jonas, *Isolationism in America, 1935–1941* (Ithaca, NY: Cornell University Press, 1966); J Doenecke, 'Power, markets and ideology: the isolationist response to Roosevelt policy, 1940–1941', in L P Liggio and J J Martin (eds), *Watershed of Empire: Essays on New Deal Foreign Policy* (Colorado Springs: Ralph Myles, 1976), 132–61; T E Mahl, *Desperate Deception: British Covert Operations in the United States, 1939–1944* (Washington: Brassey's, 1998); J W Baird, *The Mythical World of Nazi War Propaganda, 1939–1945* (Minneapolis: University of Minnesota Press, 1974), 170–2.

52. R W Steele, *Propaganda in an Open Society. The Roosevelt Administration and the Media, 1933–1941* (Westport, CT: Greenwood, 1985), 171 ff.

53. Boelcke, *The Secret Conferences of Dr Goebbels*, 25.4.1941, 152–3.

54. Boelcke, *The Secret Conferences of Dr Goebbels*, 13.10.1941, 185.

55. Boelcke, *The Secret Conferences of Dr Goebbels*, 24.3.1941, 128.

56. Goebbels, 'Der Frömmste unter uns allen', 23.3.1941, in *Die Zeit ohne Beispiel*, 435–9.

57. Cf. the SD report of 7.10.1940, in Boberach, *Meldungen aus dem Reich. Auswahl aus den geheimen Lageberichten des Sicherheitsdienstes der SS*, 114–5.

58. Boelcke, *The Secret Conferences of Dr Goebbels*, 24.3.1941, 128.

59. Goebbels, '*Das alte Lied*', 8.4.1941, in *Die Zeit ohne Beispiel*, 456 f.

60. Goebbels, '*Im Gelächter der Welt*', 16.2.1941, in *Die Zeit ohne Beispiel*, 391–2.

61. 'Europa und Amerika. Fehlerquellen im Aufbau des amerikanischen Volktums', *Schulungs-Unterlage No. 18* (Munich: Reichsorganisationsleitung der NSDAP, Hauptschulungsamt, 1942).

62. A Rosenberg, 'Wird Eli Eli über Horst Wessel siegen?', *VB*, 17.7.1938, 3.

63. R Ley, *Roosevelt verrät Amerika* (Berlin: Verlag der Deutschen Arbeitsfront, 1942), passim.

64. P H Merkl, *Political Violence under the Swastika. 581 Early Nazis* (Princeton, NJ: Princeton University Press, 1975), esp. 169, 487 ff, 522.

65. Hitler, Address to Wilhelmshaven, 1.4.1939.

66. Hitler, Speech at the Reichstag, 28.4.1939, in Domarus, *Hitler*, II, 1177–9.

67. United States, Department of State, Publication No. 3023, *Nazi-Soviet Relations 1939–1941. Documents from the Archives of the German Foreign Office* (Washington: Government Printing Office, 1948), 353.

68. J Goebbels, 'Das Tor zum neuen Jahrhundert', *Die Zeit ohne Beispiel*, 584–9, available at GPA (translation by Randall Bytwerk).

69. E Kris, H Speier, *German Radio Propaganda: Report on Home Broadcasts during the War* (London/New York/Toronto: Oxford University Press, 1944), 213 ff.

70. J Streicher, 'Bolschewismus und Synogoge', *Der Stürmer*, no. 36, September 1941, 1, available at GPA (translation by Randall Bytwerk).

71. Hitler, Speech at the Berlin Sportpalast, 3.10.1941, in Domarus, *Hitler*, II, 1761; the second quote taken from E Kris, H Speier, *German Radio Propaganda: Report on Home Broadcasts During the War* (New York: Oxford University Press, 1944), 357–8.

72. Hitler, Speech to the Reichstag, 11.12.1941, in Domarus (ed.), *Hitler*, II, 1801 ff; Goebbels, 'Buch und Schwert', Speech at the opening of the German Book Week, 26.10.1941, in his *Das eherne Herz. Reden und Aufsätze aus den Jahren 1941/42* (Munich: Zentralverlag der NSDAP, 1943), 70 ff.

73. *Das Sowjet-Paradies. Ausstellung der Reichspropagandaleitung der NSDAP. Ein Bericht in Wort und Bild* (Berlin: Zentralverlag der NSDAP, 1942), 9, available at GPA (translation by Randall Bytwerk).
74. Boberach, *Meldungen aus dem Reich. Auswahl aus den geheimen Lageberichten des Sicherheitsdienstes der SS*, No. 309 (17.8.1942), 251–4.
75. BA, R 55/602, 13, 19 (opinion reports, 12.6/26.6.1942). On the image of Russia and the Russians amongst the Germans see T Stenzel, *Das Rußlandbild des 'kleinen Mannes'. Gesellschaftliche Prägung und Fremdwahrnehmung in Feldpostbriefen aus dem Ostfeldzug (1941–1944/45)* [Osteuropa Institut München (Mitteilungen, No. 27, 1998)], 41 ff; Hillgruber, 'Das Rußlandbild der führenden deutschen Militärs vor Beginn des Angriffs auf die Sowjetunion', in Hillgrüber (ed.), *Die Zerstörung Europas. Beiträge zur Weltkriegsepoche, 1914 bis 1945* (Berlin: Propyläen, 1988), 256–72.
76. Goebbels, 'Die sogenannte russische Seele', *Das eherne Herz*, 398–405, available at GPA (translation by Randall Bytwerk).
77. Yad Vashem Archives, TR-3/1156 (Memorandum, Josef Israel Loewenherz – Head of Jewish Community in Vienna, 1.6.1942). On the event see Kershaw, *Popular Opinion and Political Dissent*, 178; W Benz, W H Pehle (eds), *Lexikon des deutschen Widerstandes, 1933–1945* (Frankfurt: Fischer Verlag, 1994), 225–7.
78. J Goebbels, Speech at the Berlin Sportpalast, 19.2.1943, 173–4.
79. Geobbels, Speech at the Berlin Sportpalast, 19.2.1943, 171 ff, 183; J Goebbels, 'Der Krieg und die Juden', *Das Reich*, 9.5.1943, 1. Note that prior to June 1941, Nazi propaganda had made ample references to the 'annihilation' of European culture, but exclusively associated with the west (and Britain in particular). See for example, A Rosenberg, 'Die Überwindung des Versailler Diktats', Speech delivered at Danzig, 15.4.1940, in Seraphin, *Das Politische Tagesbuch Alfred Rosenbergs*, 398 ff.
80. A Hitler, Speech to the Reichstag, 11.12.1941, in Domarus, *Hitler*, II, 1794–811.
81. A Hitler, Speech to the Reichstag, 30.1.1939, in Baynes (ed.), *The Speeches of Adolf Hitler*, 738–41.
82. *Goebbels Diary*, 9.3.1943.
83. A Hitler, Speech at Munich, 8.11.1943, in Domarus, *Hitler*, II, 1935–7.
84. This of course was not overlooked by public opinion. The difference between the 'colossus with clay feet' of 1941 and the significantly more apprehensive 'colossus' of 1943 was noted by the population, as SD reports clearly show. See Boberach, *Meldungen aus dem Reich. Auswahl aus den geheimen Lageberichten des Sicherheitsdienstes der SS*, 7.2.1944, 398.
85. J Goebbels, 'Überwundene Winterkrise. Rede im Berliner Sportpalast', *Der steile Aufstieg* (Munich: Zentralverlag der NSDAP, 1944), 287–306.
86. Goebbels, 'Die alte Front', 26.6.1941, in *Die Zeit ohne Beispiel*, 510–11.
87. H–A Jacobsen (ed.), *Generaloberst Halder: Kriegstagebuch* (Stuttgart: Kohlhammer, 1962), 46–8; and for a translation of the relevant excerpt, J Noakes, G Pridham (eds), *Nazism 1919–1945*, Vol. 3: *Foreign Policy, War and Racial Extermination* (Exeter: Exeter University Press, 2001), 790–1.
88. See, for example, Goebbels, 'Mimikry', 20.7.1941; 'Die Deutschen vor die Front!', 27.7.1941, both in *Die Zeit ohne Beispiel*, 526–36.
89. Hitler, Broadcast to the German Nation, 3.10.1941, in Domarus, *Hitler*, II, 1760–1.
90. Boberach, *Meldungen aus dem Reich. Auswahl aus den geheimen Lageberichten des Sicherheitsdienstes der SS*, 6.10.1941, 169–71.
91. Goebbels, 'Die Deutschen vor die Front!', 27 July 1941; 'Die Sache mit der Stalin-Linie', 17.8.1941, in *Die Zeit ohne Beispiel*, 532–6 and 555–60 respectively.

92. In sequence: J Goebbels, 'Aus Gottes eigenem Land', 9.8.1942, in his *Das eherne Herz*, 426; 'Nun, Volk, steh auf, und Sturm brich los!', speech at the Berlin Sportpalast, 18.2.1943, in his *Der steile Aufstieg*, 172.
93. J Goebbels, 'Überwundene Winterkrise', 5.6.1943, in his *Der steile Aufstieg*, 301–2.
94. A Hitler, Address to the Reichstag, 11.12.1941, in Domarus, *Hitler*, II, 1794–811.
95. Boberach, *Meldungen aus dem Reich. Auswahl aus den geheimen Lageberichten des Sicherheitsdienstes der SS*, 15.12.1941, 184–5.
96. Boelcke, *The Secret Conferences of Dr Goebbels*, 16.12.1941, 194–5.
97. Boelcke, *The Secret Conferences of Dr Goebbels*, 14.2.1942, 211–12.
98. For example, R Ley, *Roosevelt verrät Amerika! Amerika als Zerrbild europäischer Lebensordnung*, Schulungs-Unterlage.
99. See, for example, Goebbels, 'Abbau der Illusionen', 25.5.1942; 'Der Tonnagekrieg', 21.6.1942, in his *Das eherne Herz*, 325 ff and 351–8 respectively.
100. Hitler, Address to the Reichstag, 6.4.1942, in Domarus, *Hitler*, II, 1771 ff.
101. H Boog, 'Strategischer Luftkrieg in Europa und Reichsluftverteidigung 1943–1944', *DRZW*, Vol. 7: *Das Deutsche Reich in der Defensive. Strategischer Luftkrieg in Europa, Krieg im Westen und in Ostasien 1943–1944/45* (Stuttgart: Deutsche Verlags-Anstalt, 2001), 3–15.
102. For example, Goebbels, '*Schwarze Wolken über England*', 25.4.1942, in his *Das eherne Herz*, 299–300.
103. Boelcke, *The Secret Conferences of Dr Goebbels*, 28.1.1943, 324–5.
104. Boelcke, *The Secret Conferences of Dr Goebbels*, 8.11.1942, 295–6; see also Baird, *The Mythical World of Nazi War Propaganda*, 200 ff. On the 'gangster' theme see Hitler's 8.11.1942 speech, in Domarus, *Hitler*, II, 1935 ff.
105. For example Goebbels, 'Überwundene Winterkrise', Speech delivered at the Berlin Sportpalast, 5.6.1943, in his *Der steile Aufstieg*, 279–86 (passim).
106. Hitler, Speech of 8.11.1943 in Munich, in Domarus, *Hitler*, II, 1935–7.
107. Goebbels, 'Unsterbliche deutsche Kultur', Speech at the Opening of the 7th Greater-German Exhibition, 26.7.1943, 339–46.
108. Goebbels, 'Nun, Volk steh auf, und Sturm brich los!', in his *Der steile Aufstieg*, 167–204 ['Total War' speech (18.3.1943)], available at GPA (translation by Randall Bytwerk).
109. BA, NS 18/80, 85 (Propagandaparolen No. 48, 9.2.1943).
110. Cf. BA, R 55/502, 452–3 (Scharping radio commentary, 16.3.1944).
111. Goebbels, 'Das höhere Gesetz' *Das Reich*, 24.9.1944.
112. Boelcke, *The Secret Conferences of Dr Goebbels*, 12.2.1943, 439–41.
113. Jeffrey Herf, "Der Krieg und die Juden. NS Propaganda in Zweiteu Weltkrieg", in *DRZW*, Vol. 9/2, 159–201.
114. Boberach, *Meldungen aus dem Reich. Auswahl aus den geheimen Lageberichter des Sicherheitsdienstes der SS*, 13.7.1944, 437–8; BA, R 55/601, 44–45 (Tätigkeitsbericht, 17.7.1944). See the first tangible indications of this change of perception in the SD report for 7.2.1944, 398.
115. J Goebbels, 'Widerstand um jeden Preis', *Das Reich*, 22.4.1945, 2, available at GPA (translation by Randall Bytwerk).
116. A Hitler, Radio Address to the German Volk, 24.2.1945, in Domarus, *Hitler*, II, 2203–6.
117. BA, NS 6/135 (Report from Karlsruhe, 13.2.1945).
118. J Goebbels, 'Widerstand um jeden Preis', *Das Reich*, 22.4.1945, available at GPA (translation by Randall Bytwerk).
119. J Goebbels, 'Unser Hitler', VB, 20.4.1945, 1.

4 From 'Short Campaign' to 'Gigantic Confrontation': NS Propaganda and the Justification of War, 1939–41

1. For the Versailles Treaty's provisions for Austria see G L Weinberg, *The Foreign Policy of Hitler's Germany. Starting World War II, 1937–1939* (Chicago: Chicago University Press, 1980), 170 ff; A Sharp, *The Versailles Settlement* (New York: Macmillan, 1991). For a background to the Anschluß issue see K S Stadler, *The Birth of the Austrian Republic, 1918–1921* (Leyden: A W Sijthoff, 1966); A P Low, *The Anschluss Movement 1918–1919 and the Paris Peace Conference* (Philadelphia: APS, 1974).

2. R Douglas, 'Chamberlain and Appeasement', in Mommsen, Kettenacker (eds), *Fascist Challenge*, 83 ff; Weinberg, *The Foreign Policy of Hitler's Germany*, chs 10–11; M Geyer, 'The Dynamics of Military Revisionism in the Interwar Years. Military Policy between Rearmament and Diplomacy', in W Deist (ed.), *The German Military in the Age of Total War* (Leamington Spa: Berg, 1985), 100–51 (here 114 ff); Kallis, *Fascist Ideology*, ch. 4.

3. W Wette, *DRZW*, Vol. 1, 638–58.

4. S Reichman, A Golan, 'Irredentism and Boundary Adjustments in Post-World War I Europe', in N Chazan (ed.), *Irredentism and International Politics* (Boulder, CO: Lynne Rienner, 1991), 51–68.

5. Kershaw, *The 'Hitler-Myth'*, 132–9; and, for a contemporary account, L Hill (ed.), *Die Weizsäcker-Papiere, 1933–1950* (Frankfurt: Propyläen, 1974), 157–8.

6. W Wette, *DRZW*, Vol. 1, 658–64.

7. Hitler, Speech at the Reichstag, 28.4.1939, in Domarus, *Hitler*, II, 1177–9.

8. J Goebbels, 'Die große Zeit', *Die Zeit ohne Beispiel*, 70–4, available at GPA (translation by Randall Bytwerk).

9. J Goebbels, 'Die große Zeit', *Die Zeit ohne Beispiel*, 70–6, available at GPA (translation by Randall Bytwerk).

10. E Hadamovsky, *Weltgeschichte im Sturmschritt* (Munich: Zentralverlag der NSDAP, 1939), 340 ff.

11. Taylor, *The Origins of the Second World War*, 69 f, 177 ff; R Boyce, 'Introduction', in R Boyce, E M Robertson (eds), *Paths to War. New Essays on the Origins of the Second World War* (Basingstoke/London: Macmillan, 1989), 1–32.

12. J Goebbels, 'Krieg in Sicht', 25 February 1939, in *Die Zeit ohne Beispiel*, 47.

13. Goebbels, 'Danzig vor der Entscheidung: Rede vor der Danziger Bevölkerung', 17 June 1939, in *Die Zeit ohne Beispiel*, 179–80.

14. Goebbels, 'Quo vadis, Polonia', 5.5.1939, 127–34.

15. R Eatwell, *Fascism: A History* (London: Vintage, 1995), 136–7. Note that Tim Mason maintained that Ribbentrop and Hitler were perfectly aware of the high-risk strategy that they were following: T Mason, *Sozialpolitik im Dritten Reich* (Opladen: Westdeutscher Verlag, 1977), 40 ff; T Mason, R Overy, 'Debate: Germany, "domestic crisis" and war in 1939', *Past and Present*, 122 (1989), 205–40 (here 219 ff); T Mason, 'Intention and explanation. A current controversy about the interpretation of National Socialism', in G Hirschfeld, L Kettenacker (eds), *Der 'Führerstaat'. Mythos und Realität. Studien zur Struktur und Politik des Dritten Reiches* (Stuttgart: Klett-Cotta, 1981), 23–42.

16. Goebbels, 'Bajonette als Wegweiser', 13.5.1939, in *Die Zeit ohne Beispiel*, 139–40.

17. M Coulondre, French Ambassador in Berlin, to M Georges Bonnet, Minister for Foreign Affairs, Berlin, Doc. 197, 17.8.1939, in *French Yellow Book*, ed. by Ministère des Affaires Etrangères (Paris, 1940).

18. Goebbels, 'Die Einkreiser', 20.5.1939, in *Die Zeit ohne Beispiel*, 144 ff.
19. See, for example, Dwinger, *Der Tod in Polen*.
20. A Hitler, Speech to the Reichstag, 1.9.1939, in Domarus, *Hitler*, II, 1312–17.
21. Griffin, *The Nature of Fascism*, ch. 4.
22. H P von Strandmann, 'Imperialism and revisionism in interwar Germany', in Mommsen, W J, Osterhammel (eds), *Imperialism and After. Continuities and Discontinuities* (London/Boston/Sydney: Allen and Unwin, 1986), 93 ff.
23. T Mason, 'The legacy of 1918', in A Nicholls, E Matthias (eds), *German Democracy and the Triumph of Hitler – Essays in Recent German History* (London: George Allen, 1971), 215–40; cf. G G Bruntz, *Allied Propaganda and the Collapse of the German Empire in 1918* (Stanford, CA: Stanford University Press, 1938).
24. Kallis, *Fascist Ideology*, ch. 6.
25. M R Lepsius, *'Charismatic Leadership'*; Kershaw, *'Hitler-Myth'*; and his 'How effective was Nazi propaganda?', in D Welch (ed.), *Nazi Propaganda: The Power and the Limitations* (London: Croom Helm, 1983), 180–205.
26. Orlow, *The History of the Nazi Party 1933–1945*, 2 vols; M Kater, *The Nazi Party. A Social Profile of Members and Leaders, 1919–45* (Oxford: Oxford University Press, 1983); A L Unger, *The Totalitarian Party. Party and People in Nazi Germany and Soviet Russia* (London: Cambridge University Press, 1974).
27. Boberach, *Meldungen aus dem Reich. Auswahl aus den geheimen Lageberichten des Sicherheitsdienstes der SS*, No. 1 (9.10.1939), 34 ff; No. 5 (18.10.1939), 39–40. On 'Operation White' see H Rohde, 'Hitlers Erster "Blitzkrieg" und seine Auswirkungen auf Nordosteuropa', *DRZW*, Vol. 2: *Die Errichtung der Hegemonie auf dem europäischen Kontinent* (Stuttgart: Deutsche Verlags-Anstalt, 1979), 111–36.
28. Boberach, *Meldungen aus dem Reich. Auswahl aus den geheimen Lageberichten des Sicherheitsdienstes der SS*, No. 1 (9.10.1939), 33.
29. Cf. A Speer, *Inside the Third Reich* (New York: MacMillan, 1970), 229 ff.
30. Goebbels, New Year Speech 1939/40, available at GPA (translation by Randall Bytwerk).
31. Domarus, *Hitler*, II, 1418; Weinberg, *The Foreign Policy of Hitler's Germany*, 107 ff; Rohde, *DRZW*, Vol. 2, 244 ff.
32. On the 'integrative' functions of propaganda, see Introduction.
33. W D Smith, *The Ideological Origins of Nazi Imperialism* (Oxford: University Press, 1986).
34. Boelcke, *The Secret Conferences of Dr Goebbels*, 6.5.1940, 38–9 and 30.5.1940, 47; cf. J Goebbels, 'Gelobt sei, was hart macht', 28.2.1940, in *Die Zeit ohne Beispeil*, 243 ff.
35. Boelcke, *The Secret Conferences of Dr Goebbels*, 13.4.1940, 31; 10.5.1940, 39.
36. Boelcke, *The Secret Conferences of Dr Goebbels*, 10.5.1940, 39.
37. Steinert, *Hitler's War and the Germans*, 50–72; Kershaw, *The Hitler-Myth*, 152–7.
38. Goebbels, 'Zeit ohne Beispiel', 26.5.1940, in his *Die Zeit ohne Beispiel*, 289 ff.
39. Boelcke, *The Secret Conferences of Dr Goebbels*, 23.6.1940, 59 ff; H Umbreit, 'Der Kampf um die Vormachtstellung in Westeuropa', *DRZW*, Vol. 2: *Die Errichtung der Hegemonie auf dem europäischen Kontinent* (Stuttgart: Deutsche Verlags-Anstalt, 1979), 260–4.
40. Benno Wundshammer, 'Zerstörer kämpfen über London', in *Bomben auf England. Kleine Kriegshefte No. 8* (Munich: Zentralverlag der NSDAP, 1940), 1–5, available at GPA (translation by Randall Bytwerk).
41. Boelcke, *The Secret Conferences of Dr Goebbels*, 7.9.1940, 87.
42. See, for example, 'Der Vernichtungsbefehl Churchills', *Hamburger Illustrierte*, no. 40 (28.9.1940), 2–3; H W Koch, 'The Strategic Air Offensive against Germany', *Historical Journal* 34 (1991): 117–41.

43. J Goebbels, 'Die Zeit ohne Beispiel', in *Die Zeit ohne Beispiel*, 26.5.1940, 289–95.
44. H Boog, 'Luftwaffe und unterschiedsloser Bombenkrieg bis 1942', in H Boog (ed.), *Luftkriegführung im Zweiten Weltkrieg. Ein internationaler Vergleich* (Bonn: Herford, 1993), 435–68.
45. Boberach, *Meldungen aus dem Reich. Auswahl aus den geheimen Lageberichten des Sicherheitsdienstes der SS*, No. 114 (12.8.1940), 108 ff.
46. K A Maier, 'Der operative Luftkrieg bis zur Luftschlacht um England', *DRZW*, Vol. 2: *Die Errichtung der Hegemonie auf dem europäischen Kontinent* (Stuttgart: Deutsche Verlags-Anstalt, 1979), 329–44.
47. J Goebbels, 'Jahreswechsel 1940/41', 31.12.1940, in *Die Zeit ohne Beispiel*, 351–8.
48. B Stegemann, 'Die Erste Phase der Seekriegführung bis zum Frühjahr 1940', *DRZW*, Vol. 2: *Die Errichtung der Hegemonie auf dem europäischen Kontinent* (Stuttgart: Deutsche Verlags-Anstalt, 1979), 182 ff; and his 'Die zweite Phase der Seekriegführung bis zum Frühjahr 1941', *DRZW*, Vol. 2: *Die Errichtung der Hegemonie auf dem europäischen Kontinent* (Stuttgart: Deutsche Verlags-Anstalt, 1979), 345–9.
49. Boelcke, *The Secret Conferences of Dr Goebbels*, 28.10.1940, 107.
50. Boelcke, *The Secret Conferences of Dr Goebbels*, 11.10.1940, 102 ff.
51. Boberach, *Meldungen aus dem Reich. Auswahl aus den geheimen Lageberichten des Sicherheitsdienstes der SS*, No. 130, 7.10.1940, 114–9.
52. A Fredborg, *Behind the Steel Wall: A Swedish Journalist in Berlin 1941–43* (New York: Viking, 1944), 60–1.
53. BA, NS 18/199, 19–26 (RPL to all Gau-PL and NSDAP members, 10.10.1940).
54. Kallis, *Fascist Ideology*, 181–4.
55. W Michalka: 'From the Anti-Comintern Pact to the Euro-Asiatic Bloc: Ribbentrop's alternative concept to Hitler's foreign policy programme', in Koch (ed.), *Aspects of the Third Reich*, 267–84; 'Joachim von Ribbentrop: from wine merchant to foreign minister', in R Smelser, R Zitelmann (eds), *The Nazi Elite* (Houndmills/London: Longmann, 1993), 165–72; 'Die nationalsozialistische Aussenpolitik im Zeichen eines "Konzeptionen-Pluralismus" – Fragestellungen und Forschungsaufgaben', in M Funke (ed.), *Hitler, Deutschland und die Mächte. Materialien zur Außenpolitik des Dritten Reiches* (Düsseldorf: Droste-Verlag, 1977), 59–63.
56. M Knox, *Mussolini Unleashed, 1939–1941. Politics and Strategy in Fascist Italy's Last War* (Cambridge: Cambridge University Press, 1982), 251 ff; Uffizio Storico del Esercito, *La prima offensiva britannica in Africa settentrionale*, Vol. I (Rome: USE, 1979); J J Sadkovich, 'The Italo-Greek war in context: Italian priorities and Axis diplomacy', *Journal of Contemporary History*, 28 (1993): 493–64.
57. J Goebbels, 'Wenn der Frühling auf die Berge steigt', in *Die Zeit ohne Beispiel*, 415–6.
58. D Vogel, 'Das Eingreifen Deutschlands auf dem Balkan', *DRZW*, Vol. 3: *Der Mittelmeerraum und Südosteuropa. Von der 'non belligeranza' Italiens bis zum Kriegseintritt der Vereinigten Staaten* (Stuttgart: Deutsche Verlags-Anstalt, 1984), 448–85.
59. Boelcke, *The Secret Conferences of Dr Goebbels*, 6.4.1941, 131–2.
60. Boelcke, *The Secret Conferences of Dr Goebbels*, 4.4.1941, 131.
61. Boelcke, *The Secret Conferences of Dr Goebbels*, 6.4.1941, 132.
62. Vogel, *DRZW*, Vol. 3, 485–514; Flannery, *Assignment to Berlin*, ch. 15.
63. Boelcke, *The Secret Conferences of Dr Goebbels*, 30.5.1941, 170–1. See Goebbels, 'Aus dem Lande der unbegrenzten Möglichkeiten', *Das Reich*, 25.5.1941, in *Die Zeit ohne Beispiel*, 486–91; cf. 'Winston Churchill', *Das Reich*, 2.2.1941, 1, in *Die Zeit*

ohne Beispiel, 380–4; and W Diewerge, *Das Kriegsziel der Weltplutokratie. Dokumentarische Veröffentlichung zu dem Buch des Präsidenten der amerikanischen Friedensgesellschaft Theodore Nathan Kaufman 'Deutschland muß sterben'* (Berlin: Zentralverlag der NSDAP, 1941).

64. Boelcke, *The Secret Conferences of Dr Goebbels*, 5.6.1941, 174.
65. Semmler, *Goebbels*, 14.5.1941; *Goebbels Diary*, 14.5.1941; Boelcke, *The Secret Conferences of Dr Goebbels*, 13/15.5.1941, 162–5.
66. Balfour, *Propaganda in War 1939–1945*, 217–9.
67. D Irving, *Goebbels: Mastermind of the Third Reich* (London: Parforce, 1996), 640–1, where Goebbels' similar comments at the Ministerial Conference of 15.5.1941 are also quoted.
68. Flannery, *Assignment to Berlin*, 199 ff.
69. Balfour, *Propaganda in War 1939–1945*, 221–2; cf. *Goebbels Diary*, 26.5.1941.
70. BA, NS 18/195, 125 (Tiessler to Gauleiter Trautmann, 26.7.1941). On the V-campaign see R Seth, *The Truth-Benders. Psychological Warfare in the Second World War* (London: Leslie Frewin, 1969), 125–38.
71. See, for example, Boberach, *Meldungen aus dem Reich. Auswahl aus den geheimen Lageberichten des Sicherheitsdienstes der SS*, No. 194 (16.6.1941), 149 ff.
72. Fredborg, *Behind the Steel Wall*, 137.
73. Fredborg, *Behind the Steel Wall*, 32–4; Flannery, *Assignment to Berlin*, 256 ff.
74. Boelcke, *The Secret Conferences of Dr Goebbels*, 5.6.1941, 174–5.
75. Domarus, *Hitler*, II, 1672–3 (Directive 24 regarding Operation 'Barbarossa', March 1941).
76. E Klink and others, 'Der Krieg gegen die Sowjetunion bis zur Jahreswende 1941/42', *DRZW*, Vol. 4: *Der Angriff auf die Sowjetunion* (Stuttgart: Deutsche Verlags-Anstalt, 1987), 713 ff.
77. IMT, XVII, 250 ff (Hans Fritzsche's testimony).
78. J Goebbels, 'Die alte Front', *Das Reich*, 26.6.1941, in *Die Zeit ohne Beispiel*, 508–13.
79. J Goebbels, 'Die alte Front', 26.6.1941, in *Die Zeit ohne Beispiel*, 508–13.
80. Zeitgeschichtliche Sammlunger (ZgS), 101, 20.8.1941; Boelcke, *The Secret Conferences of Dr Goebbels*, 11.4.1942, 223–4.
81. J Goebbels, 'Die Deutschen vor die Front!', in *Die Zeit ohne Beispiel*, 535.
82. DGFP, D, 12, 660; M Muggeridge (ed.), *Ciano's Diary, 1939–1943* (London: Heinemann, 1947), 22.6.1941.
83. See, for example, Jacobsen (ed.), *Generaloberst Halder*, II, 257–61; G L Weinberg, *A World at Arms. A Global History of World War II* (New York: Cambridge University Press, 1994), 193; Michalka, 'From the Anti-Comintern Pact to the Euro-Asiatic Bloc'; 281–4; 'Die nationalsozialistische Außenpolitik', 55–62; R J Overy, *Goering: The Iron Man* (London: Routledge, 1984), ch. 5, esp. 190–1.
84. See Rosenberg's plans for the administration of the eastern provinces in DGFP, D, 12, 649; E Hancock, *The National Socialist Leadership and Total War, 1941–1945* (New York: St. Martin's Press, 1991), 29 ff; B Wegner, ' "My honour is loyalty": the SS as a military factor in Hitler's Germany', in W Deist (ed.), *The German Military in the Age of Total War* (Leamington Spa: Berg, 1985), 220–39; J Fest, *The Face of the Third Reich* (Harmondsworth: Penguin, 1972), 171–90; J Ackermann, *Himmler als Ideologe* (Göttingen: Musterschmidt, 1970); J Ackermann, 'Heinrich Himmler: Reichsführer – SS', in R Smelser, R Zitelmann (eds), *The Nazi Elite* (Basingstoke/ London: Macmillan, 1993), 98–112; P Padfield, *Himmler: Reichsführer-SS* (New York: Holt, 1991).
85. Seraphin, *Das Politische Tagesbuch Alfred Rosenbergs*, 29.5/21.6.1941; Cecil, *The Myth of the Master Race*, 187 ff. See, in general, D Welch, *The Third Reich: Politics and Propaganda* (London: Routledge, 2002), 130–4.

86. The Directive is discussed in R Manvell, H Fränkel, *Heinrich Himmler* (London: Heinemann, 1965), 113 ff.
87. Quoted in J M Rhodes, *The Hitler Movement* (Stanford: Hoover Institution Press, Stanford University, 1980), 119.
88. T Jersak, "Die deutsche Kriegsgesellschaft und der Holocaust", *DRZW*, Vol. 9/1, 309: *Die deutsche Kriegsgesellschaft, 1939–1945. Politisierung, Vernichtung, Überleben.*

5 From Triumph to Disaster: NS Propaganda from the Launch of 'Barbarossa' until Stalingrad

1. Boberach, *Meldungen aus dem Reich. Auswahl aus den geheimen Lageberichten des Sicherheitsdienstes der SS*, No. 356 (4.3.1943); Steinert, *Hitler's War and the Germans*, 184 ff.
2. W Stephan, *Joseph Goebbels: Dämon einer Diktatur* (Stuttgart: Union Deutsche Verlagsgesellschaft, 1949), 226 ff.
3. Balfour, *Propaganda in War 1939–1945*, 227–8; BA, NS 18/1193, 117 (Tießler to Bormann, 30.6.1941); ZgS (BA) 101/20, 30.6; *Goebbels Diary*, 30.6.1941.
4. Goebbels, 'Der Schleier fällt', *Das Reich*, 6.7.1941, in *Die Zeit ohne Beispiel*, 520–5; cf. Boelcke, *The Secret Conferences of Dr Goebbels*, 5.7.1941, 177.
5. Irving, *Goebbels*, 652–3.
6. BA, NS 18/242, 1 (Propaganda Action Plan for the Eastern Occupied Territories).
7. BA, R 58/205 (SD public opinion report, 24.7.1941).
8. Cf. BA, NS 18/1193, 128 (Propagandaparolen No. 8, 8.11.1941).
9. Balfour, *Propaganda in War 1939–1945*, 233 ff. Hitler and his entourage believed that, after the Stalinist purges of the late 1930s, the Red Army had lost most of its fighting potential: Klink and others, *DRZW*, Vol. 4, 38–97.
10. Boberach, *Meldungen aus dem Reich. Auswahl aus den geheimen Lageberichten des Sicherheitsdienstes der SS*, 4.8 and 21.8.1941.
11. Boelcke, *The Secret Conferences of Dr Goebbels*, 2.8.1941, 178–81.
12. Klink and others, *DRZW*, Vol. 4, 736–52; E Murawski, *Der deutsche Wehrmachtsbericht 1939–1945; Ein Beitrag zur Untersuchung der geistigen Kriegsführung. Mit einer Dokumentation der Wehrmachtberichte vom 1.7.1944 bis zum 9.5.1945* (Boppard: Boldt Verlag, 1962), 77–91.
13. Klink and others, *DRZW*, Vol. 4, 760–75.
14. Hitler, Speech in Berlin Sportpalast, 3.10.1941, in Domarus, *Hitler*, II, 1760–1.
15. Dietrich, *The Hitler I Knew*, 101 ff; Semmler, *Goebbels*, 9.10.1941, 54–5.
16. Boelcke, *The Secret Conferences of Dr Goebbels*, 5.9.1941, 181–2.
17. Murawski, *Der deutsche Wehrmachtsbericht 1939–1945*, 61–3.
18. Boelcke, *The Secret Conferences of Dr Goebbels*, 13.10.1941, 185–6.
19. Dietrich, *12 Jahre mit Hitler*, 123–4.
20. H Fritzsche testimony at Nuremberg: IMT, Vol. 17, 258–9 (27.6.1946).
21. Boelcke, *The Secret Conferences of Dr Goebbels*, 7.12.1941, 192–3.
22. Boelcke, *The Secret Conferences of Dr Goebbels*, 4.10.1941, 184.
23. Goebbels, 'Wenn oder wie?', in his *Das eherne Herz*, 77–84 (9.11.1941).
24. For the speech see Domarus, *Hitler*, II, 1775–8; I Kershaw, *Hitler*, II: *Nemesis, 1936–45* (London: Allen Lane, 2000), 436–7.
25. BA, NS 18/242, 36 (RPL, Propagandaaktion, 19.9.1941).
26. The *Propagandaparolen* were introduced in the second half of 1941 as a general statement of strategy for the short-term conduct of propaganda by the RMVP. They were issued by the ministry's Propaganda Division (*Hauptamt Pro*), initially

every fortnight, later on in the war less frequently [BA, NS 18/1193, 1 (Hauptamt Pro, 1941 – n.d.)]. Whilst the intended function of the *Parolen* was to supply binding overall principles for the bulk of regime and party propaganda activities, they merely reflected the RMVP's (and Goebbels's) ideas; therefore, they were neither binding for, nor truly representative of, the propaganda output of other agencies in the polycratic structures of wartime NS propaganda.

27. BA, NS 18/80, 13 (Propagandaparolen No. 5, November 1941).
28. Semmler, *Goebbels*, 28.8.1941, 50–1.
29. Boelcke, *The Secret Conferences of Dr Goebbels*, 18.11.1941, 191–2.
30. BA, NS 18/242, 1–13 (Propagandaplan für den Kriegswinter 1941/42, September 1941).
31. 'Erläuterungen zur Propaganda-Aktion 1941/42', *Politischer Informationsdienst, Gauleitung der NSDAP*. Salzburg, Gaupropagandaamt 1(1941), no. 9, 3–16.
32. BA, NS 18/242, 25–31 (RPL to all NSDAP authorities, 12.9.1941).
33. Diewerge, *Das Kriegsziel der Weltplutokratie*.
34. S Friedländer, *Prelude to Downfall: Hitler and the United States 1939–1941* (New York: Knopf, 1967), 47 ff.
35. See, amongst others, R S Thompson, *A Time for War: Franklin D Roosevelt and the Path to Pearl Harbor* (New York: Prentice Hall, 1991), and R B Stinnett, *Day of Deceit: The Truth about FDR and Pearl Harbor* (New York: Free Press, 1999).
36. Hitler, Address to the Reichstag, 11.12.1941, in Domarus, *Hitler*, II, 1801–10.
37. The losses of the first stage of 'Barbarossa' are discussed in B R Kroener, 'Die Personellen Ressourcen des Dritten Reiches im Spannungsfeld zwischen Wehrmacht, Bürokratie und Kriegswirtschaft, 1939–1942', *DRZW*, Vol. 5/1: *Organisation und Mobilisierung des deutschen Machtbereichs. Kriegsverwaltung, Wirtschaft und personelle Ressourcen 1939–1941* (Stuttgart: Deutsche Verlags-Anstalt, 1988), 877–87.
38. Fredborg, *Behind the Steel Wall*, 43–4; for the three-million figure of prisoners see Boelcke, *The Secret Conferences of Dr Goebbels*, 14.10.1941, 188–9.
39. Boelcke, *The Secret Conferences of Dr Goebbels*, 7.12.1941, 192–3. For the idea of 'realism' in Goebbels's propaganda see L W Doob, 'Goebbels' Principles of Propaganda', *Public Opinion Quaterly*, 14 (1950), 437–8.
40. Boelcke, *The Secret Conferences of Dr Goebbels*, 19.12.1941, 197–8.
41. R–D Müller, G R Ueberschär, *Hitler's War in the East. A Critical Assessment* (Providence/Oxford: Berghahn Books, 2002), Part C; Baird, *The Mythical World of Nazi War Propaganda*, 172–4.
42. Fredborg, *Behind the Steel Wall*, 55–6.
43. Fredborg, *Behind the Steel Wall*, 62–7; Kershaw, *The Hitler-Myth*, 176–7.
44. J Goebbels, 'Ruf zur Gemeinschaftshilfe. Aufruf zur Sammlung von Wintersachen für unsere Front', 21.12.1941, in *Das eherne Herz*, 131–7.
45. J Goebbels, 'Die Angeber', 14.9.1941, in *Die Zeit ohne Beispiel*, 573–8.
46. Klink and others, *DRZW*, 790 ff.
47. Goebbels, *Der steile Aufstieg*, vii–xiv (Introduction by M A Schirmeister).
48. See, for example, VB, 10.10.1941.
49. Boelcke, *The Secret Conferences of Dr Goebbels*, 17.11.1941, 190–1; cf. Hitler, Speech in Munich, 9.11.1941, in Domarus, *Hitler*, II, 1771–81.
50. A Hitler, Speech at the Berlin Sportpalast, 3.10.1941, in Domarus, *Hitler*, II, 1763 ff.
51. A Hitler, 'Order of the day to the German troops on the eastern front', 2.10.1941, in Domarus, *Hitler*, II, 1756–7.

52. B Pietrow–Ennker, 'Die Sowjetunion in der Propaganda des Dritten Reiches: Das Beispiel der Wochenschau', *Militärgeschichtliche Mitteilungen*, 46 (1989), 79 ff; P Brandt, 'German perceptions of Russia and the Russians in modern history', *Debatte: Review of Contemporary German Affairs*, 11 (2003), 39–59.
53. Kroener, *DRZW*, Vol. 5/1, 871–927.
54. Boelcke, *The Secret Conferences of Dr Goebbels*: 7.12.1941 and 27.2.1942; cf. the comments about the 'yellow peril', 10.3.1942, 217–8.
55. *Goebbels Diary*, 30.1.1942.
56. Boelcke, *The Secret Conferences of Dr Goebbels*, 28.12.1941, 198–9.
57. For example BA, NS 18/80, 70 (Propagandaparolen No. 40, 18.8.1942).
58. Cf. Boelcke, *The Secret Conferences of Dr Goebbels*, 10.3.1942, 217–8.
59. BA, NS 18/80, 70 (Propagandaparolen No. 40, 18.8.1942); cf. BA, NS 18/1193, 146.
60. A Fürst von Urach, *Das Geheimnis japanischer Kraft* (Berlin: Zentralverlag der NSDAP, 1943); see also Boberach, *Meldungen aus dem Reich. Auswahl aus den geheimen Lageberichten des Sicherheitsdienstes der SS*, No. 306 (6.8.1942), 243 ff, for information about the awkwardness which many Germans experienced in trying to appreciate the successes of Japan, even if the latter was a racially 'different' and 'non-Christian' country.
61. J Goebbels, 'Blick über die Weltlage' in his, *Das eherne Herz*, 213–4.
62. Boelcke, *The Secret Conferences of Dr Goebbels*: 23.2.1942, 213–4; 26.3.1942, 219.
63. On the reduction of food rations and the propaganda preparation for these measures, see BA, NS 18/80, 32 (Propagandaparolen No. 31, 15.2.1942); 180, 155 (Propagandaparolen No. 12, 12.1.1942).
64. J Goebbels, 'Blick über die Weltlage' in his, *Das eherne Herz*, 214.
65. For example Boberach, *Meldungen aus dem Reich. Auswahl aus den geheimen Lageberichten des Sicherheitsdienstes der SS*, No. 253 (22.1.1942), 197 ff.
66. Kershaw, *The Hitler-Myth*, 176 ff.
67. Phochner (ed.) *The Goebbels Diaries* (London, 1948), 24.2.1942.
68. 'Alles nur für den Sieg. Der Sieg allein entscheidet!', *Monatsblätter der Gaupropagandaleitung Weser-Ems der NSDAP*, 7 (1942), 19, available at GPA (translation by Randall Bytwerk).
69. Welch, *The Third Reich*, 111–12.
70. Boelcke, *The Secret Conferences of Dr Goebbels*, 2.4.1942, 222.
71. Hitler, speech to the Reichstag, 26.4.1942, in Domarus, *Hitler*, II, 1865–75.
72. B Wegner, 'Der Krieg gegen die Sowjetunion 1942/43', *DRZW*, Vol. 6: *Der globale Krieg. Die Ausweitung zum Weltkrieg und der Wechsel der Initiative 1941–1943* (Stuttgart: Deutsche Verlags-Anstalt, 1990), 868 ff.
73. Boelcke, *The Secret Conferences of Dr Goebbels*, 13.7.1942, 258.
74. Boelcke, *The Secret Conferences of Dr Goebbels*: 13.5.1942, 236–7; 10.6.1942, 242; 3.7.1942, 251; 22.7.1942, 262.
75. BA, NS 18/80, 62 (Propagandaparolen No. 32, 22.5.1942).
76. BA, NS 18/80, 71 (Propagandaparolen No. 40, 18.8.1942); cf. similar comments in BA, NS 18/1193, 146.
77. Boelcke, *The Secret Conferences of Dr Goebbels*, 22.7.1942, 262.
78. Boelcke, *The Secret Conferences of Dr Goebbels*: 22.5.1942, 238; and 6.7.1942, 253, respectively.
79. Boelcke, *The Secret Conferences of Dr Goebbels*, 27.2.1942, 214–5; cf. 7/9.7.1942, 254–6.
80. See Boelcke, *The Secret Conferences of Dr Goebbels*, 15.7.1942, 260, where Goebbels noted that 'a change has occurred in public reaction to the attitude of the

Russians. Our thesis that the Russian army is being kept together by commissars wielding the knout is no longer believed; instead, the conviction is gaining more ground every day that the Russian soldier is a convinced believer in bolshevism and fights for it'.

81. Boelcke, *The Secret Conferences of Dr Goebbels*, 7–9 July 1942, 254–7.
82. For example, Boberach, *Meldungen aus dem Reich. Auswahl aus den geheimen Lageberichten des Sicherheitsdienstes der SS*, No. 309 (17.8.1942), 248–9; Steinert, *Hitler's War and the Germans*, 155 ff.
83. Boelcke, *The Secret Conferences of Dr Goebbels*, 15.8.1942, 269.
84. For the operations in Stalingrad see Wegner, *DRZW*, Vol. 6: *Der globale Krieg. Die Ausweitung zum Wettkrieg und der Wechsel der Initiative 1941–1943* (Stuttgart: Deutsche Verlags-Anstalt, 1990), 962–1063.
85. Semmler, Goebbels, 16.12.1942; generally see A Beevor, *Stalingrad* (Harmondsworth: Penguin, 1998), passim, esp. 266 ff.
86. Boelcke, *The Secret Conferences of Dr Goebbels*, 18.9.1942, 279.
87. A Hitler, Address at the Opening of the 'Winter Relief Campaign', Berlin, 30.9.1942, in Domarus, *Hitler*, II, 1913–24; cf. his 8.11.1942 speech in Munich for the commemoration of the 1923 putsch in Domarus, *Hitler*, II, 1935–8. See also Public Records Office (PRO) – Foreign Office (FO), Documents 371/30928 (report on Hitler's speech, 1.10.1942). Note Dietrich's postwar assertion that the communiqué about the city's capture had been ready on Hitler's desk since mid-August – Dietrich, *The Hitler I Knew*, 95–6.
88. H Fritzsche, *Hier spricht Hans Fritzsche* (Zürich: Interverlag, 1948), 220–1.
89. Boelcke, *The Secret Conferences of Dr Goebbels*: 24.8.1942, 271; 18.9.1942, 278.
90. Kershaw, *The Hitler-Myth*, 185–6; cf. A–F Ruth, *Der Schattenmann: Tagebüchaufzeichnungen, 1938–1945* (Berlin, 1947), 18.9.1942.
91. Kris and Speier, *German Radio Propaganda*, 112 ff.
92. Boelcke, *The Secret Conferences of Dr Goebbels*, 12.11.1942, 298.
93. Semmler, *Goebbels*, 16.12.1942, 59; IMT, Vol. 19 (Fritzsche interrogation) 13.11.1947.
94. BA, R 55/524, 1–28 (Fritzsche broadcasts, November–December 1942).
95. Irving, *Goebbels*, 726.
96. Wegner, *DRZW*, Vol. 6, 997–1063.
97. Fredborg, *Behind the Steel Wall*, 152–3.
98. Boelcke, *The Secret Conferences of Dr Goebbels*, 7.10.1942, 287.
99. Boelcke, *The Secret Conferences of Dr Goebbels*, 12.9.1942, 275.
100. Boelcke, *The Secret Conferences of Dr Goebbels*, 6/8/12/14.11.1942, 294–9; R Stumpf, 'Der Krieg im Mittelmeerraum 1942/43: die Operationen in Nordafrika und im Mittleren Mittelmeer', *DRZW*, Vol. 6, 710–39.
101. Boelcke, *The Secret Conferences of Dr Goebbels*, 14.11.1942, 299. For the importance of 'rumours' and enemy broadcasts see ch. 6.
102. ZgS (BA) 109/39, 15.11.1942. Interestingly, this comment may be taken as a veiled criticism of Hitler himself – the Führer had misleadingly given the impression that Germany had not abandoned anything in north Africa in his 9.11.1942 speech. In late December Goebbels apparently criticised those 'dilettantes at work on the Russian front', but Semmler was convinced that 'he can only have referred to the Führer' (26.12.1942, 62).
103. Boelcke, *The Secret Conferences of Dr Goebbels*, 23/25/26.11.1942, 300–2.
104. Cf. *Goebbels Diary*, 10.5.1943.
105. Balfour, *Propaganda in War 1939–1945*, ch. 36, 288 ff; Stumpf, *DRZW*, Vol. 6, *Der globale Krieg. Die Ausweitung zum Weltkrieg und der Wechsel der Initiative 1941–1943*, 648–709.

106. SD reports (26.11/3.12.1942) in US National Archives (NA), SS, T–175, Roll 264, 2758190.
107. Boelcke, *The Secret Conferences of Dr Goebbels*, 317 – where an excerpt from the *OKW* report of 16.1.1943 is quoted. The word had been banned from propaganda information by Goebbels in October 1942 (Boelcke, *The Secret Conferences of Dr Goebbels*, 286–8).
108. Kershaw, *Hitler*, II, 550; the speech in Domarus, *Hitler*, II, 1976–80.
109. A J Berndt, von Wedel, *Deutschland im Kampf*, no. 83–4 (Berlin: Verlagsansalt Otto Stollberg, February 1943), 52–3.
110. BA, NS 18/80, 80–89 (Propagandaparolen 47 and 48, 2.3/9.3.1943); BA, NS 18/1193, 171 (Propagandaparolen 49, 17.2.1943).
111. Hans Schwarz van Berk, 'Die offenen Verlustlisten', *Das Reich*, 14.2.1943, 3.
112. BA, NS 18/180, 85 (Propagandaparolen 48, 9.2.1943).
113. 'Das ist Heldentum!', *Zeitschriften-Dienst*, 5.2.1943, translated and available at http://www.calvin.edu/academic/cas/gpa/zd1.htm
114. Goebbels' speech at the Berlin Sportpalast ('Führer befiehl, wir folgen!'), 30.1.1943, in his *Das eherne Herz*, 138–50; Goebbels, 'Die harte Lehre' (7.2.1943), in Ibid., 159–66; Boelcke, *The Secret Conferences of Dr Goebbels*, 327–8.
115. Kershaw, *The Hitler-Myth*, 189 ff; Steinert, *Hitler's War and the Germans*, 190 ff.; Beevor, *Stalingrad*, 396 ff.

6 NS Propaganda and the Loss of the Monopoly of Truth (1943–44)

1. Doob, *Public Opinion and Propaganda* (Hamden, CT: Archon Books, 1966), chs 11 and 13.
2. C J Friedrich, Z K Brzezinski, *Totalitarian Dictatorship and Autocracy* (New York/ Washington/London: Praeger, 1965), 17 ff.
3. J Habermas, *Structural Transformation of the Public Sphere* (Cambridge, MA: MIT Press, 1989); 'The Public Sphere: An Encyclopedia Article,' in S E Bronner and D Kellner (eds), *Critical Theory and Society. A Reader* (New York: Routledge, 1989), 136–42. See, in general, H D Lasswell, D Lerner, H Speier (eds), *Propaganda and Communication in World History*, Vol. 2: *The Emergence of Public Opinion in the West* (Honolulu: University of Hawaii Press, 1980).
4. Boelcke, *The Secret Conferences of Dr Goebbels*, 16.12.1942, 309.
5. Boberach, *Meldungen aus dem Reich. Auswahl aus den geheimen Lageberichten des Sicherheitsdienstes der SS*, No. 359 (15.2.1943), 296; cf. Balfour, *Propaganda in War 1939–1945*, 344–5, who quotes a 1943 opinion report that underlined the dramatic increase in rumours, jokes and other 'non-conformist' attitudes inside the Reich.
6. BA, R 58/179, 38 (Tätigkeitsbericht, 4.1.1943); cf. Welch, 'Manufacturing a Consensus', *Contemporary European History*, 1–15; D Welch, 'Nazi Propaganda and the Volksgemeinschaft: Constructing a People's Community', *Journal of Contemporary History*, 2 (1993), 229–30.
7. D J K Peukert, *Inside Nazi Germany: Conformity, Opposition, and Racism in Everyday Life* (New Haven: Yale University Press, 1987), chs 3, 7; on the propaganda preparation for the announcement of the reduction in rations, see BA, NS 18/80, 32 (Propagandaparolen No. 15, 2.1942).
8. Hitler, speech at the Berlin Sportpalast, 30.1.1942, in Domarus, *Hitler*, II, 1829 f.
9. Boelcke, *The Secret Conferences of Dr Goebbels*, 22.10.1942, 289.

10. BA, NS 18/77, 28 (Gutterer to Goebbels, 12.1.1943).
11. BA, NS 18/77, 37 (Tießler to Goebbels, 16.2.1943).
12. BA, NS 18/80, 88 (Propagandaparolen No. 50, 23.2.1943).
13. Boelcke, *The Secret Conferences of Dr Goebbels*, 27.9.1942, 280.
14. For Fritzsche's commentary see BA, R 55/524, 49 (3.2.1943); for opinion reports BA, R 55/531, 91–8.
15. Boelcke, *The Secret Conferences of Dr Goebbels*, 4.1.1943, 312–3; cf. Semmler, *Goebbels*, 3.3.1943, 72–3.
16. Semmler, *Goebbels*, 14.2.1943, 69–70.
17. 'Lehrgang der Gau- und Kreispropagandaleiter der NSDAP', *Unser Wille und Weg*, 9 (1939), 133–9.
18. J Goebbels, 'Die Standhaftigkeit der Herzen', in his *Der steile Aufstieg*, 35–6.
19. Balfour, *Propaganda in War 1939–1945*, 306 ff.
20. Goebbels's journalistic record is discussed in Balfour, *Propaganda in War 1939–1945*, 115 ff; for *Das Reich* see Abel, *Presselankung in NS-Staat*, 74–106.
21. J Goebbels, 'Der totale Krieg', *Das Reich*, 17.1.1943.
22. See, for example, the almost concurrent campaign against 'black-marketeers' in BA, NS 18/80, 46 (Propagandaparolen No. 22, 23.2.1943), where the action was scheduled to begin on 27.2.1943.
23. I Fetscher, *Joseph Goebbels im Berliner Sportpalast 1943 – 'Wollt ihr den totalen Krieg?'* (Hamburg: Europäische Verlagsanstalt, 1998); Balfour, *Propaganda in War 1939–1945*, 322 ff.
24. Goebbels, 'Nun, Volk, steh auf, und Sturm brich los!', in his *Der steile Aufstieg*, 167–204; for an analysis see G Moltmann, 'Goebbels' Speech on Total War, 18.2.1943', in H Holborn (ed.), *Republic to Reich: The Making of the Nazi Revolution* (New York: Vintage Books, 1973), 298–342; Welch, *The Third Reich*, 107 ff, available at GPA (translation by Randall Bytwerk).
25. P Longerich, 'Joseph Goebbels und der Totale Krieg. Eine unbekannte Denkschrift des Propagandaministers vom 18. Juli 1944', *Vierteljahrshefte für Zeitgeschichte*, 35 (1987), 289 ff; G Moltmann, 'Goebbels' Rede zum totalen Krieg am 18. Februar 1943', *Vierteljahrshefte für Zeitgeschichte*, 12 (1964), 13; Bramsted, *Goebbels and National Socialist Propaganda 1925–1945*, 262 ff.
26. BA, R 55/612, 6 (Tätigkeitsbericht, 22.2.1943); Boberach, *Meldungen aus dem Reich. Auswahl aus den geheimen Lageberichten des Sicherheitsdienstes der SS*, 22.2.1943, 298–300; Steinert, *Hitler's War and the Germans*, 189–90; Kershaw, *Hitler*, II, 561 ff.
27. Steinert, *Hitler's War and the Germans*, 189; Boelcke, *The Secret Conferences of Dr Goebbels*, 22.2.1942, 335–6.
28. W von Oven, *Mit Goebbels bis zum Ende* (Buenos Aires. Dürer-Verlag. 1949), Vol. II, 90 ff.
29. Balfour, *Propaganda in War 1939–1945*, 327–8.
30. BA, NS 18/80, 90 ff (Propagandaparolen Nos. 54–55, 5.3.1943).
31. A Speer, *Inside the Third Reich* (London: Book Club Associates, 1971), 256–7; Kershaw, *Hitler*, II, 561–4. See also ch. 2.
32. NSDAP, Reich Propaganda Command, 'Antibolschewistische Propaganda', 22.2.1943, NSDAP, in NA, T-81/23/20711; cf. Semmler, *Goebbels*, 13.3.1943, 74–5.
33. BA, NS 18/180, 48 (Propagandaparolen No. 48, 9.2.1943).
34. BA, NS 18/77, 18–21 (Reichsring to RPL, 22.2.1943).
35. BA, NS 18/77, 26 ('Anweisung für antibolshewistische Propaganda-Aktion', 20.2.1943).

36. BA, NS 18/77, 32 (Reichsring, Vorlage, 18.2.1943).
37. BA, NS 18/1193, 171 (Propagandaparolen No. 49, 17.2.1943), available at GPA (translation by Randall Bytwerk).
38. BA, NS 18/180, 96 (Propagandaparolen No. 51, 15.3.1943).
39. Boelcke, *The Secret Conferences of Dr Goebbels*, 5.3.1943, 337.
40. Wegner, *DRZW*, Vol. 6, 845–54.
41. Boelcke, *The Secret Conferences of Dr Goebbels*, 11/13.3.1943, 339–42.
42. Note that, in his diary, Goebbels also mentioned Hitler's desire to capitalise on the Kharkov success, thwarted only by Goebbels' insistence to play down the affair. See Baird, *The Mythical World of Nazi War Propaganda*, 197; *Goebbels Diary*, 23.3.1943.
43. Semmler, *Goebbels*, 14.3.1943, 76.
44. *Goebbels Diary*, 14.5.1943.
45. Herzstein, *The War that Hitler Won: Goebbels and the Nazi Media Campaign*, 388–90.
46. Welch, *The Third Reich*, 103–4; Peukert, *Inside Nazi Germany*, 125–44.
47. Boelcke, *The Secret Conferences of Dr Goebbels*, 16.9.1942, 277.
48. Shirer, *Berlin Diary*, 403–4.
49. BA, R 55.602, 118 (Reichsarbeiterdienst Breslau, 'Bericht über die Einstellung der Bauern zu ihren polnischen and ukrainischen Hilfskräften in den Standorten der Lager des RADwJ', 3.12.1942). See in general 'Ein Briefwechsel, der zu denken gibt', *Der Hoheitsträger* 6 (March 1943), 23–4.
50. BA, NS 18/1193, 158 (Propagandaparolen No. 43, 12.9.1942).
51. J N Kapfener, *Rumours. Uses, Interpretations and Images* (New Brunswick: Transactions Press, 1990).
52. Flannery, *Assignment to Berlin*, 256 ff.
53. Semmler, *Goebbels*, 8.6.1941, 40–1.
54. Semmler, *Goebbels*, 8.6.1941, 40–1.
55. Baird, *The Mythical World of Nazi War Propaganda*, 134–5.
56. On the function of 'silence' in propaganda see Ellul, *Propaganda*, 56–7.
57. Cf. Semmler, *Goebbels*, 11.10.1941, 55–6.
58. Boberach, *Meldungen aus dem Reich. Auswahl aus den geheimen Lageberichten des Sicherheitsdienstes der SS*, No. 338, 26.11.1943, 338 ff.
59. Baird, *The Mythical World of Nazi War Propaganda*, 200.
60. Boberach, *Meldungen aus dem Reich. Auswahl aus den geheimen Lageberichten des Sicherheitsdienstes der SS*, No. 367, 15.3.1943, 306–7; No. 403, 27.9/4.10, 357 ff. See also Balfour, *Propaganda in War 1939–1945*, 335 ff.
61. BA, NS 18/80, 49 (Propagandaparolen No. 25, 20.4.1943).
62. BA, R 55/601, 15 (Tätigkeitsbericht, 12.4.1943); Boberach, *Meldungen aus den Reich. Auswahl aus den geheimen Lageberichten des Sicherheitsdienstes der SS*, No. 314 (3.9.1942), 257 ff (rumours about massive impending attack on Frankfurt); No. 385, 24.5.1943, 323 (rumours about 30,000 dead per day as a result of air raids). Cf. similar claims that British planes had dropped leaflets about imminent, highly destructive air raids.
63. Boberach, *Meldungen aus dem Reich. Auswahl aus den geheimen Lageberichten des Sicherheitsdienstes der SS*, 1/15.7.1943; NA, SS, T-175/265/2759632.
64. A L Unger, 'The Public Opinion Reports of the Nazi Party', *Public Opinion Quarterly*, 29 (1965/66), 565–82; A L Smith Jr, 'Life in Wartime Germany: General Ohlendorf's Opinion Service', *Public Opinion Quarterly*, 36 (1972), 1–7; Balfour, *Propaganda in War 1939–1945*, 323–5; *Goebbels Diary*, 21.4.1943.
65. Bormann, Rundschreiben, NA, 198/42, 18.12.1942, CGD, T-580, Roll 15, Folder 176A; cf. *Goebbels Diary*, 18.12.1942.

66. See, for examples, comments made in Boberach's *Meldungen aus dem Reich: Die geheime Lageberichte des Sicherheitsdienstes der SS*, SD report for 27.1.1944.
67. Smith A L Jr, *Public Opinion Quarterly*, 4–7; Baird, *The Mythical World of Nazi War Propaganda*, 205 ff.
68. Stuiber, *Medien in Deutschland*, 182 ff.
69. Friedrich and Brzezinski, *Totalitarian Dictatorship and Autocracy*, 17 ff; H Arendt, *The Origins of Totalitarianism* (New York: Harcourt Brace Jovanovich, 1973, 5th ed.), 180 ff.
70. S Nicholas, *Echo of War. Home Front Propaganda and Wartime BBC 1939–45* (New York: Manchester University Press, 1996); O'Sullivan, 'Listening Through: The Wireless and World War II', in P Kirkham and D Thomas (eds), *War Culture: Social Change and Changing Experience in World War Two Britain* (London: Lawrence & Wishart, 1995); Doherty, *Nazi Wireless Propaganda*.
71. See relevant comments in Boberach's *Meldungen aus dem Reich: Die geheime Lageberichte des Sicherheitsdienstes der SS*, 8.6.1943.
72. For example Boelcke, *The Secret Conferences of Dr Goebbels*, 26.8.1942, 271–2, where Goebbels urges his subordinates to counter Soviet pessimistic reports about Stalingrad, which he considered highly suspicious.
73. Baird, *The Mythical World of Nazi War Propaganda*, 195–7.
74. Boelcke, *The Secret Conferences of Dr Goebbels*, 13/14.7.1942, 258.
75. BA, NS 18/77, 32 (Reichring to local RPL offices, 18.2.1943); cf. Jeffrey Herf, ' "Der Krieg und die Juden". Nationalsozialialistische Propaganda in Zweiten Weltkrieg', in *DRZW*, Vol. 9/2, 159–202.
76. BA, NS 18/77, 35 (Reichsring to local RPL offices, 18.11.1943).
77. PRO FO 898/458 (23.6.1944); 898/457; BA, NS 18/77, 35 (Führungshinsweis No. 6–7, 18.11.1943).
78. C Cruickshank, *The Fourth Arm: Psychological Warfare 1938–1945* (London: Davis-Poynter, 1977), ch. 7; D Lerner, *Psychological Warfare against Nazi Germany: The Sykewar Campaign, D-Day to VE-Day* (Cambridge, MA/London: MIT Press, 1971), ch. 8.
79. Cruickshank, *The Fourth Arm*, chs 3 and 5.
80. On 'black' and 'white' propaganda see Jowett and O'Donnell, *Propaganda and Persuasion*, 8–10.
81. PRO FO 898/60 (18.6.42).
82. G R Ueberschär (ed.), *Das Nationalkomitee 'Freies Deutschland' und der Bund Deutscher Offiziere* (Frankfurt am Main: S. Fischer Taschenbuch Verlag, 1995); K P. Schoenhals, *The Free German Movement: A Case of Patriotism or Treason?* (Westport, CT: Greenwood Press, 1989); H Bungert, *Das Nationalkomitee und der Westen: Die Reaktion der Westalliierten auf das NKFD und die Freien Deutschen Bewegungen 1943–1948* (Stuttgart: Franz Steiner Verlag, 1997); P Steinbach, 'Nationalkomitee Freies Deutschland und der Widerstand gegen den Nationalsozialismus', *Exilforschung. Ein Internationales Jahrbuch*, 8 (1990), 61–91.
83. J D Carnes, *General zwischen Hitler und Stalin. Das Schicksal des Walther von Seydlitz* (Düsseldorf: Droste, 1980); B Scheurig, *Freies Deutschland: Das Nationalkomitee und der Bund Deutscher Offiziere in der Sowjetunion, 1943–1945* (Munich: Mymphenburger Verlagshandlund, 1961; new eds 1984 and 1993).
84. On this issue see M Knox, 'Expansionist zeal, fighting power, and staying power in the Italian and German dictatorships', in R Bessel (ed.), *Fascist Italy and Nazi Germany: Comparisons and Contrasts* (Cambridge: Cambridge University Press, 1996), 113–33.

85. E A Shils, M Janowitz, 'Cohesion and disintegration in the Wehrmacht in World War II', in D Katz (ed.), *Public Opinion and Propaganda* (New York: Holt, 1954), 553–82.

86. J Pipes, 'Germans against Germany in WW II, the NKFD and BDO', in www. feldgrau.com/nkfd-bdo.html; cf. Ueberschär, *Das Nationalkomitee 'Freies Deutschland' und der Bund Deutscher Offiziere*, 183–91.

87. An indication of this can be found in rumours throughout 1943 that most prominent (and generally disliked) party leaders had abandoned the country: see Boberach, *Meldungen aus dem Reich. Auswahl aus den geheimen Lageberichten des Sicherheitsdienstes der SS*, 8.7.1943, 333–4.

88. J Goebbels, 'Unser Hitler' (Radio Speech on Hitler's Birthday, 19.4.1942), in his *Das eherne Herz*, 286–94.

89. Semmler, *Goebbels*, 12.12.1941, 57.

90. Kershaw, *The Hitler-Myth*, chs 5–6.

91. For the T-4 programme see H Friedlander, *The Origins of Nazi Genocide: From Euthanasia to the Final Solution*. (Chapel Hill, NC: University of North Carolina Press, 1995); M Burleigh, *Ethics and extermination: Reflections on Nazi genocide* (New York: Cambridge University Press, 1997); I Kershaw, *Popular Opinion and Political Dissent*, 336 ff; S Baranowski, 'Consent and Dissent: The Confessing Church and Conservative Opposition to National Socialism', *Journal of Modern History*, 59 (1987), 53–78.

92. Hitler, Radio Address to the German People, 15.5.1942.

93. Kershaw, *The Hitler-Myth*, 178 ff; Welch, *The Third Reich*, 206 ff; N Reeves, *The Power of Film Propaganda: Myth or Reality?*(New York: Cassell, 1999), 105–11.

94. Hitler, Speech to the Reichstag, 26.4.1942, in Domarus, *Hitler*, II, 1867 ff.

95. Boberach, *Meldungen aus dem Reich. Auswahl aus den geheimen Lageberichten des Sicherheitsdienstes der SS*, No. 279, 27.4.1942, 231–2.

96. Cruickshank, *The Fourth Arm*, 83.

97. H Boberach (ed.), *Meldungen aus dem Reich: Die geheime Lageberichte des Sicherheitsdienstes der SS, 1938–1945* (Herrsching: Pawlak Verlag, 1984), Vol. 11, 4279.

98. Kershaw, *The 'Hitler-Myth'*, 217 ff; Steinert, *Hitler's War and the Germans*, 270 ff; cf. O Buchbender and R Stern (eds), *Das andere Gesicht des Krieges* (Munich: Beck, 1982), 21–3.

99. Boberach (ed.), *Meldungen aus dem Reich: Die geheime Lageberichte des Sicherheitsdienstes der SS*, 4981–2; for the speech's reception see Steinert, *Hitler's War and the Germans*, 195–6; Aryeh L Unger, 'The Public Opinion Reports of the Nazi Party', *Public Opinion Quarterly*, 29/4 (1965–66): 572–3; Kershaw, *The 'Hitler-Myth'* 196–7.

100. Domarus, *Hitler*, II, 1998 ff; Boelcke, *The Secret Conferences of Dr Goebbels*, 3.2.1943, 327–8. The figure given by Hitler for total losses in the war was 542,000.

101. Semmler, *Goebbels*, 21.3.1943, 80.

102. NA T-81/13072.

103. G Kirwin, 'Allied bombing and Nazi domestic propaganda', *European History Quarterly*, 15 (1985), 341–62; Kershaw, *The 'Hitler-Myth'*, 201 ff; Welch, *The Third Reich*, 116–17.

104. Herzstein, *The War that Hitler Won: Goebbels and the Nazi Media Campaign*, 421–31.

105. BA, R 55/601, 102 (Tätigkeitsbericht, 4.9.1944); Speer, *Inside the Third Reich*, 256–7.

106. Kershaw, *Hitler*, II, 598 ff.

107. See, for example, *Goebbels Diary*, 25 / 27.7.1943.
108. *Goebbels Diary*, 25.7.1943.
109. See, for example, *Goebbels Diary*, 11.9.1943, 357, and Kershaw, *Hitler*, II, 600–1, on how Goebbels literally forced Hitler to deliver a speech to the people on the situation that had arisen after Mussolini's overthrow in Italy and the intensification of air warfare inside Germany (speech in Domarus, *Hitler*, II, 2305 ff).
110. *Goebbels Diary*, 9.9.1943; cf. Unger, *Public Opinion Quarterly*, 581–2.
111. Kershaw, *The Hitler-Myth*, ch. 8; Herzstein, *The War that Hitler Won: Goebbels and the Nazi Media Campaign*, chs 11–12.
112. J Petley, *Capital and Culture: German Cinema 1933–45* (London: BFI, 1979), 106–11.
113. J Goebbels, 'Unser Hitler', 19.4.1942, in his *Der eherne Herz*, 286–94; cf. 'Ein Wort zum Luftkrieg', 4.8.1943, in Goebbels, *Der steile Aufstieg*, 400–5. On the film see Hull, *Film in the Third Reich*, 213–5; Welch, *Propaganda and the German Cinema*, 174–85; E Leiser, *Nazi Cinema* (New York: Collier Books, 1975); translation of E Leiser, '*Deutschland Erwache: Propaganda im Film des Dritten Reiches* (Düsseldorf: Droste, 1987),113–18, 121–2.
114. Hitler, Address to the NSDAP Gauleiters in Berlin, 24.2.1945, in Domarus, *Hitler*, II, 2203–6.
115. A Bullock, *Hitler: A Study in Tyranny* (New York / Evanston: Harper Torchbook, 1964); 779 f; *Goebbels Diary 1945*, 20/21.3.1945.
116. *Goebbels Diary 1945*, 20/21.3.1945; cf. his speech to the Reichstag, 26.4.1942, in Domarus, *Hitler*, II, 1865–75.
117. H Trevor–Roper (ed.), *Le testament politique de Hitler* (Paris: 1959), 6.2.1945.
118. Semmler, *Goebbels*, 18.7.1943, 91–3.
119. *Goebbels Diary*, 3.3.1943. For the importance of touring those areas affected by air raids see *Goebbels Diary*, 6.11.1943. As early as in autumn 1942, Goebbels was busy touring bomb-affected areas – see BA, NS 18/347, 56 (Tießler to RPL, Vorlage). An example of a speech accompanying his public appearance: Elberfelder ('In vorderster Reihe'), 18.6.1943, in Goebbels, *Der steile Aufstieg*, 323–3. See also H Heiber (ed.), *Goebbels* (London: Robert Hale & Co, 1972), 299 ff. His speech at Essen (which was also severely affected by an air raid in the spring of 1943) was received very favourably by the local population – see BA, R/55, 601, 15 (Tätigkeitsberichte, 12.4.1943). See also the coverage of Goebbels' visit to Hamburg: 'Goebbels in Hamburg', *Hamburger Fremdenblatt* (19.8.1943), 1.
120. Semmler, *Goebbels*, 10.7.1943, 88–9.
121. Goebbels, 'Unser Hitler', 20.4.1943, in his *Der steile Aufstieg*, 252–62.
122. Goebbels, 'Die Realitäten des Krieges', 22.8.1943, in his *Der steile Aufstieg*, 422–30.
123. Semmler, *Goebbels*, 17.6.1944, 131; the jokes are recorded in Boberach's *Meldungen aus dem Reich: Die geheime Lageberichte des Sicherheitsdienstes der SS*, 27.12.1943, 386–8.
124. Z Zeman, *Nazi Propaganda* (London: Oxford University Press, 1973, 2nd ed.), 10 ff.
125. BA, R55/612, 19 (Leiter Pro to Goebbels, 2.1.1945); 76 (Bericht aus RPL Klagenfurt, 1.1.1945).
126. H Trevor-Roper, *The Last Days of Hitler* (New York: Macmillan, 1947), 118 ff; K Koller, *Der letzte Monat: Die Tagebuchaufzeichnungen des ehemaligen Chefs des Generalstabes der deutschen Luftwaffe vom 14. April bis zum 27. Mai 1945* (Mannheim: Wohlgemuth, 1949), 20 ff.
127. United States, Office of United States Chief of Counsel for Prosecution of Axis Criminality, *Nazi Conspiracy and Aggression* (Washington: Government Printing Office, 1946–1948), VI, 259–63, No. 3569-PS.

7   The Winding Road to Defeat: The Propaganda of Diversion and Negative Integration

1. Goebbels, 'Unser Hitler', VB, 20.4.1945, and in H Heiber (ed.), *Goebbels Reden 1932–1945* (Düsseldorf: Droste, 1991), 447 ff.
2. Doob, 'Goebbels' Principles', 427 ff.
3. Boberach, *Meldungen aus dem Reich. Auswahl aus den geheimen Lageberichten des Sicherheitsdienstes der SS*, No. 377, 19.4.1943, 313; no. 385, 24.5.1943, 325.
4. Doob, 'Goebbels' Principles of Propaganda', 442.
5. Hitler, Speech at Munich, 8.11.1942, in Domarus, *Hitler*, II, 1935–42; for the reactions see Boberach, *Meldungen aus dem Reich. Auswahl aus den geheimen Lageberichten des Sicherheitsdienstesdes SS*, No. 336, 19.11.1942, 274–5.
6. BA, R 55/520, 128 (Scharping commentary, 22.4.1943).
7. BA, R 55/524, 198 ff (Fritzsche commentary, 12.6.1943).
8. Goebbels, 'Überwundene Winterkrise', Speech at the Berlin Sportpalast, *Der steile Aufstieg*, 294–5, available at GPA (translation by Randall Bytwerk).
9. For example, Boberach, *Meldungen aus dem Reich. Auswahl aus den geheimen Lageberichten des Sicherheitsdienstes der SS*, no. 365, 8.3.1943, 365.
10. BA, R 55/524, 77 (Fritzsche commentary, 3.3.1943).
11. Goebbels, 'Im Schatten des Waffenkrieges', *Das Reich*, 18.7.1943, 1.
12. For example, BA, R 55/601, 16 (Tätigkeitsbericht, 12.4.1943); Boberach, *Meldungen aus dem Reich. Auswahl aus den geheimen Lageberichten des Sicherheitsdienstes der SS*, 1.7.1943, 331.
13. J P Fox, 'Der Fall Katyn und die Propaganda des NS-Regimes', *Vierteljahrshefte für Zeitgeschichte*, 30 (1982): 462–99; E Fröhlich, 'Katyn in neuem Licht? Goebbels und der Mord an den polnischen Offizieren im 2. Weltkrieg', *Geschichte in Wissenschaft und Unterricht*, 37 (1986): 234–40.
14. J Goebbels, 'Das große Wagnis', 16.5.1943, in his *Der steile Aufstieg*, 272 ff.
15. Boberach, *Meldungen aus dem Reich. Auswahl aus den geheimen Lageberichten des Sicherheitsdienstes der SS*, no. 377, 19.4.1943, 313–7.
16. Herzstein, *The War that Hitler Won: Goebbels and the Nazi Media Campaign*, 229–31.
17. Boberach, *Meldungen aus dem Reich. Auswahl aus den geheimen Lageberichten des Sicherheitsdienstes der SS*, no. 373, 5.4.1943, 309.
18. Goebbels, 'Überwundene Winterkrise', speech at the Berlin Sportpalast, 5.6.1943, in his *Der steile Aufstieg*, 297–8.
19. BA, R 55/524, 196 (Fritzsche commentary, 12.6.1943).
20. BA, R 55/525, 31 (Fritzsche commentary, 31.3.1943).
21. BA, R 55/520, 166 (Scharping commentary, 19.8.1943). The original manuscript of the commentary is heavily edited, revealing the desperate attempt of NS propaganda to keep up with developments and transmit the most positive message possible, given the circumstances.
22. Goebbels, 'Im Schatten des Waffenkrieges', *Das Reich*, 18.7.1943, 1.
23. Baird, *The Mythical World of Nazi War Propaganda*, 207 ff; P Nello, *Un fedele disubbidiente. Dino Grandi da Palazzo Chigi al 25 Luglio* (Bologna: Mulino, 1993); R De Felice, *Mussolini l'alleato*, Vol. I: *L'Italia in guerra (1940–1943) – crisi e agonia del regime* (Turin: Einaudi, 1996).
24. Balfour, *Propaganda in War 1939–1945*, 350–1. Note that Goebbels refrained from making even a single reference to the situation in Italy in his *Das Reich* editorials until well into September.
25. *Goebbels Diary*, 28.7.1943.

26. See, for example, Boberach, *Meldungen aus dem Reich. Auswahl aus den geheimen Lageberichten des Sicherheitsdienstes der SS*, 29.7.1943, 34 ff.

27. M Knox, *Mussolini Unleashed, 1939–1941*, 231 ff; J J Sadkovich, 'The Italo-Greek war in context', *Journal of Contemporary History*, 493–64; Kallis, *Fascist Ideology* (London: Routledge, 2000), 175–81.

28. BA, R 55/525, 32 (Fritzsche commentary, 31.3.1943).

29. Boberach, *Meldungen aus dem Reich. Auswahl aus den geheimen Lageberichten des Sicherheitsdienstes der SS*, 16.8.1943, 344 ff.

30. J Goebbels, 'Das Schulbeispiel', *Das Reich*, 19.9.1943, 1.

31. Cf. BA: R 55/525, 78 (Fritzsche commentary, 18.10.1943); R 55/520, 452 (Scharping commentary, 16.3.1944).

32. BA, NS 18/1193, 229 (Propagandaparolen No. 60, 9.9.1943).

33. Hitler, Speech at Munich, 8.11.1943, in Domarus, *Hitler*, II, 2050–9.

34. NA, Bormann, Bekanntgabe, 69/44, 23.3.1944, 'Italien: Verbot der Kritik am Faschismus', CGD, T-580, Roll 16.

35. BA, R 55/601, 61 (RPL Tätigkeitsbericht, 24.7.1944).

36. Sir C Webster and N Frankland, *The Strategic Air Offensive against Germany, 1939–1945*, Vol. I (London: HMSO, 1961); Koch, 'The strategic air-offensive against Germany', *The Historical Journal*, 34 (1991), 117–41; G W Feuchter, *Geschichte des Luftkriegs* (Frankfurt: Athenaeum, 1962).

37. J Goebbels, 'Blick über die Weltlage', 15.2.1942, in his *Das eherne Herz*, 209 ff.

38. J Goebbels, 'Der Luft- und Nervenkrieg', 14.6.1942, in his *Das eherne Herz*, 347–8.

39. A Hitler, speech at the Berlin Sportpalast, 30.9.1942, in Domarus, *Hitler*, II, 1917–18.

40. *The Times*, 3.5.1942, 1. On the attacks see S Burgdorff, C Habbe (eds), *Als Feuer vom Himmel fiel … Der Bombenkrieg in Deutschland* (Hamburg: DVA, 2003); L Wilde, *Bomben über Lübeck. Dokumentation über die Zerstörung Lübecks beim Luftangriff vom. 28/29 März 1942* (Lübeck: Verlag Schmidt-Römhild, 2000); J Friedrich, *Der Brand: Deutschland im Bombenkrieg 1940–1945* (Berlin: Propyläen Verlag, 2002), 122 ff.

41. H R Trevor–Roper, *Hitler's Table Talk 1941–44: His Private Conversations* (London: Redwood Press, 1953), 30.5.1942; cf. Semmler, *Goebbels*, 10.7.1943, 88–90.

42. A Klein, *Köln im Dritten Reich. Stadtgeschichte der Jahre 1933–1945* (Cologne: Greven Verlag, 1983); M Rüther, *Köln, 31. Mai 1942. Der 1000-Bomber-Angriff* (Cologne: Hohn, 1992).

43. Toni Winkelnkemper, *Der Großangriff auf Köln. Ein Beispiel* (Berlin: Franz Eher Verlag, 1942).

44. H Boog, 'Der Anglo-Amerikanische Strategische Luftkrieg über Europa und die deutsche Luftverteidigung', *DRZW*, Vol. 6: *Der globale Krieg. Die Ausweitung zum Weltkrieg und der Wechsel der Initiative 1941–1943* (Stuttgart: Deutsche Verlags-Anstalt, 1990), 506–68.

45. Boelcke, *The Secret Conferences of Dr Goebbels*, 11.8.1942, 267–8; Balfour, *Propaganda in War 1939–1945*, 341.

46. For example J Goebbels, 'Bewährung der Jugend', 25.10.1942, in his *Der steile Aufstieg*, 45.

47. J Goebbels, 'Der Luft- und Nervenkrieg', 14.6.1942, in his *Das eherne Herz*, 349.

48. On the idea that air raids were an Allied substitute for the 'second front' see R Beaumont, 'The Bomber Offensive as Second Front', *Journal of Contemporary History*, 22 (1987), 3–19.

49. Boelcke, *The Secret Conferences of Dr Goebbels*, 10/11.5.1942, 235.

50. E R Beck, *Under the Bombs: The German Home Front, 1942–1945* (Lexington: University Press of Kentucky, 1986); R J Overy, *The Air War, 1939–1945* (New York: Stein and Day, 1980), 5 ff.
51. This was acknowledged by the regime authorities – see BA, NS 18/180, 119 (Tießler to RPL, 28.10.1942).
52. BA, R 55/604, 52 (Schäffer to RPA Bochum, 19.1.1943). For the air raid on Essen see N Krüger, 'Die März-Luftangriffe auf Essen 1943. Vorgeschichte, Verlauf und Folgen', in Krüger (ed.), *Essen unter Bomben. Märztage 1943* (Essen: Klartext-Verlag, 1984), 14–37.
53. BA, R 55/601, 52 (Tätigkeitsbericht, 17.7.1944).
54. Boelcke, *The Secret Conferences of Dr Goebbels*, 221, 232 and 277 respectively.
55. Semmler, *Goebbels*, 22.11.1943, 108 ff.
56. Boelcke, *The Secret Conferences of Dr Goebbels:* 12.9.1942, 276; 10.10.1942, 245.
57. Boog, 'Strategischer Luftkrieg in Europa und Reichsluftverteidigung 1943–1944', *DRZW*, Vol. 7, 16–35.
58. For example, Boberach, *Meldungen aus dem Reich. Auswahl aus den geheimen Lageberichten des Sicherheitsdienstes der SS*, No. 385, 24.5.1943, 323–5.
59. J Goebbels, 'Überwundene Winterkrise', 5.6.1943, in his *Der steile Aufstieg*, 289 ff, available at GPA (translation by Randall Bytwerk).
60. J Goebbels, 'Überwundene Winterkrise', 5.6.1943, in his *Der steile Aufstieg*, 293 ff.
61. Hans Schwarz van Berk, 'Die ungeahnten Folgen', *Das Reich*, 2.7.1943, 4.
62. For example Semmler, *Goebbels*, 25.12.1944, 172–3; Boelcke, *The Secret Conferences of Dr Goebbels*, 7.12.1941, 192.
63. BA, NS 18/180, 120 (Propagandaparolen 54, 22.4.1943); cf. BA, NS 18/193, 133 (Tießler to RPL, 30.4.1942).
64. M Middlebrook, *The Battle of Hamburg* (New York: Charles Scribner's Sons, 1980); J Szodrzynski, 'Das Ende der "Volksgemeinschaft"? Die Hamburger Bevölkerung in der "Trümmergesellschaft" ab 1943', in F Bajohr, J Szodrzynski (eds), *Hamburg in der NS-Zeit* (Hamburg: Ergebnisse Verlag, 1995), 281–303; Boog, 'Strategischer Luftkrieg in Europa', *DRZW*, Vol. 7, 35–45.
65. Semmler, *Goebbels*, 26.7.1943, 94.
66. 'Vergeltung für den Tod an der Ruhr', *Hamburger Fremdenblatt*, 19.6.1943, 1; cf. his speech in Dortmund, analysed in R Blank, 'Die Stadt Dortmund im Bombenkrieg', in G E Sollbach (ed.), *Dortmund. Bombenkrieg und Nachkriegsalltag 1939–1948* (Hagen: Lesezeichen Verlag Dierk Hobein, 1996), 33–4; and his memorial speech at Elberfelder Town Hall (18.6.1943) in his *Der steile Aufstieg*, 323–30; Boog, 'Strategischer Luftkrieg in Europa', *DRZW*, Vol.7, 320–55.
67. J Goebbels, 'Am längeren Hebelarm', 14.8.1943, in his *Der steile Aufstieg*, 416–7.
68. Kershaw, *The Hitler-Myth*, 182–5.
69. *Goebbels Diary*, 19.6.1943.
70. Steinert, *Hitler's War and the Germans*, 318.
71. R Schabel, *Die Illusion der Wunderwaffen. Die Rolle der Düsenflugzeuge und Flugabwehrraketen in der Rüstungspolitik des Dritten Reiches* (Munich: Oldenbourg Wissenschaftlicher Verlag, 1994); H D Hölsken, *Die V-Waffen. Entstehung, Propaganda, Kriegseinsatz* (Stuttgart: Deutsche Verlags-Anstalt, 1984).
72. R Blank, 'Kriegsalltag und Luftkrieg an der "Heimatfront"', in *DRZW*, Vol. 9/1: *Die deutsche Kriegsgesellschaft, 1939 bis 1945* (Munich: Deutsche Verlag-Anstalt, 2004), 435 ff; Bramsted, *Goebbels and National Socialist Propaganda 1925–1945*, 320 ff.

73. Semmler, *Goebbels*, 17.6.1944, 131.
74. Boberach, *Meldungen aus dem Reich: Die geheimen Lageberichten des Sicherheitsdienstes der SS*, No. 5428, 2.7.1943.
75. Steinert, *Hitler's War and the Germans*, 318 ff; W von Oven, *Mit Goebbels bis Zum Ende* (Buenos Aires. Düror–Verlag, 1949), Vol. II, I, 5.1.1944, 170.
76. See, for example, Hitler's radio address, 10.9.1943, in Domarus, *Hitler*, II, 2034–9.
77. J Goebbels, 'Zum Sieg mit Schwert und Pflug' [text of Berlin Sportpalast speech, 4.10.1943), *Hamburger Fremdenblatt*, 4.10.1943; reprinted in Heiber (ed.), *Goebbels*.
78. Blank, *Dortmund*, 435–6.
79. *Akten der NSDAP*, Vol. 2, *Stadt Oberhausen*, Report about Kreisleitung Oberhausen, 18.12.1943.
80. J Goebbels, Speech 15.4.1944, in Heiber (ed.), *Goebbels*.
81. Steinert, *Hitler's war and the Germans*, 204 ff.
82. Blank, *Dortmund*, 438–40.
83. Semmler, *Goebbels*, 17.6.1944, 131.
84. Kirwin, 'Allied bombing and Nazi domestic propaganda', *European History Quarterly*, 15 (1985), 576 ff; R Beaumont, 'The Bomber offensive as Second Front', *Journal of Contemporary History*, 22(1987), 14 f; Boog, 'Strategischer Luftkrieg in Europa' *DRZW*, Vol. 7, 367–79.
85. J Goebbels, 'Die Schacht um Berlin', *Das Reich*, 13.2.1944, available at GPA (translation by Randall Bytwerk).
86. Semmler, *Goebbels*, 17.6.1944, 131; cf. 10.6.1944, 129 (comment on the postponement of the launch).
87. Harald Jansen, 'Erste V.1-Bilanz' *Das Reich'*, 2.7.1944, 4.
88. See for example *Goebbels Diary*, 18.6.1944; Berndt and von Wedel, *Deutschland im Kampf*, 109 ff. Boog, 'Strategischer Luftkrieg in Europa', *DRZW*, Vol. 7, 385–98.
89. BA, R 55/601, 47–49 (Tätigkeitsbericht, 17.7.1944).
90. Harald Jansen, 'Erste V.1-Bilanz', *Das Reich*, 2.7.1944, 4.
91. BA, R 55/601, 47 (Tätigkeitsbericht, 17.7.1944).
92. Boog, 'Strategischer Luftkrieg in Europa', *DRZW*, Vol. 7, 398–403.
93. BA, R 55/601, 60–1 (Tätigkeitsbericht, 24.7.1944); BA, R 55/601, 92 (Tätigkeitsbericht, 28.8.1944).
94. BA, R 55/602, 143 (RPA Westfalen-Süd report to Schäffer, 14.11.1944); cf. BA, R 55/601, 215 (Tätigkeitsbericht, 14.11.1944).
95. BA, R 55/601, 156 (RPL Tätigkeitsbericht, 9.10.1944); see also Hölsken, 113 ff, Boog, 'Strategischer Luftkrieg in Europa', *DRZW*, Vol. 7, 411 ff.
96. Hitler, Speech at Munich, 8.11.1943, in Domarus, *Hitler*, II, 2054 ff.
97. Boberach, *Meldungen, aus dem Reich. Auswahl aus den geheimen Lageberichten des Sicherheitsdienstes der SS*, 'Meldung zur Führerrede vom 8.11.1943' (11.11.1943), 357–60; see also Kershaw, *The Hitler-Myth*, 211 ff.
98. *Rede des Reichsministers Dr. Goebbels auf der Reichs-und Gauleiter Tagung in München*, February 23, 1944 (Munich: Franz Eher, 1944).
99. Goebbels, 'Das höhere Gesetz', *Das Reich*, 24.9.1944, 1, available at GPA (translation by Randall Bytwerk).
100. Balfour, *Propaganda in War 1939–1945*, 354.
101. BA, R 55/520, 224 (Scharping commentary, 23.8.1943).

102. *Zeitschriften-Dienst,* 27.1.1943, 1–2, available at GPA (translation by Randall Bytwerk).
103. BA, R 55/ 520, 275 (Scharping commentary, 18.10.1943).
104. BA, R 55/520, 180 (Scharping commentary, 13.11.1943).
105. A Seaton, *The Russo–German War, 1941–1945* (London: Arthur Baker Limited, 1971), 426–7.
106. Goebbels Diary, 6.11.1943.
107. Balfour, *Propaganda in War 1939–1945,* ch. 38.
108. Cf. the attempt of NS propaganda to dispel any wishful thinking that a defeat of Germany will result in the punishment of only the Nazi leadership in BA, NS 18/77, 32 (Reichsring to RPL authorities, 18.2.1943).
109. Goebbels, 'Vor einem neuen Jahr', *Das Reich,* 2.1.1944, 1, available at GPA (translation by Randall Bytwerk).
110. Boog, 'Strategischer Luftkrieg in Europa', *DRZW,* Vol. 7, 75–80.
111. Goebbels, 'Die Schlacht um Berlin', *Das Reich,* 13.2.1944, 3.
112. Goebbels, 'Das ist nicht mehr Krieg, das ist Mord', VB, 27.5.1944, 1; Balfour, *Propaganda in war 1939–1945,* 373–4; Steinert, *Hitler's War and the Germans,* 236–8.
113. Cf. J Goebbels, 'Die 30 Kriegsartikel für das deutsche Volk', 26.9.1943, Article 3. Interestingly, the need to embrace more radical measures and intensify the 'total war' against the enemy, was reflected in SD public opinion reports, with people complaining about the 'total war in paper' that the NS regime was waging – see Boberach, *Meldungen aus dem Reich. Auswahl aus den geheimen Lageberichten des Sicherheitsdienstes der SS,* 17.2.1944, 404–6.
114. Boberach, *Meldungen aus dem Reich. Auswahl aus den geheimen Lageberichten des Sicherheitsdienstes der SS,* 7.2.1944, 395–6.
115. J Goebbels, 'Die 30 Kriegsartikel für das deutsche Volk', *Das Reich,* 26.9.1943, reprinted in *Der steile Aufstieg,* 468 (Article 11).
116. F D Roosevelt, Radio Address about Teheran and Cairo Conferences, 24.12.1943, in F D Roosevelt, *The Great Speeches of President Roosevelt* (Washington: Presidential Publishers, 1947), 313–9.
117. ZgS (BA) 3/1673, Sonderlieferung 24/44 (31.5.1944).
118. Goebbels's speech in Heiber, *Goebbels,* 286–304.
119. Boberach, *Meldungen aus dem Reich. Auswahl aus den geheimen Lageberichten des Sicherheitsdienstes der SS,* 11.11.1943, 359–60.
120. Goebbels, Speech at Berlin, 7.12.1943, in Heiber, *Goebbels,* 311–2.
121. BA, R 55/520, 452 (Scharping commentary,14.3.1944).
122. Boberach, *Meldungen aus dem Reich. Auswahl aus den geheimen Lageberichten des Sicherheitsdienstes der SS,* 27.12.1943, 388.
123. Steinert, *Hitler's War and the Germans,* 234 ff.
124. Boberach, *Meldungen aus dem Reich. Auswahl aus den geheimen Lageberichten des Sicherheitsdienstes der SS,* 7.2.1944, 398–9; cf. similar feelings noted in the later report about Ukraine, 20 April 1944, 417 ff.
125. Ibid., 6.4.1944, 411; cf. the report of 17.2.1944, 404–5.
126. Ibid., 4.5.1944, 420–2.
127. Steinert, *Hitler's War and the Germans,* 240–1; Boberach, *Meldungen aus dem Reich. Auswahl aus den geheimen Lageberichten des Sicherheitsdienstes der SS,* 20.4, 4.5.1944.
128. Domarus, *Hitler,* II, 2101.

129. D Vogel, 'Deutsche und Alliierte Kriegführung im Westen', *DRZW*, Vol. 7: *Das Deutsche Reich in der Defensive*. *Strategischer Luftkrieg in Europa, Krieg im Westen und in Ostasien 1943–1944/45* (Stuttgart: Deutsche Verlags-Anstalt, 2001), 451–501.

130. Balfour, *Propaganda in war 1939–1945*, 374 ff.

131. Cf. Goebbels, 'Am längeren Hebelarm', 14.8.1943, in his *Der steile Aufstieg*, 414–21.

132. Steinert, *Hitler's War and the Germans*, 239–41; Boberach, *Meldungen aus dem Reich. Auswahl aus den geheimen Lageberichten des Sicherheitsdienstes der SS*, 20.4.1944 503–9.

133. Goebbels, 'In neunzig Tagen', *Das Reich*, 20.1.1944, 1.

134. *Goebbels Diary*, 13, 16.5.1944.

135. For 'Operation Overlord' see Vogel, *DRZW*, Vol. 7, 502–80.

136. Steinert, *Hitler's War and the Germans*, 258 ff; Baird, *The Mythical World of Nazi War Propaganda*, 223–5; cf. Boberach, *Meldungen aus dem Reich. Auswahl aus den geheimen Lageberichten des Sicherheitsdienstes der SS*, 8.6.1944, 427–8.

137. BA, R 55/602, 78 (Wilke to RMVP, Abt Pro, Meldung No. 5402, 12.6.1944).

138. G Jannsen, *Das Ministerium Speers. Deutschland Rüstung im Krieg* (Berlin, Frankfurt, Vienna: Ullstein Verlag, 1968), 238–40.

139. J Goebbels, 'Die Hintergründe der Invasion', *Das Reich*, 18.6.1944, 1–2.

140. BA, R 55/601, 48 (RPL Tätigkeitsbericht, 17.7.1944); cf. Irving, *Goebbels*, 825 ff.

141. 'Der Sinn der Abwehrschlacht in Italien', VB, 22.5.1944, 1–2, available at GPA (translation by Randall Bytwerk).

142. Goebbels Diary, 6.6.1944.

143. N von Below, *Als Hitler Adjutant, 1937–1945* (Mainz: von Hase und Köhler, 1980), 372–3.

144. *Zeitschriften-Dienst*, 9.6.1944, 1, available at GPA (translation by Randall Bytwerk).

145. *Rom, Berlin Rom Tokio. Monatschrift für die Vertiefung der kulturellen Beziehungen der Völker des weltpolitischen Dreiecks*, VI (June 1944), 2–3. For public reactions see Boberach, *Meldungen aus dem Reich. Auswahl aus den geheimen Lageberichten des Sicherheitsdienstes sdienstes der SS*, 7.6.1944, 430.

146. BA, R 55/601, 59 (RPL Tätigkeitsbericht, 24.7.1944).

147. BA, R 55/601, 44 (RPL Tätigkeitsbericht, 17.7.1944); cf. Steinert, *Hitler's War and the Germans*, 260 ff.

148. BA, R 55/601, 74 (RMVP Tätigkeitsbericht, 15.8.1944). On the German retreat from France see J Ludewig, *Der deutsche Rückzug aus Frankreich 1944* (Freiburg: Verlag Rombach, 1994).

149. Boberach, *Meldungen aus dem Reich. Auswahl aus den geheimen Lageberichten des Sicherheitsdienstes der SS*, 13.7.1944, 437–43; Steinert, *Hitler's War and the Germans*, 262–4.

150. Steinert, *Hitler's War and the Germans*, 58.

151. Steinert, *Hitler's War and the Germans*, 269–71; G R Ueberschär, 'Gegner des Nationalsozialismus 1933–1945. Volksopposition, individuelle Gewissensentscheidung und Rivalitätskampf konkurrierender Führungseliten als Aspekte der Literatur über Emigration und Widerstand im dritten Reich zwischen dem 35 und 40. Jahrestag des 20. Juli 1944 (Bericht aus der Forschung)', *Militärgeschichtliche Mitteilungen*, 35 (1984), 141–95.

152. BA, NS 18/1674, 148 (SD report, 24.7.1944).

153. NA, Hitler, 'Erlaß des Führers über den totalen Kriegseinsatz vom. 25. Juli 1944', CGD, T-580, Roll 17, 179.

154. J Goebbels, 'Der Befehl der Pflicht', *Das Reich*, 6.8.1944, 1.
155. J Goebbels, 'In den Stürmen der Zeit', *Das Reich*, 20.8.1944, 1.
156. Steinert, *Hitler's War and the Germans*, 270–2.
157. H-A Jacobsen, *Spiegelbild einer Verschwörung: die Opposition gegen Hitler und der Staatsstreich vom 20. Juli 1944 in der SD-Berichterstattung* (Stuttgart: Seewald Verlag, 1984), Vol. 1, 6–7.
158. The two speeches (3.8/3.10.1944) can be found in H Heiber, *Goebbels Reden 1932–1945* (Düsseldorf: Droste, 1991), 360–428.
159. Jacobsen, *Spiegelbild einer Verschwörung*, 1–5; BA, R 55/601, 65 (Tätigkeitsbericht, 7.8.1944).
160. The text of Hitler's radio address can be found in Domarus, *Hitler*, II, 2127–9.
161. H Trevor-Roper, *Goebbels Diary 1945*, 23.3.1945.
162. BA, R 55/602: 2 (report from RPL Baden, 28.7.1944); 9 (report from RPL Thuringia, 28.7.1944).
163. BA, R 55/609, 133 (Tätigkeitsbericht, 8.8.1944).
164. Goebbels, 'In den Stürmen der Zeit', *Das Reich*, 20.8.1944, 1.
165. See the RPL 'opinion reports': BA, R 55/601, 58 (24.7.1944) and 102 (4.9.1944); Steinert, *Hitler's War and the Germans*, 271–3.
166. Irving, *Goebbels*, ch. 55.
167. ZgS (BA) 109/52, 44, quoted in Steinert, *Hitler's War and the Germans*, 287–8.
168. Hitler, Address to the German Nation, 30.1.1945, in Domarus, *Hitler*, II, 2195–8.
169. H Trevor-Roper, *Goebbels Diary 1945*, 2.4.1945.
170. J Streicher, 'Das Grauen im Osten', *Der Stürmer*, issue 8, 2.1945, available at GPA (translation by Randall Bytwerk).
171. Quoted in J Noakes, G Pridham (eds), *Nazism: A Documentary Reader, 1919–1945*, Vol. IV: *The German Home Front in World War Two* (Exeter: University of Exeter Press, 1998), 652.
172. BA, R 55/601, 197 (Tätigkeitsbericht, 30.10.1944).
173. J Goebbels, 'Die Urheber des Unglücks der Welt', *Das Reich*, 21.1.1945, 1.
174. Vogel, *DRZW*, Vol.7, 502.
175. Goebbels, Speech at Cologne, 3.10.1944, in Heiber, *Goebbels* 425.
176. Goebbels, 'Die Urheber des Unglücks der Welt', *Das Reich*, 7.10.1944, 3.
177. A Armstrong, *Unconditional Surrender: The Impact of the Casablanca Policy on World War II* (New Brunswick: Rutgers University Press, 1971), 69 ff.
178. H Goitsch, *Niemals* (Munich: Zentralverlag der NSDAP, 1944).
179. *Goebbels Diary 1945*, 28.2.1945; 'Das Jahr 2000', *Das Reich*, 25.2.1945, 1–2.
180. Heiber, *Goebbels*, 432; cf. his last editorial 'Widerstand um jeden Preis', *Das Reich*, 22.4.1945, 1–2.
181. See, for example, VB, 7.11.1944, 1 and 3; BA, R 55/601, 156 (RPL Tätigkeitsbericht, 9.10.1944).
182. See the RPL 'opinion report' for 9.10.1944 in BA, R 55/601, 156.
183. Semmler, *Goebbels*, 2.11.1944, 163.
184. *RGB*, 1944, I, 73–5; BA, R 55/601, 184 (Tätigkeitsbericht, 23.10.1944); BA, R 55/602, 143–4 (RPA Westfalen-Süd to RMVP, 14.11.1944); Steinert, *Hitler's War and the Germans*, 279–81.
185. Vogel, *DRZW*, Vol.7 619–34.
186. Irving, *Goebbels*, 876–7.
187. See the RPL 'opinion reports': BA, R 55/601, 249 ff (19.12.1944) and 261 ff (26.12.1944).
188. 'Unser Führer', *Das Reich*, 6.1.1945, 1.

189. BA, R 55/601, 284 (RPL Tätigkeitsbericht, 21.2.1945).
190. Cf. BA, R 55/601, 204 (RPL Tätigkeitsbericht, 7.11.1944).
191. See, for example, his references in his 28.2.1945 radio address, in Heiber, *Goebbels*, 441–2.
192. Heiber, *Goebbels*; cf. 'Die Weltkrise', *Das Reich*, 17.12.1944, 1.
193. Goebbels, 'Unser Hitler', VB, 20.4.1945, 1, available at GPA (translation by Randall Bytwerk).
194. Heiber, *Goebbels*, 340 ff.
195. Cf. Hans–Ulrich Arntz, 'Berlin, ein Riesenigel', *Das Reich*, 18.3.1945, 4, available at GPA (translation by Randall Bytwerk).

8 Cinema and Totalitarian Propaganda: 'Information' and 'Leisure' in NS Germany, 1939–45

1. S Kracauer, *From Caligari to Hitler: A Psychological History of the German Film* (Princeton: Princeton University Press, 1974).
2. A Hewitt, *Fascist Modernism: Aesthetics, Politics, and the Avant-Garde* (Stanford: Stanford University Press, 1993), 163 ff.
3. A Gramsci, *Selection from Prison Notebooks* (London: Lawrence and Wishart, 1971), 440 ff; C Buci–Glucksmann, 'Hegemony and consent: a political strategy', in A S Sassoon (ed.), *Approaches to Gramsci* (London: Writers and Readers, 1982), 116–26.
4. Jowett and O'Donnell, *Propaganda and Persuasion*, 90 ff, 187 ff.
5. J Wulf, *Theater und Film im Dritten Reich*, 26 ff, 283.
6. See the forthcoming volume edited by D Welch and Roel vande Winkel, *Cinema under the Swastika* (Basingstoke: Palgrave, 2006).
7. S Deren, *The Cradle of Modernity: Politics and Art in Weimar Republic (1918–1933)* (unpublished MSc thesis Middle East Technical University, Ankara, 1997), 129–63; T G Plummer (ed.), *Film and Politics in the Weimar Republic* (New York: Holmes and Meier, 1982).
8. See, for example, the case of Leni Riefenstahl's *Blaue Licht* in T Elsaesser, *Weimar cinema and after: Germany's historical imaginary* (London/New York: Routledge, 2000); Rentschler, *The Ministry of Illusion*, ch. 1; Hoffman, *The Triumph of Propaganda*, 128–31.
9. Wulf, *Theater und Film im Dritten Reich*, 359–60.
10. Witte K, 'Revue als montierte Handlung. Versuch, die Filme zu beschreiben', in Belach, *Wir tanzen um die Welt. Deutsche Revuefilme 1933–45* (Munich: Hanser, 1979), 219 ff.
11. On Goebbels's views on cinema see ch. 1.
12. Knox, 'Expansionist Zeal', 113–33.
13. H–G Happel, *Der historische Spielfilm im Nationalsozialismus* (Frankfurt: Rita Fischer, 1984).
14. G Lange, *Das Kino als moralische Anstalt. Soziale Leitbilder und die Darstellung gesellschaftlicher Realität im Spielfilm des Dritten Reiches* (Frankfurt/New York: Peter Lang, 1994).
15. Kracauer, *From Caligari to Hitler*, 275 ff.
16. Taylor, *Film Propaganda*, Introduction; Jowett and O'Donnell, *Propaganda and Persuasion*, 92–4.
17. T J Saunders, *Hollywood in Berlin. American Cinema and Weimar Germany* (Berkeley: University of California Press, 1994); Hoffman, *The Triumph of Propaganda*, 74 ff.
18. BA, R 109/I, 1079 (Ufa management conference, 14.5.1935).

19. R vande Winkel, 'Nazi Newsreels in Europe, 1939–1945: the many faces of Ufa's foreign weekly newsreel (Auslandstonwoche) versus German's weekly newsreel (Deutsche Wochenschau)', *Historical Journal of Film, Radio and Television*, 24/1 (2004): 5–34; K Kremeier, *The Ufa Story. A History of Germany's Greatest Film Company, 1918–1945* (London: University of California Press, 1999), 270 ff.

20. H Traub, 'Zur Entwicklungsgeschichte der Ufa-Wochenschauen', in *25 Jahre Ufa-Wochenschau* (Berlin, 1939), 18–21; cf. BA, R 109/I, 2433 (Ufa Situation Report for the period 1–30.9.1939, 2.10.1939).

21. P Dietrich, 'Ausbau und Erneuerung des deutschen Filmtheaterparks', *Der Deutsche Film*, 9/1939, 241–2.

22. F Hippler, *Die Verstrickung. Einstellungen und Rückblenden von Fritz Hippler* (Düsseldorf: Droste, 1982), 196.

23. Herzstein, *The War that Hitler Won: Goebbels and the Nazi Media Compaign*, 232–3.

24. M S Phillips, 'The Nazi control of the German Film Industry', *Journal of European Studies*, 1 (1971), 37–68.

25. Kremeier, *The Ufa Story*, 270–1.

26. J Eckhardt, 'Abbild und Sinnbild. Von der Gestaltung der Wirklichkeit in Wochenschau und Kulturfilm', in B Drewniak, *Der deutsche Film 1938–1945. Ein Gesamtüberblick* (Düsseldorf: Droste, 1987).

27. H Barkhausen, *Filmpropaganda für Deutschland im Ersten und Zweiten Weltkrieg* (Hildesheim/Zürich/New York: Olms Presse, 1982), 235–43.

28. Hesrzstein, *The War that Hitler Won*, 233.

29. Barkhausen, *Filmpropaganda für Deutschland in Ersten und Zweiten Weltkrieg*, 242–3.

30. Herzstein, *The War that Hitler Won*, 234–6.

31. See the SD reports for 4.3.1943, in Boberach, *Meldungen aus dem Reich. Auswahl aus den geheimen Lageberichten des Sicherheitsdienstes der SS*, No. 364, 300–1; cf. the change in the tone of the opinion reports about the Wochenschau in BA, R 109 II/67.

32. H K Smith, *Last Train From Berlin* (New York: Alfred Knopf 1942), 157.

33. BA, R 109/II, 67 (Hinkel to Deutsche Wochenschau GmbH, 20.5.1944).

34. BA, R 109/II, 67 (OKW/PRO to PK, 30.3.1943).

35. Herzstein, 246–51.

36. BA, R 109/II, 67 (Chief of Sicherheitspolizei to Hinkel, 25.5/7.6.1944).

37. BA, R 109/II, 67 (Chief of Sicherheitspolizei to Hinkel, 13.7.1944).

38. BA, R 109/II, 67 (Chief of Sicherheitspolizei to Hinkel, 17.5.1944).

39. Quoted in Kremeier, *The Ufa Story*, 342.

40. BA, R 109/II, 67 (Arbeitsstatut des Hautpschriftleiters der deutschen Wochenschau).

41. BA, R 55/663, 79 (Hinkel to State Secretary of the RMVP, 31.7.1944); 81 (Hinkel to Goebbels, 3.8.1944).

42. BA, R 109/II, 67 (Deutsche Wochenschau GmbH to RMVP State Secretary Naumann, 25.1.45).

43. BA, R 190/II, 67 (Hinkel to Naumann, 25.1.45).

44. BA, R 109/II, 67 (Hinkel to Deutsche Wochenschau, 30.1.45); cf. BA, R 55/663, 19 (Hinkel to Gutterer, 8.12.44).

45. BA, R 109/II, 67 (Deutsche Wochenschau to Naumann, 25.1.1945; Hinkel to Auslandsfilmreferat, 30.1.1945).

46. S Hornshøj–Møller and David Culbert, ' "Der ewige Jude" (1940): Joseph Goebbels' unequalled monument to anti-Semitism', *Historical Journal of Film, Radio and Television*, 12 (1992), 41–68; D Hollstein, *Antisemitische Filmpropaganda* (Munich/Berlin: Verlag Dokumentation, 1971), 21 ff and 108–117; D S Hull, *Film in the Third Reich: A Study of German Cinema, 1933–1945* (Berkeley: University of California Press, 1969), 157–77.

47. Leiser, *Nazi Cinema*, 36 ff, 157–8; Boberach, *Meldungen aus dem Reich. Auswahl aus den geheimen Lageberichten des Sicherheitsdienstes der SS*, No. 145, 28.11.1940, 124 ff; Wulf, *Theater und Film im Dritten Reich*, 397–413.

48. N Reeves, *The Power of Film Propaganda: Myth or Reality?* (New York: Cassell, 1999), 114–7.

49. S Hornshøj-Møller, *Der ewige Jude. Quellenkritische Analyse eines antisemitischen Propagandafilms* (Göttingen: Institut für Wissenschaftlichen Film, 1995).

50. Taylor, *Film Propaganda*, 142–4; cf. H. Herma, 'Goebbels' conception of propaganda', *Social Research*, 10 (1943), 200–18.

51. BA, NS 18/40 (Cerff to Gutterer, 23.1.1942) and 24 (Tießler to Gutterer, 4.3.1942), respectively.

52. BA, NS 18/349, 21–22 (Tießler to Fischer, Stabsleiter of RPL, 23.2.1942).

53. BA, R 55/663,149 (Hinkel to Goebbels, 15.11.1944).

54. Quoted in Kremeier, *The Ufa Story*, 310.

55. Cf. Kracauer, *From Caligari to Hitler*, 278 ff.

56. BA, NS 18/349, 78 (RPL to all Gauleiters, 20.7.1940).

57. P Cadars, F Courtade, *Histoire du cinéma nazi* (Paris: E. Losfeld, 1972), 215 ff.

58. Kracauer, *From Caligari to Hitler*, 291 ff.

59. BA, NS 18/348, 229 (Hesse to Bormann, 3.2.1941); 228 (Tießler to Goebbels, n.d).

60. Kracauer, *From Caligari to Hitler*, 288.

61. Taylor, *Film Propaganda*, 145 ff.

62. BA, NS 18/663, 40 (Hinkel to Goebbels, 8.5.1944), where the RMVP agreed to provide DM 61,500 for the film *Die Russen flüchten vor den Bolschewisten*; and BA, NS 18/663, 50 (Hinkel to State Secretary, 23.10.1944), where RM 28,500 were allocated to the production of a film about the 'anti-religious attitude of the Soviet authorities'.

63. BA, NS 18/347, 114–33 (1941 Tobis Production Plan for *Kulturfilme*).

64. BA, NS 18/834, 1–2 (Hippler to Goebbels/Hippler to Rosenberg, 28.8/4.9.1942 respectively) for the initial refusal; BA, NS 18/663, 45–6 (Goebbels to Rosenberg/ Hippler to Goebbels, 20.10.1944), where the production of the 'Schulungsfilm' *Wenn morgens Krieg ist* is approved for the *Ufa Sonderprodution* programme.

65. H–G Voigt, ' "Verräter vor dem Volksgericht". Zur Geschichte eines Films', in Bengt von zur Mühlen, A von Klewitz (eds.), *Die Angeklagten des 20. Juli vor dem Volksgerichtshof* (Berlin-Kleinmachnow: Chronos, 2001), 398 ff.

66. BA, R 55/663, 28 (Hinkel to Goebbels, 31.8.1944).

67. BA, NS 18/349, 96 (Tießler to Fischer, 15.1.1942); 82 (Tießler to Krämer, Stabsamt, 8.2.1943); cf. BA, NS 18, 347, 10–12 (Leiter F, Report on film production, 1943), where the film appears as 'rejected', 9.2.1943.

68. Rentschler, *The Ministry of Illusion*, 113 ff.

69. P Meers, 'Is There an Audience in the House? – film audiences – Critical Essay', *Journal of Popular Film and Television*, 29 (2001), 138–47.

70. Rentschler, *The Ministry of Illusion*, ch. 6; S Tegel, ' "The demonic effect": Veit Harlan's use of Jewish extras in Jud Süss', *Holocaust and Genocide Studies*, 14 (2000), 215–41.

71. J Ellul, *The Formation of Men's Attitudes* (New York: Alfred A. Knopf, 1965), 43 ff, 178 ff.

72. See, for example, the post-war attempts of directors such as Leni Riefenstahl and Veit Harlan to present themselves as reluctant but dutiful executors of an otherwise alien regime vision in their film productions: V Harlan, *Im Schatten meiner Filme* (Gütersloh: Sigbert Mohn, 1966); L Riefenstahl, *Memoiren* (Munich/ Hamburg: Knaus, 1987).

73. Taylor, *Film Propaganda*, 196; H–J Eitner, *Kolberg : Ein preußischer Mythos 1807/1945* (Berlin: Quintessenz-Verlag, 1999); P Paret, '*Kolberg* (1945) as a historical film and historical document', *Historical Journal of Film, Radio and Television*, 14 (1994): 433–48; D Culbert, '*Kolberg*: Film, Filmscript and Kolobrzeg Today', *Historical Journal of Film, Radio and Television*, 14 (1994), 433–66; R Giesen, M Hobsch, *Hitlerjunge Quex, Jud Süss und Kolberg: Die Propagandafilme des Dritten Reiches* (Berlin: Schwarzkopf und Schwarzkopf Verlag, 2003).

74. BA, R 55/663, 3 (State Secretary of the RMVP to RPA Leader Pommerania, 19.10.1944).

75. K Riess, *Das gab's nur einmal – Die große Zeit des deutschen Films* (Vienna: Molden Taschenbuch Verlag, 1977), 3, 205–6.

76. Kremeier, *The Ufa Story*, 350–2.

77. Kremeier, *The Ufa Story*, 358–60.

78. BA, R 55/663, 266–71 (Hinkel to Goebbels, 15.10.1944).

79. BA, R 55/663, 3 (State Secretary to Popp, Gauleiter of Pommerania, 19.10.1944).

80. BA, R 55/663, 6 (Hinkel to Goebbels, 6.12.1944).

81. *Film Kurier*, 21.12.1944, 4.

82. Harlan, *Im Schatten meiner Filme*, 187.

83. Culbert, '*Kolberg*' 451–2; cf. his 'Joseph Goebbels and his diaries – Adolph Hitler's propaganda minister', in *Historical Journal of Film, Radio and Television*, 15 (1995), '*Kolberg*', 143–9.

84. B Winston, 'Triumph of the Will – reinterpretation of Leni Riefenstahl's Nazi-era film', *History Today*, January 1997, 24–8; cf Taylor, *Film Propaganda*, 162–73.

85. W von Oven, *Mit Goebbels bis zum Ende* (Buenos Aires. Dürer-Verlag, 1949), Vol. I, 58 ff.

86. Rentschler, *The Ministry of Illusion*, 179–81.

87. Kremeier, *The Ufa Story*, 303–4.

88. On this connection see generally Welch, *Propaganda and German Cinema*, ch. 5; D Welch, 'Hitler's History Films', *History Today*, 52 (2002), 20–25.

89. R C Lutz, 'False history, fake Africa, and the transcription of Nazi reality in Hans Steinhoff's "Ohm Krüger"', *Literature-Film Quarterly*, 25 (1997), 188–92.

90. Welch, *Propaganda and the German, Cinema*, 270.

91. Kallis, *Fascist Ideology*, 34–5.

92. BA, R 58/157 (SD report, 27.1.1941).

93. Welch, *Propaganda and the German Cinema*, 173–4.

94. BA, NS 18/347, 114–128 (report on *Die Entlassung*); Welch, *Propaganda and the German Cinema*, 274 ff.

95. BA, NS 18/283, 31–35 (report on *Die Entlassung*, 27.7.1942). The whole folder contains detailed accounts of reactions to the screening of the film prior to its eventual release.

96. Cf. *Goebbels Diary*, 23.11.1942 and 26.9.1942 respectively.

97. BA, NS 18/283, 6 (Rosenberg to Bormann, 25.9.1942).

98. BA, NS 18/283, 9 (Tießler to Goebbels, 5.10.1942); Welch, *Propaganda and the German Cinema*, 172–4.

99. In general see K Kanzog, '*Staatspolitisch besonders wertvoll*'. *Ein Handbuch zu 30 deutschen Spielfilmen der Jahre 1934–1945* (Munich: Mankred Hattendorf, 1994), 297–311; Petley, *Capital and Culture*, 106 ff.

100. See ch. 4.

101. *Goebbels Diary*, 28.1.1942.

102. *Goebbels Diary*, 19.2.1942.

103. Welch, *Propaganda and the German Cinema*, 176.

104. BA, NS 18/347,10–2 (1943 Report on Film Production), where the film is listed with the comment 'propagiert'.
105. Hull, *Film in the Third Reich*, 224–5.
106. Welch, *Propaganda and the German Cinema*, 134–44.
107. S Lowry, *Pathos und Politik: Ideologie in Spielfilmen des Nationalsozialismus* (Tübingen: Niemeyer, 1991).
108. See, for example, the series of reports on the reception of each weekly Wochenschau in BA, R 109/II, 67. On the NSDAP opinion reports see Unger, 'Public opinion reports', 565–82, esp. 569–70 for monitoring of films.
109. Albrecht, *Nationalsozialistische Filmpolitik*.
110. BA, NS 18/349, 44 (Gauleitung Sachsen – Notice to Tießler, 11.3.43).
111. BA, NS 18/834 (Gauleitung Württemberg – Notice for Räther, 22.10.43).
112. Quoted in Kremeier, *The Ufa Story*, 310; K Witte, 'Gehemmte Schaulust. Momente des deutschen Revuefilms', in Belach, *Wir tanzen um die Welt*, 7–52.
113. BA, NS 18/834, 1–2 (Tießler to Hippler, 28.8.42).
114. BA, NS 18/834, 35 ff.
115. BA, NS 18/348, 32 (Tießler's Aktennotiz, 17.6.1943).
116. The unpopularity of Nazi rule in the Protectorate had seriously concerned the RMVP since 1939. A few months after the outbreak of the war there were massive student demonstrations in Prague that resulted to the closure of the universities. The matter was extensively debated in the RMVP's Ministerial Conference – see Boelcke, *The Secret Conferences of Dr Goebbels*, 30.10.1939, 2–3.
117. BA: NS 18/348 (Gauleiter Sudetengau to Goebbels, 18.3.43); NS 18/349, 156 (26.3.43, Tießler to RMVP Film Abteilung).
118. BA, NS 18/349, 158 (Film Abt to Tießler, 5.12.42).
119. BA, NS 18/834, 48 (Gauleitung Wartheland – Notice for Tießler, 24.9.43).
120. Hull, *Film in the Third Reich*, 241 ff; Kremeier, *The Ufa Story*, 348–9.
121. Hull, *Film in the Third Reich*, 240–3.
122. BA, NS 18, 349, 275 (Übersicht – Film Beurteilung 1943).
123. Belach, *Wir tanzen um die Welt*, 134–6.
124. BA, NS 18/349, 2 (Rudolf Haake to Rassenpolitisches Amt, 4.9.1942).
125. BA, NS 18/347, 39 (Party Chancellery, Report from Madgeburg-Anhalt, 9.12.1941).
126. BA, NS 18/349, 31 (Tießler to Party Chancellery, 1.11.1941).
127. Herzstein, *The War that Hitler Won*, 294 f; H Goedecke, W Krug, *Wir beginnen das Wunschkonzert* (Berlin/Leipzig: Nibelungen Verlag, 1940); Belach, *Wir tanzen um die Welt*, 184 ff; Bathrick D, 'Making a National Family with the Radio: The Nazi Wunschkonzert', *Modernism/Modernity*, 4 (1997), 115–27.
128. M M Semati and P J Sotirin. 'Hollywood's transnational appeal: hegemony and democratic potential?' *Journal of Popular Film and Television*, 26 (1999), 176–88; cf. M Horkheimer, T Adorno, *Dialectic of Enlightenment* (New York: Herder and Herder, 1972), 121 ff; T Adorno, 'The Culture Industry reconsidered' in *The Culture Industry: Selected Essays on Mass Culture* (New York: Routledge, 1991).
129. Balfour, *Propaganda in War 1939–1945*.
130. B Kleinhans, *Ein Volk, ein Reich, ein Kino. Lichtspiel in der brauen Provinz* (Cologne: PapyRossa Verlag, 2003), 14–5, 79.
131. P Schaper, *Kinos in Lübeck. Die Geschichte der Lübecker Lichtspieltheater und ihrer unmittelbaren Vorläufer 1896 bis heute* (Lübeck, 1987).
132. Kleinhans, *Ein Volk, ein Reich, ein Kino*, 86.
133. For the penetration of the German countryside during the NS period see N von Keeken, *Kinokultur in der Provinz. Am Beispiel von Bad Hersfeld* (Frankfurt et al.: Lang, 1993); Kleinhans, *Ein Volk, ein Reich, ein Kino*, 117–57.

134. Kracauer *From Caligari to Hitler*, 277–8; Welch, *Propaganda and the German Cinema*, 19–20.
135. J Spiker, *Film und Kapital. Der Weg der deutschen Filmwirtschaft zum national-sozialistischen Einheitskonzern* (West Berlin: Spiess 1975), 196–7.
136. H Traub, *Die Ufa. Ein Beitrag zur Entwicklungsgeschichte des deutschen Filmschaffens* (Berlin: UFA-Buchverlag, 1943), 157 ff.
137. BA, NS 18/834, 42 (RMVP Führerinformation No. 0061, 12.5.42).
138. A J Sander, *Jugend und Film* (Berlin: NSDAP, 1944), 72 ff; Herzstein, *The War that Hitler Won: Goebbels and the Nazi Media Compaign*, 417 ff.
139. *Goebbels Diary*, 21.12.1941.
140. Kremeier, *The Ufa Story*, 301–11; Herzstein, 267; Rentschler, *The Ministry of Illusion*, 269 ff.
141. NA T-580/626 (report for summer–autumn 1941).
142. BA, NS 18/834, 42 (Führerinformation No. 0061, 12.5.42).
143. BA, R 55/663, 98 (Hinkel to Goebbels, 11.2.44).
144. BA, R 55/663, 17 (Hinkel to Goebbels, 5.12.44).
145. BA, NS 18/834 (Tießler to RMVP, 9.10.42).
146. BA, R 55/663, 287 (Hinkel to Goebbels, 12.12.44).
147. BA, R 55/663, 282 (Hinkel to Goebbels, 21.12.44).
148. BA, R 55/663, 127 (Hinkel to Goebbels, 26.4.44).
149. Herzstein, *The War that Hitler Won: Goebbels and the Nazi Media Compaign*, 270 ff.
150. BA, NS 18/834, 70 (Vertrauliche Information, 16.11.43).
151. Sington and Weidenfeld, 48 ff (in Herzstein, *The war that Hitler Won: Goebbels and the Nazi Media Compaign*, 268).
152. Herzstein, *The War that Hitler Won: Goebbels and the Nazi Media Compaign*, 317 ff.
153. BA, R 55/664, 266 (Hinkel to Goebbels, 16.10.44).
154. BA, R 109/I, 1716, 1577 (Ufa management meeting, 16.11.44).
155. J C Fest, *The Face of the Third Reich* (New York: Pantheon Books, 1970), 150 ff.

Conclusions: Legitimising the Impossible?

1. Dietrich, *The Hitler I Knew*, 113.
2. A Speer, *Inside the Third Reich*, 414–6.
3. D Roberts, *The Poverty of Great Politics*, chs 1–3; J Herf, *Reactionary Modernism. Technology Culture and Politics in Weimar and the Third Reich* (Cambridge: Cambridge University Press, 1984).

Bibliography

Primary sources

Archival material

Archivio Centrale dello Stato, Ministero di Cultura Popolare.
Bundesarchiv (BA) Berlin.
Public Records Office (PRO, UK National Archives) – Foreign Office (FO) Documents.
US National Archives (NA).
Zeitgeschichtliche Sammlungen (ZSg) [Bundesarchiv].

Newspapers and Periodicals

Das Reich.
Der Stürmer.
Hamburger Fremdenblatt.
Hamburger Illustrierte.
Rom Berlin Rom Tokio. Monatschrift für die Vertiefung der kulturellen Beziehungen der Völker des weltpolitischen Dreiecks.
Schulungs-Unterlage (Munich: Reichsorganisationsleitung der NSDAP, Hauptschulungsamt, 1942).
The Times.
Unser Wille und Weg.
Völkischer Beobachter (VB).
Zeitschriften-Dienst.

Published documents

Akten der NSDAP, Vol 2: *Stadt Oberhausen.*
Boberach H (ed.), *Meldungen aus dem Reich. Auswahl aus den geheimen Lageberichten des Sicherheitsdienstes der SS, 1939–44* (Neuwied/Berlin: Luchterhand, 1965).
Boberach H (ed.), *Meldungen aus dem Reich: Die geheime Lageberichte des Sicherheitsdienstes der SS, 1938–1945* (Herrsching: Pawlak Verlag, 1984), vols 17.
Boelcke W A (ed.), *The Secret Conferences of Dr Goebbels. The Nazi Propaganda War, 1939–43* (New York: E P Dutton & Co, 1970).
Documents on German Foreign Policy (DGFP), Series D.
French Yellow Book ed. by Ministere Des Affaires Estrangeres (Paris 1940).
Reichsgesetzblatt (RGB), *1933–1945.*
Trials of War Criminals before the Nuremberg Military Tribunals under Control Council Law No. 10 October 1946–April 1949, 15 vols (Washington, DC, 1949–1953).
Uffizio Storico del Esercito, *La prima offensiva britannica in Africa settentrionale*, Vol. I (Rome: USE, 1979).
United States, Department of State, Publication no. 3023, *Nazi–Soviet Relations 1939–1941. Documents from the Archives of the German Foreign Office* (Washington: Government Printing Office, 1948).
Trevor–Roper H R, *Hitler's Table Talk 1941–44: His Private Conversations* (London: Redwood Press, 1953).

Trevor–Roper H (ed.), *La testament politique de Hitler*, (Paris: 1959).
Noakes J, Pridham G (eds), *Nazism: A Documentary Reader, 1919–1945*, Vol. 3: *Foreign Policy, War and Racial Extermination* (Exeter: Exeter University Press, 2001).
Noakes J, Pridham G (eds), *Nazism: A Documentary Reader, 1919–1945*, Vol. 4: *The German Home Front in World War Two* (Exeter: University of Exeter Press, 1998).

Memoirs and Diaries

Below N von, *Als Hitler Adjutant, 1937–1945* (Mainz: von Hase und Köhler, 1980).
Dietrich O, *12 Jahre mit Hitler* (Munich: Atlas-Verlag, 1955).
Dietrich O, *The Hitler I Knew* (London: Methuen and Co, 1957).
Flannery H W, *Assignment to Berlin* (London: The Right Book Club, 1943).
Fredborg A, *Behind the Steel Wall: A Swedish Journalist in Berlin 1941–43* (New York: Viking, 1944).
Fritzsche H, *Hier spricht Hans Fritzsche* (Zürich: Interverlag, 1948).
Harlan V, *Im Schatten meiner Filme* (Güterloh: Sigbert Mohn, 1966).
Hippler F, *Die Verstrickung. Einstellungen und Rückblenden von Fritz Hippler* (Düsseldorf: Droste, 1982).
Jacobsen H–A (ed.), *Generaloberst Halder: Kriegstagebuch* (Stuttgart: Kohlhammer, 1962), 2 vols.
Kordt E, *Nicht aus den Akten …* (Stuttgart: Union Deutsche Verlagsgesellschafft, 1950).
Lochner L P (ed.), *The Goebbels Diaries* (London: Hamish Hamilton, 1948). [referenced as *Goebbels Diary*. Trevor–Roper's diary volume for 1945 is referenced as *Goebbels Diary 1945*.]
Martin H–L, *Unser Mann bei Goebbels. Verbindungsoffizier des Oberkommandos der Wehrmacht beim Reichspropagandaminister 1940–1944* (Neckargemünd: Scharnhorst Buchkameradschaft, 1973).
Oven W von, *Mit Goebbels bis zum Ende* (Buenos Aires: Dürer-Verlag 1949), Vol. I.
Riefenstahl L, *Memoiren* (Munich/Hamburg: Knaus, 1987).
Semmler R, *Goebbels: The Man Next to Hitler* (London: Westhouse, 1947).
Shirer W L, *Berlin Diary. The Journal of a Foreign Correspondent, 1934–1941* (London: Hamish Hamilton, 1942).
Speer A, *Inside the Third Reich* (London: Book Club Associates, 1971).

Speeches

Baynes N H (ed.), *The Speeches of Adolf Hitler*, Vol. I (London: Oxford University Press, 1942).
Domarus M (ed.), *Hitler: Reden und Proklamationen*, Vol. II: *Untergang (1939–1945)* (Würzburg: Schmidt, 1963).
Goebbels J, *Das Eherne Herz. Reden und Aufsätze aus den Jahren 1941/42* (Munich: Zentralverlag der NSDAP, 1943).
Goebbels J, *Der steile Aufstieg* (Munich: Zentralverlag der NSDAP, 1944).
Goebbels J, *Die Zeit ohne Beispiel* (Munich: Zentralverlag der NSDAP, 1941).
Heiber H (ed.), *Goebbels* (London: Robert Hale & Co, 1972).
Roosevelt F D, *The Great Speeches of President Roosevelt* (Washington: Presidential Publishers, 1947).
Rede des Reichsministers Dr. Goebbels auf der Reichs-und Gauleiter Tagung in München, 23.2.1944 (Munich: Franz Eher, 1944).
Rosenberg A, *Deutsche und europäische Geistesfreiheit [Rede auf einer Weltanschauliche Feierstunde der NSDAP in Prag 16.1.1944]* (Munich: Zentralverlag der NSDAP, 1944).

Other contemporary publications

'Amerika als Zerrbild europäischer Lebensordnung', *Schulungs-Unterlage* n. 19 (Der Reichsorganisationsleitung der NSDAP, Munich: Hauptschulungsamt, 1942).

Belling C, *Der Film in Staat und Partei* [Film in State and Party] (Berlin, 1936).

Berndt A J, von Wedel, *Deutschland im Kampf*, no. 83–4 (Berlin: Verlagsansalt Otto Stollberg, February 1943).

Bruntz G G, *Allied Propaganda and the Collapse of the German Empire in 1918* (Stanford, CA: Stanford University Press, 1938).

Daitz W, *Der Weg zur Volkswirtschaft, Großraumwirtschaft und Großraumpolitik* (Dresden: Zentralforschungsinstitut für Nationale Wirtschaftsordnung und Großraumwirtschaft, 1943).

Didier F, *Europa arbeitet in Deutschland. Sauckel mobilisiert die Leistungsreserven* (Munich: Zentralverlag der NSDAP, 1943).

Dietrich P, 'Ausbau und Erneuerung des deutschen Filmtheaterparks', *Der Deutsche Film* 9/1939, 241–2.

Diewerge W, *Das Kriegsziel der Weltplutokratie. Dokumentarische Veröffentlichung zu dem Buch des Präsidenten der amerikanischen Friedensgesellschaft Theodore Nathan Kaufman 'Deutschland muß sterben'* (Berlin: Zentralverlag der NSDAP, 1941).

Dwinger E E, *Der Tod in Polen. Die Volksdeutsche Passion* (Jena: Eugen Diederichs Verlag, 1940).

Europa. Handbuch der politischen, wirtschaftlichen und kulturellen Entwicklung des neuen Europa, edited by Deutsches Institut für Außenpolitische Forschung (Leipzig: Helingsche Verlagsanstalt, 1943).

Goedecke H, Krug W, *Wir beginnen das Wunschkonzert* (Berlin/Leipzig: Nibelungen Verlag, 1940).

Goitsch H, *Niemals* (Munich: Zentralverlag der NSDAP, 1944).

Hadamovsky E, *Weltgeschichte im Sturmschritt* (Munich: Zentralverlag der NSDAP, 1939).

Handbuch der deutschen Tagespresse, 1937.

Ley R, *Internationaler Völkerbrei oder Vereinigte National-Staaten Europas?* (Berlin: Verlag der DAF, 1943).

Ley R, *Roosevelt verrät Amerika* (Berlin: Verlag der Deutschen Arbeitsfront, 1942).

Parteitag der Ehre vom 8. bis 14. September 1936. Offizieller Bericht über den Verlauf des Reichsparteitages mit sämtlichen Kongreßreden (Munich: Zentralverlag der NSDAP, 1936).

Rosenberg A, *Der völkische Staatsgedanke: Überlieferung und Neugeburt* (Munich: Deutschvölkische Buchhandlung, 1924).

Rosenberg A, *Neugeburt Europas als werdende Geschichte* (Halle: Max Niemeyer, 1939).

Sander A J, *Jugend und Film* (Berlin: NSDAP, 1944).

Six F A (ed.), *Jahrbuch der Weltpolitik 1942* (Berlin: Junker und Dünnhaupt, 1942).

Sowjet-Paradies. Das Ausstellung der Reichspropagandaleitung der NSDAP. Ein Bericht in Wort und Bild (Berlin: Zentralverlag der NSDAP, 1942).

Traub H, *Die Ufa. Ein Beitrag zur Entwicklungsgeschichte des deutschen Filmschaffens* (Berlin: UFA-Buchverlag, 1943).

Urach A F von, *Das Geheimnis japanischer Kraft* (Berlin: Zentralverlag der NSDAP, 1943).

Winkelnkemper T, *Der Großangriff auf Köln. Ein Beispiel* (Berlin: Franz Eher Verlag, 1942).

Wundshammer B, 'Zerstörer kämpfen über London', in *Bomben auf England. Kleine Kriegshefte* n. 8 (Munich: Zentralverlag der NSDAP, 1940).

Secondary sources

Abel K D, *Presselenkung im NS-Staat. Eine Studie zur Geschichte der Publizistik in der nationalsozialistischen Zeit* (Berlin: Colloquium Verlag, 1990).

Ackermann J, *Himmler als Ideologe* (Göttingen: Musterschmidt, 1970).

Ackermann J, 'Heinrich Himmler: Reichsführer – SS', in Smelser R, Zitelmann R (eds), *The Nazi Elite* (Houndmills/London: Macmillan, 1993), 98–112.

Adorno T, 'The culture industry reconsidered' in *The Culture Industry: Selected Essays on Mass Culture* (New York: Routledge, 1991).

Ajzen I, Fishbein M, *Understanding Attitudes and Predicting Social Behavior* (Englewood Cliffs: Prentice-Hall, 1980).

Albrecht G, *Nationalsozialistische Filmpolitik. Eine soziologische Untersuchung über die Spielfilme des Dritten Reichs* (Stuttgart: Ferdinand Enke Verlag Stuttgart, 1969).

Andrews H D, 'Hitler and Bismarck: a history', *German Studies Review*, 14 (1991), 511–32

Armstrong A, *Unconditional Surrender: The Impact of the Casablanca Policy on World War II* (New Brunswick: Rutgers University Press, 1971).

Aster S, *1939: The Making of the Second World War* (London: History Book Club, 1973).

Baird J W, *The Mythical World of Nazi War Propaganda, 1939–1945* (Minneapolis: University of Minnesota Press, 1974).

Balfour M, *Propaganda in War 1939–1945: Organisation, Policies and Publics in Britain and Germany* (London: Routledge, 1979).

Baranowski S, 'Consent and dissent: The confessing church and conservative opposition to National Socialism', *Journal of Modern History*, 59 (1987), 53–78.

Barkhausen H, *Filmpropaganda für Deutschland im Ersten und Zweiten Weltkrieg* (Hildesheim/Zürich/New York: Olms Presse, 1982).

Barnes J J, Barnes P P, *Hitler's 'Mein Kampf' in Britain and America: A Publishing History 1930–39* (New York: Cambridge University Press, 1980).

Bast J, *Totalitärer Pluralismus. Zu Franz L. Neumanns Analyse der politischen und rechtlichen Struktur der NS-Herrschaft* (Tübingen: J C B Mohr, 1999).

Bathrick D, 'Making a national family with the radio: The Nazi Wunschkonzert' *Modernism/Modernity*, 4 (1997), 115–27.

Beck E R, *Under the Bombs: The German Home Front, 1942–1945* (Lexington: University Press of Kentucky, 1986).

Beevor A, *Stalingrad* (Harmondsworth: Penguin, 1998).

Behn M, 'Gleichschritt in die "neue Zeit". Filmpolitik zwischen SPIO und NS', in H–M Bock, M Töteberg (eds), *Das Ufa-Buch* (Frankfurt: Zweitausendeins, 1992), 341–69.

Belach H, *Wir tanzen um die Welt. Deutsche Revuefilme 1933–45* (Munich: Hanser, 1979).

Benz W, Pehle W H (eds), *Lexikon des deutschen Widerstandes, 1933–1945* (Frankfurt: Fischer Verlag, 1994).

Bergmeier H J P, Lotz R E, *Hitler's Airwaves: The Inside Story of Nazi Radio Broadcasting and Propaganda Swing* (New Haven, CT: Yale University Press, 1997).

Bern D J, *Beliefs, Attitudes and Human Affairs* (Belmont: Brooks/Cole, 1970).

Birken L, *Hitler as Philosophe. Remnants of the Enlightenment in National Socialism* (Westport, CT/London: Praeger, 1995).

Blank R, 'Die Stadt Dortmund im Bombenkrieg', in G E Sollbach (ed.), *Dortmund. Bombenkrieg und Nachkriegsalltag 1939–1948* (Hagen: Lesezeichen Verlag Dierk Hobein, 1996), 15–55.

Boelcke W A, *Die Macht des Radios* (Frankfurt: Ullstein, 1977).

Boog H, 'Strategischer Luftkrieg in Europa und Reichsluftverteidigung 1943–1944', *DRZW*, Vol. 7: *Das Deutsche Reich in der Defensive. Strategischer Luftkrieg in Europa, Krieg im Westen und in Ostasien 1943–1944/45* (Stuttgart: Deutsche Verlags-Anstalt, 2001), 3–417.

Boog H, 'Der Anglo-Amerikanische Strategische Luftkrieg über Europa und die deutsche Luftverteidigung', *DRZW*, Vol. 6: *Der globale Krieg. Die Ausweitung zum Weltkrieg und der Wechsel der Initiative 1941–1943* (Stuttgart: Deutsche Verlags-Anstalt, 1990), 429–68.

Boog H, 'Luftwaffe und unterschiedsloser Bombenkrieg bis 1942', in H Boog (ed.), *Luftkriegführung im Zweiten Weltkrieg. Ein internationaler Vergleich* (Bonn: Herford, 1993).

Boster R J, Mongeau P, 'Fear-arousing persuasive messages', in R N Bostrum, N H Westley (eds), *Communication Yearbook 8*, (Beverly Hills, CA: Sage, 1984), 330–75.

Boyce R, 'Introduction', in Boyce R, Robertson E M (eds), *Paths to War. New Essays on the Origins of the Second World War* (Basingstoke/London: Macmillan, 1989), 1–32.

Bracher K D, *Die nationalsozialistische Machtergreifung. Studien zur Errichtung des totalitären Herrschaftssystems in Deutschland 1933/34* (Cologne 1960).

Bracher K D, 'The role of Hitler: perspectives of interpretation', in W Laqueur (ed.), *Fascism: A Reader's Guide* (Harmondsworth: Penguin, 1979), 211–55.

Bracher K D, *Totalitarismus und Faschismus. Eine wissenschaftliche und politische Begriffskontroverse* (Munich / Vienna: IZG, 1980).

Bramsted E J, *Goebbels and National Socialist Propaganda 1925–1945* (East Lansing: Michigan State University Press, 1965).

Brandt P, 'German perceptions of Russia and the Russians in modern history', *Debatte: Review of Contemporary German Affairs*, 11 (2003), 39–59.

Broszat M, *The Hitler State: The Foundation and Development of the Third Reich* (London: Longman, 1981).

Brown J A C, *Techniques of Persuasion. From Propaganda to Brainwashing* (Baltimore: Penguin, 1963).

Buchbender O, *Das tönende Erz: Deutsche Propaganda gegen die Rote Armee im Zweiten Weltkrieg* (Stuttgart: Seewald, 1978).

Bucher P, 'Goebbels und die Deutsche Wochenschau. Nationalsozialistische Filmpropaganda im Zweiten Weltkrieg 1939–1945', *Militärgeschichtliche Mitteilungen*, 40 (1986), 53–70.

Buci–Glucksmann C, 'Hegemony and consent: a political strategy', in Sassoon A S (ed.), *Approaches to Gramsci* (London: Writers and Readers, 1982), 116–26.

Bullock A, *Hitler: A Study in Tyranny* (New York/Evanston: Harper Torchbook, 1964).

Bungert H, *Das Nationalkomitee und der Westen: Die Reaktion der Westalliierten auf das NKFD und die Freien Deutschen Bewegungen 1943–1948* (Stuttgart: Franz Steiner Verlag, 1997).

Burgdorff S, Habbe C (eds), *Als Feuer vom Himmel fiel … Der Bombenkrieg in Deutschland* (Hamburg: DVA, 2003).

Burleigh M, *Ethics and Extermination: Reflections on Nazi Genocide* (New York: Cambridge University Press, 1997).

Cadars P, Courtade F, *Histoire du cinéma nazi* (Paris: E. Losfeld, 1972).

Caplan J, *Government without Administration. State and Civil Service in Weimar and Nazi Germany* (Oxford: Clarendon Press, 1988).

Caplan J, 'National Socialism and the theory of the state', in T Childers, J Caplan (eds), *Reevaluating the Third Reich* (New York/London: Holmes & Meier, 1993), 98–102.

Carnes J D, *General zwischen Hitler und Stalin. Das Schicksal des Walther von Seydlitz* (Düsseldorf: Droste, 1980).

Cecil R, *The Myth of the Master Race. Alfred Rosenberg and Nazi Ideology* (London: Bratsford, 1972).

Coser L A, *The Sociology of Max Weber* (New York: Vintage Books, 1977), 223 ff.

Craig G A, *Germany 1866–1945* (Oxford: Oxford University Press, 1978).

Cruickshank C, *The Fourth Arm: Psychological Warfare 1938–1945* (London: Davis-Poynter, 1977).

Culbert D, '*Kolberg*: film, filmscript and Kolobrzeg today', *Historical Journal of Film, Radio and Television*, 14 (1994), 449–66.

Cuthbert D, 'Joseph Goebbels and his diaries – Adolph Hitler's propaganda minister' in *Historical Journal of Film, Radio and Television* 15 (1995), 143–9.

Dahl P, *Radio. Sozialgeschichte des Rundfunks für Sender und Empfänger* (Reinbek: Freies Sender Kombinat/AG Radio, 1983).

Das Deutsche Reich und der Zweite Weltkrieg (DRZW).

Vol. 1: *Kriegsbeginn und Kriegsziele* (Stuttgart: Deutsche Verlags-Anstalt, 1979).

Vol. 2: *Die Errichtung der Hegemonie auf dem europäischen Kontinent* (Stuttgart: Deutsche Verlags-Anstalt, 1979).

Vol. 3: *Der Mittelmeerraum und Südosteuropa. Van der 'non belligeranza' Italiens bis zum Kriegseintritt der Vereinigten Staaten* (Stuttgart: Deutsche Verlags-Anstalt, 1984).

Vol. 4: *Der Angriff auf die Sowjetunion* (Stuttgart: Deutsche Verlags-Anstalt, 1987).

Vol. 5/1 : *Organisation und Mobilisierung des deutschen Machtbereichs. Kriegsverwaltung, Wirtschaft und personelle Ressourcen 1939–1941* (Stuttgart: Deutsche Verlags-Anstalt, 1988).

Vol. 5/2: *Organisation und Mobilisierung des deutschen Machtbereichs, Zweiter Halbband: Kriegsverwaltung, Wirtschaft und personelle Ressourcen 1942–1944/45* (Stuttgart: Deutsche Verlags-Anstalt, 1989).

Vol. 6: *Der globale Krieg. Die Ausweitung zum Weltkrieg und der Wechsel der Initiative 1941–1943* (Stuttgart: Deutsche Verlags-Anstalt, 1990).

Vol. 7: *Das Deutsche Reich in der Defensive. Strategischer Luftkrieg in Europa, Krieg im Westen und in Ostasien 1943–1944/45* (Stuttgart: Deutsche Verlags-Anstalt, 2001).

Vol. 9/1: *Die Deutsche Kriegsgesellschaft 1939 bis 1945. Politisierung, Vernichtung, Überleben* (Stuttgart: Deutsche Verlags-Anstalt, 2003).

Vol. 9/2: *Die deutsche Kriegsgesellschaft 1939–1945. Ausbeutung, Deutungen, Ausgrenzung* (Stuttgart: Deutsche Verlags-Anstalt, 2005).

De Felice R, Mussolini l'alleato, Vol. I: L'Italia in guerra (1940–1943) – crisi e agonia del *regime* (Turin: Einaudi, 1996).

De Felice R, *Mussolini il fascista*, Vol. II: *L'organizzazione dello Stato Fascista, 1925–1929* (Turin: Einaudi, 1968).

Deren S, *The Cradle of Modernity: Politics and Art in Weimar Republic (1918–1933)* (unpublished MSc thesis Middle East Technical University, Ankara, 1997).

Diehl-Thiele, P, *Partei und Staat im Dritten Reich. Untersuchung zum Verhältnis von NSDAP und allgemeiner innerer Staatsverwaltung, 1933–1945* (Munich: CH Beck Verlag, 1971).

Diller A, *Rundfunkpolitik im Dritten Reich* (München: DTV, 1980).

Doenecke J, 'Power, markets and ideology: the isolationist response to Roosevelt policy, 1940–1941' in L Liggio P, Martin J J (eds), *Watershed of Empire: Essays on New Deal Foreign Policy* (Colorado Springs: Ralph Myles, 1976), 132–61.

Doherty M A, *Nazi Wireless Propaganda: Lord Haw–Haw and British Public Opinion in the Second World War* (Edinburgh: Edinburgh University Press, 2000).

Doob L W, *Public Opinion and Propaganda* (New York: Henry Holt and Co, 1948).

Doob L W, 'Goebbels' principles of propaganda', *Public Opinion Quarterly*, 14 (1950), 419–42.

Douglas R, 'Chamberlain and appeasement', in W. J. Mommsen, J Kettenacker (eds), *The Fascist Challenge and the policy of Appeasement* (London: Allen & Unwin, 1983), 79–88.

Drechsler N, 'Die Funktion der Musik im deutschen Rundfunk 1933–1945', *Musikwissenschaftliche Studien*, 1988.

Dussel K, *Deutsche Rundfunkgeschichte. Eine Einführung* (Konstanz: UVK-Medien, 1999).

Dutton D, *Neville Chamberlain* (London: Arnold; New York: Oxford University Press, 2001).

Eatwell R, *Fascism: A History* (London: Vintage, 1995).

Eatwell R, 'Towards a new model of generic fascism', *Journal of Theoretical Politics*, 2 (1992), 161–94.

Eckhardt J, 'Abbild und Sinnbild. Von der Gestaltung der Wirklichkeit in Wochenschau und in Kulturfilm' in B Drewniak (ed.), *Der deutsche Film 1938–1945. Ein Gesamtüberblick* (Düsseldorf: Droste, 1987).

Eitner H–J, *Kolberg: Ein preußischer Mythos 1807/1945* (Berlin: Quintessenz-Verlag, 1999).

Eley G, 'What produces fascism: pre-industrial traditions or the crisis of the capitalist state', *Politics and Society*, 12 (1983), 76–82.

Ellul J, *Propaganda: The Formation of Men's Attitudes* (New York: Knopf, 1971).

Elsaesser T, *Weimar Cinema and after: Germany's Historical Imaginary* (London/New York: Routledge, 2000).

Fest J C, *The Face of the Third Reich* (New York: Pantheon Books, 1970; Harmondsworth: Penguin, 1972).

Fetscher I, *Joseph Goebbels im Berliner Sportpalast 1943. 'Wollt ihr den totalen Krieg?'* (Hamburg: Europäische Verlagsanstalt, 1998).

Feuchter G W, *Geschichte des Luftkriegs* (Frankfurt: Athenaum, 1962).

Fox J P, 'Der Fall Katyn und die Propaganda des NS-Regimes', *Vierteljahrshefte für Zeitgeschichte* (*VfZ*), 30 (1982), 462–99.

Fraenkel E, *The Dual State* (New York: Octagon Books, 1969).

Frei N, 'Nationalsozialistische Presse und Propaganda', in M Broszat und H Möller (eds), *Das Dritte Reich. Herrschaftsstruktur und Geschichte* (Munich: Beck Verlag, 1986), 152–75.

Frei N, Schmitz J, *Journalismus im Dritten Reich* (Munich: Beck, 1999, 3rd ed.).

Friedlander H, *The Origins of Nazi Genocide: From Euthanasia to the Final Solution.* (Chapel Hill, NC: University of North Carolina Press, 1995).

Friedländer S, *Prelude to Downfall: Hitler and the United States 1939–1941* (New York: Knopf, 1967).

Friedrich C J, 'The unique character of totalitarian society', in C J Friedrich (ed.), *Totalitarianism* (New York: Grosset & Dunlap, 1954), 47–60.

Friedrich C J, Brzezinski Z K, *Totalitarian Dictatorship and Autocracy* (Cambridge, MA: Harvard University Press, 1956).

Friedrich J, *Der Brand: Deutschland im Bombenkrieg 1940–1945* (Berlin: Propyläen Verlag, 2002).

Fröhlich E, 'Katyn in neuem Licht? Goebbels und der Mord an den polnischen Offizieren im 2. Weltkrieg', *Geschichte in Wissenschaft und Unterricht*, 37 (1986), 234–40.

Führer K C, 'Auf dem Weg zur 'Massenkultur'. Kino und Rundfunk in der Weimarer Republik', *Historische Zeitschrift*, 262 (1996), 739–81.

Geyer M, 'Restorative elites, German society and the Nazi pursuit of goals', in R Bessel (ed.), *Fascist Italy and Nazi Germany. Comparisons and Contrasts* (Cambridge: Cambridge University Press, 1996), 139–40.

Geyer M, 'The dynamics of military revisionism in the interwar years. Military policy between rearmament and diplomacy', in W Deist (ed.), *The German Military in the Age of Total War* (Leamington Spa: Berg, 1985), 100–51.

Giesen R, Hobsch M, *Hitlerjunge Quex, Jud Süß und Kolberg: Die Propagandafilme des Dritten Reiches* (Berlin: Schwarzkopf und Schwarzkopf Verlag, 2003).

Ginsberg B, *The Captive Public. How Mass Opinion Promotes State Power* (New York: Basoc Books, 1986).

Goebel G, 'Der Deutsche Rundfunk bis zum Inkrafttretten des kopenhagener wellenplans', *Archiv für das Post- und Fernmeldewesen*, 6 (1950), pp. 335–53.

Goldhagen D J, *Hitler's Willing Executioners. Ordinary Germans and the Holocaust* (London: Abacus 1997).

Gramsci A, *Selection from Prison Notebooks* (London: Lawrence and Wishart, 1971).

Griffin R, 'Da capo, con meno brio: towards a more useful conceptualization of generic fascism', *Erwägen, Wissen, Ethik*, 15/3 (2004): 361–77.

Griffin R, 'Fascism's new faces (and new facelessness) in the 'post-fascist' epoch', *Erwägen, Wissen, Ethik*, 15/3 (2004): 287–301.

Griffin R, 'Grey cats, blue cows, and wide awake groundhogs: notes towards the development of a 'deliberative ethos' in fascist studies', *Erwägen, Wissen, Ethik*, 15/3 (2004): 429–41.

Griffin R, 'Revolution from the right: fascism', in D Parker (ed.), *Revolutions and the Revolutionary Tradition in the West 1560–1991* (London: Routledge, 2000), 185–201.

Griffin R, 'Fascism is more than reaction', *Searchlight*, 27/4 (1999): 24–6.

Griffin R, *The Nature of Fascism* (London/New York: Routledge, 1994).

Habermas J, *Structural Transformation of the Public Sphere* (Cambridge, MA: MIT Press, 1989).

Habermas J, 'The public sphere: an encyclopedia article', in Steven E Bronner and Douglas Kellner (eds), *Critical Theory and Society. A Reader* (New York: Routledge, 1989), 136–42.

Hagemann W, *Publizistik im Dritten Reich. Ein Beitrag zur Methode der Massenführung* (Hamburg: Hansischer Gildenverlag, 1948).

Hale O J, *The Captive Press in the Third Reich* (Princeton, NJ: Princeton University Press, 1973).

Hancock E, *The National Socialist Leadership and Total War, 1941–1945* (New York: St. Martin's Press, 1991).

Happel H–G, *Der historische Spielfilm im Nationalsozialismus* (Frankfurt: Rita Fischer, 1984).

Hassell U, von, *The von Hassell Diaries* (London: Hamish Hamilton, 1948).

Hauner M, 'The professionals and the amateurs in National Socialist foreign policy: revolution and subversion in the Islamic and Indian world', in G Hirschfeld, L Kettenacker (eds), *Der 'Führerstaat'. Mythos und Realität* (Stuttgart: Kett–Cotta, 1981), 305–28.

Hauner M, 'A German Racial Revolution?', *Journal of Contemporary History*, 19 (1984), 671–90.

Hehl U, von, *Nationalsozialistische Herrschaft* (Munich: R Oldenbourg Verlag, 1996).

Herf J, *Reactionary Modernism: Technology, Culture and Politics in Weimar and the Third Reich* (Cambridge: Cambridge University Press, 1984).

Herf J, ' "Der Krieg und die Juden". Nationalsozialistische Propaganda im Zweiten Weltkrieg', in *DRZW*, Vol. 9/2: *Staat und Gesellschaft im Kriege*, 159–202.

Herzstein R E, *The War that Hitler Won: The Most Famous Propaganda Campaign in History* (London: Hamish Hamilton, 1979).

Hewitt A, *Fascist Modernism: Aesthetics, Polics, and the Avant-Garde* (Stanford: Stanford University Press, 1993).

Hilberg R, *The Destruction of the European Jews* (London: WH Allen, 1961).

Hildebrand K, 'Monokratie oder Polykratie?', in G Hirschfeld, L Kettenacker (eds), *Der 'Führerstaat'. Mythos und Realität. Studien zur Struktur und Politik des Dritten Reiches* (Stuttgart: Klett–Cotta, 1981), 73–96.

Hildebrand K, 'Nationalsozialismus oder Hitlerismus?', in M Bosch (ed.), *Persönlichkeit und Struktur in der Geschichte* (Düsseldorf: Droste, 1977), 55–61.

Hill L (ed.), *Die Weizsäcker-Papiere, 1933–1950* (Frankfurt: Propyläen, 1974).

Hillgruber A, 'Das Rußlandbild der führenden deutschen Militärs vor Beginn des Angriffs auf die Sowjetunion', in Hillgruber (ed.), *Die Zerstörung Europas. Beiträge zur Weltkriegsepoche, 1914 bis 1945* (Berlin: Propyläen, 1988), 256–72.

Hirt A, 'Die deutsche Truppenbetreuung im Zweiten Weltkrieg: Konzeption, Organisation und Wirkung', *Militärgeschichtliche Zeitschrift*, 59 (2000), 407–35.

Hoffman I, *The Triumph of Propaganda – Film and National Socialism 1933–1945* (Providence / Oxford: Berghahn Books, 1996).

Hollstein D, *Antisemitische Filmpropaganda* (Munich / Berlin: Verlag Dokumentation, 1971).

Hölsken H D, *Die V-Waffen. Entstehung, Propaganda, Kriegseinsatz* (Stuttgart: Deutsche Verlags-Anstalt, 1984).

Horkheimer M, Adorno T, *Dialectic of Enlightenment* (New York: Herder and Herder, 1972).

Hornshøj-Møller S, *Der ewige Jude. Quellenkritische Analyse eines antisemitischen Propagandafilms* (Göttingen: Institut für Wissenschaftlichen Film, 1995).

Hornshøj-Møller S, Culbert D, ' "Der ewige Jude" (1940): Joseph Goebbels' unequalled monument to anti-Semitism', *Historical Journal of Film Radio and Television*, 12 (1992), 41–68.

Hovland C I, Janis I L, Kelly H H, *Communication and Persuasion. Psychological Studies of Opinion Change* (New Haven: Yale University Press, 1953).

Hull D S, *Film in the Third Reich: A Study of German Cinema 1933–1945* (Berkeley: University of California Press, 1969).

Hull D S, 'Forbidden fruit: the harvest of the German cinema, 1939–1945', *Film Quarterly*, 14/4 (1961), 16–30.

Hüttenberg P, *Die Gauleiter* (Stuttgart: Deutsche Verlag-Anstalt, 1969).

Irving D, *Goebbels: Mastermind of the Third Reich* (London: Parforce, 1996).

Jacobsen H–A, *Nationalsozialistische Außenpolitik 1933–1945* (Frankfurt: Alfred Metzner Verlag, 1968), 90–160.

Jacobsen H–A, *Spiegelbild einer Verschwörung: die Opposition gegen Hitler und der Staatsstreich vom 20. Juli 1944 in der SD-Berichterstattung* (Stuttgart: Seewald Verlag, 1984), 2 vols.

Jannsen G, *Das Ministerium Speers. Deutschland Rüstung im Krieg* (Berlin/Frankfurt/Vienna: Ullstein Verlag, 1968).

Jersak T, "Die deutsche Kriegsgesellschaft und der Holocaust", *DRZW*, Vol. 9/1: *Die deutsche Kriegsgesellschaft, 1939–1945*. Politisierung, Vernichting, Überleben.

Jonas M, *Isolationism in America, 1935–1941* (Ithaca, NY: Cornell University Press, 1966).

Jowett G S, O'Donnell V, *Propaganda and Persuasion* (Newbury Park / London / New Delhi: Sage, 1992).

Kallis A, 'Der Niedergang der Deutungsmacht. Die nationalsozialistische Propaganda im Kriegsverlauf', in *DRZW*, Vol. 9/2: *Staat und Gesellschaft im Kriege*, 202–50 (Stuttgart: Deutsche Verlags-Anstalt, 2005).

Kallis A, 'The "regime model" of fascism: a typology', *European History Quarterly*, 30 (2000), 77–104.

Kallis A, ' "Fascism", "para-fascism" and "fascistization": on the similarities of three conceptual categories', *European History Quarterly*, 33 (2003), 219–49.

Kallis A, *Fascist Ideology. Territory and Expansionism in Italy and Germany, 1919–1945* (London: Routledge, 2000).

Kallis A, 'Race, "value" and the hierarchy of human life: ideological and structural determinants of National Socialist policy-making', *Journal of Genocide Research*, 7 (2005), 5–30.

Kallis A, 'To expand or not to expand? Territory, generic fascism and the quest for an "ideal fatherland" ', *Journal of Contemporary History*, 38 (2003), 238–60.

Kanzog K, *'Staatspolitisch besonders wertvoll'. Ein Handbuch zu 30 deutschen der Spielfilmen Jahre 1934–1945* (Munich: Mankred Hattendorf, 1994).

Kapfener J N, *Rumours. Uses, Interpretations and Images* (New Brunswick: Transactions Press, 1990).

Kater M, *The Nazi Party. A Social Profile of Members and Leaders, 1919–45* (Oxford: Oxford University Press, 1983).

Keeken N, von, *Kinokultur in der Provinz. Am Beispiel von Bad Hersfeld* (Frankfurt/Berlin/Bern/New York/Paris/Wien: Lang, 1993).

Kershaw I, *Hitler, II: Nemesis, 1936–45* (London: Allen Lane, 2000).

Kershaw I, 'How effective was Nazi Propaganda?', in D Welch (ed.), *Nazi Propaganda: The Power and the Limitations* (London: Croom Helm, 1983), 180–205.

Kershaw I, *Popular Opinion and Political Dissent in the Third Reich: Bavaria, 1933–45* (Oxford: Clarendon, 1983).

Kershaw I, ' "Working towards the führer": reflections on the nature of the Hitler dictatorship', in I Kershaw, M Lewin (eds), *Stalinism and Nazism: Dictatorships in Comparison* (Cambridge: Cambridge University Press, 1997), 88–107.

Kershaw I, *The Hitler-Myth. Image and Reality in the Third Reich* (Oxford/New York: Oxford University Press, 1989).

Kershaw I, *The Nazi Dictatorship. Problems and Perspectives of Interpretation* (London: Edward Arnold, 1995, 4th ed.).

Kirk T, McElligott A (eds), *Working towards the Führer: Essays in Honour of Sir Ian Kershaw* (Manchester: Manchester University Press, 2004).

Kirwin G, 'Allied bombing and Nazi domestic propaganda', *European History Quarterly*, 15 (1985), 341–62.

Klein A, *Köln im Dritten Reich. Stadtgeschichte der Jahre 1933–1945* (Cologne: Greven Verlag, 1983).

Kleinhans B, *Ein Volk, ein Reich, ein Kino. Lichtspiel in der brauen Provinz* (Cologne: PapyRossa Verlag, 2003).

Klingler W, *Nationalsozialistische Rundfunkpolitik 1942–1945. Organisation, Programm und die Hörer* (Dissertation: Mannheim, 1983).

Klink E et al., 'Der Krieg gegen die Sowjetunion bis zur Jahreswende 1941/42', DRZW., Vol. 4: *Der Angriff auf die Sowjetunion* (Stuttgart: Deutsche Verlags-Anstalt, 1987), 451–1087.

Knox M, 'Expansionist zeal, fighting power and staying power in the Italian and German dictatorships' in R Bessel (ed.), *Fascist Italy and Nazi Germany: Comparisons and Contrasts* (Cambridge: Cambridge University Press, 1996) 113–33.

Knox M, *Mussolini Unleashed, 1939–1941. Politics and Strategy in Fascist Italy's Last War* (Cambridge: Cambridge University Press, 1982).

Koch H W, 'Hitler's programme and the genesis of operation "Barbarossa" ', in H W Koch (ed.), *Aspects of the Third Reich*, (New York: St. Martin's Press, 1985), 285–322.

Koch H W, 'The strategic air offensive against Germany; the early phase, May–September 1940', *The Historical Journal*, 34 (1991), 117–41.

Koehl R, 'Feudal aspects of National Socialism', *American Political Science Review*, Vol. LVI/4 (1960): 921–33.

Kohlmann–Viand D, *NS-Pressepolitik im Zweiten Weltkrieg. Die 'Vertraulichen Informationen' als Mittel der Presselenkung* (Munich: Saur, 1991).

Koller K, *Der letzte Monat. 14. April–27. Mai 1945. Tagebuchaufzeichnungen des ehemaligen Chefs des Generalstabs der Luftwaffe* (Mannheim: Wohlgemuth, 1949).

Kornhauser W, 'Mass Society', *International Encyclopedia of the Social Sciences* (New York: Macmillan, 1968).

Kornhauser W, *The Politics of Mass Society* (New York: Free Press, 1959).

Koszyk K, *Deutsche Presse, 1914–1945*, Part III (Berlin: Colloquium, 1972).

Kracauer S, *From Caligari to Hitler: A Psychological History of the German Film* (Princeton, NJ: Princeton University Press, 1974).

Kremeier K, *The Ufa Story. A History of Germany's Greatest Film Company, 1918–1945* (London: University of California Press, 1999).

Kris E, Speier H, *German Radio Propaganda: Report on Home Broadcasts During the War* (New York: Oxford University Press, 1944).

Kroener B R, 'Die personellen Ressourcen des Dritten Reiches im Spannungsfeld zwischen Wehrmacht, Bürokratie und Kriegswirtschaft, 1939–1942', *DRZW*, Vol. 5/1: *Organisation und Mobilisierung des deutschen Machtbereichs. Kriegsverwaltung, Wirtschaft und personelle Ressourcen 1939–1941* (Stuttgart: Deutsche Verlags-Anstalt, 1988), 693–1002.

Krüger N, 'Die März-Luftangriffe auf Essen 1943. Vorgeschichte, Verlauf und Folgen', in Krüger (ed.), *Essen unter Bomben. Märztage 1943* (Essen: Klartext-Verlag, 1984), 14–37.

Lange G, *Das Kino als moralische Anstalt. Soziale Leitbilder und die Darstellung gesellschaftlicher Realität im Spielfilm des Dritten Reiches* (Frankfurt / New York: Peter Lang, 1994).

Larson C, 'The German Press Chamber', *Public Opinion Quarterly*, 9 (October 1937), 53–70.

Lasswell H D, Lerner D, Speier H (eds), *Propaganda and Communication in World History*, Vol. 2: *The Emergence of Public Opinion in the West* (Honolulu: University of Hawaii Press, 1980).

Leiser E, *Nazi Cinema* (New York: Collier Books, 1975); translation of Leiser E, *'Deutschland Erwache': Propaganda im Film des Dritten Reiches* (Düsseldorf: Droste, 1987; originally published in 1968).

Lepsius M R, 'Charismatic leadership: Max Weber's model and its applicability to the rule of Hitler', in C F Graumann and S Moscovici (eds), *Changing Conceptions of Political Leadership* (New York: Springer–Verlag, 1986).

Lerg W B, *Rundfunkpolitik in der Weimarer Republik* (Munich: DTV, 1980).

Lerg W, Steininger R (eds), *Rundfunk und Politik 1923–1973. Beiträge zur Rundfunkforschung* (Berlin: Spiess, 1975).

Lerner D, 'Effective propaganda: conditions and evaluation', in D Lerner (ed.), *Propaganda in War and Crisis. Materials for American Policy* (New York: Stewart, 1951).

Lerner D, *Psychological Warfare against Nazi Germany: The Sykewar Campaign, D-Day to VE-Day* (Cambridge, MA/London: MIT Press, 1971).

Longerich P, 'Nationalsozialistische Propaganda', in K D Bracher, M Funke, H–A Jacobsen (eds), *Deutschland 1933–1945. Neue Studien zur nationalsozialistischen Herrschaft*, (Düsseldorf: Droste–Verlag, 1992), 291–314.

Longerich P, 'Joseph Goebbels und der Totale Krieg. Eine unbekannte Denkschrift des Propagandaministers vom 18. Juli 1944', *Vierteljahrshefte für Zeitgeschichte*, 35 (1987), 289 ff.

Longerich P, *Propagandisten im Krieg. Die Presseabteilung des Auswärtigen Amtes unter Ribbentrop* (Munich: Oldenburg, 1987).

Low A P, *The Anschluss Movement 1918–1919 and the Paris Peace Conference* (Philadelphia: APS, 1974).

Lowry S, *Pathos und Politik: Ideologie in Spielfilmen des Nationalsozialismus* (Tübingen: Niemeyer, 1991).

Ludewig J, *Der deutsche Rückzug aus Frankreich 1944* (Freiburg: Verlag Rombach, 1994).

Lutz C R, 'False history, fake Africa and the transcription of Nazi reality in Hans Steinhoff's "Ohm Krüger" ', *Literature-Film Quarterly* 25 (1997), 188–92.

Lyttelton A, 'Fascism in Italy: The Second Wave', *Journal of Contemporary History*, 1 (1966), 75–100.

Mahl T E, *Desperate Deception: British Covert Operations in the United States, 1939–1944* (Washington: Brassey's, 1998).

Maier K A, 'Der Operative Luftkrieg bis zur Luftschlacht um England', *DRZW*, Vol. 2: *Die Errichtung der Hegemonie auf dem europäischen Kontinent* (Stuttgart: Deutsche Verlags-Anstalt, 1979), 329–44.

Mann M, *Fascists* (Cambridge: Cambridge University Press, 2004).

Mann M, 'The contradictions of continuous revolution', in I Kershaw, M Lewin (eds), *Stalinism and Nazism* (Cambridge: Cambridge University Press, 1997), 135–57.

Manvell R, Fraenkel H, *Heinrich Himmler* (London: Heinemann, 1965).

Marlin R, *Propaganda and the Ethics of Persuasion* (New York: Broadview Press, 2002).

Marvick D (ed.), *Harold D Lasswell on Political Sociology* (Chicago/London: The University of Chicago Press, 1977).

Mason T, 'Intention and explanation. A current controversy about the interpretation of National Socialism', in G Hirschfeld, L Kettenacker (eds), *Der 'Führerstaat'. Mythos und Realität. Studien zur Struktur und Politik des Dritten Reiches* (Stuttgart: Klett-Cotta, 1981), 23–42.

Mason T, *Sozialpolitik im Dritten Reich* (Opladen: Westdeutscher Verlag, 1977).

Mason T, 'The legacy of 1918', in A Nicholls, E Matthias (eds), *German Democracy and the Triumph of Hitler – Essays in Recent German History* (London: George Allen, 1971), 215–40.

Mason T, Overy R, 'Debate: Germany, "domestic crisis" and war in 1939', *Past and Present*, 122 (1989), 205–40.

McQuail D, *Mass Communication Theory: An Introduction* (London—Beverly Hills/New Delhi: Sage, 2003, 4th ed.).

Meers P, 'Is There an audience in the house? – film audiences – critical essay', *Journal of Popular Film and Television*, 29 (2001), 138–47.

Merkl P H, *Political Violence under the Swastika. 581 Early Nazis* (Princeton, NJ: Princeton University Press, 1975).

Messerschmidt M, 'Außenpolitik und Kriegsvorbereitung', *DRZW*, Vol. 1: *Kriegsbeginn und Kriegsziele* (Stuttgart: Deutsche Verlags-Anstalt, 1979), 535–701.

Meyer zu Uptrup W, *Kampf gegen die 'jüdische Weltverschwörung'. Propaganda und Antisemitismus der Nationalsozialisten 1919 bis 1945* (Berlin: Metropol Verlag, 2003).

Michalka W, 'From the Anti-Comintern Pact to the Euro-Asiatic Bloc: Ribbentrop's alternative Concept to Hitler's foreign policy programme', in Koch (ed.), *Aspects of the Third Reich*, (New York: St Martin's Press, 1985), 267–84.

Michalka W, 'Die nationalsozialistische Außenpolitik im Zeichen eines "Konzeptionen-Pluralismus" – Fragestellungen und Forschungsaufgaben', in M Funke (ed.), *Hitler, Deutschland und die Mächte. Materialien zur Außenpolitik des Dritten Reiches* (Düsseldorf: Droste-Verlag, 1977), 59–63.

Michalka W, *Ribbentrop und die deutsche Weltpolitik 1933–1940. Außenpolitische Konzeptionen und Entscheidungsprozeße im Dritten Reich* (Munich: Wilhelm Fink Verlag, 1980).

Michalka W, 'Joachim von Ribbentrop: from wine merchant to foreign minister', in R Smelser, R Zitelmann (eds), *The Nazi Elite* (Houndmills/London: Longmann, 1993), 165–72.

Middlebrook M, *The Battle of Hamburg* (New York: Charles Scribner's Sons, 1980).

Milward A S, 'The Reichsmark Bloc and the International Economy', in H W Koch (ed.), *Aspects of the Third Reich* (New York: St. Martin's, 1985), 331–59.

Milward A S, *The German Economy at War* (London: The Athalone Press, 1965).

Moeller F, *Der Filmminister. Goebbels und der Film im Dritten Reich* (Berlin: Henschel Verlag, 1998).

Moltmann G, 'Goebbels' speech on total war, 18.2.1943', in H Holborn (ed.), *Republic to Reich: The Making of the Nazi Revolution* (New York: Vintage Books, 1973), 298–342.

Mommsen H, 'Working towards the Führer: reflections on the nature of the Hitler dictatorship', in I Kershaw, M Lewin (eds), *Stalinism and Nazism* (Cambridge: Cambridge University Press, 1997), 75–87.

Muggeridge M (ed.), *Ciano's Diary, 1939–1943* (London: Heinemann, 1947).

Müller R–D, 'Albert Speer und die Rüstungspolitik im Totalen Krieg', *DRZW*, Vol. 5/2: *Organisation und Mobilisierung des deutschen Machtbereichs: Kriegsverwaltung, Wirtschaft und personelle Ressourcen 1942–1944/45* (Stuttgart: Deutsche Verlags–Anstalt, 1989), 275–375.

Müller R–D, Ueberschaer G R, *Hitler's War in the East. A Critical Assessment* (Providence/Oxford: Berghahn Books, 2002).

Murawski E, *Der deutsche Wehrmachtsbericht 1939–1945. Ein Beitrag zur Untersuchung der geistigen Kriegsführung. Mit einer Dokumentation der Wehrmachtberichte vom 1.7.1944 bis zum 9.5.1945* (Boppard: Boldt Verlag, 1962).

Nello P, *Un fedele disubbidiente. Dino Grandi da Palazzo Chigi al 25 Luglio* (Bologna: Mulino, 1993).

Neumann F, *Behemoth: The Structure and Practice of National Socialism* (London: Victor Gollancz, 1944).

Nicholas S, *Echo of War. Home Front Propaganda and Wartime BBC 1939–45* (Manchester: Manchester University Press, 1996).

Nyomarkay J, *Charisma and Factionalism in the Nazi Party* (Minneapolis: University of Minnesota Press, 1967).

O'Sullivan N, *Fascism* (London: Dent 1983).

O'Sullivan T, 'Listening through: the wireless and World War II', in P Kirkham, D Thomas (eds), *War Culture: Social Change and Changing Experience in World War Two Britain* (London: Lawrence & Wishart, 1995), 173–86.

Orlow D, *The History of the Nazi Party 1933–1945* (Pittsburgh: Pittsburgh University Press, 1969–1973), 2 vols.

Overy R J, *Goering: The Iron Man* (London: Routledge, 1984).

Overy R J, *The Air War, 1939–1945* (New York: Stein and Day, 1980).

Padfield P, *Himmler: Reichsführer-SS* (New York: Holt, 1991).

Padover K S, 'The German motion picture today: the Nazi cinema', *Public Opinion Quarterly*, 3 (1939), 142–6.

Paret P, '*Kolberg* (1945) as a historical film and Historical Document', *Historical Journal of Film, Radio and Television*, 14 (1994), 433–48.

Pater M, '*Rundfunkangebote*', in I Marßolek, A von Saldern (eds), *Radio im Nationalsozialismus. Zwischen Lenkung und Ablenkung, Zuhören und Gehörtwerden*, Vol. 1 (Tübingen: Diskord, 1998), 129–242.

Petley J, *Capital and Culture: German Cinema 1933–45* (London: BFI, 1979).

Peukert D J K, *Inside Nazi Germany: Conformity, Opposition, and Racism in Everyday Life* (New Haven, CT: Yale University Press, 1987).

Phillips M S, 'The Nazi control of the German film industry', *Journal of European Studies*, 1 (1971), 37–68.

Pietrow–Ennker B, 'Die Sowjetunion in der Propaganda des Dritten Reiches: Das Beispiel der Wochenschau', *Militärgeschichtliche Mitteilungen*, 46 (1989), 79–120.

Plummer T G (ed.), *Film and Politics in the Weimar Republic* (New York: Holmes and Meier, 1982).

Pohle H, *Der Rundfunk als Instrument der Politik. Zur Geschichte des deutschen Rundfunks von 1923/38*, (Hamburg: Eigenverlag, 1955).

Qualter T H, *Opinion Control in the Democracies* (New York: St Martin's Press, 1985).

Quanz C, *Der Film als Propagandainstrument Joseph Goebbels* (Cologne: Teiresias, 2000).

Rahn W, 'Der Seekrieg im Atlantik und Nordmeer', *DRZW*, Vol. 6: *Der globale Krieg. Die Ausweitung zum Weltkrieg und der Wechsel der Initiative 1941–1943* (Stuttgart: Deutsche Verlags-Anstalt, 1990), 275–428.

Reeves N, *The Power of Film Propaganda: Myth or Reality?* (New York: Cassell, 1999).

Reichman S, Golan A, 'Irredentism and boundary adjustments in post–world War I Europe', in N Chazan (ed.), *Irredentism and International Politics* (Boulder, CO: Lynne Rienner, 1991), 51–68.

Rentschler E, *The Ministry of Illusion. Nazi Cinema and Its Afterlife* (Cambridge, MA and London: Harvard University Press, 1996).

Rhodes J M, *The Hitler Movement* (Stanford, CA: Hoover Institution Press, Stanford University, 1980).

Riess K, *Das gab's nur einmal – Die große Zeit des deutschen Films* (Vienna: Molden Taschenbuch Verlag, 1977).

Rimmele D, 'Anspruch und Realität nationalsozialistischer Rundfunkarbeit vor 1933 in Hamburg', in W Lerg, R Steininger (eds), *Rundfunk und Politik 1923–1973. Beiträge zur Rundfunkforschung* (Berlin: Spiess, 1975), 135–57.

Roberts D, *The Poverty of Great Politics. Understanding the Totalitarian Moment* (London: Routledge, 2006).

Robins K, Webster F, Pickering M, 'Propaganda, information and social control', in J Hawthorn (ed), *Propaganda, Persuasion and Polemic* (London: Edward Arnold, 1987, 2nd ed.), 1–17.

Rohde H, 'Hitlers Erster "Blitzkrieg" und seine Auswirkungen auf Nordosteuropa', *DRZW*, Vol. 2: *Die Errichtung der Hegemonie auf dem europäischen Kontinent* (Stuttgart: Deutsche Verlags-Anstalt, 1979), 79–233.

Rüther M, *Köln, 31. Mai 1942. Der 1000-Bomber-Angriff* (Cologne: Hohn, 1992).

Sadkovich J J, 'The Italo-Greek war in context: Italian priorities and Axis diplomacy', *Journal of Contemporary History*, 28 (1993), 493–64.

Salter S, 'Structures of consensus and coercion: workers' morale and the maintenance of work discipline, 1939–1945', in D Welch (ed), *Nazi Propaganda. The Power and the Limitations* (London/Canberra: Croom Helm, 1983), 88–116.

Saunders T J, *Hollywood in Berlin. American Cinema and Weimar Germany* (Berkeley: University of California Press, 1994).

Schabel R, *Die Illusion der Wunderwaffen. Die Rolle der Düsenflugzeuge und Flugabwehrraketen in der Rüstungspolitik des Dritten Reiches.* (Munich: Oldenbourg Wissenschaftlicher Verlag, 1994).

Schaper P, *Kinos in Lübeck. Die Geschichte der Lübecker Lichtspieltheater und ihrer unmittelbarer Vorläufer 1896 bis heute* (Lübeck, 1987).

Scheel K, *Krieg über Ätherwellen. NS-Rundfunk und Monopole 1933–1945* (Berlin: Deutscher Verlag der Wissenschaften, 1970).

Scheurig B, *Freies Deutschland: Das Nationalkomitee und der Bund Deutscher Offiziere in der Sowjetunion, 1943–1945* (Munich: Mymphenburger Verlagshandlund, 1961; new eds 1984 and 1993).

Schmidt F, *Presse in Fessel. Das Zeitungsmonopol im Dritten Reich* (Berlin: Verlag Archiv und Kartei, 1947).

Schmidt–Leonhardt H, *Das Schriftleitergesetz* (Berlin, 1944).

Schmitt C, *Staat, Bewegung und Volk. Die Dreigliederung der politischen Einheit* (Hamburg: Hanseatische Verlagsanstalt, 1934).

Schneider I, *Radio-Kultur in der Weimarer Republik. Eine Dokumentation* (Tübingen: Gunter Narr Verlag, 1984).

Schoenberner G, 'Ideologie und Propaganda im NS-Film: Von der Eroberung der Studios zur Manipulation ihrer Produkte', in U Jung (ed.), *Der deutsche Film. Aspekte seiner Geschichte von den Anfängen bis zu Gegenwart* (Trier: Wissenschaftlicher Verlag, 1993), 91–110.

Schoenhals K P, *The Free German Movement: A Case of Patriotism or Treason?* (Westport, CT: Greenwood Press, 1989).

Schöllgen G, *A Conservative against Hitler. Ulrich von Hassell, Diplomat in Imperial Germany, the Weimar Republic and the Third Reich, 1881–1944* (Basingstoke/London: Macmillan, 1991).

Schreiber G, 'The Mediterranean in Hitler's strategy in 1940. "Programme" and military planning', in Deist W (ed.), *The German Military in the Age of Total War* (Leamington Spa: Berg, 1985), 248–67.

Schütte W, *Regionalität und Föderalismus im Rundfunk. Die geschichtliche Entwicklung in Deutschland 1923–1945* (Frankfurt: 1971), 34–78.

Seaton A, *The Russo–German War, 1941–1945* (London: Arthur Baker Limited, 1971).

Semati M M, Sotirin P J, 'Hollywood's Transnational Appeal: Hegemony and Democratic Potential?', *Journal of Popular Film and Television*, 26 (1999), 176–88.

Seraphin H G, *Das Politische Tagebuch Alfred Rosenbergs 1934/5 und 1939/40* (Göttingen/Berlin/Frankfurt, 1956).

Sharp A, *The Versailles Settlement* (New York: Macmillan, 1991).

Shils E A, Janowitz M, 'Cohesion and disintegration in the Wehrmacht in World War II', in D Katz (ed.), *Public Opinion and Propaganda* (New York: Holt, 1954), 553–82.

Smelser R, *Robert Ley: Hitler's Labor Front Leader* (Oxford: Berg, 1988).

Smith A L, Jr, 'Life in wartime Germany: General Ohlendorf's opinion service', *Public Opinion Quarterly*, 36 (1972), 1–7.

Smith H K, *Last Train From Berlin* (New York: Alfred Knopf 1942).

Smith W D, *The Ideological Origins of Nazi Imperialism* (Oxford: University Press, 1986).

Sørensen G, 'The dual state and fascism', *Totalitarian Movements and Political Religions*, 2 (2001), 25–40.

Spiker J, *Film und Kapital. Der Weg der deutschen Filmwirtschaft zum nationalsozialistischen Einheitskonzern* (West Berlin: Spiess, 1975).

Stadler K S, *The Birth of the Austrian Republic, 1918–1921* (Leyden: A W Sijthoff, 1966).

Stegemann B, 'Die Erste Phase der Seekriegführung bis zum Frühjahr 1940', *DRZW*, Vol. 2: *Die Errichtung der Hegemonie auf dem europäischen Kontinent* (Stuttgart: Deutsche Verlags-Anstalt, 1979), 159–88.

Stegemann B, 'Die Zweite Phase der Seekriegführung bis zum Frühjahr 1941', *DRZW*, Vol. 2: *Die Errichtung der Hegemonie auf dem europäischen Kontinent* (Stuttgart: Deutsche Verlags-Anstalt, 1979), 159–88.

Steinbach P, 'Nationalkomitee Freies Deutschland und der Widerstand gegen den Nationalsozialismus', *Exilforschung. Ein Internationales Jahrbuch*, 8 (1990), 61–91.

Steinert M G, *Hitler's War and the Germans: Public Mood and Attitude During the Second World War* (Athens, OH: Ohio University Press, 1977).

Stenzel T, *Das Rußlandbild des 'kleinen Mannes'. Gesellschaftliche Prägung und Fremdwahrnehmung in Feldpostbriefen aus dem Ostfeldzug (1941–1944/45)* [Osteuropa Institut München (Mitteilungen, No. 27, 1998)].

Stephan W, *Joseph Goebbels: Dämon einer Diktatur* (Stuttgart: Union Deutsche Verlagsgesellschaft, 1949).

Stinnett R B, *Day of Deceit: The Truth about FDR and Pearl Harbor* (New York: Free Press, 1999).

Strandmann H P von, 'Imperialism and revisionism in interwar Germany', in Mommsen, W J Osterhammel (eds), *Imperialism and After. Continuities and Discontinuities* (London/Boston/Sydney: Allen and Unwin, 1986), 90–119.

Streit C, *Keine Kameraden. Die Wehrmacht und die sowjetischen Kriegsgefangenen, 1941–1945* (Bonn: Dietz Verlag, 1991).

Struve W, *Elites against Democracy: Leadership Ideals in Bourgeois Political Thought in Germany, 1890–1933* (Princeton, NJ: Princeton University Press, 1973).

Stuiber H–W, *Medien in Deutschland*, Vol 2: *Rundfunk*, Part I (Konstanz: UVK–Medien, 1998).

Stumpf R, 'Der Krieg im Mittelmeerraum 1942/43: die Operationen in Nordafrika und im Mittleren Mittelmeer', *DRZW*, Vol. 6: *Der globale Krieg. Die Ausweitung zum Weltkrieg und der Wechsel der Initiative 1941–1943* (Stuttgart: Deutsche Verlags-Anstalt, 1990), 569–759.

Szodrzynski J, 'Das Ende der "Volksgemeinschaft"? Die Hamburger Bevölkerung in der "Trümmergesellschaft" ab 1943', in Bajohr F, Szodrzynski J (eds), *Hamburg in der NS-Zeit* (Hamburg: Ergebnisse Verlag, 1995), 281–303.

Taithe B, Thornton T, 'Propaganda: a misnomer of rhetoric and persuasion?', in B Taithe, T Thornton (eds), *Propaganda. Political Rhetoric and Identity, 1300–2000* (Stroud: Sutton Publishing, 1999), 1–24.

Taylor A J P, *The Origins of the Second World War* (London: Hamish Hamilton, 1961).

Taylor P M, *Munitions of the Mind. A history of propaganda from the ancient world to the present era* (Manchester: Manchester University Press, 2003, 3rd ed.).

Taylor R, *Film propaganda: Soviet Russia and Nazi Germany* (London/New York: IB Tauris, 1998).

Tegel S, ' "The demonic effect": Veit Harlan's use of Jewish extras in Jud Süss', *Holocaust and Genocide Studies*, 14 (2000), 215–41.

Thompson R S, *A Time for War: Franklin D Roosevelt and the Path to Pearl Harbor* (New York: Prentice Hall, 1991).

Töteberg M, 'Unter den Brücken. Kino und Film im totalen Krieg', in M Töteberg and H–M Bock (eds), *Das Ufa-Buch* (Frankfurt: Zweitausendeins, 1992), 466–8.

Traub H, 'Zur Entwicklungsgeschichte der Ufa-Wochenschauen' in *25 Jahre Ufa-Wochenschau* (Berlin, 1939) 18–21.

Trevor–Roper H, *The Last Days of Hitler* (New York: Macmillan, 1947).

Trevor–Roper H–R, 'Hitlers Kriegsziele', *Vierteljahrshefte für Zeitgeschichte*, 8 (1960), 127.

Triandis H C, *Interpersonal Behavior* (Monterey: Brooks/Cole, 1977).

Ueberschär G R (ed.), *Das Nationalkomitee 'Freies Deutschland' und der Bund Deutscher Offiziere* (Frankfurt am Main: S. Fischer Taschenbuch Verlag, 1995).

Ueberschär G R, 'Gegner des Nationalsozialismus 1933–1945. Volksopposition, individuelle Gewissensentscheidung und Rivalitätskampf konkurrierender Führungseliten als Aspekte der Literatur über Emigration und Widerstand im Dritten Reich zwischen dem 35 und 40. Jahrestag des 20. Juli 1944 (Bericht aus der Forschung)', *Militärgeschichtliche Mitteilungen*, 35 (1984), 141–95.

Umbreit H, 'Der Kampf um die Vormachtstellung in Westeuropa', *DRZW*, Vol. 2: *Die Errichtung der Hegemonie auf dem europäischen Kontinent* (Stuttgart: Deutsche Verlags-Anstalt, 1979), 235–328.

Unger A L, 'The Public Opinion Reports of the Nazi Party', *Public Opinion Quarterly*, 29 (1965/66), 565–82.

Unger A L, *The Totalitarian Party. Party and People in Nazi Germany and Soviet Russia* (London: Cambridge University Press, 1974).

Uzulis A, *Nachrichtenagenturen im Nationalsozialismus. Propagandainstrumente und Mittel der Presselenkung* (Frankfurt: P Lang, 1995).

Vande Winkel R, 'Nazi Newsreels in Europe 1939–1945: the many faces of Ufa's foreign weekly newsreel (Auslandstonwoche) versus German's weekly newsreel (Deutsche Wochenschau)', *Historical Journal of Film, Radio and Television* 24 (2004), 5–34.

Vogel D, 'Das Eingreifen Deutschlands auf dem Balkan', *DRZW*, Vol. 3: *Der Mittelmeerraum und Südosteuropa. Von der 'non belligeranza' Italiens bis zum Kriegseintritt der Vereinigten Staaten* (Stuttgart: Deutsche Verlags-Anstalt, 1984), 417–515.

Vogel D, 'Deutsche und Alliierte Kriegführung im Westen', *DRZW*, Vol. 7: *Das Deutsche Reich in der Defensive. Strategischer Luftkrieg in Europa, Krieg im Westen und in Ostasien 1943–1944/45* (Stuttgart: Deutsche Verlags-Anstalt, 2001), 419–642.

Voigt H–G, ' "Verräter vor dem Volksgericht". Zur Geschichte eines Films', in Bengt von zur Mühlen, A von Klewitz (ed.), *Die Angeklagten des 20. Juli vor dem Volksgerichtshof* (Berlin: Kleinmachnow: Chronos, 2001).

Wedel H von, *Die Propagandatruppen der deutschen Wehrmacht* (Neckargemünd: Scharnhorst Buchkameradschaft, 1962).

Weber M, 'Politics as vocation', in H Gerth and C Wright Mills (ed.) *Max Weber: Essays in Sociology* (New York: Oxford University Press, 1985).

Webster Sir C, Frankland N, *The Strategic Air Offensive against Germany, 1939–1945*, Vol. I (London: HMSO, 1961).

Wegner B, 'Der Krieg gegen die Sowjetunion 1942/43', *DRZW*, Vol. 6: *Der globale Krieg. Die Ausweitung zum Weltkrieg und der Wechsel der Initiative 1941–1943* (Stuttgart: Deutsche Verlags-Anstalt, 1990), 761–1093.

Wegner B, ' "My Honour is Loyalty": the SS as a Military Factor in Hitler's Germany', in W Deist (ed.), *The German Military in the Age of Total War* (Leamington Spa: Berg, 1985), 220–39.

Weinberg G L, *A World At Arms: A Global History of World War II* (New York: Cambridge University Press, 1994).

Weinberg G L, *The Foreign Policy of Hitler's Germany. Starting World War II, 1937–1939* (Chicago: Chicago University Press, 1980).

Welch D, vande Winkel R (eds), *Cinema and the Swastika. The International Expansion of the Third Reich Cinema* (Basingstoke/New York: Palgrave Macmillan, 2007).

Welch D, 'Nazi Propaganda and the Volksgemeinschaft: constructing a people's community', *Journal of Contemporary History*, 39 (2004), 213–38.

Welch D, *The Third Reich: Politics and Propaganda* (London: Routledge, 2002).

Welch D, 'Hitler's history films', *History Today*, 52 (2002), 20–25.

Welch D, *Propaganda and the German Cinema, 1933–1945* (London/New York: IB Tauris, 2001, rev. ed.).

Welch D, 'Manufacturing a consensus: Nazi propaganda and the building of a national community (Volksgemeinschaft)', *Contemporary European History*, 2 (1993), 1–15.

Wette W, 'Ideologien, Propaganda und Innenpolitik als Voraussetzungen der Kriegspolitik des Dritten Reiches', *DRZW*, Vol. 1: *Kriegsbeginn und Kriegsziele* (Stuttgart: Deutsche Verlags-Anstalt, 1979), 25–176.

Wilde L, *Bomben über Lübeck. Dokumentation über die Zerstörung Lübecks beim Luftangriff vom. 28/29. März 1942* (Lübeck: Verlag Schmidt-Römhild, 2000).

Williams W A, 'The legend of isolationism in the 1920s', in Williams WA, The *Tragedy of American Diplomacy* (New York: Dell, 1962), 104–59.

Winston B, 'Triumph of the will – reinterpretation of Leni Reifenstahl's Nazi-era film', *History Today*, January 1997, 24–8.

Witte K, 'Film im Nationalsozialismus', Wolfgang Jacobsen (ed.), *Geschichte des deutschen Films* (Stuttgart/Weimar: J B Metzler 1993), 119–70.

Wright J, *Terrorist Propaganda* (New York: St Martin's, 1990).

Wulf J, *Theater und Film im Dritten Reich* (Gütersloh: Sigbert Mohn Verlag, 1964).

Wulf J, *Presse und Funk im Dritten Reich. Eine Dokumentation* (Reinbek: Rowohlt, 1966).

Zeman Z, *Nazi Propaganda* (London: Oxford University Press, 1973, 2nd ed.).

Internet Resources

German Propaganda Archive (GPA):

http://www.calvin.edu/cas/gpa (translations by Randall Bytwerk)

Index

AA (*Auswärtiges Amt*), 34, 49–53, 60, 77, 107
  foreign press conference, 50
  KA-R, 50
  radio activities, 50–1
  see also Ribbentrop, Joachim von
Afifa, 200
Agfa, 59, 214
air warfare, 10, 11, 143, 167, 176, 192
  on Berlin, 162–3, 192, 193, 200
  on Bochum (1944), 164–5
  against Britain, 102–3, 166
  on Cologne (1943), 151, 161
  escalation of (1943–44), 30–1, 87, 115, 151, 155, 160, 163, 165, 167, 182
  on Essen (1943), 162
  fears of biological attack, 139
  against Germany, 59, 102, 160–8
  Goebbels admits effect of, 137, 155
  on Hamburg (1943), 164
  impact on film production, 61, 200, 203, 211, 214, 215
  leaflets dropped during air raids, 142
  on Lübeck (1942), 140, 160, 215
  on Rostock (1942), 160
  rumours about, 142
  see also Luftwaffe; Eagle Offensive; German public
Algeria, 127
Amann, Max, 18, 26–7, 28, 29–30, 45, 47, 48
Anschluß (1938), 25, 30, 93, 94, 116
anti-Bolshevism, *see under* Discourses
anti-British propaganda, *see under* Discourses
anti-Semitism, *see under* Discourses; *see also* Jews
anti-plutocratic theme, *see under* Discourses
anti-US propaganda, *see under* Discourses; *see also* USA; Roosevelt, Franklin D
Ardennes offensive (1944), 182–3
Athenia, sinking of (1939), 11

Außenpolitisches Amt (APA), 52
  see also Rosenberg Alfred
Austria, 67, 93, 116
  film production, 24, 210, 214
  see also Anschluß; Dollfuss, Schuschnigg
Axis, 68, 69, 76, 86, 91, 104, 105, 117, 157, 170, 175
  alliance of 'young peoples', 74
  Italian contribution to, 121, 158–9
  plans for reorganisation of Europe, 88

Balfour, Michael, 7
Balkans, 51, 104–6, 158
Barbarossa, *see* Operation Barbarossa
Bavaria Film AG, 24, 189
BBC, 107, 108, 142, 143, 160
  see also Counter-propaganda
BDO (*Bund Deutscher Offiziere*), 144
Berghof, 148
Berk, Hans Schwarz van, 128, 163
Berlin
  air raids, 102, 143, 162–3, 171, 192, 211
  centre of party and state activity, 43–4
  cinema activities in, 215, 216, 218
  Goebbels as 'Defender of Berlin', 43
  Goebbels as Gauleiter of Berlin, 59, 135
  home of 'Goebbels network', 46, 51
  occupied (1945), 218
  Red Army in the outskirts (1945), 152
  western Allies in the outskirts (1945), 183
Berndt, Alfred-Ingemar, 34–5, 36, 54, 55, 60
  see also NS radio
Bessarabia, 136
Bismarck, Otto von, 68, 187, 202, 204, 205, 206, 207
Bismarck (1940), 204–5, 206
Bismarck, battle with HMS Hood (1941), 107
Blomberg–Fritzsch affair (1938), 56
Bolshevik revolution (1917), 74, 77

Bormann, Martin, 41, 46, 49, 56, 61, 107, 114, 131, 135, 140, 150, 160, 205, 220
Bormann network, 53–5
controls access to Hitler, 53–6, 149
Hitler's secretary (1943–45), 53, 149
relations with Goebbels, 53–5
relations with Tießler, 54–5
'Bormann network', 53–5
Braeckow, Ernst, 48, 60
Brauchitsch, Walther von, 113, 143, 146
Britain, 69, 70, 74, 77, 83, 85, 86, 87, 88, 91, 100, 101, 105, 106, 107, 108, 110, 111, 117, 122, 128, 131, 136, 138, 139, 140, 141, 142, 143, 144, 147, 154, 155, 157, 160, 161, 162, 163, 164, 165, 167, 169, 171, 183, 201, 202, 204, 206, 207
Athenia incident, 11
declares war on Germany, 72, 95, 98
German attack on (1940), 102, 104, 119, 203
guarantee to Poland (1939), 96
plutocratic, 72–3, 84, 102, 116
propaganda, 7
relations with the Soviet Union, 77, 83, 87
retaliation against, 174
US aid, 75–6
see also Churchill; Operation Sea Lion
Brzezinski, Zbigniew, 7–8
Bulgaria, 105, 108

Carl Peters (1941), 201, 203, 204
Catholic Church, 3, 146
Caucasus, 123
Chamberlain, Neville, 72, 73
charisma, 8, 9, 17, 44, 50, 53, 55, 66, 148, 219
charismatic community (*Gemeinde*), 34, 42
see also Hitler
Cherbourg, 176
Churchill, Winston, 85, 157, 163, 173, 180
1943 plan for postwar Germany, 180
attacked by NS propaganda, 73, 76, 83, 106, 116, 128

Jewish-Bolshevik-plutocratic conspiracy, 88–9, 117
presented as 'criminal', 161
'puppet' of the Jews, 84
responsible for cultural destruction, 161
see also Britain; Conferences
cinema, 15, 18, 19, 21, 22
as propaganda medium, 185–8
see also NS cinema
Cologne, 33, 151, 177, 178
air raid (5.1942), 161–2
Conferences
Casablanca (1943), 86, 87, 157
Quebec (1944), 180
Teheran (1943), 173
Yalta (1945), 88, 181
Counter-propaganda
enemy broadcasts, 11, 38, 141–2, 143–5;
British, 141–4; Soviet, 144–5
impact of, 145
leaflets, 11, 79, 132, 142–3, 179
see also BBC, NS Radio
Crete, battle of (1941), 106, 107, 139
see also Operation Marita
Crimea, 170, 173
Czech crisis (1938), 50, 93–4, 98
Czechoslovakia, 30, 45, 50, 93, 98, 210
dissolution of (1939), 94–5
see also under Pacts

DACHO (*Dachorganisation der Filmschaffenden Deutschland*), 20
DAF (*Deutsche Arbeitsfront*), 21, 45, 52, 60, 70, 86, 213
Danzig, 96–8, 211
Das Reich, 80, 107, 114, 128, 133, 151, 158, 163, 167, 171, 175, 180
DD (*Drahtlose Dienst*), 37, 49, 60
Der ewige Jude (1940),, 194–5
Der größe König (1942), 150, 205–6
Der Stürmer, 74, 179
Deulig, 189
Deutsche Filmvetriebs GmbH, 215
Deutsche Wochenschau GmbH, 190, 191, 194
Deutsche Wochenschauzentrale, 189
see also newsreel, NS cinema

DFT (*Deutsche Filmtheater-Gesellschaft*),
213
Die Entlaßung (1942), 202, 204,
206, 211
Die Goldene Stadt (1942), 210
Die Große Liebe (1942), 211, 212
Die Rotschilds (1941), 201, 206, 207
Dienststelle Rosenberg, 52
Dietrich, Otto, 30, 50, 53, 56, 115, 157,
174, 182, 189, 219
antipathy to Rosenberg, 52
appointed *Reichspressechef*, 27–8
Dietrich network, 46–9
dismissed (1945), 60
Heß affair, 107
loss of influence, 60–1
role in press, 30, 45, 61
'special announcements', 37, 111
Stalingrad campaign, 133
*Tagesparolen des Reichspressechefs der
NSDAP*, 48, 49
triumphalism, 112, 113, 119, 125
views on Europe, 70
'Dietrich network', 46–9
Diewerge, Wolfgang, 34, 35,
36, 116
discourses
long-term positive themes, 65–70:
elitism, 66; Europe, 68–70,
121, 131–2, 136, 174, 183;
Hitler-cult, 66–7; ideal
fatherland, 65–6; rebirth, 65–6,
67–9
long-term negative themes, 70–92:
anti-Bolshevik, 76–83, 135–7;
anti-British, 72–4, 76;
anti-plutocratic, 72–6; anti-USA,
75–6; anti-western, 72–6;
Jewish-Bolshevik-plutocratic
conspiracy, 83–92, 115–17, 159
DNB (*Deutsche Nachrichtenbüro*), 36, 37,
46, 48, 189
Dönitz, Karl, 155, 218
Dortmund, 164
Dreßler-Andreß, Horst, 32, 33, 37

Eagle air offensive (1940), 102
Egypt, 104
Eher Verlag, 26, 28, 29
El-Alamein, 128

Ellul, Jacques, 1, 199
Enabling Act (1933), 30
Essen, 162
Europe, *see under* Discourses, NS
propaganda
'Euthanasia' programme (T-4) (1939–41),
3, 4, 146

Fangauf, Eberhard, 189
fascism, 16, 65, 70
aesthetics, 23
fascistisation, 18
Feldzug in Polen (1939), 194, 196, 197
Feuertaufe (1940), 194, 196
Filmkreditbank, 20
First World War, 2, 73, 85, 154, 197, 204,
213
cinema production, 188
German defeat, 74, 98, 205
radio, 30–1
Fraenkel, Ernst, 40, 41
France, 51, 72, 73, 88, 93, 95, 96, 100,
104, 165, 176, 190, 200, 201, 207,
211
attack on (1940), 101
declares war on Germany (1939), 98
liberation of Paris (1944), 181
Franco, Francisco, 140
Frankfurt, 151
Frederick the Great, 68, 150, 177, 205,
206, 207
Fredericus (1936), 201
Fridericus Rex (1922), 205
Fritzsche, Hans, 11, 36, 48, 75, 101, 107,
113, 126, 127, 154, 155, 157, 158
anti-Semitic views, 74
flexibility, 49, 60
importance for Goebbels, 60
Radio Commissioner for Political
Matters (1942), 35–6
Stalingrad commentary (1943), 132
Funk, Walther, 47

Gallipoli, 175
Gauleiters, 17, 59, 135, 177, 208, 210
German minorities, *see Volksdeutsche*
German public
admiration for Soviets, 124
against war, 64, 98
Barbarossa, 108–9, 112–13

German public – *continued*
  effect of air raids on, 162
  feelings towards Poland, 97
  Haltung, 4, 5, 81, 91, 153, 164, 165, 218
  hatred against enemies, 172
  Hitler, 146–8, 149, 151–2
  miracle weapons, 165–8
  peak of support for war (1940), 101
  questioning Hitler (1944), 178
  resistance to NS propaganda, 3–4,
    130–2, 138, 148, 181–2, 208–9
  resistance to western powers, 90–1, 182
  Stimmung, 4, 5, 38, 58, 89, 91, 112,
    124, 140, 145, 151, 153, 160, 164,
    167, 168, 171, 174, 178, 181, 218
  surrender in the west (1945), 182
  talk of 'leadership crisis' (1943), 148
  views about Italy, 121, 158–60, 176
  views about Japan, 120–1
Gesamtdeutschland, 68, 95, 96
Gibraltar, 104
Glasmeier, Heinrich, 33, 36
Gneisenau, August Neithardt von, 170
Goebbels, Joseph, 4, 5, 12, 14, 19, 20,
    21, 27, 28, 30, 32, 33, 34, 35, 36, 41,
    47, 48, 49, 50, 51, 52, 57, 67, 75, 79,
    92, 95, 100, 101, 102, 105, 113, 115,
    116, 118, 119, 120, 121, 122, 123,
    136, 138, 140, 141, 143, 144, 145,
    146, 147, 148, 150, 153, 154, 155,
    162, 169, 171, 175, 178, 179, 180,
    182, 183, 187, 189, 195, 197, 198,
    200, 205, 206, 208, 210, 211, 212,
    213, 218
  admiration for Churchill, 163
  admits war may be lost (1943), 132–3
  anti-Bolshevism, 78, 80–1, 87–8
  anti-Semitism, 84–5
  attacks Churchill (1943), 85–6
  Baarova affair, 45
  Badoglio's 'betrayal' (1943), 158–9
  cautious about Stalingrad campaign
    (1942), 125
  creates diversion for Operation
    Barbarossa (1941), 106, 107, 139
  criticises newsreel (1944), 192–3
  criticises NS propaganda, 114, 137
  criticises OKW, 127–8, 161
  Danzig, 96–7
  deals with counter-propaganda, 142

decides to stay in Berlin, 184
Defender of Berlin, 43
exaggerated influence, 43–6, 219–22
fear propaganda, 82, 89–90
frustration with Katyn coverage
  (1943), 156
Gauleiter of Berlin, 59, 135
Goebbels network, 16, 43–6, 56, 62,
  126, 156, 201, 207, 219–21
handling of Stalingrad campaign,
  125–9
Jewish-Bolshevik-plutocratic
  conspiracy, 83, 84, 88, 108–9
justifies war (1939), 72–3
limits of his power, 7–10
measures to restore newsreel's
  popularity, 191–4
measures to revive cinema (1942–45),
  215–16
'never another crisis' (1943), 133
peace, 96
plays down loss of north Africa (1943),
  156–7
Plenipotentiary for Total War (1944),
  43, 54, 177, 181
puts pressure on Hitler to appear in
  public, 149, 223
relations with Bormann, 53–5
relations with Dietrich, 47–9, 111, 112
relations with OKW, 56–7, 107–8
'resistance at any price' (1945), 90–1
revenge (*Vergeltung*), 163–8, 173, 174
role in NS cinema, 22–6, 61, 186,
  216–17
role in NS propaganda, 17–18
role in NS radio, 37–8
strengthens position (1943–45), 59–2
suicide (1945), 184
total war speech (2.1943), 81–2, 84–5,
  87, 134–5
'unity of people and party' (1944), 172
unpopular, 151
views on cinema, 209
views on Europe, 70, 74, 78, 109
views on newsreel, 190
views on USA, 86
warns against false optimism (1942),
  124–5
see also NS propaganda
'Goebbels network', 43–6, 219–22

Goering, Hermann, 41, 43, 62, 128, 184, 220
GPU (1942), 202, 206
Gramsci, Antonio, 8
Greece, 104, 105
Großdeutschland, 94
Große Freiheit N 7 (1944), 211
Großraumwirtschaft, 69
Gutterer, Leopold, 59, 60

Hadamowsky, Eugen, 32, 33, 36, 54
Halder, Franz, 113
Haltung, see under German public
Hamburg, 102, 151, 162, 164, 216
Hans Westmar (1933), 195
Harlan, Veit, 200, 201, 210, 216
Hegel, Georg Wilhelm Friedrich, 41
Heimkehr (1941), 207
Herzstein, Edward, 6, 13
Hess, Rudolf, 53, 111, 140, 149
    flight to Scotland (1941), 107–8
    heads NSDAP PO, 47, 50, 60
Himmler, Heinrich, 41, 43, 46, 58, 59, 110, 184
Hindenburg, Paul von, 47, 197
Hinkel, Hans, 61, 216
    head of RMVP Film Division, 192–3, 215
    reorganisation of NS radio (1941–42), 35–6
Hitler, Adolf
    30.1.45 address, 179
    20.7.44 assassination attempt, 176–8
    1.1.45 broadcast, 151–2
    11.12.41 speech, 85, 117–18, 119
    26.4.42 speech, 123, 147
    21.3.43 speech, 147–8
    9.11.1943 speech, 168
    annihilation of Jews (1.1939 speech), 82
    assassination attempt against (7.1944), 176, 177, 181, 194, 198, 206
    attack on F D Roosevelt (1941), 85
    attacks Churchill, 84, 117
    Badoglio's 'betrayal' (1943), 159–60
    charisma, 8, 9, 17, 40–3, 44, 50, 53, 55, 66, 148, 219
    confident about collapse of the Soviet Union (1941), 120

cult, 66–7, 145–52
    erosion of (1943–45), 147–8
    staying power, 149–52
Danzig, 97–8
frustration (1945), 152
Führerprinzip, 41
infallibility, 5, 146, 206, 219
Jewish-Bolshevik conspiracy, 77, 84
Mediterranean strategy (1940–41), 104–5
parallels between Hitler and Frederick the Great, 150, 205–6
peace talks, 73, 97, 98, 99–100, 115
reclusive (1943–45), 148–9
rumours about his health, 140, 143–4
views on Europe, 79
views on Poland (1943), 82
'working towards the *Führer*', 42, 43
    see also NS propaganda
Hitler Youth (*Hitlerjugend*), 70, 187, 194, 213
Hitlerjugend Quex (1933), 187
Hollywood, 23, 187, 189
Hungary, 181, 182

Irredentism, 68, 93, 94, 95, 96
Italy
    comparison with NS Germany, 158
    Fascism, 25, 121, 210
    German operations in (1943–44), 168, 173, 175–6, 181
    surrenders (1943), 158–60
    Tripartite Pact, 108
    war (1940–41), 104, 157
    see also Mussolini; Sicily; NS propaganda, German public

Japan, 108, 117, 121
Jews, 25, 65, 67, 124, 136, 137, 175, 183
    depiction on film, 3, 15, 194–5, 199, 201, 205, 206, 207
    Entjudung, 17, 22, 23, 28, 38
    international conspiracy, 68–71, 73, 74, 76–85, 87–91, 109, 112, 114, 116, 117, 123, 133, 147, 159, 173, 183
    revenge on Germany, 179–80
    see under Discourses, Goebbels, Hitler; *see also* Streicher
Jodl, Alfred, 57
Jud Süß (1940), 3, 195, 198, 199, 201

KA-R, 50, 51
Katyn massacre, 156
Kaufman, Theodore Newman ("Nathan"),
 116–17
Keitel, Wilhelm, 41, 54, 135
 see also OKW, Wermacht
Kershaw, Ian, 8, 41, 42, 43
Kharkov, 136–7, 142, 169, 170
Kiev, 113, 118, 145
Koehl, Robert, 41, 42
Kolberg (1944), 187, 200–1, 203, 207, 216
KPD (*Kommunistische Partei
 Deutschlands*), 27
Kracauer, Siegfried, 185, 197
Kraft Durch Freude, 213
 see also DAF
Kriegler, Hans, 33, 34
Kristallnacht (11.1938), 45

La Rochelle, 200
Lammers, Hans, 51, 53, 135
Latvia, 136
Leander, Zara, 211
Lebensraum, 101
Leinen aus Irland (1939), 206
Ley, Robert, 45, 47, 52, 60, 70
Libya, 104
Linz, J J, 70
London, 45, 84, 85, 87, 97, 105, 108,
 166, 224
 air raids on, 102, 140, 141, 143, 162
Lübeck, 140, 160, 161, 213, 215
Luftwaffe, 61, 103, 107, 138, 140, 141,
 155, 163, 166, 167, 175, 196,
 failure, 167, 220
 operations against London,102, 140,
 141, 143, 162
 unable to protect German cities, 160,
 162, 164
 see also Goering, Hermann

Martin, Hans-Leo, 57
Maske in Blau (1942), 210
Memel, 30, 95
Meßter, Oskar, 188, 189
Ministry of Finance, 32, 34
Minsk, 111, 170
miracle weapons (*Wunderwaffen*), 140,
 165, 175, 178
 see also V-1, V-2, V-3, NS propaganda

modernity, 1, 25, 70, 155, 222
Molotov, Viacheslav, 52, 71, 77, 86, 108,
 110, 202, 204
Montecassino, 175
Morgenthau, Henry Jr, 180
 'Morgenthau Plan' (1944), 180–1
Münchhausen (1943), 187
Mussolini, Benito, 70, 78, 157, 178
 alarmed at German aggression
 (1938–39), 94
 kept in the dark about Barbarossa, 108
 letter from Hitler, 110
 removal from power (1943), 158–60, 178
 rescue (1943), 158–9

Napoleon Bonaparte, 170, 207
national community (*Volksgemeinschaft*),
 see under NS propaganda
National Socialism
 centralisation, 18–19
 co-ordination, 18–19
 neo-feudalism, 22, 41, 44, 45, 46, 219
 party–state relations, 55, 59
 polyocracy, 8, 38, 41
 rebirth, 65, 66, 67, 68, 69, 95, 98, 99
 revolution, 4, 16
 seizure of power (1933), 8, 17, 19, 29,
 128, 135, 179, 200
 totalitarianism, 7–10
 see also NSDAP, NS propaganda
Neubabelsberg, Ufa facilities, 193, 200,
 201
Neumann, Franz, 40
Neurath, Konstantin Freiherr von,
 45, 50
Neustadt, 162
Newsreel (*Wochenschau*), 15, 57, 61, 79,
 103, 112, 148, 156, 185, 188–94,
 196, 197, 198, 208, 209, 214
 Auslandstonwoche, 190
 centralisation, 189–90
 last newsreel (755/10), 194
 loss of popularity (1942–5), 191–2
 popularity (–1941), 190–1
 production problems (1944–45),
 193–4
 see also NS cinema
NKFD (*Nationalkomitee Freies
 Deutschland*), 144, 145
 see also counter-propaganda

Normandy, Allied landing (1944), 90, 166, 173–6
NS cinema, 19–26, 185, 186, 187, 188, 195, 199, 200, 211, 217
  anti-British films, 203–4
  anti-Semitic films, 194–5
  anti-Semitic stereotypes in, 206–7
  between reality and fiction, 187–8
  censorship, 21–2, 190
  certificates (*Prädikate*), 21–2
  continues until the end, 215–17
  decline of influence, 23–4
  deemed 'essential' for war effort, 62
  documentaries, 194–8
  Durchhaltefilme, 208
  emphasis on German production, 213–14
  entertainment tax, 20, 21
  exceptional status, 186–8
  expansion, 190, 213
  Goebbels's personal domain, 216–17
  historical films, 198–207
  ideological films, 195–6
  influence of Hollywood, 23, 187, 189
  integration, 188
  intervention of authorities, 210–12
  Jews (*Entjudung*), 22–3
  Kulturfilme, 197, 202, 206
  nationalisation (1936–41), 23–6, 186
  NS films as 'totalitarian panoramas', 197
  problems and shortages (1942–45), 62, 214–17
  Reich Cinema Law (1934), 18, 21, 22
  under Goebbels's control, 61
  Unterhaltungsfilme, 208–12
  see also newsreel, cinema
NS press, 26–31, 48, 89
  Amann Ordinances (1935), 18, 29–30
  financial crisis, 28–30
  Jewish press, 28, 29
  left-wing press, 27–8, 29
  see also Amann, Dietrich, Goebbels, Winkler, *Eher Verlag*
NS propaganda
  atrocity propaganda, 79, 89, 97, 102, 112, 116, 181
  'Bolshevik-Jewish conspiracy', 71, 80, 81, 109
  'bolshevisation of Europe', 81, 83, 87

censorship, 22
centralisation, 39
consensus, 63–4, 71
co-ordination (*Gleichschaltung*), 14, 38, 219
defeatism, 115, 131, 205
ersatz reality, 10–11
escapism, 10, 38, 198, 208, 216
fear, 5, 69, 71, 81, 82, 88, 91, 116, 121, 132, 133, 134–7, 173, 180, 182, 184
Freemasons, 159
Fortress Europe, 157
General Winter, 120–1
Habe-nichts (proletarian nations), 72, 121, 203
Haltung, 4–5
heroism, 82, 128–9, 141, 157, 163, 168, 175, 201
integration, 153–4
Italy, 121, 158–60
Japan, 120–1
Katyn massacre (1943), 156
legacy of 1918, 43, 56, 73, 74, 77, 98, 101, 116, 128, 155, 170, 177, 213, 223
miracle weapons propaganda, 165–8
monopoly of truth, 10–12, 130–1, 137–45
mouth propaganda (*Mundpropaganda*), 139
national community (*Volksgemeinschaft*), 66, 103, 133, 172, 186, 217
negative integration, 70
'never another crisis', 133, 173
north Africa, 156–7
polyocracy, 8, 9, 16–19, 30, 32, 37, 38, 39, 40, 41, 42, 44, 45, 46, 50, 55–6, 59, 111, 114, 126–7, 219–28
Propagandaparolen, 114, 121, 135
race, 77, 82, 95, 112, 120–1, 211
realism, 123–4
retaliation (*Vergeltung*) propaganda, 79, 102, 108, 155, 160, 163–8, 171, 174, 178
rumours, 139–41
sacrifice, 82, 128, 151, 157
silence about Stalingrad, 127–8

NS propaganda – *continued*
Slavs, 93, 112
'Soviet Paradise' exhibition (1942),
79–81, 135
Stimmung, 4–5
total war, 133
U-boat propaganda, 11, 86, 107, 128,
137, 154–6, 178, 183
underestimation of the Soviet Union,
109–13, 120–1
use of history, 150–2, 170
V-campaign (1941), 107–8
Winter Aid Campaigns
(*Winterhilfsspende*), 114–15, 119,
125, 126
'year of decision' (1942), 121, 124
see also Discourses, propaganda,
Goebbels, RMVP, RPL
NS radio, 1, 3, 8, 15, 18, 21, 31–8, 43, 44,
46, 48, 49, 55, 56, 57, 80, 84, 102,
107, 112, 125, 126, 134, 146, 154,
156, 166, 170, 174, 179, 182, 186,
187, 192, 206, 209
29.6.1941 twelve 'special
announcements', 37, 111
AA's role in, 50–1
broadcast announcing Stalingrad
defeat (3.2.1943), 132
centralisation, 32–3
enemy broadcasts, 11, 38, 141–2,
143–5
Goebbels-Dietrich competition, 48
Interradio, 51
news agencies, 36–7
peoples' radio (*Volksempfänger*), 34–5,
38
regional structure, 31–3
Reichssender, 33
RMVP Radio Division, 60,
shift to entertainment, 35–6, 38
Stalingrad hoax broadcasts (12.1943),
128
stations (*Sender*), 32, 33
supervisors (*Intendanten*), 33
see also radio
NSDAP (*Nationalsozialistische Deutsche
Arbeiterpartei*), 19, 20, 28, 29, 30, 47,
74, 114, 117, 135, 196, 202, 211
Austrian NSDAP, 67
cinema, 19, 20, 26, 209, 213–14

constant revolution, 18
cultural affairs, 52, 55
electoral victories, 17, 77
internal competition, 40–9, 51–5,
58–62
leader, 67
party–state dualism, 8, 26, 39, 44–6,
55, 59–62, 112, 220
press, 28–9
response to air raids, 151
role in NS state, 17–18, 40–2
RPA, 80
unity with people, 142
unpopular, 66, 145–8
see also RPL, National Socialism

Ohlendorf, Otto, 141
Ohm Krüger (1941), 201, 203, 204, 207
OKW (*Oberkommando Wehrmacht*), 34,
37, 52, 58, 59, 111, 133, 134, 137,
157, 169, 171, 176, 194, 205, 214
air raids, 161–2
film activities, 196
importance in NS wartime
propaganda, 46
newsreel, 190–2
OKW network, 56–7
OKW/WPr, 46, 57
optimism about Barbarossa, 115
PK, 34, 56–7, 190–3
radio activities, 51
relations with Goebbels, 54
relations with Ribbentrop, 54
Stalingrad, 125, 126–7
see also Wehrmacht
'OKW network', 56–7
OKW/WPr, 46, 57
Operation Barbarossa, 15, 52, 68, 75,
77–9, 83, 104, 106, 108–21, 122,
139, 144, 202, 219
drive to Moscow (1941), 113–19
impossible to complete in 1941, 115
launch (1941), 111–12
secret preparations, 106–8
Operation Citadel (1943), 141
Operation Felix, 104, 152
Operation Green (1940), 100–1
Operation Marita (1941), 105–6, 108
Operation Sea Lion (1940), 102–4,
119, 203

Operation Torch (1941), 87, 127
Operation Typhoon (1941), 113, 115–17
Operation White (1939), 71–2, 95–8,
    98–100
Opfergang (1944), 216
opinion reports, *see* SD, RPA

Pacts
    Munich Pact (1938), 64, 94, 95, 96,
        163, 173
    Non-aggression pact
        (Ribbentrop–Molotov Pact, 1939),
        71–2, 77–8, 202, 204
    Pact of Steel (1939), 108
    Tripartite Pact (1940), 108
Papen, Franz von, 33
Paracelsus (1943), 202, 203
Party Chancellery (*Parteikanzlei*), 46, 54,
    55, 60, 114, 211, 220, 224
    see also Bormann, Martin
Paulus, Friedrich von, 191
Pearl Harbour, attack on (1941), 15, 84,
    117
PK (*Propaganda Kompanien*), 34, 56–7,
    190–3, 194, 196
PO (*Politische Organisation der NSDAP*),
    47, 50, 60
    see also Hess Rudolf
Poland, 26, 30, 50, 51, 71, 73, 82,
    95, 101, 108, 116, 138, 156,
    170, 194
    British guarantee to (1939), 72, 96
    depiction in newsreel, 196–7
    feelings of Germans towards, 97
    Heimkehr, 207
    invasion (1939), 45, 97–100, 190
    see also Operation White
polyocracy, 8, 9, 16–19, 30, 32, 37,
    38, 39, 40, 41, 42, 44, 45, 46,
    50, 55–6, 59, 111, 114, 126–7,
    219–28
    see also NS propaganda
Prädikate (film certificates), 21, 197, 201,
    210, 216
Press, 31, 209
    see also NS press
Propaganda
    attitudes, 3–5
    centralisation, 6–7
    cinema, 185–8

correlation (emplotment), 64–5
    definition, 1–2, 12
    distortion, 63
    effective, 6–12, 13
    fear, 5, 89–91
    'filter' function, 63–4
    gatekeeper, 9
    impact of war, 12–13
    integration, 2, 3–6, 8, 12, 14
    leisure-entertainment, 2–3
    persuasion, 1, 9
    subpropaganda, 3
    techniques, 5–6

Race Political Office (*Rassenpolitisches
    Amt*), 211
radio
    in Germany, 31–2
    history, 3, 31
    as propaganda medium, 15
    see also NS radio
Raeder, Erich, 11
Red Army, 53, 91, 119, 121, 136, 145,
    168, 181, 182, 197
    advances, 89, 169, 170–1
    battle for Berlin, 152
    'fear' propaganda about, 79, 179
    fighting power, 120
    see also Soviet Union
Reichspost, 32, 34
*Reichsring für NS Propaganda und
    Aufklärung*, 44, 54, 55, 60, 210
    see also RMVP, Tiessler
Reichstag, 27, 79, 85, 86, 97, 117, 119,
    123, 147, 184
revisionism, 93, 94, 95, 98, 223
RFD (*Reichsfilmdrammatung*), 21
RFK (*Reichsfilmkammer*), 214
Rhineland, re-militarisation of (1936),
    67, 116
Ribbentrop, Joachim von, 41, 45,
    46, 52, 53, 56, 60, 62, 71, 108,
    110, 220
    Ribbentrop network, 49–51
    Compromises with Goebbels (1941),
        51
    Loses influence, 60–1
    see also AA
'Ribbentrop network', 49–51
Riefenstahl, Leni, 185, 201

RKK (*Reichskulturkammer*), 35, 193
    Entjudung, 22
    establishment (1933), 21, 32, 44
    Goebbels network, 32, 46
    structure, 27
    theatre, 44, 52
RMVP (*Reichsministerium für
        Volksaufklärung und Propaganda*)
    Bormann network, 54–5, 61
    central role in NS propaganda, 9
    creation (13.3.1933), 18, 32, 42–4, 47
    deals with air raids, 161, 163
    deals with counter-propaganda, 140–2
    Dietrich, 47–9
    deals with enemy broadcasts, 50–1, 60
    foreign press conference, 50
    initiates rumours, 139
    last meeting (4.1945), 184
    limits of power, 14, 18
    ministerial conference, 61
    OKW network, 56–7
    press conference, 48–9, 50
    Propaganda Division (*Hauptamt Pro*),
        34, 54, 55, 60, 114
    realism, 138
    relations with AA, 34, 50–1, 60
    relations with Sauckel/Speer, 58, 61–2
    sets up clandestine transmitters, 112
    'Soviet Paradise' exhibition (1942),
        79–80
    Stalingrad, 126–7, 147
    structure, 44–5
    theatre, 52
    see also Goebbels, NS propaganda,
        RPL, RKK
Romania, 181
Rome, evacuation of (1944), 175–6
Rommer, Erwin, 140, 156, 174
Roosevelt, Franklin D, 84–8, 128, 157,
    173, 180
    attacked by NS propaganda, 75–6
    death (12.4.1945), 183
    'gangster', 84
    'pawn' of international Jewry, 76,
        84–7, 116–17
    see also Conferences, USA
Rosenberg, Alfred, 41, 45, 47, 49, 60, 131
    antipathy to Ribbentrop, 52
    APA, 52
    cinema activities, 198, 209

criticises NS cinema, 205, 209
    Dienststelle Rosenberg, 52
    ecstatic about Barbarossa, 110
    Minister of Eastern Territories, 46,
        51–2, 70
    Rosenberg network, 61–3
    theatre, 52
    views on Europe, 69
    'Rosenberg network', 61–3
Rostock, 160, 161, 162
Rostov, 123, 161
RPA (*Reichspropagandaamt*) reports, 80,
    89, 164, 208, 210
    see also SD, Sopade
RPK (*Reuchspressekammer*), 27, 28, 29, 32,
    47, 48
RPL (*Reichspropagandaleitung*), 11, 48, 54,
    55, 58, 86, 116, 139, 167, 181, 220
    film activities, 80, 207
    Goebbels network, 17, 19, 32, 44, 46,
        60, 62
    propaganda plans, 103, 115, 122–3,
        127
    radio activities, 32
RRG (*Reichsrundfunkgesellschaft*), 31, 32,
    33, 37, 50, 60
    loss of autonomy, 36
    reorganisation (1940), 34
    see also NS radio
RRK (*Reichsrundfunkkammer*), 32, 50
    dissolution (1939), 37
Ruhr, 101, 138, 151, 163, 164
rumours
    Hitler, 140, 143–4
    Stalingrad, 139–40
RVDP (*Reichsverband der deutschen
        Presse*), 27
RVDZV (*Reichs-Verein Deutscher
        Zeitungsverleger*), 27, 28

SA (*Sturmabteilung*), 67, 195
Saar, re-incorporation of (1935), 67, 101,
    183
SA-Mann Brand (1933), 195
Sauckel, Fritz, 41, 58, 59
Schacht, Hjalmar, 47
Scharping, Rudolf, 154
Schirach, Baldur von, 70
Schmidt, Paul, 50
Schmitt, Carl, 41

Schuschnigg, Kurt von, 93
SD (*Sicherheitsdienst*), 141
  reports, 58, 67, 80, 84, 89, 90, 102,
    108, 112, 122, 125, 128, 131, 148,
    155, 165, 166, 171, 172, 173, 174,
    176, 195, 208, 210
Second World War, 6, 18, 24, 40, 65, 66,
    67, 190, 203
Semmler, Rudolf, 49, 127, 148
Sevastopol, 123
Sicily, Allied landing on (1943), 157, 158
Sieg im Westen (1940), 194, 196–7
Sopade reports, 67
  see also SD, RPA
Soviet Union
  admiration of German public for, 138
  attack on, 52, 110–12
  battle for Stalingrad, 125–9
  cinema production, 23
  counter-propaganda, 144–5
  coverage of Soviet resistance, 124
  depicted by NS cinema, 197, 202, 206
  'fear' propaganda against, 142, 156,
    181, 202
  German preparations for attack, 105–9
  impressive fighting power, 79
  in NS propaganda, 77–9, 82–91, 134–7
  negotiations with Germany (1939),
    71–2
  relations with Germany (1940–41),
    104, 108
  'Soviet Paradise' exhibition, 80–1
  underestimation of, 117–20, 158
  see also Operation Barbarossa, Stalin;
    see under Discourses
Spain, 104, 131, 136, 202
SPD (*Sozialdemokratische Partei
    Deutschlands*), 27
Speer, Albert, 43, 62, 220
  loses favour, 43, 53, 62
  minister, 46, 61
  at Nuremberg Trials, 222
  Speer network, 58–9
SPIO (*Spitzenorganisation der deutschen
    Filmwirtschaft*), 20
SS (*Schutzstaffeln*), 57, 58, 59, 110, 152,
    158
Stalin, Josef W, 80, 83, 87, 106, 131, 173
  attacked by NS propaganda, 79, 83,
    112

'puppet' of 'Jewish conspiracy', 88
  unprepared for war (1941), 108
  see also Conferences
Stalingrad, 125–9, 130, 133, 137, 141,
    144, 147, 151, 154
  advance towards (1942), 123, 124–6
  announcement of defeat, 128–9, 132
  battle for, 126–9
  impact of defeat, 5, 43, 53, 81, 88,
    132, 142
  newsreel on, 191
  rumours, 139–40
  'Stalingrad mood', 133, 156, 174
Steiner, Felix, 152
Streicher, Julius, 74, 79, 179
Sweden, 131
Switzerland, 203

Taylor, A J P, 72
Taylor, Richard, 72
Tempelhof, Ufa facilities, 193, 211
theatre, 21, 23, 44, 52, 62
Tießler, Walter, 44, 60, 210, 224
  relations with Bormann, 54, 55
  see also Reichring; RMVP
Timoshenko, Semyon, 118
Titanic (1943), 206
Tobis Film AG, 24, 189, 197
Tobruk, 127, 142
Todt, Fritz, 177
total war, 81–3, 133–6
Totalitarianism
  cinema, 187, 197
  claim to truth, 141
  comparison with liberal societies, 7–8,
    212
  Goebbels's views on, 18
  limits of NS totalitarianism, 6–11,
    221–2
  see also total war, fascism
Triumph des Willens (1935), 201
Tunis, 156

U-boats
  attack US targets, 86
  in film, 194, 196, 206
  new generation of, 183
  revival of campaign (1944), 178
  successes of, 128, 137, 154, 206
  used as propaganda diversion, 154–6

Ukraine, 81, 138, 170, 173
Universum-Film AG (Ufa)
  financial crisis, 24
  first newsreel, 189
  Kolberg, 200, 210–11, 216
  nationalised, 25, 190
  Parufamet deal (1925–27), 189
  problems (1944–45), 216
  Sonderproduktion, 194, 197
  twenty-fifth anniversary (1942), 187
USA, 7, 85, 117
  'destroyer of European civilisation',
    86–7
  'melting pot of races', 76
  Molotov's visit to, 86
  naval power, 154
  'puppet' of Jewish conspiracy, 88
  war with Germany, 75, 84, 117, 142
  see also Roosevelt Franklin D

V-1, 165–7
V-2, 165, 167–8, 178
V-3, 168
  see also miracle weapons
VDZV (*Verein Deutscher Zeitungsverleger*),
    27
Verräter vor dem Volksgericht (1944), 194,
    198
Versailles, Treaty of, 26, 64, 67, 68, 74,
    93, 94, 95, 96, 97, 98, 101, 181, 196
  see also revisionism
Volk
  annihilation of, 82, 132, 134, 172
  community of destiny
    (*Schicksalsgemeinschaft*), 151
  conspiracy against, 177
  elitism, 69, 123
  enemies of, 27, 29, 38, 65, 71,
    73, 202
  frustration of, 146–7
  historic mission of, 68
  'ideal fatherland', 65
  integration of, 89–90, 206
  praised for its resistance, 161, 163,
    170, 184
  protection of, 72
  Volksgemeinschaft, 66
  see also NS propaganda; *Volkssturm*,
    Volksdeutsche

Volksgemeinschaft, see under NS
  propaganda, Volk
Völkischer Beobachter, 95, 119, 139
Volksdeutsche (ethnic German
  minorities), 31, 50, 96–8, 207
Volkssturm (1944), 144, 145, 181, 192,
  196
  see also NS propaganda

Wächter, Werner, 58
Waffen-SS, 57
Wedel, Hasso von, 46, 57
Wehrmacht
  assists 'V-Aktion' (1941), 108–9
  betrayal of the people, 177
  confident for Allied landing (1944), 174
  contributes to *Kolberg*, 199
  effective Blitz, 99–100
  on film, 194, 196–7
  monopoly over visual material, 57
  no confidence in (1945), 182
  prepares for war (1939), 97
  propaganda activities, 46, 56–7
  rapid advance in the east (1941), 113
  reaches outskirts of Moscow (1941),
    119–20
  reports (WB), 56, 57, 79, 113, 125, 127
  resistance until the end, 79, 145
  retreat in the west (1944–45), 175–6,
    181
  show of force in the west (1940), 101
  Stalingrad, 127–9
  see also OKW, Operations, PK
Weimar Republic, 7, 16, 21, 22, 31, 74,
    185, 187
Wien Film AG, 24
Winkelnkemper, Toni, 60
Winkler, Max, 18, 24, 25, 26–7, 30, 189
Winter Aid Campaigns
  (*Winterhilfsspende*)
  (1941), 114–15, 119
  (1942), 125–6
Wir tanzen um die Welt (1939), 187
Wochenschau, see newsreel
Wünschkonzert (1940), 212
Wunderwaffen, see miracle weapons

Yalta conference, *see* Conferences
Yugoslavia, 51, 104, 105